A HISTORY OF BRITAIN

1945 THROUGH BREXIT

A HISTORY
OF BRITAIN

1945 THROUGH BREXIT

NEW EDITION

JEREMY BLACK

INDIANA UNIVERSITY PRESS

This book is a publication of

Indiana University Press
Office of Scholarly Publishing
Herman B Wells Library 350
1320 East 10th Street
Bloomington, Indiana 47405 USA

iupress.indiana.edu

The paper used in this publication
meets the minimum requirements of
the American National Standard for
Information Sciences—Permanence
of Paper for Printed Library
Materials, ANSI Z39.48–1992.

Manufactured in the
United States of America

Cataloging information is available
from the Library of Congress.

ISBN 978-0-253-06843-9 (pbk.)
ISBN 978-0-253-06845-3 (e-bk.)

First Printing 2023

For Anne Foreman

CONTENTS

Preface: From Empire to Where?   *ix*

Prime Ministers from 1945   *xiii*

Abbreviations   *xv*

1. Environment under Strain   *1*

2. Economy under Strain   *33*

3. Changing Society   *56*

4. Changing Culture   *92*

5. The After-Echoes of War, 1945–60   *119*

6. The Politics of Crisis, 1961–79   *132*

7. Thatcherism, 1979–90   *151*

8. Changing Directions, 1990–   *169*

9. British Issues, 1945–   *188*

10. European and World Questions   *201*

11. Into the Future   *231*

12. Conclusions   *237*

Notes   *247*

Selected Further Reading   *253*

Index   *255*

PREFACE

FROM EMPIRE TO WHERE?

IN JUNE 2016, Britain[1] voted to come out of the European Union (EU). Everyone rightly said that this was, and is, a pivotal historic moment. The book can in part be read as showing how Britain has got to this point and considering the consequences. This entails looking at the postwar (post–World War II) world, in particular the economic problems, political issues, and social changes leading up to Britain joining the Common Market or European Economic Community, the predecessor of the EU, in 1973. There was the deindustrialization that, without necessarily being linked to this, followed, as well as the more acute pressures arising from globalization, especially from the 1980s, notably the decline of industry, and as a related factor, of the old industrial areas, as well as the marked growth of the service economy, and the rise of London.

As a result of these and other factors, a metropolitan liberal elite emerged and came to dominate both the Conservative and the Labour parties, as well as Britain in general. In turn, there was disillusionment, notably with the rise of Scottish nationalism from the late 1960s, and later, what can be seen, in the vote to leave the EU, as the revolt of the English provinces, both rural and old urban. This vote is leading to a reshaping of Britain, economically, socially, geographically, politically, and maybe demographically, a reshaping that has already proved be deeply problematic. This summary provides a chronological dynamic for what is the first historical account of our new dramatically changing times.

Let us turn back to the start. Exhausted by war, Britain in 1945, nevertheless, was victorious and was still the world's greatest empire. That was, and is, clear. Its subsequent path and destination, however, have repeatedly been unsettled and uncertain, but they have been of consequence not only for Britain but also, to a degree, at the world scale. This is that history. Of course, the impact of the present on our understanding of the past is most readily apparent for recent history. The present to which this history appears to be trending changes constantly, as British history in 2014–23 has repeatedly demonstrated, and with those changes comes altering assessments of the past and of the significance of developments within it. This is the case not only in general but also with reference to particular topics such as environmental change or military history.

In the specific case of modern Britain, major developments in the 2010s, notably in Scottish politics and in the relations with the European mainland, led to a reading back and doing so very much looking for anticipations or, indeed, contrasts. So in the 2010s did the high rate of demographic (population) growth. This then is a history from the early 2020s of post-1945 Britain, and a history for the early 2020s. It is up to date and will also look to the future. This history will not require any prior knowledge of British history. The book will be largely designed for non-British, especially American, readers, but will also be pertinent for their British counterparts.

I have written before on parts of the period but not for more than a decade and not covering the period as a whole. Moreover, the nature of the present and our understanding of the past have both altered. The "death of Tory Britain," which appeared readily apparent during the Blair government (1997–2007) after three successive Labour victories in general elections in 1997, 2001, and 2005 is no longer the case, or at least, not as far as England is concerned. Moreover, in 2016, the Conservatives took second place in the elections to the Scottish Parliament behind the Scottish National Party, pushing Labour into third place, results that earlier, and as recently as the early 2010s, would have seemed inconceivable. The current projections for the next British parliamentary election, due by the winter of 2024–25, point to a Labour majority.

I have benefited greatly from teaching the subject and from traveling widely in the British Isles, the latter taking me to many different environments, from Holy Communion service at Holy Trinity Dalston in London, with its largely black and markedly enthusiastic congregation, to the far reaches of the Outer Hebrides. I have also been fortunate to be able to meet and talk with several of those mentioned in this text including Kenneth Baker, Tony Benn, Alec Douglas-Home, Michael Gove, Douglas Hurd, Edward Heath, Kwasi Kwarteng, John Major, Theresa May, Robert Runcie, Margaret Thatcher, and Jeremy Thorpe.

While thinking about and writing this book, I discussed themes with a number of Members of Parliament (MPs), including Ben Bradshaw, Douglas Carswell, Greg Clark, Geoffrey Clifton-Brown, Oliver Colvile, Graham Evans, Michael Gove, Damian Green, John Howell, Andrew Lansley, Julian Lewis, Oliver Letwin, David Lidington, Peter Luff, Gordon Marsden, Andrew Mitchell, and David Willetts, as well as with others, including Melvyn Bragg, Phil Collins, Richard Dales, and Frank Kitson. Clearly, this is in part a personal account, but that is true of all recent history. I would like to thank Steve Bodger, George Boyce, Roger Burt, David Coleman, Eileen Cox, Bill Gibson, David Gladstone, Sergio José Rodríguez González, Nick Lewis, Thomas Otte, Murray Pittock, Peter Spear, Peter Temple-Morris, Richard Toye, Nick White, and two anonymous readers for commenting on all or part of an earlier draft. I have benefited in considering this topic from opportunities to speak to the Foreign Policy Research Institute, the World Affairs Council, the University of Virginia's Oxford program, and Sherborne School. I am most grateful to Dan Crissman for proving a most helpful publisher. Thanks also to Theresa Quill for creating the map.

This book is dedicated to Anne Foreman, a neighbor whose friendship I greatly appreciate.

PRIME MINISTERS FROM 1945

Clement Attlee, Labour, 1945–51

Winston Churchill, Conservative, 1951–55

Anthony Eden, Conservative, 1955–57

Harold Macmillan, Conservative, 1957–63

Alec Douglas-Home, Conservative, 1963–64

Harold Wilson, Labour, 1964–70

Edward Heath, Conservative, 1970–74

Harold Wilson, Labour, 1974–76

James Callaghan, Labour, 1976–79

Margaret Thatcher, Conservative, 1979–90

John Major, Conservative, 1990–97

Tony Blair, Labour, 1997–2007

Gordon Brown, Labour, 2007–10

David Cameron, Conservative, 2010–16

Theresa May, Conservative, 2016–2019

Boris Johnson, Conservative, 2019–2022

Liz Truss, Conservative, 2022

Rishi Sunak, Conservative, 2022–

ABBREVIATIONS

BBC   British Broadcasting Corporation
Brexit Britain exiting from the EU
EEC   European Economic Community
EU   European Union
IRA   Irish Republican Army
MP   Member of Parliament (of the House of Commons)
NHS   National Health Service
NUM   National Union of Mineworkers
ONS   Office for National Statistics
SNP   Scottish National Party
UK   United Kingdom

A HISTORY OF BRITAIN

1945 THROUGH BREXIT

1

ENVIRONMENT UNDER STRAIN

POPULATION

IN WRITING ON Britain in the late twentieth century and to the present, the theme of the environment under strain principally referred, for much of the public, to "green" issues. This assessment reflected the extent to which these issues, and the related attitudes, both of which had developed from the 1960s, had been diffused more widely into the political community. In contrast, by the mid-2010s, there was, for many, a more specific and pointed concern, that of people, and more particularly their number. This concern related to anxieties about the consequences of both large-scale immigration and population aging due to higher life expectancy and, linked to that, of a future acceleration in the already-pronounced rise in population, with all the consequences that brought or allegedly brought or might bring, categories that people were often slipshod about in their comments. The population of the United Kingdom (UK) rose from 50.2 million in 1945 to 68.14 million by July 2023, and such figures were regarded as reasonably accurate and, if anything, as an underestimate.

Trends and projections indicate a continuation of the present direction of change. The population of England and Wales on Census Day, March 21, 2021, was 59.6 million, an increase of 6.3 percent since 2011 when it was 56.1 million. The population grew in each of the nine regions of England and also in Wales. Scotland's population as estimated to be 5.5 million in mid-June 2021, reflecting an increase of 8.2 percent from mid-2001. Immigration in the shape of net migration was a key element in the population of England and Wales, with the migrant share of the population rising from 8.9 percent (2001) to 13.4 percent (2011) and 16.8 percent (2021), the last 1 in 6 of the population, about 10 million in total. This is a larger growth than that due to natural change, the difference between births and deaths. Immigration is also a crucial factor in natural change, as women born overseas, but giving birth after migrating, had higher birth rates than women born in Britain. This trend is likely to continue.

Alongside birth rates and immigration, an aging population, due to higher life expectancy, is a key factor in the rise of the UK population. Indeed, over-65s are expected to be the fastest growing age group in all regions, with increases of more than 20 percent in most areas. Moreover, the number of local authority areas in which more than a quarter of residents are over sixty-five is expected to triple—from 28 to 84—between 2014 and 2024, with West Somerset having 36.5 percent of residents in that category, followed by North Norfolk, another predominantly rural area, with 34.6 percent, and the number of people in England over the age of ninety passing five hundred thousand in 2017, and reaching one million by 2034. In the 2021 census, North Norfolk had a median age of 54, Rother of 53, and East Lindsey of 52. The English region with the highest median age was the South West at 44, whereas London had the youngest, at 35. The youngest borough there was Tower Hamlets, a center of immigration, at 30. Other cities had low figures, notably Manchester and Nottingham at 31.

Regional differences in population figures and trends are projected by the Office for National Statistics (ONS) to be pronounced, with growth in Britain strongest in the South and East of England. The local authority with the highest increase in residents born outside the UK was the London borough of Barking and Dagenham, where the percentage rose from 31 to 41 in 2021, while the highest growth in EU nationals in 2011–21 was in Boston in Lincolnshire, which also provided the highest leave vote in the 2016 Brexit referendum. EU-born residents in 2011 were 2.5 million, and in 2021 3.6 million.

The 2020–21 COVID pandemic affected detailed local figures in that period, not least with movement out of London. Nevertheless, many earlier trends continued. Thus, some areas in northern England saw falls in population. Moreover, Scotland continues to not have growth rates to match those of England, in part due to much less immigration, both current and historic, and also to considerable recent emigration, both to England and abroad. The October 2016 ONS figures suggested that of the eleven largest city regions, London had the largest percentage growth in 2011–15, followed by Bristol, the West Midlands, and Greater Manchester, in that order, with Glasgow, at 1 percent, having the lowest rate of growth, followed by Liverpool at 1.2 percent.

A plethora of figures may confuse or, indeed, become tedious. The overall impression, however, is clear, and the figures tend to provide different aspects of it, as well as to help explain aspects of the situation and the trend. Moreover, looking at the figures in detail highlights important chronological and regional variations and reveals their significance. There is no sign that this situation will change. In addition, population trends provide a key product of, and focus for, developments across a range of spheres, including, crucially, economic shifts, migration, and social welfare policies. The implications of population changes for land use, resource pressures, housing, transport, and public services, notably education, health, and social care, are immense. At the same time, population is a key—arguably, the most significant—source of pressure on the environment.

NIMBYISM

Each interpretation of environmental crisis, and every discussion of future trends, focused wider issues, but also reflected the sense that Britain itself was under pressure. In reality, that has always been the case. Britain has been an inhabited landscape for thousands of years and, throughout that period, has been affected by major changes in land use, as well as by successive waves of immigration. It would be extraordinary if these processes should cease, although population growth at a great rate nearly stopped in the 1970s and 1980s, before immigration took off again in the years of Tony Blair's prime ministership (1997–2007). Nevertheless, the often vociferous aspiration for continuity and for opposition to change, on the part of many, generally tells us more about (some) attitudes than about practicalities. This aspiration is particularly expressed in terms of "nimbyism," or "not in my backyard," an opposition to development in the particular areas of those concerned.

The charge of nimbyism was regularly thrown at those who opposed change and usually in order to claim or suggest that they were privileged and selfish people who were unwilling to share the fruits of their privilege. This charge had a basis in fact and notably so in terms of opposition to new housing in rural areas or to "social housing" (housing for the poor) in affluent urban neighborhoods and also, starting in the mid-2010s, to fracking for natural gas. Strong opposition to the expansion of Heathrow Airport starting in the 2010s, especially in West London, was seen in these terms by critics.

Thus, nimbyism served a critical agenda suggesting that hostility to development represented class interest. This agenda was particularly present in the 1960s and 1980s as, respectively, Labour and Conservative governments sought to push through change. It was also more generally the case as far as local government was concerned and, notably, its often pronounced hostility to interests and views that opposed its development plans. An aspect of nimbyism was provided by what David Willetts, a modernizing, "one nation," Conservative minister in the early 2010s, referred to as "bring backery," by which imaginative use of the language he meant a conservative yearning for the past.

In reality, this placing of nimbyism, while well founded in part, also totally failed to capture the range of opposition to developments, and the extent to which much of it was well merited. The UK was not, as often presented, a battlefield of reform versus self-interest, nor of merit versus tradition, but instead, a far more complex tension of motives and causes; and nimbyism was frequently an aspect of local democracy as in opposition in Lancashire to fracking from the mid-2010s. Moreover, the extent and pace of change in the years since 1945 have been great. Linked to these, confidence about their processes and consequences has been generally limited. This has been more particularly the case after postwar optimism about a "brave new world" ebbed in the 1970s and 1980s, and in many respects, was shattered, a process repeated across the political spectrum, albeit for different reasons, over the past decade.

Nimbyism also had a pronounced regional dynamic. It was particularly notable in the South and Midlands of England, although its consequences can be UK-wide, as with the surcharge for flood protection on buildings' insurance policies. There is a connection between nimbyism and the major population growth after 1980 in southern England. In its turn, this growth, and the major restrictions placed on it in terms of planning permission, had a great and lasting impact on house prices. Nimbyism therefore played a role in the misguided increased building on floodplains in the crowded South.

ENVIRONMENT

In discussing the environment, and indeed other issues, we have to distinguish between change and crisis. Furthermore, we have to accept the dependence of the latter on perception and, more specifically, on clashing perceptions. The intensity of change is in part a matter of perception. We also need to distinguish between issues specific to Britain and, what is far more common, the British manifestations of wider, often global, trends—for example, climate change and rising population. None of these points minimize the extent of change in Britain. Climate change has been held responsible for a range of developments, including the greater numbers of sharks and jellyfish in British waters, both especially notable since 2016. Thus, Portuguese men-o-war and bioluminescent jellyfish became more common.

As humans are not the sole species, it is valuable to appreciate the extent to which it is often not the human environment that is most under strain but, instead, those of animals and plants. In both instances (and each encompasses a broad range of cases), there were many issues posed by the nature of sharing territory. The usual approach would be to comment on the advance of humans at the expense of other animals, notably birds and butterflies, and to focus, in particular, on the destruction of animal habitats, such as hedgerows, copses (small woods), and ponds.

These changes are indeed occurring, as they have long done. In particular, the loss of habitats for plant and animal species is a long-established process.[1] However, at present, change is frequently at an unprecedented rate. At the same time, the process is far more complex. Consider Exeter, a growing city of 133,000 people, the historic county town of Devon, where I have lived since 1996. To urban dwellers there, and the overwhelming majority of the British population live in cities or towns, the situation is not one of the retreat of animals but, rather, one in which some animals adapt to living with humans and not always in a fashion that appeals to humans. The quest for garbage is a key issue. The city, like many others, including many inland cities, echoes to the sound of seagulls, who have no natural predators and who are protected by law. The seagulls have moved inland as there is now fewer fish in the sea and less fishing at sea to produce food. Trash bags and takeaway food remains discarded in the streets now provide key sources of food for seagulls, foxes, squirrels, and badgers.

Badgers and foxes have moved into the cities, often following the railway tracks into the inner cities. Both have taken up residence near me. Foxes have become a common sight in the cities, including in London. These wild animals that have no natural predators attack other animals that humans prefer, notably domestic pets and small birds. Domestic rabbits and cats are killed by foxes, and sometimes by seagulls, and the latter have also killed dogs and tortoises. Indeed, like foxes, they appear to be losing their fear of humans. There is an increasing number of attacks on humans by seagulls.

There are also periodic panics in popular newspapers when foxes attack young children, although they do so less frequently than dogs that are pets. Indeed, attacks of the latter type have been increasing, and that despite the 1999 Dangerous Dogs Act, under which particular breeds were prohibited. In 2016, a group of squirrels biting a child in Cornwall caused alarm. Less seriously, deer eat flowers in suburban as well as rural gardens. Indeed, without natural predators, the number of deer in Britain is allegedly at a historic high. Bats and squirrels nest in houses, the latter eating through electric wires.

These are simply conspicuous instances of a wider process. Trash is also attractive to smaller creatures, such as snails and woodlice. Warm environments, for example hospitals, attract cockroaches and mice. The rat population is rising rapidly and becoming more conspicuous, benefiting from less attention being paid to animal infestation, and also from the extent that traditional poisons are no longer so effective, or are prohibited, an issue that also affects dealing with moles.

The rat situation appears to have deteriorated markedly, not least as water companies are devoting less of an effort to pest control. There are frequent comments on the proximity of rats to humans and various statistics, all unsettling, about how close rats are living to the average human. This is also the case with mice. Both mice and rats can regularly be observed on the platforms of London Underground stations. "Can be," in this case, also means that I have seen them, as I have also seen a large rat walking down the pavement at midday in the scenic Somerset town of Wells.[2] In houses that lack cats, mice and squirrel infestation is often a problem, and pest controllers, or burglar alarm engineers dealing with malfunctions, often first ask householders if they have cats. Mice, rats, and other animals have adapted to opportunities in other respects than those offered by trash or eating through cables. For example, the hot water outflows of washing machines provide a means of entry into houses. As a result, glass fragments are added to the plaster in which these outflows are located. Animals also carry disease. In 2016, it was claimed that one-third of dogs carried ticks, while deer are held responsible for the spread of Lyme disease, which is becoming an increasing problem.

There is much more concern about the radical reduction of wildlife numbers in the countryside as a result of habitat loss and the chemicals used in intensive farming. Both have hit butterflies. That is also apparent in the marked diminution or disappearance of garden birds, for example, pied flycatchers, starlings, greenfinches, and even sparrows. Population growth will make this situation even worse. So may technology. In 2016, concern was expressed about the danger to birds from test flights for Amazon's drone delivery service. Also in 2016, it was predicted that one-tenth of the wild species living in Britain would soon disappear.

HEALTH

The declining effectiveness of recent remedies is a key element for microbes as well as rats and mice. As elsewhere in the world, the ability of antibiotics, the wonder drugs of the late twentieth century, to tackle infectious diseases has declined. The rise of methicillin-resistant *Staphylococcus aureus* (MRSA) and multidrug-resistant tuberculosis, among other antibiotic-resistant strands, is notable. Indeed, as a result, going to the hospital is now possibly a more dangerous activity than used to be the case or, at least, is discussed in such terms.

Given that the National Health Service (NHS), established in 1948 by the Attlee Labour government, has been a key element in subsequent national identity, that itself is a potent change. The malaise that has affected the NHS in recent years owes something to a sense of unsafe hospitals, as well as of inadequate care, notably with a major scandal surrounding the treatment of patients in the Mid-Staffordshire Hospital in the late 2000s, specifically the neglect of necessary care. This scandal, one of many, which took far too long to investigate and then report on, influenced the public and governmental discussion of the NHS in the mid-2010s. Concerns over inadequate health care in part arise from increased demand, notably from an aging population and from immigration, but the issues posed by demands for standardized care are significant, as are the difficulties of providing adequate management. At any rate, it is important to note both major commitment to the institution and also concern about its state. By 2022, there were waiting lists of 7 million people, including over 380,00 waiting more than a year, and 2.5 million were recorded as unable to work due to illness. The last is despite a vast amount of money being spent on the NHS, the largest employer in Europe. Prior to the COVID pandemic, this was 9 percent GDP, but by 2022 this had risen to about 12 percent. Yet, each year brings dire warnings, from within the NHS, that unless more is spent, there will be a breakdown in services.

When the NHS was established, the government could not afford to finance an actuarial system of national health insurance (or, with its socialist approach, did not seek to do so), with the result that the taxpayer has been landed with a financial bottomless pit. The European-style insurance-based healthcare systems are restricted to those who go "privately." Labour and, even more, the trade unions show reluctance about any change at all that is designed to increase efficiency, even if it came from the Blair government of 1997–2007, and, as in the 2015 general election and the 2016 Labour leadership contest, complain at once about alleged privatization of the NHS. The danger is that this national icon, this essentially very good but often inefficient and badly run nationalized industry, staggers on until the day comes when it will either be reformed or will bankrupt the country. Both Conservative and Labour governments have sought to reform the NHS since the 1980s, but, by 2022, in the aftermath of the COVID pandemic, ambulance response times were poor and falling, while there were serious problems in hospital accident and emergency units.

The population aging is partly an inheritance of past declines in the birth rate. The age structure of the population had changed totally as a result, in large part, of the fall in the birth rate from the use of family planning. Contraceptive developments dramatically increased the ability of women to control their own fertility. These developments played a major role in the emancipation of women, as well as in the "sexual revolution," a change in general sexual norms, from the 1960s onward. After 1921, when Marie Stopes founded the Society for Constructive Birth Control, it became increasingly acceptable socially for women to control their own fertility. Contraceptives became widely available and notably so from the 1960s. In addition, after the 1967 Abortion Act, the number of legal abortions in the United Kingdom was 184,000 in 1990, rising to 214,000 in 2021.. Meanwhile, the fertility of the approximately 20 percent of couples (about 10 percent of adults) who were infertile was enhanced by new techniques such as in vitro fertilization.

Average life expectancy for all age groups consistently rose during the twentieth century, the major exception being those aged between fifteen and forty-four during the 1980s. Average life span increased by an average of two years every decade in the 1960s–1990s. Longer life expectancy, which was only slightly tempered by the COVID pandemic, is gradually becoming more important and will be the dominant factor after the mid-twenty-first century, when population aging due to past declines in the birth rate will slow down in part as a result of a higher birth rate. Population aging led to a new age structure as a result of the increasing number of pensioners, and to problems of dependency posed by the greater number of people over eighty-five: 12.6 percent of Norfolk's population were over sixty-five in 1951 and only 9.2 percent a century earlier. But by 1990, the percentage was 19.6.

As a result of this trend, Britain's potential support ratio (of working-age to retirement-age citizens) is predicted to be 2.4 by 2050. The actual ratio is worse than the demographically defined one as workforce participation is much less than 100 percent. However, forecasts of dependency mostly rely on fixed boundaries of working age, which are misleading; these forecasts exaggerate the problem of population aging as they take no account of the shift upward in retirement age.

Alongside increased longevity, not all illnesses retreated, which was unsurprising as people do not live forever, while the population rose. The assault on health came from a variety of directions. Although other factors also play a role, high and rising rates of obesity helped to explain high and rising rates of type 2 diabetes and of heart disease; the latter is particularly acute in Scotland. In England, blood pressure rates are especially high in the North and in the West Midlands. This underlines the strong local and regional character of disease rates and health indicators.

The leading causes of death have changed considerably, with decreases in the number of deaths from cerebrovascular disease and ischemic heart disease, and an increase in deaths from dementia and Alzheimer's disease, which together became leading causes of death from the late 2000s, and for men over 80 starting in 2015, and for women over 80 in 2009 and since 2011. Lung cancer rates fell as people gave up smoking, which represented a major change in social norms and behavior. In 2007, smoking in enclosed public places was prohibited. In 2012–15, adult smoking numbers fell by nearly one million. However, due in part to much increased testing, rates of prostate cancer, the most common killer for men in 2019, rose from 7.7 to 51 cases per 100,000 people from 1979 to 2008, while greater exposure to the sun led to a marked increase in skin cancer, the tenth most common for men and fifth for women in 2019, with 2,500 deaths annually from melanoma, the deadliest form, by the mid-2010s. Mouth cancer rose over a third in the 2010s. During 1979 to 2008, cancer rates as a whole rose from 329 to 388 per 100,000 people, but having peaked in 2013 thereafter fell. Rates rose particularly strongly among women, increased drinking, obesity, and later childbirth, all being significant factors, although not necessarily being aligned as better detection for breast cancer, helped lessen death rates. Indeed, cancer survival rates doubled from 1979 to 2008. At the same time, a 2016 review focused on substandard care across much of the country, including late diagnosis, poor survival rates, and delayed treatment. Britain had the lowest cancer survival rates in Western Europe.

Aside from cancer, the massive increase in the importation, treatment, and burying of hazardous waste from the 1980s led to concern about possible health implications. Moreover, in 2014, there were 2,248 deaths related to drug misuse. Possibly as a result of increasing car exhaust emissions, respiratory diseases, such as asthma, definitely rose. Exhaust emissions are responsible for 9,000 excess deaths in London alone each year, diesels being a particular problem. Tuberculosis made a comeback after 1987, partly due to refugees and immigrants from countries where it was more common, but also as a result of HIV infection, homelessness, and the appearance of drug-resistant strains. There were 282 tuberculosis deaths in the UK in 2012, but the rate declined from 2011.

Although AIDS (acquired immunodeficiency syndrome) developed in the 1980s as a new killer, leading to an emphasis on "safe sex," antibiotics, by then, dealt with most other sexually transmitted diseases. At the same time, the development of resistant strains of venereal disease, notably gonorrhea, became a problem in the 2010s, as did chlamydia.

More generally, pain was increasingly held at bay by more effective and selective painkillers, bringing relief to millions suffering from illnesses such as arthritis and muscular pain. This was an important counter to the health problems created by greater longevity. Thus, the condition of the people really changed. They became healthier and longer living. Nutrition improved considerably, average height increased for both men and women, and the country became affluent and health conscious enough to emphasize (correctly) the newly perceived, very serious, and rapidly growing problem of the overweight. The latter dramatically drove up diabetes and other rates.

THE PRESSURES OF CHANGE

As with health, it is important to note that the man-made environment is one that is not completely under the control of humans. Given the house-building, road construction, and agrarian changes that have an impact on natural environments, it is all too easy to forget the vulnerabilities of this environment, but they were many. The manifestations vary. For example, the ponds or "water features" that adorned many gardens from the 1990s, a clear sign of affluence, consumerism, and media-driven fashion, and one that benefited frog life, also became breeding grounds for mosquitoes. These are annoying rather than a health problem in Britain, but there are possible future consequences of a return to malaria alongside climate change: England used to have malaria. The goldfish and tadpoles humans put in these ponds became targets for herons, seagulls, and other birds. Conversely, the increase of estrogens in river water affected the sexual characteristics of some fish and may have had an impact on human health. So also with the antibiotics given automatically to farm animals in order to protect them from illness, antibiotics also frequently used with fish farming, antibiotics that increased human vulnerability. Cleaner rivers have led to more fish and seals being seen in rivers and their estuaries including the Thames, but the 2022 annual report by Defra, the Department for Environment, Food and Rural Affairs, indicated that in 2021 only 16 percent of England's rivers and inland waters were of good ecological status, and 63 percent moderate. The Environment Agency of 2022 indicated that there was a sewage spill every 2.5 minutes in England and Wales. Weak enforcement was a problem, as were leaks from sewage works as well as agricultural pollution.

At the macrolevel, discussion of climate change, specifically, but not only, global warming, accelerated environmental concern and led to a range of predictions, including coastal flooding due to higher sea levels, more extreme weather conditions, and possibly a fundamental northward shift in the Gulf Stream, leading to a colder Britain. Were such a shift in the Gulf Stream to occur, and, in contrast, temperatures at present are consistently rising, an indication of the conditional points more generally true for the climate, the shift would be a crucial change to the very fundamentals of British life: the nature of the climate is important not only to the economy, in the shape of agriculture and fishing, but also to the character of sociability, the value and longevity of the existing housing stock, and the effectiveness of the transport system.

At present, the trend is clearly toward more stormy winters and higher summer temperatures, with more violent wind and rain conditions episodically around the year. Each created issues for the sustainability of particular communities and practices. Rising sea and river levels linked to climate change and global warming were in part responsible for flooding in early 2020, affecting the government's response to the early stages of the COVID pandemic. The impact of floods could be devastating, as in Oxfordshire in 2007, a year in which flooding affected 55,000 homes and killed 13 people.

In policy terms, floods raised fundamental questions about the advisability of building on floodplains and about the impact on water runoff of development, especially house building, that made it harder for rain to move downward through the soil, for example, the tarmacking of front gardens in order to provide space for more cars to park. Changes in agricultural practice could also make it harder for rain to move downward, especially the switch to corn. It proved relatively easy to highlight the issue of climate change when discussing floods, although in practice, it was often difficult to differentiate between such change and the more specific impact of particular human policies and practices. The capacity of the infrastructure to cope with climate change was highlighted repeatedly when the railway to southern Devon and Cornwall was cut near Dawlish after the seawall was breached and part of the line washed away. The inability of modern Britain to provide and sustain an infrastructure comparable to that of the Victorians became an issue.

In the waters around Britain, climate change had major consequences. Thus, the increase in sea temperature led to the departure for cooler waters of plankton and to a consequent fall in the stocks of the fish that fed on them. This fall ensured that there are more jellyfish and crab as their fish predators have declined. In turn, this situation leads to a very different maritime ecosystem.

Yet, to put climate trends in perspective, fundamental changes can also occur for other reasons. For example, the consequences of the end of the ice ages continue with the rising of landmasses that had been covered and weighed down by ice. In Britain, this has led to a tilting of the country as the ice was deeper closer to the North Pole. There is uplift in Scotland and northern England. Shorelines in northern and western Britain, especially in northwestern

Scotland, thus contain raised beaches. In contrast, a downwarp is especially apparent in East Anglia and South-East England, which are sinking, with consequent pressures on coastal defenses and especially so in the Thames estuary and East Anglia. More locally, there are also changes in the water table.

Repeatedly, alongside international and national environmental trends, there were regional and local ones. For example, on the whole, lowland species were more seriously affected than highland counterparts by housing developments and agricultural changes. The 2007–11 survey by the British Trust for Ornithology indicated an increase in overall populations of woodland, farmland, and migrant perching birds in northern England and Scotland and a decline in the more populous south of England. Climate change was partly responsible for these changes, but development pressures in the South were significant. Such trends became even more apparent at local levels, as development pressures had an impact in particular watersheds, valleys, hillsides, or fields.

POLLUTION

Pollution might benefit some wildlife, such as the bacteria found in human waste. For humans, however, pollution is generally undesirable, although some regretted the loss of the "smell of jobs," a loss particularly prominent where there had been chemical works, or in the town of Bridgwater in Somerset where the cellophane works opened in 1937, which employed much of the population, gave a characteristic odor to the locality; they closed in 2005 and were destroyed in 2015. Across the UK, the range of pollution, from sewage outflows to oil spills, was, and remains, formidable. For example, lead emissions from traffic and emissions from aircraft were issues, and the latter had a major impact in the 2010s in the debate over the increase in airport runways in the South-East of England. The respective impact of Heathrow and Gatwick airports on air quality and noise became key elements in the bitter debate between their protagonists and opponents in the 2010s. Oil spills were also an occasional issue.

Meanwhile, high-stack emissions from power stations spread pollution far and wide. Although the Clean Air Act of 1956 brought major changes to the cities, and sulfur dioxide emissions were reduced by the use of cleaner techniques at power stations, there was a rise in nitrogen oxides, ammonia, and photochemical smog. In addition, industrial pollution was responsible for "acid rain," which damaged woodland, rivers, and lakes.

The "green agenda" increasingly came to the fore in the 2000s and, more particularly, with the Conservative–Liberal Democrat coalition government of 2010–15, largely due to pressure from the Liberal Democrats. The agenda focused on "clean energy," especially sun- and wind-powered generation, although with interest also in other sources such as biomass. However, this agenda faced difficulties as a consequence of economic and fiscal issues, more particularly the crises in government finances, which led to a downturn in investment on "green" remedies, but also highlighted the extent to which a lack of funds made it difficult to replace clearly polluting entities, especially coal-fired power stations.

There was also a growing realization that what have appeared remedies in turn repeatedly created new problems. This was the case with diesel-powered buses and cars, which were soon associated with a marked deterioration in air quality in cities, notably in London. In turn, the prospects for electric cars were affected by the rising cost of electricity, and by the question of vulnerability to power cuts. In addition, wind turbines were controversial. It was claimed that they were dangerous to birds, although the Royal Society for the Protection of Birds (RSPB) supports wind turbines provided they are located correctly. It was claimed that they were eyesores, although that is a matter of opinion. The difficulties and costs of eventually dismantling them attracted attention, but many of the claims were exaggerated. The interest and agendas in each case of apparent "green" remedy varied greatly, but the common characteristic was a lack of agreement.

What was most notable at the national level was a change in the landscape and seascape. Wind turbines altered many a vista on land and at sea and were threatened on many more. This was particularly apparent in upland areas. On land, sun-powered units spread across both agricultural land and also on the roofs of buildings, including small ones. Equally, wildlife could flourish under the sun-powered units on agricultural land and not least because pesticides were generally not used there.

WATER

As across history and around the world, water was an issue. This might not seem an obvious factor for a country noted for its rain, and at a time of increasing global population and concern, water availability was certainly far greater than in much of the world. Nevertheless, in Britain the major rise in the population and the significant increased per capita (per person) use of water placed great demand on supplies. Far more dwellings had integral toilets, baths, and showers than in the 1940s, and usage markedly increased. A daily shower, rather than, as in the past, a wash (often a "strip wash" with a flannel) or an occasional bath, became a norm. This was not least because, thanks to improvements in the convenience of power and usage within houses—for example, with gas-powered hot-water boilers and electric showers—there was an immediate availability of plentiful supplies of hot water. This was very different to the situation in the 1950s. In addition, the real cost of such hot water decreased, as did the cost of hot water (and water and heating as a whole) as a percentage of household budgets. So also with washing machines, dishwashers, and the plentiful employment of hosepipes for washing cars and watering gardens. Social assumptions about cleanliness were also significant to the increased use of water for showers and washing machines. Many television advertisements focused on cleanliness and on smelling fragrant.

There were also important pressures on water supplies. The irrigation of crops increased, especially in East Anglia where the mass cultivation of vegetables was linked to the production of standard-condition crops, such as peas, for the supermarkets. East Anglian agriculture was also the focus for other pressures in the shape of a degree of local public dislike of the immigrant (notably Polish) labor that provided much of the workforce, even though there was not a comparable willingness to do the work on the part of some of the local unemployed.

As a result of the greater national usage of water, and notably in the South and East of England, there was the depletion of natural aquifers and a marked fall in ground-water levels. Irrigation poses major problems for these levels. This usage caused the seasonal, or permanent, disappearance of rivers or sections of rivers, and of ponds. Moreover, the major political problems facing the acquisition of land for reservoirs meant that new capacity did not keep pace with the major rise in the population. This continues to be a problem and will be exacerbated by the devolution of authority and powers to regional governments where that develops and by the growing complexity of planning. In particular, the clash between urban and rural interests emerges very much with reservoirs.

Water shortages became an annual issue, notably in late summer. Greater demands for water exacerbated droughts, such as those of 1976, 1995, 2006, and 2022, and led to concerns about possible droughts in other years. These demands encouraged both frequent hosepipe bans and other measures to limit consumption, as well as the more general practice of water metering as a means to reduce usage. This was a significant development and comparable to the charge basis for energy supplies.

There was a contrary tendency, especially among sections of the public, to treat utilities as public services in which the extent to which usage set charges should be limited. This attitude became less plausible with availability issues but also with the privatization of utility providers in the 1980s. Nevertheless, important vestiges remained, notably in reduced charging for the elderly, especially transport, fuel, medicine, and television costs. The bus pass became a badge of pride for the elderly, providing free local travel that was paid for by means of transfers from local governments to the bus operators. Given that many of the elderly were better off, thanks to their inflation-proof pensions and accumulated assets, than the average worker, this transfer lacked social and generational fairness. So too with medicines, which are provided free to those aged sixty or above, irrespective of their wealth. However, hostility to means testing was a staple of the Labour approach to social welfare, but there were also practicable issues involved, notably the cost of administering means testing.

As so often in modern Britain, there was a strong regional dimension to the water situation. Major and sustained population rises in the South of England, where rainfall and ground-water levels anyway were lower and there were fewer reservoirs, exacerbated the strain on water supplies and emphasized the serious problems arising from the continued absence of a national water grid. As a result, the reuse of water is especially high in the South-East, with recycled water in London on average flowing through nine people thanks to the effective system of treatment plants. This is an aspect of national circumstances that people preferred not to think about, one that also reflected a more general lack of engagement with the value of engineering and of applied knowledge. Another spatial variation was provided by regulation: water in Scotland, where the supply is plentiful, is publicly administered by the relevant boards. In contrast, England and Wales were the preserve of private utility suppliers, and there has been extensive investment by French water companies.

Under pressure from agricultural fertilizers, industrial waste, and sewage, water quality was also an issue. In 2009, a survey of rivers indicated that the majority did not meet European Union (EU) standards for cleanliness. The value of such surveys, notably the annual one of beaches, in encouraging pressure for improvement, indicates the need to devise an effective post-EU replacement in order to prevent a fall in standards.

Concern about water quality encouraged a major boom in the sale of bottled water, although consumerism and the ready response by producers and retailers also played a role in that boom. The identification of bottled water with natural sources of water in mountainous or hilly terrain—for example, Highland Scotland or the Long Mynd in Shropshire—further underlined the sense of the desirability of rural life and underlined concerns about its city counterpart. This contrast drew on long-standing themes in British culture and ones for which consumerism provided new images, issues, and opportunities.

AGRICULTURE

Agricultural changes were scarcely unique to Britain. At the same time, the density of Britain's population and the major place of the landscape in the national self-image ensured that they were particularly sensitive issues. There were also regional and political dimensions to these changes, while a more general sense of a loss of continuity contributed to a feeling of crisis. Malaise was particularly pronounced from the 1990s. The factors varied by agricultural sector and frequently coincided with high land values and, less consistently, with good product prices in some sectors. Indeed, some farmers became very wealthy. Nevertheless, key issues in the malaise included foreign competition, especially for pig production, public health crises in meat production, falling consumption of dairy products, and the major and distorting role of supermarket chains as mass purchasers, notably for milk but, in practice, for all foodstuffs. Foreign competition was exacerbated by the entry of Eastern Europe into the EU, while Brexit affected the subsidy system. The net effect was to reduce the income of many farmers, and tenant farmers did not benefit, as landowners did, from the rise in the capital value of land.

Land, both agricultural and forestry, was purchased for investment by nonrural interests, which created a further source of tension. So too was the generational issue, as with the questions, for all of the population, of jobs and housing. Farmers found that their children could not, or did not want to, stay on the land and certainly could not secure a reasonable standard of living if they did. The fate of family farming was especially contentious in Northern Ireland where there were many such farms. In Britain as a whole, the sense of a lack of a future for agriculture contributed powerfully to the more general malaise, one that matched that among much of the urban working class.

The regulatory context could be significant. For example, the abolition in 1994 of the statutory Milk Marketing Board for England and Wales, part of the move toward privatization, in practice changed the regulation of the dairy industry from a state-controlled producer corporatism to control by retailers, and thus to a buyers' market. This market was dominated by supermarket chains, with the established practice of milk delivery to homes largely ceasing as it proved impossible to compete with less expensive supermarket purchases. The daily pint of milk delivered in a glass bottle that was returned for washing and reuse was replaced by larger containers, purchased in supermarkets, containers that were made of plastic and became part of the trash put out with the waste. Criticism of supermarkets over the prices paid to farmers became particularly prominent starting in the mid-2010s. It was linked to criticism of supermarkets for not stocking local products but instead, preferring central distribution systems that relied on mass producers.

These moves adversely affected dairy farmers, especially small-scale farmers, and led to a change in the texture of rural life as many farmers either went bankrupt or sold up, resulting in bigger farms, or altered their land use—for example, cultivating corn or oilseed rape—such that there was less grassland. Some farmers switched to high-value cheese production. This reflected a search for niche economic activities. Another instance of such diversification was provided by the development of wine production which also benefited from climate change. The regional character of dairying introduced an important regional dynamic to the resulting changes in agriculture. It was particularly pronounced in upland Britain and in Western England.

The control over agriculture by regulations and financial mechanisms affected not only financing but also land use. The taking of land out of cultivation in order to meet "set-aside" regulations designed to control production or for environmental reasons encouraged a nonproductivity that seemed bizarre to many and that also led to fields being covered with weeds. Although many farmers benefited from agricultural subsidies, others disliked the regulations, as well as competition from Continental suppliers. As a result, the agricultural interest was very publicly divided in the 2016 EU referendum.

Pressures on farming hit the remainder of the rural economy, as well as that of small towns. The resulting consequences were specific and general, particular and cumulative, and changes in measurable criteria, as well as those in broader assumptions and senses of identity. The rural working population largely ceased to be a matter of agricultural workers, often being replaced by commuters to work in towns, while the fall in agricultural jobs meant that many of the young did not stay on the land but instead moved to the towns. As a result, there was a transformation in the demographics of counties where agriculture was prominent, such as Norfolk, where static overall population totals in 1951–81 could not conceal major changes.

More generally, a fabric of local life, integration and identity provided by agricultural markets and local food processing was lost. Markets that were central to local identity, for example that in Holsworthy in Devon, closed or were threatened. In addition, agricultural mechanization and the problems of rural towns led to a depopulated feel in parts of rural Britain. As a result, a marked contrast with the rural situation in areas within commuting distance of the cities developed. In these latter areas, there was a different sense of loss of identity.

Moreover, rural society felt ignored, notably under the Blair governments (1997–2007). This issue came to the fore in the early 2000s and particularly over the "Right to Roam" under the Countryside and Rights of Way Act of 2000; over the banning, in England and Wales in 2004, of the long-established practice of fox hunting with hounds; and over the taxation of petrol as rural inhabitants on average drove farther.

There was a clear element of social tension in the banning of fox hunting. Activities that involved the death of animals but were patronized by the "working class," notably hunting with ferrets, were not prohibited, nor was leisure fishing, an activity in which a large number participated and across all social groups. More generally, the discussion of public policy has to be aware of the political dimensions and notably those focused on social images. For example, fox hunting, which, in practice, included, among participants or supporters, many country people who were not affluent or members of the rural elite, was regarded, on the Left, with great hostility as an elitist practice. There was a deliberate effort to have a go at perceived rural "toffs," with no knowledge whatsoever of the ways of the countryside or the surprisingly class-less support for hunting.

A survey of adults in 2003 indicated that two-thirds had never met a farmer. Previous points of identification with the countryside and farming were lost or became less significant. Whereas many, the young in particular, had visited the countryside for leisure, notably for youth hosteling, camping, rambling, bicycling, and so on, up to the 1960s, these activities became less prominent in large part due to the rise in foreign travel from the 1960s. So also across society. Many prominent figures of the 1950s—for example, the Liverpool-born Selwyn Lloyd, Conservative foreign secretary from 1955 to 1960—focused on "country pursuits" in Britain, such as hunting, shooting, fishing, walking, eating cream teas, and so on. By the 1980s, such activity had become less prominent. Instead, more time was spent on the Continent.

The location of second homes was instructive. Insofar as they had them, many British families had theirs in Continental Europe, notably southern France and Spain, and for the 2000s, inexpensive air services developed to serve these families, as well as those who had settled abroad, with services, for example, to Angers, Avignon, Bergerac, Bordeaux, Brest, Nantes, Nice, Perpignan, Quimper, Rennes, and Toulouse in France and to a similar range in Italy, Portugal, and Spain. In contrast, in France, Germany, Spain, Norway, and Sweden, the norm was to have second homes within the country in question and to look after the land that came with them. This encouraged a greater identification with the countryside than in Britain. However, in Scotland, vacationing at home is, and has long been, very common.

Furthermore, in Britain, although the numbers of people experiencing rural life declined, rural "values" remained strong and not just in elite culture but also among the middle class. A classic instance was visits to stately homes owned by the National Trust, the largest private landowner and an organization with a 2022 membership of 5.7 million. Thanks in part to the spread of car ownership, leisure moved into the countryside for more people.

The management of agriculture led to a number of crises. The 2001 outbreak of foot-and-mouth disease arose from the mishandling of contaminated waste by a pig farm and resulted in Britain prohibiting the feeding of kitchen waste to animals. During the crisis, a ban on the movement of livestock was imposed by the government; public footpaths were closed to prevent the spread of the virus; the EU prohibited the export from Britain of animals and meat products, which accentuated tension between Britain and France; and there was a mass cull (slaughter) of at least four million animals. Across the countryside, smoldering pyres of carcasses became a common sight. The disease was wiped out, but the crisis was traumatic for much of rural Britain and created ugly images of British agriculture. Moreover, the crisis further accentuated urban-rural tensions. Urban claims that farmers were neglectful were wide of the mark, but so were the views of farmers that town dwellers who walked across the countryside habitually brought problems, including spreading disease. Many farmers illegally blocked public footpaths after the government ban on their use was lifted, usually with a barbed wire fence, and this practice continues to be a problem.

The vulnerability of the human food system was shown again with the rise of bovine tuberculosis among cattle. This led to an increase in the number of cattle slaughtered in England and Wales to more than 38,000 in 2012 and to a marked decrease in cattle rearing in southern England where the disease was most pronounced. Indeed, the geography of cattle rearing changed.

There was great controversy over whether this disease should be countered by the vaccination of cattle and/or by the culling of badgers which were alleged to spread the disease, controversy which again indicated how far farmers were regulated by national agencies and by ones with which they had only limited influence. Farmers were not permitted to kill badgers on their land. From 2013, the government licensed the killing of badgers in selected parts of England by authorized marksmen, but this policy was condemned: the potency of sentimental urban attitudes toward animals came into play. Badger culls were opposed by animal rights groups, most of whom were town dwellers, an instance of largely urban pressure-group politics having an impact on farming. In practice, badgers are vicious animals and kill other animals, particularly hedgehogs, the fate of which became an issue in 2016.

The issue allegedly led to a fair amount of low-level lawbreaking on the part of farmers, notably the killing of badgers by illegal means—for example, leaving around apples in which paracetamol pills had been inserted—and then taking the dead badgers and putting them by the roadside as if they were roadkill. Other illegal means were allegedly used against foxes and seagulls. However, the extent of such activity is unclear. For example, badgers are, indeed, run down by cars. As so often, rumor may not be helpful. With badgers as with foxes, there was the infantilization of social attitudes, seeing animals as delightful characters from children's fiction, rather than as predators or prey or as competitors in the use of the natural environment. These attitudes were linked to the trend of the uncontrolled growth of the animal population.

Changes in agriculture were not alone in affecting the face of rural Britain. Other nonurban activities, especially forestry, fishing, mining, and quarrying, either declined or dramatically cut their workforces. These cuts had an impact on male employment, as the jobs had principally been for unskilled men or rather, men with highly specialized skills but often limited formal education, which was a situation often misleadingly described as unskilled. The cuts in workforces affected local settlements and the sense of identity that continuity bound up in these jobs. This was very much seen with fishing communities, both large and small. A crucial aspect of local identity, all the tin mines in Cornwall (long Britain's leading producer) were closed as they became internationally uncompetitive, the last in 1998.

Attempts to introduce new mines faced major opposition at the planning stage, as in the early 2010s with the big new tungsten mine at Hemerdon, Devon, opened in 2015, the first metal mine to be opened in Britain in forty-five yearsand in 2021–22 to a new coal mine in Cumbria, which would have been the first in thirty years. Nevertheless, some branches of mining remained significant, notably of salt in Cheshire; of potash, a key ingredient in making fertilizer, in East Cleveland; and of aggregate for the railways, as at Meldrum, Devon. However, production facilities were repeatedly hit by the limited investment or disinvestment linked to short-termism.

ENERGY

A key element of controversy over the environment was that of energy provision and use. The decline of coal as a fuel source increased the contentiousness of energy issues. So too did the doubts about nuclear fuel that increased from the 1960s and, even more, the 2000s. Britain had played a major role in the development of nuclear power in the 1950s, and it had then been seen as a clean and modern alternative to coal in the generation of electricity.

Politics repeatedly played a major role in discussions about energy. From the early 1970s, the National Union of Miners (NUM) and Arab oil producers both posed major problems for stable energy provision. Indeed, energy provision was a major issue in the national and international politics of the 1970s and 1980s, threatening the very stability of the economy and the government. However, thanks to Britain becoming a major producer of oil and natural gas from the mid-1970s, as a result of the extraction of both in major quantities from the North Sea, the issue of energy then ebbed. The defeat of the NUM in its 1984–85 strike (see chapter 7) was also important in the declining political significance of energy.

By the 2010s, however, there were growing concerns that "the lights may go off" due to energy shortages. Power stations were not built to keep up with estimated peak demand from a rapidly rising population that had high expectations of energy provision. Nor were they built to cope with the obsolescence of existing power plants and the fall in the production of natural gas and oil from the North Sea; with 4.5 million barrels of oil equivalent a day, 2000 had been the peak year of production there. Green policies were also a factor, in particular in the move from coal-fired power stations. As a consequence, there was a highly risky energy policy, with a great possibility of being unable to meet the country's energy requirements. By 2015, 24.7 percent of electricity production was from renewables, notably wind turbines and solar panels, with Scotland producing about half the UK output. The Scottish government is focusing greatly on renewables, and in 2016, the world's first large-scale tidal energy farm was launched in the Pentland Firth near Inverness. Drax in South Yorkshire in England, the biggest power station in Britain, converted three of its six units to burning wood pellets, which qualify as renewables, and not, as before, coal. Of the 337.7 terawatt hours of electricity generated in 2015, gas-fired power stations supplied 99.8 and renewables 83.3, but the share of coal-fired power stations fell due to carbon taxes. As a result, output from nuclear power stations rose 10 percent to 20.8 percent of national electricity output, compared to 22.6 percent for coal. In the coalition negotiations in 2010 with the Conservatives, the Liberal Democrats had to drop their manifesto pledge to close the nuclear power stations.

The use of coal-generated electricity, much of the coal imported, continued to fall, and in 2016, there were periods when coal power output fell to zero.

The decline of coal thus arose as much from environmentalism, notably the ambitious "green" targets from the Blair government of 1997–2007, as earlier, from the politicized issues of labor relations that had encouraged the Thatcher government in the 1980s to focus on the North Sea.

However, concern about the availability of power led to pressure to delay the phasing-out of coal-power stations. This concern also encouraged government support for the building of new nuclear plants to replace what was to be decommissioned. Both were major issues in infrastructural improvement (or at least maintenance). The new nuclear plant came to focus on the projected Hinkley Point B power station in Somerset, which was designed to meet 7 percent of power needs, and the related issue of Chinese and French financing and management was important to public finances and foreign policy in the mid-2010s. In turn, concerns about Chinese influence encouraged caution, while, in 2022, the Russian invasion of Ukraine led to a major increase in worry about energy availability, security, and costs. These were part of the cost-of-living crisis that gathered pace in 2022 as well as in post-Brexit discussions about European policy. The lack of adequate disposal facilities for nuclear waste is another issue. Governments have pressed for disposal deep underground but have not yet identified a suitable and safe location to construct such a facility.

With some honorable exceptions, successive governments have avoided necessary decisions on the future, with particular reference to nuclear power but also with much else. There was a particular contention starting in the late 2010s about the role of renewables, notably wind farms, both on- and offshore, as well, very differently, about fracking from oil shale. Indeed, division over the latter helped precipitate the fall of the Truss government in 2022: divisions between local and national, and between environmental sensitivity and energy needs, were fully revealed. The difficulties of facing up to realities in a democracy, and of confronting the political, fiscal, and social consequences, have become more apparent. As both cause and consequence, politicians have become smaller in stature and real achievement.

GARBAGE

The growing and more consumerist society produced greater and greater quantities of trash, much of it nondegradable and some of it toxic. By 2002, about 30 million metric tons of garbage was being produced, with the figure growing at an annual rate of 3 percent. Kitchen and garden waste and newspapers and magazines were the largest categories of household waste. The decline in the reusable forms of goods, notably of diapers, which, instead, became disposable, was a major factor as well. Thus, garbage increased per capita at the same time as the number of people rose—a challenging combination, and one that caused particular issues in urban rivers.

The management of waste created major problems for communities, notably due to greater public sensibilities about the means and locations of landfill and far more regulation of both. Finding suitable landfill sites became a serious problem, but there was widespread opposition to the alternative of incineration (burning) due to fears about the production of toxic fumes charged with dangerous chemicals. This situation resulted in increasing pressure for the recycling of waste, itself a major aspect of "green" policies, and in attempts by local government to ensure this outcome by regulations and charges.

In practice, it was difficult to alter public attitudes but not impossible. Much of the population accepted the discipline of dividing their garbage between color-coded bins, depending on its being recyclable or not, and if so, in which forms, just as most of the smoking population gave up smoking in pubs, restaurants, and cinemas when it was prohibited in 2007. These bins became part of the visual landscape, notably of city streets, and the old-fashioned metal bin was replaced by colorful plastic versions. In turn, protecting these bins from seagulls, squirrels, and foxes became an issue, one that was particularly troublesome in seaside towns.

Littering, however, remained a major problem and, indeed, a growing one. *Litter and Flytipping in England*, a 2015 report by a House of Commons Select Committee, observed, correctly, that "England is a litter-ridden country compared to most of Europe, North America and Japan." Factors cited included a marked rise in fast-food debris, as well as the impact of foxes, and the issues created by a lack of commitment to cleaning the front gardens of properties, especially if they were communal and/or the responsibility of tenants. In 2016, cyclists were accused of causing the death of deer in Richmond Park, London, by dropping litter. The situation continued to deteriorate thereafter.

At the same time, there were improvements, notably in the cleanliness of some beaches from the 1990s, in the mass public litter picks of the 2010s, and in the introduction then of charges for supermarket plastic bags. These charges encouraged many to reuse more-durable bags.

NOISE AND LIGHT

Noise and light pollution became both issues and problems, each recognizably different to earlier periods and each accelerating in their impact. The Countryside Commission's map of tranquil areas showed that an area five times the size of the large county of Kent was lost to tranquility in England between the early 1960s and the early 1990s and notably so in lowland areas. Light pollution ensured that it was increasingly difficult across much of the country to see stars in the night sky or to see as many stars as in the past. The Council for the Protection of Rural England and the British Astronomical Association reported that by 2000, only 11 percent of England was free from light pollution. More locally, sleep was affected by continuous lighting. Light pollution was a largely new concept or, at least, a largely new one in those terms. This indicated the significance of environmentalism and the extent to which many people felt under pressure. Light also helped define local and regional experiences. For example, in Devon, there was light pollution from the spreading of cities, notably Plymouth and Exeter, but, in contrast, also the "black hole" of Dartmoor, which is largely uninhabited moorland.

Concern over noise divided communities and families. Traffic was an especially potent source of noise. By the late 1990s, noise was the biggest source of complaints to local authorities, indeed ahead of garbage. Noise affected relations between people, in particular intergenerational relations, and brought rights and responsibilities, notably feelings of freedom and privacy, into conflict. Amplifiers and other sound systems accentuating the impact of music proved especially contentious. Disputes about noise came to play a role across the fabric of society. In rural areas, newcomers objected to the noise made by church bells. In restaurants and shops, the provision of Muzak, background noise, led in the 2010s to a greater level of complaint. Generational issues played a role, notably the hearing problems of the elderly.

TRANSPORT

Tranquility was particularly affected by the continued rise of the car, which was central to consumerism and to mobility, the two of which were closely linked. The rise in road transport was rapid. After a fall in car ownership during World War II (1939–45 for Britain), its rise accelerated rapidly, especially after petrol rationing stopped in 1953. In terms of thousand million passenger miles, private road transport shot up from 47 in 1954 to 217 in 1974, an increase from 39 percent to 79 percent of the total. This gain was made at the expense of bus, coach, and rail transport. The percentage of goods traffic moved by road rose from 37 in 1952 to 58.3 in 1964, exacerbating the poor finances of British Rail. There were nearly 4 million cars in the UK in 1950, just under 5 million in 1960, almost 10 million in 1970, 20.7 million in 1990, 29.3 million in 2010, and 32.9 million registered in 2022. This rise was far greater than that in the population, and car ownership rose from 224 per 1,000 people in 1971 to 380 per 1,000 in 1994. Two-car families became more common, as, albeit to a lesser extent, did three-car families, although ownership and usage remain far lower than in the United States. In 2015, British motorists bought 2.6 million new cars; there were also many purchasers of secondhand cars, a practice made much easier by online information. A fictional reference to the sense of remorseless and destructive change was offered in Douglas Adams's popular radio series and novel *The Hitchhiker's Guide to the Galaxy* (1979), which rested on the idea that Earth had been demolished to further an interstellar bypass.

People used cars more for work, shopping, and leisure. Indeed, cars can be seen in a very positive light as well as in a democratizing one, permitting working people to more easily access jobs, leisure, and education than previously. The average distance traveled each day per person rose to about twenty miles by 2000, which was an increase of three-quarters over a quarter century. This increase helped drive a demand for more space, for both roads and associated infrastructure, such as garages and parking. In addition, many cars became larger, notably on the American model, and particularly as SUVs enjoyed popularity from the 2000s. They affected other car users as well as other road users, notably cyclists, riders, and pedestrians. There was a social as well as regional dimension in the response to SUVs, as in their description as "Chelsea tractors," a term that captured antipathy to wealthy Londoners with second homes in the countryside.

The attempt by planners to limit car usage by authorizing new developments in which houses or flats had no or few parking spaces proved of only limited effectiveness. Quarrels between neighbors over street parking increased greatly and offered a variation on "road rage," which, itself, became a problem. Indeed, a classic cause of small-scale altercations, brawls, and vandalism arose from homeowners or tenants assuming (wrongly) that parking at the street-side curb outside their dwelling should be used only by them and responding in a hostile manner when others parked there.

Another aspect of road rage developed from anger with cyclists breaking traffic regulations, especially driving through red lights and on pavements. In turn, cyclists complained about other road users and demanded special lanes. The net effect was more acrimonious individual relations and a marked rise in tension. Cyclists became more effective in their lobbying because young, affluent Londoners increasingly cycled to work beginning in the 2010s; their deaths in accidents attracted very favorable treatment of the victims, and cycle paths were installed there from the 2010s.

Car culture interacted with other aspects of social development. It was linked, for example, to changes in employment patterns. In place of factories or mines dependent on large labor forces, most modern industrial concerns are capital intensive and employ less labor. They are often located away from the central areas of cities and on flat and relatively open sites with good road links. As an aspect of the Americanization of much of British life, car park space and access roads are considered important to the attraction of sites, as also with business, science, and shopping "parks."

Related changes in location have also been of great importance in such areas as education, health, shopping, and retirement. Thus, junior schoolchildren, who, in the 1940s, '50s, '60s, and '70s, usually went to school by walking, cycling, or bus, as I did (walking every weekday to the bus station to take a bus to school, with the reverse each evening), came increasingly to be driven. This was a factor that was well understood to contribute to obesity, which rose greatly among children, and also to social differentiation.

The impact of the car proved hard to resist and was particularly apparent in rural areas. It facilitated the mobility of most rural consumers but was also linked to the closure of many rural schools, shops, pubs, churches, and post offices, greatly affecting the fabric of rural life and the nature of community. By 2000, 42 percent of rural parishes had no permanent shop, 49 percent no school, and 75 percent no daily bus service. All of these factors encouraged dependence on cars. Whereas in 1960 there were 75,000 pubs, by 2020 there were 47,000. Many of these closed pubs were in urban areas where some were changed into houses, including the one in London where my sister lived until recently. However, many villages lost their pubs, and those that did had their sense of community challenged. As a result, rural councils sought to refuse change of use consent in order to prevent pubs from being sold for housing.

Economic factors played a major role as many pubs belonged to breweries and they tended to charge their publicans high rents. In turn, the ability to meet these was hit by the competition provided by supermarket sales of alcohol, and notably through the supermarket price promotions that caused a political storm in the early 2010s. As also with milk prices, supermarkets were an easy target, deservedly so, and across the political spectrum. Politicians did not devote comparable attention to the difficult impact of drunk-driving laws on the use of rural pubs. While such legislation was fully understandable, the consequences were severe. There was also a class element. The wealthy could afford higher prices and the conversion of some pubs to restaurants, as well as taking taxis to and from pubs. In contrast, the ploughman (of whom there were far fewer) could rarely now afford "the ploughman's lunch" of bread and cheese in many such pubs; nor were the meals offered intended for ploughmen.

Meanwhile, rising levels of car and truck use put major strain on both the national road network and on local services, as did the greater size and heavier axle weight of trucks, which caused particular problems for bridges. Under EU regulations, Britain was obliged to accept larger trucks. These changes led to pressure to supplement and upgrade existing roads and bridges.

In turn, improvements to the national network, such as the 117-mile M25 round London and the extension of the M40 from Oxford to the West Midlands, were heavily used as traffic responded to new opportunities. The M25 was already inadequate when Thatcher opened the first section in 1986, leading to widening of sections in 2009. The M40 was extended because the M1, opened in 1959, could no longer provide an adequate route to match demand for road traffic from London to the West Midlands. In Cambridgeshire, between 1982 and 1995, traffic on the mostly new A14 and the new M11 increased by close to 300 percent; in the same period, it grew there by over 100 percent on the older-established A10. Road transport provided one among many instances of the serious lack of expenditure on infrastructure. This was in particular a failure of the Thatcher government and was linked to it cutting public expenditure as a whole.

Most freight was moved by road as a result of improvements in the road network but also due to problems with rail transport, including the inflexibility and limitations of the system and strikes. Indeed, the hostile attitude of the rail unions toward labor-saving improvements discouraged investment in rail. There was a comparison with the role of the NUM and investment in coal. Aside from frequent strikes, as in the 1990s, strikes that recurred in 2016–17 and 2022, there were the issues posed by serious rivalry between the different rail unions. Warehousing and distribution increasingly responded to road-based supplies. Distribution systems previously reliant on rail, notably letters and newspapers, switched to road. This had major consequences at the local level, with buildings, routes, staff, and vehicles becoming redundant as a result of such changes.

At the same time, although only used by a minority of the population, there was a steady growth of passenger traffic by rail in the 2000s and 2010s, a growth that put enormous pressure on the system in part because of the failure to maintain capacity. Seriously overcrowded trains became far more common, which contributed greatly to the problems and stress of travel. New capacity was limited, and in this and so much else, the problems of the planning system and of Britain, especially England, being a crowded island were much to the fore.

The regional dimension became more contentious, not least with complaints outside the South-East that investment was overly concentrated there, notably the Elizabeth line across London opened in 2022. There were particular problems in the 2000s and 2010s with overcrowding on trains in the North of England and around Bristol, while investment was focused on train links into London, on which there was also serious overcrowding. The lack of a good east-west rail system, especially from Leeds to Manchester, in northern England became controversial, but in 2021 the original 2014 plan for an improved system between Liverpool and Hull via Manchester and Leeds was scaled down. There is a social dimension, as areas that were poor, such as Lincolnshire, tended to have inadequate services. So also with other largely rural areas, such as East Anglia, Mid-Wales, the Welsh borders, and North Devon.

One of the biggest government projects, HST-2, for a new high-speed train line from London to Birmingham and then on to the North, was presented as a way to provide transport capacity as well as to contribute to Northern growth, specifically that of the "Northern Powerhouse" called for from 2014 by George Osborne, chancellor of the exchequer from 2010 to 2016. This project created great local controversy as the projected route cut across areas of great natural attraction, especially north Buckinghamshire.

At the same time, the course of HST-2, like the contemporaneous dispute over airport runways at Heathrow and Gatwick, led to considerable debate over whether the British were incapable of seeing through major infrastructure projects. Comparisons were drawn with China, France, Japan, the Netherlands, and Spain, and notably in railway and airport construction. Much was made of the complexities and delays of the planning system, and of the propensity to appeal against projects. In practice, aside from securing funding, the difficulty of securing and maintaining project consistency, in what was a crowded country with clashing interests, was the key problem. The fiscal strain arising as a result of the COVID pandemic led to the cancelation in 2022 of the branch to Leeds.

HOUSING

Housing demand was a constant feature of the period, from postwar rebuilding in the late 1940s to repeated calls in the early twentieth century from across the political spectrum to build more homes in order to respond to a rapidly rising population. Housing policy saw competing interests: central and local government, builders, owners, landlords private and public, tenants private and public, would-be purchasers, lenders, and others. Moreover, there were very different markets across the country and also the pressures of strong social and individual assumptions about place, location, space, and cost. A history of Britain in these years can be written around these myriad tensions.

In contrast to the United States, housing costs were/are higher in what is a more crowded country, and the role of the state in regulation is much stronger. This is particularly so in limiting green-field development and low-density

sprawl. Thus, as part of the bout of policy initiatives and regulations that fol-
lowed World War II and linked to a wider process of urban renewal,[3] New
Towns were designed to complement Green Belts, greenfield areas outside
cities that were intended to prevent their continual expansion. The first New
Town, Stevenage, to the north of London, was chosen in 1946, the year of the
New Towns Act, which was followed by a new Town and Country Planning
Act in 1947. The London Green Belt, which was given legislative aspiration
in 1938, was finally secured with an Act of 1959. An aspect of regional planning was provided by the designation of "overspill" development areas beyond
the Green Belt: for London, this was especially so of expansion at the towns
of Basingstoke, Ipswich, and Northampton. Many new and greatly expanded
towns, however, translated old social problems to new sites, as with Peterlee. In
addition, Green Belts led to increased commuting from new housing beyond
them, for example from Wantage to Oxford. Insufficient thought was given to
the idea of Green Wedges as opposed to Green Belts.

The long-term consequences of housing provision, in terms of social
norms, tensions, and structure, remain unclear, but it would be inappropriate to ignore the issue or to neglect its close relationship with environmental
trends. Aside from the cost of housing, there are issues of quality. Much of the
older housing that was cleared from the scene, in both town and country, was
unsatisfactory. However, much was not, being perfectly capable of improvement to good standard. Very often, the problem was not the housing but the
poverty of the inhabitants and the excessive number of their children, not that
it was considered widely acceptable to discuss the latter. The wholesale flat-
tening of such areas and the movement of their inhabitants to new estates
destroyed old communities and eliminated some working-class owner occupation, not to mention private renting, replacing them with council tenure to
the great political benefit of the Labour Party.

Rural housing was also affected. For example, the chaumers and bothies
(one- or two-room huts), in which many male Scottish farmworkers lived in
claustrophobic and insanitary conditions, disappeared in the 1960s. In a 1946
John Rhode novel, the landowner "was rather annoyed about those two cot-
tages being condemned. He said it was nonsense, and that they could be made
to last for years yet . . . he told me to look round and find a better site on which
to build two new ones."[4]

All housing built in New Towns was built to Parker Morris standards,
which were reasonable. These standards were extended to all council (public) housing in 1969, although many councils had already adopted them by
then. Outdoor toilets became a thing of the past as far as new housing was

concerned. In part, public housing was, and is, cramped because of overoc-cupancy, rather than the inherent nature of the accommodation. Aside from crowdedness, however, there is the danger that a new generation of substan-dard housing is being built, notably housing with damp, an issue raised in Parliament in 2016. The absence of a minister knowledgeable in all aspects of housing provision is readily apparent. Consistently, much new build has been of indifferent quality, while parking and garden space are both very limited.

In contrast to the Continent, where living in apartments is the urban norm, high-density housing is unpopular in Britain, notably in England, and the desired norm is of a house with separate entry to the road and usually with a garden. That, however, cannot be afforded by most, and planners have long sought not to fulfil this norm. It is notable that much advertising and many television "soaps" depict housing that is more generous, indeed far more gen-erous, in space than the crowded circumstances of much, indeed most, of the population. This contrast between image and reality is true for all countries but is particularly true of Britain. It can also be seen with "show houses" in new developments, with such houses having very misleading small furniture, especially beds, in order to make them appear bigger.

The contrast between image and reality can accentuate social tension and also intergenerational issues, as adult children frequently cannot afford the space and lifestyle enjoyed by their parents. In part, this is due to the changed priorities of the young: their emphasis on vacations, entertainment, and con-sumption, rather than belt-tightening to save deposits and pay mortgages. This situation contributes greatly to pressure for the transfer of funds from parents to children. This pressure invites both family disputes and questions of public policy, more particularly not only house building and death duties, but also the provision and payment of long-term care for the elderly, and par-ticularly how far adequate and affordable care can be provided in care homes or if people stay in their houses. For many, the capital value of their house is the key security and, in practice, their private pension, which helps explain sensitivity about house prices.

Again, the generational experience has been very different, being greatly affected by population trends, housing provision, financing, and government policy, including the right-to-buy revolution for council housing in the 1980s and the revival of private renting after the 1988 Housing Act. In the 1950s and 1960s, although interest (borrowing) rates could be high, it was relatively easy for young adults with steady jobs to move into the property market, but that has ceased to be the case and across more and more of the country. The cost of deposits is high, and interest rates rose markedly in 2016 after a long period of low rates. What was largely a London issue has become one across most of the country. The number of new houses remains well below needs.

BRITISH *HEIMATS*?

The environment, both natural and built, is under pressure. The relationship between this and the popular sense of identity is complex because the latter has tended not to attract much attention and notably so for England. In contrast, interest in nationalism has led to much more attention being devoted to such a sense in Scotland, Wales, and Northern Ireland (see chapter 9). In these three, history, or at least an approach to history, is crucial to particular feelings about what Germans call *Heimat*, which can be loosely translated as homeland. The English counterpart has been largely subsumed or translated into a Britishness. In both Englishness and Britishness as understood by the English, the natural and built environments play an inconsistent role. In particular, the notion of the desirable nature of both of these environments held in the North of England, and of the relationship between them, is consciously different to that in the South. In turn, each is carefully differentiated in a local patterning of experience and perception.

What this situation means in terms of identity, and how far there is such an identity separate to more international, if not global, attitudes and trends, are questions that are significant for what follows in the book and notably so in the cultural and political sections. There are reasonable questions as to whether the English are less prone to the question of homeland than the Scots, Welsh, or Northern Irish, and whether the key element within England is regional or national. Immigration has had such resonance as an issue in part due to English nationalism. In addition, the Brexit vote had a very high correlation with "English, not British" identity in England. Indeed, the English identity is slowly, albeit only partially, emerging from the catch-all British identity, now that the Scots, Welsh, and Northern Irish, especially the Scots, are vocal in asserting their identity. The issues of civic politics are also relevant: issues that confronted politicians from the mid-2000s as they sought to define and ground a public patriotism.

CONCLUSIONS

The number of people per square kilometer in 2008 was 244.2 in the UK, 109.3 in France, and 31 in the United States. In all three, regional variations were marked, but as indicated, the base figure varied greatly. In Britain, population and environmental pressure was most acute in England. High population density is readily apparent in the South-East of England where population and population growth are concentrated. In many respects, despite policies of regional development, government policy, especially since 1979, has also helped drive population concentration. British Broadcasting Corporation (BBC) payments to staff in the 2010s to move from London to Salford near Manchester were only one consequence of a major problem in which the culture and significance of major provincial cities in England have been marginalized over time. In March 2014, the BBC screened a program, "Mind the Gap: London vs the Rest," which captured much attention. On June 23, 2014, George Osborne announced in a speech in Manchester, "The powerhouse of London dominates more and more. . . . We need a Northern Powerhouse." Northern consciousness was the focus of a major BBC radio series in 2016, "The Matter of the North." It remains an issue.

A sense of crowdedness became more common in South-East England and, increasingly, elsewhere. One clear manifestation was the critical stage in cemetery provision by the 2010s, with many graveyards filling up. The environmental pressures from a rising population are felt differently across the country, most clearly in urban areas, and these differences are important to regional and social perceptions and politics. Government responses are sometimes actively unhelpful. Notably, in 2001, in order to address global warming, the government cut the duty on low-sulfur diesel and reduced company car taxes on diesels. This policy led to an increase in diesel car registrations from 3.45 million (13 percent of the total) to 8.2 million (28 percent), which reduced carbon emissions but, however, greatly increased the emission of nitrogen oxide and particulates. In 2022, the government banned the sale of new cars powered solely by engines that use diesel fuel.

It is likely that environmental pressure will continue to be the case and will become more important, possibly much more important, as the population rise continues. This is a crucial factor for both the natural environment and for its built counterpart.

2

ECONOMY UNDER STRAIN

BRITAIN, THE COUNTRY that invented the Industrial Revolution in the eighteenth century and became the "Workshop of the World" in the nineteenth, also became unwillingly "postindustrial" after 1945. This change had major consequences: for the country itself, for its society and culture as well as its economy, and for Britain's relations with the rest of the world.

Problems had been long coming and were systemic. Nineteenth-century British industry had faced serious international competition, notably from rapid and large-scale industrialization in the United States and in Germany. By the late nineteenth century, having been passed by both, Britain was no longer the foremost manufacturing country in the world and some sections of the economy were in major difficulties. As a result, prefiguring aspects of Britain from 1945, there was both a pronounced sense of imperial overstretch and a related call for political reform and social regeneration—a call that helped drive the politics of the 1900s and early 1910s, notably with an unsuccessful campaign for tariff reform in the shape of protectionism. The two world wars, the Great Depression of the 1930s, and the protectionism to which it gave rise placed even more of a strain on the British economy and on the world trading system in which it flourished. However, Britain's competitors were also greatly affected.

In 1945, despite all its problems, Britain still had one of the leading economies in the world. Would-be rivals, notably Germany and Japan, were in ruins as a result of war damage, especially bombing, and China, France, Italy, and the Soviet Union had been badly affected by occupation and other wartime strains. In 1945, Britain remained a major manufacturing country, with its significant heavy industry based on steelmaking, engineering, and shipbuilding and drawing on extensive coal production. Light industry was also very important, including the manufacture of consumer goods, notably cars. Britain was particularly important in services, having, for example, the foremost merchant marine in the world, as well as the leading insurance market. Britain was also a key banking center, indeed the largest outside the United States.

This was no longer the situation by 2016. Although Britain remained the second largest player in world finance and in other branches of services, including popular music and related leisure activities, industrial decline was pronounced and was felt to be pronounced. Alongside success in particular manufacturing sectors, notably pharmacy, and a marked revival in car making encouraged by high demand, there had been a more general decline, both absolute and relative, and notably as Britain lost comparative advantage and gained comparative disadvantage. Once major industrial players, such as ICI in chemicals, were no longer present or as prominent. Areas in which Britain had previously done well, such as small arms munitions, had been seriously affected by disinvestment including, in this case, the closure of factories. Short-termism was repeatedly a key factor in investment decisions, and in encouraging the decision to close plants.

Manufacturing decline had a particularly devastating impact as much of the social and regional structures and geography of the country had derived from nineteenth-century industrialization. This was true in particular of the North and Midlands of England, of South Wales, and of the Central Belt of Scotland but was also the case for other regions where industry had been prominent, even if not locally or regionally dominant. For example, printing ceased to be prominent in Exeter, which, instead, became one of the many cities in which "business parks" were really primarily centers for retail and wholesale, rather than for manufacturing. Printing, which had also been important in other centers such as Watford, was one of the industries affected by globalization. In this case, printing was increasingly carried out in South and East Asia, with material eventually sent there online. So also, for example, with the drawing of architectural plans.

Economic decline also became a key political narrative in Britain, one that led politicians and government frequently, even consistently, to reject the existing situation and to seek new solutions. As a result, the economic story cannot be divorced from that of politics. For the population, monthly figures of unemployment and quarterly figures of trade frequently encouraged a sense of drama and despair. That the unemployment figures were monthly, not quarterly, proved especially important. Industrial disputes repeatedly drove this decline onto a public stage that politicians could not control or, as damaging, give the impression of being able to control.

Economic change was generally perceived as decline, which was true as far as relative international position was concerned. It was also the case as far as absolute activity was concerned in many, but not all, sectors. This decline repeatedly undermined the policies of governments. This situation encouraged an already-strong tendency to governmental intervention in the economy, and the failure of this intervention further led to a sense of political failure, if not impotence. Political contention on this point then encouraged further intervention. In practice, economic decline was only relative. Growth in GDP and in GDP per head has been considerable over the period.

NATIONALIZATION

In the late 1940s, the answer apparently was nationalization, the state ownership of the economy, or of what were presented as its key sectors. Pushed by the trade unions that were crucial to its composition, that was the policy of the Labour governments of 1945–51, and much of the economy was nationalized, including the gas industry, electricity supply, coal mining, steel production, the railways, the Bank of England, and the hospitals. Much of the population was brought into state employment, which underlined the possibilities for central planning, as did the shortage of resources in the private sector and notably of liquidity after World War II, as well as the damage and disruption of that conflict when state direction had been insistent.

At the same time, nationalization was very much an ideology for the peacetime economy, one advanced without any real understanding of how capitalism worked, how to value assets, and how to secure a return on assets and investment. Nationalization was in practice a panacea for unoriginal thinking by a Socialist Party with little idea how to run anything and whose main contribution was to keep Communism at bay. If, however, Labour was inadequate for government and helped to cause further systemic problems, the Conservatives were painfully slow to adapt to the new postwar world. Britain muddled along, although its role in designing the new German trade unions showed that it knew what to do.

Nationalization owed much to a left-wing ideal of a planned, corporatist state, one that, in practice, only appeared to work due to the global "long boom" from 1945 to the early 1970s. Even before that ended, the deficiencies of the model were clear, and it collapsed under the strain of world recession in the 1970s. The same was true of the Communist planned economies of Eastern

Europe. In the late 1940s, nationalization appeared the counterpart to the social policies of Labour. The two were joined in the creation, as the key element of a new welfare state, of the National Health System (NHS), and notably as a centralized system of state provision, rather than of the state payment, via social insurance, of a variety of independent health providers.

Nationalization remained the Labour panacea until the 1990s, under Tony Blair, brought a change in policy for the party. It was seen anew in the 1970s. Indeed, in 1975, the recently elected Labour government took the majority of the shares in the newly consolidated car manufacturer British Leyland and also created the British National Oil Corporation. In 1977, British Aerospace and British Shipbuilders were created as nationalized industries. This was not an exhaustive list of nationalizations in the 1970s.

Although it bitterly opposed steel nationalization, and denationalized it in 1953, the Conservatives largely supported state ownership in the 1950s. Moreover, whatever his rhetoric, both in opposition and eventually when he gained office in 1970, Edward Heath was driven to abandon his stance and to back nationalization in the early 1970s in order to save industries threatened by closure. The Conservatives only changed policy (and not immediately so) as Margaret Thatcher introduced a very different approach after she became party leader in 1975. Ideology, the political issues bound up with public-sector issues, and the pressures of economic failure all encouraged a new approach that led to large-scale privatization in the 1980s.

INDUSTRIAL PROBLEMS

There had been long-term relative economic decline from the 1870s, but the situation deteriorated markedly in the late twentieth century. Between 1960 and 1981, the UK annual growth in GDP was lower than that of all the other eighteen OECD countries. As a result, the average standard of living fell beneath that of West Germany, Japan, France, and Italy in the post-1960 period. There were serious problems with underinvestment, low industrial productivity, limited innovation, poor management (particularly production management), and obstructive trade unions. A sense of decline, pervasive at times, was especially characteristic in the 1970s.

Ironically, the discovery of large quantities of oil in the North Sea in 1970 and its production from 1975, at a time of higher oil prices, was to help ease Britain's balance-of payments problem. However, this production did not prevent continued economic decline relative to competitors who lacked that resource. Thus, the oil masked the consequences of this decline from most of the population, creating, at the same time, a dangerous dependence and sense of entitlement, especially on the part of unskilled labor, but also across society, including among the middle class and notably so in the public sector.

Just as the political context for the economy changed greatly, so did the economic one for politics and society. Until the 1970s, there was a strong labor market for skilled and semiskilled workers, and also many jobs for the unskilled and in both manufacturing and in other sectors. Employment remained high and expanded to include more jobs for women. Full employment was important to widespread affluence. Moreover, a sense of relative economic decline, and especially so in relation to the United States and West Germany, was not accompanied by one of crisis until the major devaluation of sterling in 1967, one that had been strongly resisted by the Labour government. However, in the meanwhile, the economic fundamentals were poor, and especially poor in relation to other leading economies. British industry was becoming steadily less efficient and competitive, and was largely providing a healthy impression because of a prolonged boom in the Western, indeed world, economy as a whole. This boom powered growth between 1945 and 1973 and made it apparently possible to afford and pursue everything: full employment, social welfare, and international influence.

During this boom, industries in which Britain had played a crucial role, such as cotton, woollen, and linen textiles, declined markedly. Shipbuilding was a long-established heavy industry in which Britain had led the world. From the late 1950s, however, shipbuilding lost orders to the lower charges of new foreign shipyards, notably in Japan. In addition, the latter were able to promise earlier and more reliable delivery dates, which was a result of the absence in Britain of modern shipyards able to offer flow-line production and the resulting higher productivity. This absence reflected a lack of investment in Britain, one that was born of short-term attitudes and of limited governmental and management planning for the long term. Labor problems, notably strikes, were also a serious issue and one that greatly discouraged innovation and investment.

Crises hit shipbuilding hard. In particular, the economic crisis caused by the quadrupling of oil prices in 1973 led to a decline in orders for new ships, a decline that exposed inefficiencies in UK shipbuilding. As a result, by the end of 1981, the number of shipbuilding sites had fallen from twenty-seven to fifteen, and the gross registered tonnage launched fell from 1,281,000 in 1974 to 46,000 in 1987. Moreover, countries such as South Korea that pursued sales regardless of profitability hit Britain hard in the 1980s, ensuring that investment in Britain faced few profitable outcomes. However, a lack of investment from the late 1950s was also a factor.[1]

More generally across the UK, deindustrialization was a problem and not only in traditional heavy industries, as had been the case in the 1930s. Poor labor relations and indifferent management were systemic issues, and there was persistent concern about low productivity. The trade unions frequently acted in a disruptive fashion, and this was more serious because they were an integral part of Labour, which was a governing or potentially governing political party. Whole industries went down the drain thanks in part to unions supported by Labour: for example, shipbuilding and the docks. Management was often as bad. The different class and social status of management and worker were far too evident for comfort. While the workers had egg and chips in the canteen, the board of directors had gin and tonics and a three-course lunch in the comfortable boardroom. These divisions, and the linked cultural and social differences, exacerbated labor relations. Workplace trade unionism became a greater problem, with anarchic local bargaining led by shop stewards, many of whom readily resorted to strikes. Restrictive practices, bitter interunion disputes, and poor productivity were all linked and also contributed to questions of social and political order. New factories, such as in car manufacturing, faced these problems as well. Certain regions, notably Merseyside, the region centered on Liverpool, proved particularly difficult for labor relations, but they were an issue across much of industrial Britain.

Thus, the construction of an effective postwar manufacturing economy did not proceed as far in Britain as elsewhere in Western Europe. This was very much the case, for example, with the docks. In 1947, the Labour government introduced a Dock Labour Scheme, which brought a measure of job security. However, the scheme lessened the worker freedoms enjoyed under the earlier, casual system of employment, and the dockers, traditionally militant, resented the discipline of the new system. There were dock strikes during each year of the 1945–51 Labour government, leading to the deployment of troops. Subsequently, the unionized dockers did not respond well to the change in working practices required by containerization, and this negative attitude encouraged the shift in freight business to Rotterdam in the Netherlands. The first British container ship sent to Australia, the *Encounter Bay*, sailed from Rotterdam in 1969 because of an industrial dispute at Tilbury, the new port for London. Subsequently, Felixstowe, where the labor force was less unionized, and therefore more flexible in working practices, became a much more important port than London.

The difficult history of the docks indicated the problems posed by bad labor relations and, in particular, the difficulties they posed for responding to possibilities for transformation. More generally, dock labor was an aspect of the resistance by low-skill workers to working techniques and technology that needed fewer workers. Many of these techniques required workers with more skills. Compounding these problems, low-skill workers used industrial muscle to press for high-skill wages, and the consequence was to help make activities and companies uneconomic. This was also a problem, for example, with train conductors (ticket checkers) and manual workers on the railways. There was resistance to new working practices, as in 2016–17 with a dispute over driver-only trains leading to major disruption on Southern Railway.

Alongside the decline of heavy industry, such as steel and shipbuild-ing, more recent spheres of growth, notably the chemical and car industries, did not meet their potential and, often, decayed. The very public problems of British Leyland, the government-run car manufacturer, notably with labor relations in the 1970s and 1980s, helped dramatize to the public the acute dif-ficulties of the economy and encouraged a sense of serious intractability. In addition, as Leyland cars declined in quality, these problems had a subliminal impact in reducing public support for the nationalized industries.

Similarly, alongside decline in the traditional heavy industrial areas, such as the North-East of England, there were difficulties in industrial activity in newer areas, such as Fife. For example, synthetic fiber plants, established there in the 1960s, closed in the early 1980s. Alongside national trends, there were clear regional and local dimensions to the economic crises of the 1970s and 1980s. For example, Liverpool and Glasgow, the ports that specialized in impe-rial trade, suffered from the uncertainties and instabilities of the late-colonial and postcolonial world, which reinforced other problems in these docks.[2] Although the trade unions, and the public as a whole, did not appreciate the point, the rest of the world did not owe them a living. Although London suf-fered much deindustrialization as a manufacturing center, it also benefited greatly from the expansion of financial services and of production tasks linked to the media.

Wales demonstrated the reasons for economic dynamism and its spatial variations. This dynamism was linked to major social changes, not least the growth of a white-collar workforce for whom traditional loyalties had scant interest. This was a workforce living not in the valleys, the center of coal pro-duction, but on the north and south coasts and in the Cardiff urban region. Expansion in service industries and, in particular, in administrative agen-cies based in Cardiff (declared capital of Wales by Parliament in 1955), cre-ated much new employment, as did investment, especially from Japan, in new industrial plants, several linked to the car industry. These plants were concen-trated in South Wales, the economic importance of which was boosted by a new proximity to markets, thanks to the opening of the Severn Bridge (which had been called for since the 1930s) and the extension of the M4 motorway from London to Bristol into South Wales over the bridge. Opened in 1966, the bridge was at once a major symbol of modernity and, in practice, a problematic design. It was eventually supplemented by a second bridge over the Severn estuary.

A new geography of wealth and employment greatly favored Cardiff and, to a lesser extent, the towns of Bridgend, Newport, Swansea, and Wrexham. Conversely, coal and, later, steel were badly hit in Wales, as was long-established metal smelting in the Swansea area. The collapse of coal mining in one of its traditional centers was not followed by effective inward investment. The expansion of steel in the late 1940s, in particular in the massive Port Talbot steelworks opened in 1951, was succeeded by closures and massive layoffs, with the steelworks there threatened by closure in 2016. In June 2016, Scunthorpe (in Lincolnshire), the second largest UK steel plant after Port Talbot, was sold by the Indian-owned Tata Steel for £1 to a European investment company after being on the market for three years. Despite the cushioning of social security, economic problems had a serious impact on the social framework in Wales as elsewhere. Unemployment rose, and traditional mining and heavy industrial centers, such as Merthyr Tydfil, became linked to dissatisfaction and notably so in the EU referendum in 2016. The previous year, Tata had mothballed the last two Scottish steel works, although in 2016 the rolling plate mill at Motherwell was reopened to produce steel for wind farms and other manufacturing.

In a long-standing process, traditional blue-collar male workers suffered the most from globalization and, more particularly, from the end of economic protectionism in the shape of import tariffs and other restrictive practices. Whereas in 1951, 70 percent of the workforce was "manual," by 2000 it was 37 percent as a result of industrial decline. The crisis of much of the remaining British steel industry in 2016 underlined this issue. Linked to this decline, there was a fall in the percentage of national wealth enjoyed by the working class, as well as in much of their individual real income, a process also seen more generally across the West. Conversely, the rise of service industries created greater opportunities for social mobility.

Transfer payments to the regions with a weaker economy became a key element in public finances, not least due to unemployment payments and income support. Northern Ireland and Scotland were particular beneficiaries of transfer payments, but so was much of northern England, including Merseyside. Labour used the system to direct funds to its political fiefdoms, and they, in turn, provided solid electoral support until the late 2000s. This system proved the basis for Labour politics, notably in Scotland and North-East England,

and was to be continued by Gordon Brown, the Labour prime minister from 2007 to 2010, in his use of £1.6 billion of public money to save the Dunfermline Building Society and his decision to concentrate naval shipbuilding on Rosyth, running down Portsmouth (in southern England) in contrast. This choice had important knock-on economic consequences.

The political character of social policy and regional economic support did not tend to attract much attention, but it was a key element, and what to Americans are "pork barrel" politics were much in evidence, although not at the rate seen in the United States. The excellent road system constructed in the North-East of England by Labour was an aspect of this politics, as were Conservative concerns about rail season-ticket prices for commuters into London. A rewriting of the history of the period in these terms would be rewarding, but the evidence behind political support for specific policy choices in regional investment is frequently suggestive, rather than conclusive. It was easier for government to intervene when industries were nationalized. Aside from privatization, EU competition provisions limited the options for blatant government intervention.

By the mid-1980s, Britain was importing more manufactured goods than it exported. This reflected in part the crisis in British industry, which had been greatly exacerbated by 1970s' trade union militancy and early 1980s' Conservative fiscal policies (see chapter 7). The changing balance of priorities within the economy was also important. This balance was responsive to the sectors in which Britain enjoyed competitive advantage and also to social priorities and political drives. Politicians, of all major parties, repeatedly spoke of the need for a manufacturing renaissance, and they have frequently continued to do so in the 2010s, but they found it difficult to provide any coherent or effective policies to that end. For example, the West Midlands, still a key area for manufacturing and engineering in the 1960s, was badly affected by deindustrialization, with, by 2015, the second highest unemployment rate of any UK region (equal with Northern Ireland) and the third lowest economic output per head in England.

FINANCE

It proved easier to disguise deindustrialization as a result of the extraction of large quantities of oil from under the North Sea, and it proved easier to ensure a regulatory structure that helped service industries, notably the financial sector. The latter benefited under Thatcher from a "bonfire of regulations," in the so-called Big Bang in 1986. In this, restrictions on the activities of financial concerns were removed or relaxed, with, for example, the end of both minimum commissions on the stock market and of banning foreign banks and firms from membership of the stock exchange. Old demarcations were scrapped, and the nature of trading moved from "open outcry" on the exchange floor to trading on screen. More generally, Thatcherism represented a move, however qualified, to neoliberalism, with the attendant reduction in the role and power of the state and its quest to cut the economy free. This move reflected both a strand in intellectual and political thought and also views on the part of some major figures in the Confederation of British Industry and in other "think tanks" and groups that were influential under Thatcher. In November 1985, Thatcher accordingly rejected the advice of the Bank of England and Treasury that Britain join the European Exchange Rate Mechanism (ERM), and it only did so in 1990.

The new situation in financial regulation helped the accumulated skill and entrepreneurial ability focused on banking, share dealing, and insurance, all spheres that expanded greatly, producing secondary (related) growth. The hyperactive open trading floor became an important image of the new London and the bonus culture a matter of public report and criticism. The profits and bonuses reflected a high level of activity, as well as an ability to respond to opportunities. Thus, the City (the name given to the financial sector that was centered in that part of London) proved effective at developing trading in new financial instruments, such as euro bonds in the 1960s, being helped by a US tax on interest. The City also played a major role in the recycling of oil wealth on the global scale from newly affluent producers (including Britain thanks to North Sea oil) both to investment opportunities and to those short of liquidity.

Partly as a result of such activity, the City became more prominent in the British economy and also more closely linked into a world network of financial centers, the other key points in which were New York, Tokyo, and Hong Kong. London benefited from its time-zone position, which enabled it to do business while New York, Tokyo, Hong Kong, and later, Shanghai, the other leading financial centers, were all open. Timekeeping reflected this, with clocks in financial institutions also showing the time in these centers.

At the same time, the City's financial place within Europe was challenged by Frankfurt in Germany, although as part of this challenge, German, Swiss, French, and Scandinavian banks established themselves in London, especially by purchasing British merchant banks. For example, Deutsche Bank bought Morgan Grenfell. This process was encouraged by Britain's membership of the European Economic Community (later European Community and then European Union) and by a liberal attitude to takeovers and the related inward investment. The effectiveness of the City, despite the relative decline of the

British economy as a whole, and particularly of manufacturing, and despite the loss of sterling's role as a stable international reserve currency, owed much to the liberal attitude of the government to the growing role of overseas banks in the City. This role led to the large-scale arrival of overseas financial interests. For example, the Swiss bank UBS became one of the biggest investment banks in London, employing just over 5,400 people there in early 2016, in part because Switzerland, which is not in the EU, lacked a financial services passporting deal with the EU.

Inward investment in Britain was a key development that was eased by this arrival of overseas financial interests. Investment brought not only liquidity but also the repatriation abroad of profit which affected the value of the service sector to the economy and to public finances. Meanwhile, a speculative building boom changed the face of London, not least with large Modernist buildings that had the functionalism of large, open trading floors. Rising property values, for both business and residential properties, were linked to the City's growth. In fashionable London nightclubs such as Annabel's, people were asked if they worked in the City.

The City tended to take an indirect role in politics, although the support of many City individuals for the Conservative Party was important to its finances. City interests tended to make their point privately to the chancellor of the exchequer, in effect the finance minister, and he was generally in effect the deputy prime minister, a situation particularly seen with Gordon Brown (1997–2007) and George Osborne (2010–16), and in effect with Kwasi Kwarteng (2022, very briefly) and Jeremy Hunt (2022–). As an instance of City influence, favorable tax regimes for "non-doms," nondomiciled residents, those classed as foreign residents, were important to the City and were introduced and maintained accordingly. The key City interests were globalization and stability, and these helped explain strong opposition on its part in 2014 to the prospect of Scottish independence and even more in 2016 to leaving the EU.

In turn, the reputation of banks had been badly hit, especially from the late 2000s, by public criticism of high salaries, notably bonuses, and the poor performance that contributed to the financial crisis of 2008, notably short-termism. As a result, the very fact that banks took a position encouraged hostility on those grounds. This was notably so with foreign banks, as in 2016 when J. P. Morgan was criticized for opposing Brexit.

Prior to Brexit, London was the financial capital of Europe and either the world's leading financial center or second only to New York. Being in the EU helped the City to become more global, with US, Asian, and EU banks, asset managers, and insurers using London and EU "passporting" arrangements, as a hub to operate across Europe and way beyond. The resulting liquidity pool and skill base brought many advantages, and Britain made money financing other economies. After Brexit, London will become an offshore center, with regulatory decisions made elsewhere, especially in the Eurozone by the European Central Bank, although to trade for overseas clients, certain regulatory rules always have to be complied with: for example, US rules for US clients. For banking regulation, it is the global international rules that are supreme, not the rules of the individual states or bodies such as the EU. Outside the EU, London is likely to benefit from being less regulated. The importance of the EU to the City can be overstated. It is the openness to foreign investment, the British trading culture, the thriving support "industries" and professions, and the fact that money and finance are international and have no borders that are at the heart of the City's success.

In 2022, pressure from the financial markets brought to an abrupt close first the fiscal plans of the Truss government and then the government itself. In a sense, this was another demonstration of the City's power, although that was as part of an international financial system.

REGIONAL DIMENSIONS

The financial sector was heavily concentrated in London, albeit with other important locations, notably Edinburgh. The sector could afford the high rents of London; and the attraction of business closeness, of living in London, and of the ease of partners finding jobs there outweighed other considerations. The sector brought jobs to the educated, both male and female, but offered little to traditional blue-collar male workers, other than, crucially, providing much of the tax revenue that was used to support social welfare payments. Moreover, most major back-office centers are in other parts of the country, sometimes in former industrial towns. These are very big employers, albeit without many of the highly paid jobs. Just to take the banks, for whom there are very many thousands employed in this fashion, Barclays does so in Coventry, Glasgow, Liverpool, and Northampton; Lloyds in Brighton, Bristol, and Halifax; HSBC in Birmingham; Santander in Liverpool and Milton Keynes; and RBS in Southend.

Always significant, the regional geography of Britain's economy became more pronounced in this period. Nevertheless, at the local level, the ease of commuting reduced such contrasts and notably between urban and rural areas or, rather, their industrial and agricultural counterparts. Thus, London's commuting pool spread across much of southern Britain, while, in general, journey-to-work areas across Britain increased and continue to increase.

Weekly commuting became more common, further lessening contrasts. In part as a result of commuting, local and regional geographies changed. Thus, Newcastle pulled in commuters and shoppers from northern County Durham and southern Northumberland, and Bristol from Somerset. Once-poor rural areas, such as southern Norfolk and northern Kent, became part of London's commuter belt. Transport improvements, both rail and road, were important to this process, but so too was the willingness of commuters to travel for more of the day and to spend more on commuting, and the extent to which more family economies depended on both adults working and the consequent need for commuting. The compromises involved in such choices became an important staple of conversation and dissension. That so many were willing to commute in this fashion contributed to greater economic productivity but was also linked to social differentiation as many children were as a result entrusted to low-paid childminders (the overwhelming majority women) by more affluent parents. One side effect was to undermine the value of gender as an analytical unit in economic activity and, instead, to underline the significance of class.

On the national level, there was a regional and local differentiation related to the stage of production. In particular, increasingly separate from production tasks, many of which went abroad, management and research and development jobs were concentrated in South East England. There, the city of Milton Keynes, a "New Town," had the fastest-growing economy outside London between 1997 and 2011, while, also in the South-East, Croydon saw significant expansion starting in the late 2000s with major growths in technology companies.

No other part of the country saw office development to compare with that in London. One Canada Square, a pyramid-topped 235-meter-high skyscraper in Canary Wharf, built in 1988–91, and then Britain's tallest skyscraper, symbolized the development of the Docklands in East London as a modern business hub focused on financial services. This project was very much encouraged by the Thatcher government. To that end, a development corporation that was removed from the control of the Labour local authorities was established in order to circumvent these authorities, their hostility to the financial sector, and their concern about the interests and housing opportunities of their traditional constituents. The opening of the Thames Barrier in 1984 protected the area from sea surges. The number of jobs based in the Canary Wharf development quadrupled from 27,400 to 100,500 between 2001 and 2012.

New communications links and methods and the financing and politics behind them played important roles in this development. In particular, a new train system, the Docklands Light Railway, was put in to link the Docklands to the City, and it was provided with remotely controlled trains that greatly reduced exposure to the poor labor relations and expensive overmanning of the London Tube (underground railway) system, a situation that led to repeated Tube strikes, as in 2015 before twenty-four-hour services were introduced in 2016. London's geography was transformed as a result of the development of Docklands, and a new urban landscape was pushed to the fore, one that, in turn, became influential elsewhere. In 2016, London had the best access to 4G in Britain. Mobile phone users in London could get a 4G signal 69.7 percent of the time, compared to 35.4 percent in Wales.

CRIME

As a very different trend, crime also appeared to become more linked to financial services, although fraud has long had a relationship with money, and much of the appearance was due to the rise of investigative journalism. The willingness of newspapers to report fraud, notably involving banks, was also significant, although frequently, there was a reluctance to engage with the issue until less-prominent publications had established the point.

It is not usual to discuss films in sections on the economy, but there is a pertinent one about the transforming role of money, *The Long Good Friday* (1980). This was voted by *Empire* magazine in 1997 as the best British movie ever made. As a reminder of the multiple dimensions of change, experience, and imagination, the film was controversial when it came out because it suggested that the Provisional Irish Republican Army (IRA; see chapter 9), then engaged in a terrorist campaign against Britain, was well-nigh invincible. The resulting controversy helped delay the film's release but also distracted attention from the film's vivid depiction of a Britain in change. The protagonist, Harold Shand, brilliantly played by Bob Hoskins, was a self-made millionaire businessman, with bold ambitions for Thames-side property development in London. He was also corrupt, and his "corporation" spanned crime and business. Criminal London was presented as awash with new money but also under pressure from stronger international forces. Wooing mafia-linked American investors to back his property plans, Shand was attacked by a shadowy group using extreme violence. This turns out to be the IRA, who had been inadvertently crossed by Shand's gang over drug running. The IRA destroy a Docklands pub, a classic symbol of community life.

Much of the film was shot on location in London and revealed a city changing under the influence of the property development and new money expressed by Shand. In turn, he was a focus for globalization as London was laid open to transformative outside influences. The world of crime was indeed changing fast. Traditional forms of crime, notably of protection rackets, intimidation, prostitution, and illegal gambling, remained important. From the 1960s, however, they were affected by the possibilities and profits linked to the rise of drug use. Moreover, greater volatility arose from the removal by the police of established criminal gangs, notably those of the Krays in East London and of Charlie Richardson in South London. The new gangs that replaced them were more international in ambition and composition, and globalization affected the world of crime, not least with drug smuggling and distribution.

Compared to most states, the linkage between crime and politics was limited. It was most pronounced in the case of the IRA, which was active in smuggling and intimidation, but mainstream politics tended to seek funds from the trade unions (Labour) and legitimate businesses (Conservatives), and those business figures who pursued political ambitions, such as James Goldsmith, the founder of the 1990s' Referendum Party, were legitimate businessmen. The Krays socialized with some politicians, and questions were asked about the financial probity and links of others, notably Reginald Maudling, the Conservative home secretary in the early 1970s. Other politicians involved in fraudulent or highly questionable activities included John Stonehouse of Labour in the 1960s. In 2023, the police questioned Nicola Sturgeon, the recently resigned First Minister of Scotland, in a corruption enquiry. Dodgy businessmen who sat as Members of Parliament included Robert Maxwell. On the whole, however, the business of crime did not encompass politics.

TECHNOLOGY

In practice, economic change frequently met with a negative response but generally did not lead to a violent one. Nevertheless, there were significant episodes. Thus, in 1986, when Rupert Murdoch broke the restrictive practices of the print unions, notably the need to pay for typesetting, by moving the production of his newspapers from Fleet Street in Central London to a new production site at Wapping in London's docklands, there was violent picketing. It was thwarted by the police, who were certain of government support. Murdoch was also successful because he could turn to the Electricians Union to provide an alternative labor force to that of the print unions. The Electricians Union was one in which Communist control had already been defeated after a long battle. Commentators emphasized the political nature of the dispute. Murdoch supported Thatcher, notably with the populist *Sun*, but also with the *Times*, while the print unions looked to the Left. Many commentators were to be critical of Murdoch's management style and political preferences, but the luddite print workers scarcely deserve much sympathy.

The move of newspapers to new production practices reflected radical changes in technology, particularly the end of hot-metal printing. This was an aspect of a more general technological transformation that Britain shared with the rest of the world. Companies moved to digital technology, Britain becoming a center of innovation and development in the digital economy. Individuals moved online, and by 2020, adults were spending, on average, twenty-five hours a week online, compared to ten hours in 2005. Many industries were affected. For example, betting online rose, although that was not necessarily at the expense of over-the-counter betting. Instead, both were primarily affected by employment and interest rates.

Since 2008

In contrast to London's dynamism as a world city, the Local Government Association reported, in 2014, that underemployment and underachievement among sixteen to twenty-four-year-olds was especially acute in Northern cities, particularly Sheffield, Leeds, Newcastle, and Manchester. Class and regional distinctions repeatedly interacted in these and other respects. There is also much poverty in particular locations across the country, including towns in the South-East—such as Chatham—and those in eastern Kent—for example, Dover and Margate—as well as in parts of London, notably Tower Hamlets. Company start-ups were fewest in such places. In Scotland, there is much deprivation in Glasgow, and in Wales in old coal-mining areas. In contrast to investment in London, that by foreign companies elsewhere was more limited.

At the same time, distance from London and the South was not the sole factor. For example, the North West of England has economic output per head of population that is the highest in England outside the South and London. Whereas the rate of business start-ups in the West Midlands is the second lowest in England, the East Midlands has the second highest rate of any UK region, and Darlington in the North-East had significant growth in the mid-2010s. "Ten Years of Tax: How Cities Contribute to the National Exchequer," a July 2016 report by the Centre for Cities, noted that London generated almost as much tax as the next thirty-seven largest UK cities combined, with a percentage rise of 24.8 percent from 2004–5 to 2014–15. Most of the other nine fast-rising tax-paying cities were in the South-East, including Cambridge, Oxford, and Ipswich. Manchester's tax rose by 1 percent, but it fell in many industrial cities, including Birmingham, Bradford, Glasgow, Huddersfield, Leeds, and Preston. This contrast reflected not only wages but also house prices in the shape of inheritance, land, and property taxes. To take another survey and set of indicators, the Barclays Prosperity Map, issued in August 2016 and based on data to April 2016, calculated scores based on median household wealth, gross domestic product (GDP) per capita, the unemployment rate, average household expenditure and house prices, working hours, and charitable giving. This showed greater prosperity in every region compared to the prior year, with the ranking region index score as follows:

London 0.78
South-East 0.58
Eastern England 0.42
South-West 0.37
Northern Ireland 0.34
East Midlands 0.30
Scotland 0.27
North-West 0.26
West Midlands 0.23
Yorkshire and the Humber 0.21
North East 0.12

As far as cities were concerned, there was a major contrast between London (0.78), Reading (0.75), and Cambridge (0.56) on the one hand, and Birmingham (0.26), Manchester (0.26), Liverpool (0.15), and Newcastle (0.11) on the other hand. London was Europe's largest urban economy, accounting for a quarter of UK GDP, while cities contribute 60 percent of national output, more than in any other European country. However, the other cities were below the European average in skills, innovation, and productivity.

The backdrop to problems in parts of Britain was that of a continual deterioration of the economy as a whole, at least in relative terms, from the 2010s. Nevertheless, prior to Brexit, the British economy tended to outperform that of France where the labor market was far more rigid and labor relations more difficult. Debt, however, was a key aspect of the British experience, one linked to the financial revolution or deregulation of the 1980s, and to the politics of borrowing to pay, rather than increasing taxes. Indeed, the budget balance as a percentage of GDP was about –3.6 percent in 2016. In 2015, the current account deficit, the difference between what the nation earns and pays abroad, rose to £96.2 billion, equivalent to 5.2 percent of GDP. This was the biggest annual gap since records began in 1948.

This increase reflected a widening in the trade balance—to £12.2 billion in the last quarter of 2015—and a fall in the income from investments abroad. This deficit was wide ranging but also specific to particular sectors and countries. In 2015, Germany exported €89 billion ($99 billion) of goods to Britain, including 810,000 vehicles. Britain had a trade deficit in goods of £62 billion a year with the EU, largely with Germany and France, and in contrast, an annual surplus in services of £15 billion.

At the same time, there was, in large part thanks to Japanese investment, a revival in mass-market car production in Britain which had seemed on the way out when in 2002 Ford closed its Dagenham factory. In 2016, three-quarters of all vehicles produced in Britain were exported, half of those to other parts of the EU. The biggest carmaker, Nissan in Sunderland, employed seven thousand workers in 2016 and, in addition, had an important supply chain. BMW reinvented the Mini, and Jaguar Land Rover was highly successful in the West Midlands. Whereas in 2003, the UK car production had stood at 1.65 million and was at 1.72 million in 2011, it fell to 1.3 million in 2019 and 860,000 in 2021.

Moreover, the ability of Britain to trade with much of the world, and notably the growing economies, was constrained by a lack of products that much of the world wished to purchase. In 2015, Britain traded more with Ireland, which is in the EU, than with India and China combined. Because of the significant growth of services in the developed world as a whole, Britain's manufacturing sector is roughly the same proportion of the economy as in France and the United States, but it faces major issues of competitiveness.

Aside from living and consuming beyond individual and collective means, a key problem was a clear-cut failure of productivity to rise from 2008. This measure, of production per hour worked, had risen steadily in the late 1990s and early 2000s, but it fell in 2009 and thereafter, found it difficult to return to the 2008 figure. Productivity is regarded as a particular British problem. In 2015, GDP per person was up only 0.3 percent on the pre-crisis peak in 2008. It is possible that the efficiency gains stemming from new technology and processes, gains so readily and repeatedly seen in the twentieth century, is proving harder to repeat and with less widespread benefits. This was not least as new technology often provides only limited employment possibilities and then only for skilled workers. Such technology may well spread.

Yet, there are also suggestions that much of the labor force, both in the public and in the private sectors, is demotivated and does not engage positively with the objectives of employers and the need to deliver a profit, an issue found with some union leaders. This is far less of a problem for the self-employed who are a key element in the economy and one of growing importance. A chronic failure to encourage a positive impression of production posed, and continues to pose, a major challenge. This failure is institutional, cultural, and social, and it provides a clear contrast with many other European states, notably Germany. The representation and perception of technical and vocational education as somehow less than academic is a persistent failure. This perception is seen in secondary and higher education and in public attitudes. There is also a gender dimension, with a stronger unwillingness among female than male graduates to follow jobs in industry. A disinclination to invest in industry is part of the equation.

Low productivity, seen for example in numerous public holidays (including the lengthy public mourning for the Queen in 2022), translated into stagnation in per capita GDP, with a marked fall in 2008–10 followed by growth by 2016 but only back to the 2008 figure. As a result both of this and of large-scale immigration, adjusted for the Consumer Price Index, average hourly wages, having risen from £9.87 in 1997, fell from £12.75 in 2009 to £11.75 in 2015. This made much of the population feel poorer and rely on borrowing and/or government welfare policies. The important service sector was affected by depressed demand, which was significant as spending was both a major expression of identity, as well as an important leisure activity. Due to the low productivity that affected profitability (a low productivity especially seen with services), and the failure of wages to rise, there was a reliance on debt to finance expenditure, a reliance encouraged by consistently low interest rates for much of the 2010s. These rates became habit-forming. They made it far easier to finance mortgages and to pay higher prices for property, which encouraged property prices to rise.

Low wages were seen as helping to maintain employment rates in Britain where the unemployment rate in March–May 2016 was 4.9 percent, the lowest since September 2005. This compared to a euro area rate of 10.2 percent that March. Figures from the ONS showed 31.7 million people in work in May 2016, the highest since records began in 1971. The UK had an employment rate of 74.4 percent, another record high. For June to August 2022, it was 75.5 percent. The contrast with the situation in the euro area helped to encourage immigration and also to make it contentious in employment terms. UK unemployment briefly fell to 3.5 percent in the summer of 2022. This situation exposed many to short-term uncertainties.

Public policy played a major role. At the same time, immigrants provided much of the low-paid labor force, including two-fifths of those working in food processing and a quarter of security guards.

Changes in the pension age, as well as fiscal policies leading to historically low interest rates encouraged people to stay in the workforce. In 2016, employment rates for people aged over fifty hit a record high, with the unemployment rate for those aged fifty to seventy-four dropping to 3.3 percent, while the employment rate for people aged between twenty-five and forty-nine has scarcely altered.

To cushion the impact of the recession and to stimulate borrowing and spending, the Bank of England cut interest rates from 5 percent to 0.5 percent in 2009, as well as expanded the money supply in a process known as quantitative easing, that was also seen elsewhere, notably in the United States. This was very much a rejection of Thatcherite monetarism. However, neither inflation rose nor the economy grew as had been anticipated. Indeed, recession appeared close in 2016, and the government, in its arguments for staying in the EU, made much of the threat of recession, a threat opponents unfairly characterized as "Project Fear." The danger came from a variety of sources, notably a decrease in economic activity. Indeed, the consumer confidence barometer fell sharply after the referendum vote for Brexit, and business confidence was also affected. In response, interest rates were cut to 0.25 percent after the Brexit vote and there was more quantitative easing.

The governmental policies of austerity in the 2010s, policies adopted in response to the level of debt left by Labour, contributed to a sense of stringency with a squeeze on public services being pressed hard by George Osborne, chancellor of the exchequer from 2010 to 2016, although there was little real austerity. Public expenditure was reordered, but government debt rose and employment remained high. The squeeze proved particularly serious in regions where public employment was especially significant—for example, the North-East of England. So also in Scotland, where, in 2013, the leading employment sectors were health, wholesale and retail, and administration. For individual workers, the possibilities of transferring to employment in the private sector were affected by regional, skill, and age factors. These problems encouraged Osborne to pursue the idea of what in 2014 was termed the Northern Powerhouse, an attempt at regional regeneration in which infrastructural investment, educational provision, and the expansion of manufacturing were all seen as significant.

Whereas the 1970s, 1980s, and 1990s recessions were followed by periods of relatively rapid above-trend growth, there has not yet been a comparable bounce back from the 2008–2009 recession to ensure a true recovery. That reflects more widespread conditions and factors in the world economy but also very much those in that of Britain. Structural factors remain difficult. For example, labor productivity in terms of GDP per hour worked in both 2014 and 2015 according to the ONS was 18 percentage points behind the rest of the G7 group of leading economies, and was 27, 30, and 35 percentage points lower than in France, the United States, and Germany, respectively. In part, this was due to underinvestment and to an overreliance on lower-paid work, although such productivity is not easy to measure. The World Economic Forum ranks Britain thirty-third in the quality of infrastructure, which reflects poor public provision, as well as difficulties in key sectors, notably rail, with trade unions. The aim of doubling British exports from 2012 to 2020, as part of the "march of the makers" called for by Osborne, was not realized.

Many businesses called for continued EU membership, including companies crucial to local economies, such as Airbus in Flintshire, Honda in Swindon, and Nissan in Sunderland, only for the voters there to vote for Brexit: 56.4 percent in Flintshire, 54.7 percent in Swindon, and 61.4 percent in Sunderland. So also for the Midlands, once the industrial heartland. The prospect is not encouraging, although many states would be glad to have Britain's problems.

The financial services industry continues to be important on the global level. Moreover, other service industries have expanded. After the United States, Britain is the second largest educator of foreign students in the world and has proved particularly successful in educating Chinese students, earning about £2 billion annually from the latter alone. At the same time, as a reminder of the interaction of economic and social trends with political issues, the rise in the number of foreign students has become problematic due to the consequences for the contentious issue of immigration. Indeed, in the 2010s and early 2020s, this caused ministerial divisions, with the Home Office determined to increase regulations on student entry, while the Department of Business welcomed the expansion of student numbers.

The Thatcherite liberalization of the 1980s continues to offer a degree of labor mobility not seen in most of Europe. Indeed, despite concerns that social welfare benefits are more significant, it is the ability to create jobs, and the freedom to fill them, that makes Britain so attractive to immigrants. The 2016 referendum debate captured an element of this, with the stress on the danger that Britain's departure would affect inward investment from non-EU companies, such as Nissan in Sunderland and Toyota in Burnaston, that wanted a production center in the EU but not one with the labor-market rigidities of so many EU states. At the same time that the private sector made insufficient investment in Britain, and notably in research, Britain's long-standing openness to foreign investment, and notably to the purchase of British assets, ensured that in 2015, Britain held about 7 percent of the world's stock of foreign direct investment, which was worth about £1 trillion. This was greater than any other economy apart from the larger US one. About half of this investment came from the EU.

Other aspects of openness included cross-border loans and data-storage hubs. The English language was another aspect of openness. Foreign labor was very important to the economy. In the 2015 Annual Population Survey, 27.9 million UK nationals and 3.1 million non-UK nationals were working. Of the 4.1 million health and social work employees, 9 percent were non-UK nationals, with 9.3 percent for wholesale, retail, and vehicle repair; 12.7 percent of the 2.97 million working in manufacturing; 6 percent of those in agriculture, forestry, and fishing; 9.2 percent in construction; and 19.4 percent as household employed. The dependence of the crucial service sector was seen by the provision by non-British workers of almost 30 percent of jobs in tourism and hospitality. Tourism represented about 7.5 percent of the economy.

The economic part of the debate on EU membership ably focused the extent to which the UK was dependent on international investment as well as on international currency inflows. Substantial outward movement from sterling holdings and the London stock market in 2016 captured the degree of foreign unease about the viability of Britain and the value of its assets outside the EU, and the very need for foreign confidence was clearly demonstrated. This dependence was in part a consequence of Britain living beyond its means and searching at all levels for ways to bridge the gap, a process also seen in the United States. In early 2016, the current account deficit was 6 percent of GDP, compared to 5.4 percent in 2015. The inflow of foreign capital was a key means to bridge the gap in the balance of payments and helped ensure the sale of British assets abroad, notably property assets, both housing and land, but also companies. Indeed, Mark Carney, the governor of the Bank of England, claimed that Britain was dependent on the "kindness of strangers" to fund its external liabilities, by buying British assets. Qatar, a major Gulf state, by 2016 had purchased a range of British assets, including "trophy" or prestige assets, such as the leading London department store, Harrods, three of London's leading hotels (Claridge's, The Berkeley, and The Connaught), a raft of property assets in Central London, and large stakes in Heathrow Airport and British Airways. China acquired stakes in Thames Water and the House of Fraser shopping chain. In 2015, Osborne told a room of British business leaders at Davos, "We want to be China's best partner in the West." Whereas the United States benefited from the dollar being the international reserve currency and from strong economic fundamentals, in order to secure this inflow, the UK lacked these strengths.

This situation underlined the weakness of the UK's political economy, which was a strand throughout the period covered by this book, and one of which politicians were well aware. If foreigners really lose confidence in the country and, in large numbers, stop taking government debt and investing, there would be a major sterling crisis that would affect living standards, as in 2022. Domestic policy is a key issue. The independence from government of the Bank of England and international confidence in the latter's commitment to containing inflation are both significant in encouraging investment in sterling-denominated assets. They were challenged by the policy offered by Labour under Jeremy Corbyn (2015–19) which advocated "a national investment bank and a network of regional investment banks to redistribute wealth and power." The risk that the Bank of England would be obliged to support these banks and their deficit financing was compounded by a lack of clarity as to Labour targets for public debt and the budget deficit. Keir Starmer, Labour leader from 2019, sought to provide reassurance on these points.

The situation is also heavily dependent on international developments— for example, a flare up of the Eurozone crisis, a failure in the Chinese economy, or a war as with that caused by the Russian invasion of Ukraine in 2022. Once, outside a major bloc, the ability of the British economy, the sixth largest in the world in 2023, to maintain growth rates, and thus invest and cope, is unclear. Without Britain, the EU is still a $14 trillion economy, compared with $16–17 trillion for the United States and $11 trillion for China. The United States is Britain's largest trading and investment partner, and Germany its second largest. How well Britain would operate as an economy, a society, a state, and a country was unclear, with assessments varying greatly and unsurprisingly so, as the world itself, including the EU, was scarcely stable. The future was viewed with considerable uncertainty from 2016 (and still is). That was not new but was more pronounced than earlier in the 2010s.

3

CHANGING SOCIETY

To BRITISH AND foreign people alive in 1945 and able to revisit the country eighty years later (a group that was a decreasing percentage of the population), it is the changes in its society that would have appeared most extraordinary. The visual transformation, of the people in the streets, and notably in the cities, would have been joined by changes in their organization, assumptions, and sense of themselves. Britain and the British have both changed profoundly since 1945. These changes had a greater impact than the doings of politicians that generally dominate historical discussion, although they cannot be separated from these doings.

A principal driver in the change in the country has been, as already suggested, a major and unprecedented growth in population since the late 1990s. This growth occurred thanks to a rise in fertility and to immigration. That, however, has not been the sole factor in social change. Both this growth as well as periods of little growth, notably the 1970s and 1980s, have been matched by rapidly rising expectations about lifestyle, as affluence became normative (although far from universal) and individuals expressed themselves through creating their own material worlds. These worlds were, at once, individualistic and, also, as a result of pressures from advertising and pricing, conformist. Both were seen in a growth area of consumerism: cosmetic surgery.

More generally, anxiety about not being able to meet assumptions about lifestyle helped encourage debt, as well as to stimulate and focus anger. The belief in social mobility was not matched by an acceptance that it could be downward. At the same time, although most people theoretically believed in upward social mobility, there was also a widespread disinclination to abandon inherited social position, however modest and, linked to this, a rejection of groups above. Envy of others was a very unattractive consequence, as sometimes was hostility to immigrants who very much represented a form of mobility.

Social changes can be masked to foreign observers who are struck by the continued distinctiveness of British class structures and assumptions, as well as by the continuity offered by much British culture, notably such popular forms as respect for the monarchy, which rose to a height with the funeral of Elizabeth II in 2022, and the making and showing of "golden age" detective stories. Television and film greatly contributed to this impression. Alongside gritty social realism, which gathered pace from the late 1960s, came television series such as *Midsomer Murders* in which, in addition to a misleading plethora of murders (which are relatively rare in Britain and notably so in rural and suburban areas), everyone lives in nice houses, including those in low-wage jobs.

As a result, there are times and contexts when social change does not appear to have been significant, and, in practice, there is a basis for this assumption. A BBC Listener Research Report of 1948 noted class and regional differences in the times when people ate their meals, factors that very much survive to the present, as do different names for meals, the evening meal variously being called dinner, tea, and supper. In 1949, the Listener Research Department justified its emphasis on social class because listening behavior was highly correlated with education,[1] again a factor that continues to the present. The mapping of Britain on the basis of the modal, or most commonly occurring category, shows that there is relatively little social mixing in neighborhoods, certainly as measured by income, housing tenure, or occupational class.[2]

In 2010–16 and 2019–22, Britain, in David Cameron and Boris Johnson, had members of the privileged social elite as the prime minister, and there was much about social differences that was scarcely new in terms of widely divergent experiences for individuals and communities. Images of class proved central in *Downton Abbey*, one of the most successful television series of the 2010s, and one broadcast on ITV. That the series was set a century earlier did not lessen its potency. The characters were treated by much of the public as personal friends. Equally, as a sign of change and to views on aspiration, many viewers were prepared to identify more closely with the servants than with the aristocrats.

Class continued to be an issue in social placing, both self-placing and the placing of others. It encourages an envious side of public observation and can lead to a misleading tendency to stigmatize others. Everyone whose parents were not bus drivers, as was the father of Sadiq Khan, the Labour mayor of London from 2016 (a point he frequently mentioned in his election campaigns), and who were well educated privately, are treated as somehow elitist. There is also a tendency to ignore the extent to which people, whatever their social background, prefer to be with those who are similar. Previous episodes of proclaimed social change had not led to the transformation that had been anticipated, hoped for, or feared. This was true of the "sixties," namely the radical values expressed in terms of the 1960s. It was also the case that particular movements, such as feminism, while achieving much, have failed to fulfill their apparent potential.

A key social change, however, one that indeed took place, alongside persistent stereotypes, was that of a major change in the working population, including, in particular, an expansion of the middle class, and notably from the 1960s. In 1900, 75 percent of the labor force were manual workers, members of the working class, and in 1951 the percentage was still 70. By 1974, the percentage had fallen to 47 and by 2000, to 37. The manufacturing base had declined, and the service sector had grown, creating a different working class, in a process that continues to the present. In the mid-2010s, about 60 percent of poll respondents described themselves as working class, but in reality, the situation is more complex. Part of the old working class can be seen as the new lower middle class and, as such, as a form of "blue-collar plus." This change has had important political consequences as many of this group tended to vote Conservative.

More generally, white collar replaced blue collar, with the change in the working class hitting the traditional character of the Labour Party and the trade unions. Moreover, as a related aspect of social change, average incomes for those in work rose appreciably, so that real disposable income for the average household rose 46 percent between 1971 and 1992. That helped account for the character of the Thatcher years (1979–90) and also for their impact. In turn, the crisis caused by high inflation in 2022 challenged assumptions.

IMMIGRATION

To suggest that change was less transformative than it might have been does not mean that change, indeed major change, did not occur. This was especially true of the ethnic transition. Whereas large-scale immigration has been central to the US experience and worldview from the outset, although not from 1922 to 1965, the political, social, and cultural impact of immigration into Britain did not become prominent until the 1950s. In 1945, Britain was a largely white and largely Christian society, with the vast majority of people being of

European descent. Yet, there were others not thus described, notably Chinese immigrants in port cities, especially London. Furthermore, a changing situation, especially of large-scale Jewish immigration from persecution in Eastern Europe, had led to press panics and to legislation in the shape of the Aliens Act of 1905.

After World War II, the situation changed dramatically, although not in a consistent pattern. There was immigration after the war as refugees who did not wish to return home settled, many of them, notably Poles, Ukrainians, and Latvians, fleeing Communist oppression. However, there was also a continued pattern of British emigration to former colonies, particularly Australia, in the search for economic opportunity. The aftereffect of the war included the emigration to the United States of large numbers of "GI brides" who had married American servicemen, brides who included all three of my aunts. Since the seventeenth century, Britain has been a country of emigration, and a loss of British-born citizens has continued to the present at the same time as large-scale immigration. Economic opportunity has played an important role in this emigration, leading, for example, to return migration from the United States during recessions there.

Reflecting the wartime experience of strong imperial links, the British Nationality Act of 1948 confirmed the existing position in guaranteeing freedom of entry from the Commonwealth and colonies. From the late 1950s, in part as a result, "nonwhite" immigration became a major feature. Large-scale immigration was the case initially with West Indians from British colonies, especially Jamaica. This immigration was a reflection of colonial links and, in part, of labor shortages in Britain where unemployment was then low. Thus, many West Indians went to work as London bus conductors. Many, however, had no job to go to and were seeking whatever work they could obtain. There was tension over the immigration, and many West Indians felt unwelcome: they were often rejected as tenants by racist landlords. Many planned to earn money and return home, although most did not do so.

From the 1960s, this immigration was supplemented by a large flow of South Asians from former British India, many from the new state of Pakistan, a Muslim state. Whereas the West Indian immigrants, who were Christian, congregated in London, those from South Asia were Muslims, Hindus, or Sikhs and focused on industrial centers in Lancashire, Yorkshire, and the Midlands, for example, the cities of Burnley, Leicester, and Wolverhampton. As with other migrant flows, there was a focus on going to areas where there were networks of support, notably from coreligionists and members of extended kinship groups. The search for economic opportunity also played a key role and helped explain why Hull, North-East England, the Central Belt of Scotland, and South Wales, all areas of industrial decline, or South-West England and East Anglia, those of little industry, received relatively few immigrants from South Asia, in contrast to the areas above.

Only a minority of immigrants from the New Commonwealth countries (the "nonwhite" former empire) came for a specific job. There was no general recruitment. Most came opportunistically: the door was open, and word spread about opportunities. Push factors were also important. They included general poverty as well as specific events, such as the upheavals arising from the building of the Mangla Dam in the Mirpur District in Pakistan, from which a high proportion of Pakistani immigrants came.

The net effect was a major change in individual communities in Britain and a challenge to traditional assumptions about nationhood. This could take bizarre forms. My mother was greatly embarrassed in the 1960s when the dog barked loudly at a West Indian postman. The dog in this part of outer London had never seen a "black" person, and my mother was worried that the postman would think her a racist. Dogs also tend to react to people who are frightened of them, and most immigrants came from communities in which there were no dogs as pets.

At one level, the accompanying transition toward a society in which there were immigrants was one that saw prejudice, discrimination, and violence. Particular sensitivity attached to a speech in 1968 by Enoch Powell, a prominent Conservative backbencher and former minister, who warned his West Midland listeners at a constituency lunch that large-scale immigration might lead to violence, using the emotive phrase "rivers of blood." In what was a divided and divisive response, he was met with criticism, notably from the Conservative Party leader, Edward Heath, who kept Powell from positions of responsibility, and also praise. In practice, there was no such violence until 1981, but the riots of that year raised major questions about race relations.

At another level, that of comparison, a major change, in the shape of large-scale immigration, occurred without large-scale problems. There was nothing in Britain to match the violence in Los Angeles, Detroit, and Newark in the 1960s. Despite much uneasiness, British society proved more flexible than might have been anticipated.

The scale of the immigration, however, combined with public concern, and a rise in unemployment, led to restrictions on immigration, especially in the 1960s and early 1970s when there was a large immigration of Asians from the former British African colony of Uganda where they were being persecuted. The first Commonwealth Immigrants Act was passed in 1962. These restrictions were accompanied by a transformation in citizenship, so as to draw a strong distinction between citizens of the United Kingdom and those living in the empire or in former imperial possessions. Previously, they had all shared a common citizenship. There was also, however, the continued anomaly, unique in Europe, that UK resident citizens of the Commonwealth and the Irish Republic can vote in UK parliamentary elections without being UK citizens, a situation that involved about one million people by the mid-2010s. These votes, notably those from Ireland, disproportionately support Labour. That Thatcher did not end the anomaly was symptomatic of her more general failure to protect the electoral position of the Conservative Party.

As a result of restrictions, immigration receded from the forefront of attention in the late 1970s and 1980s, although urban rioting in 1981 and 1985, especially in London and Liverpool, threw much attention on the issue of race relations as many (although far from all) of the rioters were of Afro-Caribbean descent. In turn, starting in the 2000s, the issue of immigration came to the fore. Immigration from Commonwealth and foreign non-EU countries rose substantially following the change in policy toward immigration from 1997 when the "primary purpose rule" intended to filter out fake marriage applications was removed by the Blair government. A more fundamental revision followed in 2000, again from the Blair government, when immigration was treated as essential to the economy. A total of 3.3 million immigrants came into the UK from 2001 to 2004. Non-EU immigration was generally higher than from the EU. In part, this immigration was for reasons of family union (e.g., family members brought in from South Asia through arranged marriages, particularly Muslim women from Pakistan) and in part as refugees notably from Afghanistan, Eritrea, Iraq, and Somalia.

In addition, in 2004, the government, alone among the major Western European states, permitted free entry for work to the new EU accession countries, in part because neither Blair nor Brown predicted the extent of immigration and therefore took up the opportunity to limit it from these countries. EU member states in Eastern Europe, especially Poland which joined in 2004, were the source of large numbers of immigrants and also led to a much greater number of Catholics in Britain. Slovakia also provided large numbers of immigrants, as, in the 2010s, did Bulgaria and Romania, which had joined the EU in 2007. By 2013, 1.24 million people born in Eastern Europe were living in the UK, compared with 170,000 in 2004. The numbers subsequently continued to grow. By the end of March 2016, 3.2 million EU nationals were living in Britain, a number that rose to 3.6 million by 2021.

The major rise in immigration contributed to a sense of governmental inadequacy. Alongside policy failures, there were deficiencies in implementation. The Home Office proved a weak instrument to control the situation, including under Theresa May, home secretary from 2010 to 2016, who, nevertheless, escaped the blame. Successive governments promised results they could not deliver. In 2008, the Labour government under Gordon Brown introduced a "points system" for non-EU immigrants who were not family members or refugees. However, the government then confronted demands for changes to benefit particular groups of employees, notably those in the financial sector. Others included football players who did not know English. There were complaints that it was difficult to find sufficient South Asian chefs for curry houses. Neither the Brown government nor its successors were able to cut immigration to the extent they promised.

The changing composition of the population from the 2000s was accentuated because, in the 1990s, births had come so close to deaths and emigration that the total number of the native, principally white British, population had been constant, at about 52 million. In the 2011 census, the 729,000 Indian-born inhabitants were the largest foreign-born group, followed by the 646,000 Poles. In the year ending March 2016, the Poles, at 831,000, exceeded the Indian-born for the first time. However, in part due to Poles returning home after Brexit as well as due to renewed immigration, the figures in the 2021 census were very different. The largest foreign-born category of residents in England and Wales was Indian-born, 920,000 or 1.5 percent of the total population, followed by those from Poland (743,000), Pakistan, Romania, Ireland, Italy, Bangladesh, Nigeria, Germany, South Africa, the USA, and Jamaica. The greatest percentage increase was from Romania: 80,000 in 2011 compared to 539,000 in 2021. The number of Italians had doubled. In comparison, the number of Irish-born had fallen.

In the early 2000s, there was particular sensitivity over illegal immigration, mostly in small boats across the Channel. Most of those coming were young men. From the start of 2018 to the summer of 2022, Iranians and Iraqis made up close to half, but in 2022 there were both increasing numbers and a rise in the percentage of Afghans and Albanians.

Immigrants provided vital labor services and skills as well as tax revenues that countered claims that they were causes of expense on social welfare. To a degree, immigrants, who were preponderantly young, also offset the structure of an aging native population. They also posed major issues. From mid-2009, 55 percent of all births in London were to mothers who had been born outside Britain. One consequence was crowding. London, the focus of immigration, saw its population rise from 6.7 million in 1988 to 7.2 million in 2001, and from mid-2007 to mid-2008 alone, London's population rose by 0.83 percent. The rise continued to 8.2 million in mid-2011 and 8.7 million in mid-2015. Reporting in October 2016, the ONS noted that immigration had helped to increase the population of Greater London by almost half a million in five years. Over one-third of all immigration to Britain was then to London.

The process of change was socially varied, although most immigrants were poor, at least in capital terms. They therefore formed part of the expanding rented sector and were badly affected by rising rents, while, in turn, providing a demand that contributed to increased rents for them and for the rest of the population.

The net effect of immigration was to turn Britain into a multiethnic, multireligious, and multicultural society. This was readily apparent at school level, as immigration and differential birth rates among new immigrants ensured that there was a particularly large school population of children born to parents who had not been born in Britain, and notably so in London, the Midlands, Lancashire, and Yorkshire. Partly as a result, although also due to concerns about integration, an emphasis on English-language proficiency as an aspect of identity and citizenship was seen both in education policy and in the 2002 Nationality, Immigration, and Asylum Act.[3]

Religious change was readily apparent. Whereas, in 1970, there were about 375,000 Hindus, Muslims, and Sikhs combined, by 1993 the figure was about 1,620,000, with the rise in the number of Muslims being especially pronounced and controversial. The trend continued. The religious landscape was affected as a consequence. In London in 1997, the largest Hindu temple outside Asia was opened. A major Sikh temple in Glasgow was a particularly prominent sequel in 2016. Many mosques were built.

These changes posed issues of acculturation, toleration, and mutual tolerance. These issues created stresses, but at the very same time, they were also handled with less difficulty than might have been anticipated. Most of British society was far less prejudiced and racist than critics frequently suggested and notably so in terms of international comparisons. A tolerant multiculturalism characterizes much of British life and has a variety of consequences. Interracial dating, marriage, and parenthood are more common than in Continental Europe, and the census indicated that the number claiming a mixed-race background doubled between 2001 and 2011 to 1.2 million, rising to 1.7 million (3 percent) by 2021. This trend ensures that more of the population have relations of mixed or different race, which is especially the case in London.

Nevertheless, interracial dating, marriage, and parenthood are rare among Muslims, which further underlines their cultural difference. In addition, in 2016, there were divisions among the Sikh community in Leicester about interracial marriage; divisions there became violent.

The consequences of demographic change were very varied. From the 1980s, a new style of speech called multicultural London English, a hybrid of West Indian, South Asian, and native English styles, became increasingly common in London, with variants in other cities with numerous immigrants. Another acceptance of different cultural traditions was seen in 2002, the year in which the citizenship test was introduced, when the celebration of the Queen's Golden Jubilee brought carnival dancers and gospel singers into the Mall. More edgy transitions were apparent in popular music, with Asian influences playing a role in the musical forms known as grime and dubstep, and also in the development of Asian-British films, which became a highly successful genre.

Ethnic identities and issues of assimilation and difference emerged as key themes in a series of novels, including Hanif Kureishi's *The Buddha of Suburbia* (1991), Zadie Smith's *White Teeth* (2000), Monica Ali's *Brick Lane* (2003), and Gautam Malkani's *Londonstani* (2006). British-born descendants of immigrants contributed much to an understanding of the creation of new, multiple identities, with Kureishi and Smith being especially successful in doing so for the benefit of readers who lack their background. Television programs sought to do the same.

However, there was also much rejection of multiculturalism, including from immigrants. Despite good intentions, multiculturalism, whether as empirical description or policy prescription, did not always lead to acculturation and integration. Indeed, far from it. There was a degree of ethnic segregation, such that between 2001 and 2011, the percentage of ethnic minorities living in wards where whites were in a minority rose from 25 to 41. Moreover, criticism of Muslim nonintegration came not only from whites but also from others—for example, Trevor Phillips, the black former head of the Equality and Human Rights Commission. In a pamphlet *Race and Faith: The Deafening Silence* (2016), Phillips claimed that Britain was "sleepwalking to catastrophe" due to multiculturalism and, specifically, the rejection of established norms by many Muslims.

The treatment of women, and not just Muslim women or non-Muslim women, by Muslim males sometimes did not correspond to the law, let alone to established social norms. This was especially so of attitudes to unmarried women. In England, in 2015–16, there were 5,700 new cases of female genital mutilation, with most of the girls being Muslims from Africa, notably Somalis. The operation of Islamic law in the UK as administered by Sharia courts or councils, a practice welcomed by Rowan Williams, the former archbishop of Canterbury, and by Lord Phillips, the former lord chief justice, deprives Muslim women in practice of the theoretical equality bestowed by domestic British law. Sharia rulings on marriage, divorce, children, property, inheritance, testimony, and appearance do not match the provisions of domestic law. Marital rape, forced marriage, and honor-based violence are particular issues.

At the local and regional levels, ethnic alignments and divides affected settlement patterns and politics, as well as assumptions about areas and neighborhoods. The desirability of living in particular town, streets, and neighborhoods was part of the equation. So, too, were tensions: for example, widespread South Asian dislike of Africans. In 2022, among South Asians, there were Hindu-Muslim disturbances in Leicester.

At the national level, ethnic alignments and divides encouraged a rise in far-Right political movements, notably the British National Party. These failed, however, to make much political impact and certainly less so than in France, Germany, Italy, and Spain. In part, this was due to British culture, but the first-past-the-post electoral system (rather than proportional representation) was also significant. The last point underlined the role of contingency. Had the 2011 referendum on proportional representation led to the introduction of this system, then it would have benefited the Liberal Democrats who sought it, as well as extreme and sectarian parties. However, the measure was rejected in a referendum result that did not cause the controversy of the 2016 referendum on the membership of the EU.

RELIGION

Shifts in religious practice did not solely arise from immigration. By the 1990s, only one in seven Britons was an active member of a Christian church, although far more claimed to be Christian believers. For most believers, as well as for the less or nonreligious, faith became less important, not only to the fabric of life but also to many of the turning points of individual lives, especially dying. This was part of a longer-term trend toward the ascendancy of secular values, albeit an ascendancy that was not as strong as many had anticipated. Baptism and confirmation became less common in relative terms, while more Christians did not marry in church. It became commonplace not to get married, or to rely on a secular ceremony, or one not in church. In addition, the beliefs of Christians changed, with traditional doctrine being neglected by many.

For example, belief in the Resurrection fell to about a half among those who claimed to be Christians. More generally, knowledge of theology and liturgy declined, and many worshippers adopted a "pick-and-mix" approach to belief and practice, one in which emotion was often to the fore. In response to the apparent view of congregants, clerics markedly cut the length of their sermons.

The weakening of the Church of England, the Anglican Church in England, a process that really began with the Catholic Emancipation Act of 1829, gathered pace in the late twentieth century. The most influential clergyman of the interwar years, William Temple, archbishop of York 1929–42 and of Canterbury 1942–44, had sought to reverse the decline of organized religion and to make England an Anglican nation again and thus to justify the Church of England's claim to speak for it. But, although he strengthened the church, Temple failed to give England a more clearly Christian character, and his inspiration of the already-developing role of the Church of England as a voice of social criticism and concern led to it being seen increasingly in a secular light.

Both the Church of England and the Scottish Episcopal Church were particularly badly hit by changes in Christian attitudes or by their declining power. For example, the repeal in 1951 of the 1735 Witchcraft Act was a response to the spiritualist lobby as it had been employed against attempts to conjure spirits upon pain of imprisonment.[4] More significantly, there was a widespread and protracted decline in attendance at Easter by Church of England congregations. In 1931, there had been 2.2 million communicants, but by 1951, the number had fallen to 1.9 million and by 2019, to 1.1 million. In addition, by 1951, a decline in attendance among Nonconformist congregations was apparent, although many, especially the Baptists and Methodists, were confident that they were growing in the 1950s. When taken as a proportion of the total population, which grew rapidly, the overall percentage attending church remained relatively small and became smaller. This was an instance of a wider change in Western Europe, one in which affluence played a role as the part of churches in communication, leisure, and entertainment declined before alternatives, while religiosity was affected by a greater degree of relativism and skepticism.[5]

The churches retained a role in education, with many state schools Protestant or Catholic foundations, and with the churches playing a modest role in their governance. However, as a consequence of the formation of the NHS, the major role of the churches in charitable functions and the provision of social welfare was largely replaced by the state. The failure in the 1990s of the "Keep Sunday Special" campaign, a campaign, to prevent shops from opening on the Sabbath, that was heavily backed by the Established Churches, confirmed the general trend.

The explicit and implicit role of religion in politics declined. Prayer Book reform had taken up much parliamentary time in the 1920s, but priorities changed thereafter. National days of prayer, announced with the approval of the government and expected to engage the general population, rather than simply church congregations, ended in 1947 when one was held with the agreement of the Labour government in response to severe economic difficulties. The Cabinet (of a Conservative government) considered another in 1957 but rejected the idea. This end reflected not just a change in the political atmosphere but also on the part of the church leaders now accepting the role and extent of secularization.

The lives of most politicians ceased to be illuminated by religious value. Whereas developments in the faith of some earlier politicians had been important, that was less the case with Wilson or Heath. Attlee was an agnostic. However, Thatcher's emphasis on self-reliance owed more to her Methodism than to her interest in Chicago School economics, and in 1989 she set herself to read all of the Old Testament. Her relations with the leadership of the Church of England were not close,[6] although Christianity remained important to Conservative political thought.[7] Blair's conversion to Catholicism was important to his baleful support for faith-based education, a support that, in practice, encouraged sectarianism, as it had notably already done in Northern Ireland. Brown was a son of a Church of Scotland cleric. Cameron's compassionate Conservatism and inclusive one-nation approach owed as much to his Anglicanism as to his desire to modernize the Conservative Party and make it electable—or maybe not. The daughter of a Church of England clergyman, May is a regular church attender at Church of England services with a strong commitment to a one-nation Conservatism, a commitment in which religion does play a role. In 2022, Johnson and Truss, prime ministers for whom religion was not prominent at all, were followed by Sunak, a practicing Hindu.

The decline of Christianity as the glue and purpose of society was readily apparent in the public sphere. From the 1960s, it became less credible to refer to a "Christian Britain." When government spoke of "community leaders," it frequently meant religious figures. However, their influence was largely restricted to non-Western communities. Among the "white" population, such figures could seek to lead but had less influence than in the past. Prelates who tried to be both leaders of the church and guides to their community found it difficult to match the expectations of an increasingly diverse society, the fate, for example, of Geoffrey Fisher, the archbishop of Canterbury from 1945 to 1961.[8]

Separately, the theological diversity of the Church of England created major and persistent problems, notably over the issue of women priests and then bishops. This issue also indicated the problems of being part of a global communion, for some sister churches, especially in Africa, were more conservative than others. Moreover, facing spiraling pension costs and inadequately funded spending commitments, the Church of England was unable to meet its liabilities. In response, it transferred not only those of parochial stipends (salaries) but also the cost of dioceses (bishoprics) and the church as a whole, to the individual parishes, creating major difficulties at that level.[9] There were many similarities between the problems of the church and those of both the country and the government.

In the early twenty-first century, Catholic prelates tended to make more comments than their Protestant counterparts on social matters, comments that were often of an illiberal and intolerant type, as with their strident opposition to homosexual marriage, which became legal under the Cameron government as a result of legislation in 2013. The Catholic prelates did not always find a widely appropriate tone. When, for example, in 2016, the Cardinal-Archbishop of Westminster arranged for a bone of Thomas Becket, a twelfth-century saint, to be sent round the country for reverence, this was treated by many non-Catholics with derision and by some Catholics with embarrassment.

The position of the established churches in the British Isles, especially England, was also challenged by the rise of "fundamentalist" Christianity, inspired by the United States; by black churches supported by African immigrants; and also by "New Age" religions and practices, notably Druidism. There was also an appreciable number of converts to Buddhism. New Age believers and Buddhist converts tended to have particular views on diet and health, and their increase was linked to such changes as the rise of interest in crystals.

Gender

If mass immigration was one transformation, another was provided by the changing position of women, the majority of the population, and more especially, by feminism. Gender relations had been disrupted during World War I (1914–18) and World War II (1939–45), often greatly so, as an aspect of more general wartime changes in social relations. Preexisting patterns of control, deference, and hierarchy were disrupted, and new freedoms were tested. However, in each case, the postwar years saw a return to more traditional patterns of behavior. More particularly, as far as women were concerned, husbands and fathers came back from the war, and the numbers of women in work fell as women were replaced in favor of ex-soldiers.

In essence, this situation was transformed from the 1960s, but the emphasis on that decade needs to be matched by an awareness of earlier changes and notably so in the 1950s. Allowing for that, the advancing of concepts of female liberation and sexual emancipation in the 1960s spelled a new world. The moral code that prevailed in 1945 was largely overthrown and in a process that was to be reflected in far-reaching legal change in the 1960s. Abortion and homosexual acts became legal, the Abortion Act of 1967 leading to a situation close to abortion on demand. The contraceptive pill made a major difference, but so too did changing attitudes toward female autonomy, birth control and sexual activity, and a drive for new personal relations.[10] Capital punishment was abolished.

These values were reflected in the arts, including popular works. Female self-assurance and competence were demonstrated by the character Emma Peel in the popular television series *The Avengers* (1961–69). In the television series *Butterflies* (1979–83), a married woman with a dull husband was tempted to seek fun elsewhere. American television imports, such as *Sex in the City* in the 2010s, also had an impact. Alongside emotional drives, women's sexual needs and imaginations came to play a greater role in literature, journalism, and films, including a sympathetic portrayal of sex leading to illegitimacy in *Bridget Jones's Baby* (2016). Interest in relationships played a role in the popularity of book clubs, which had many more female than male members. The popularity of soft pornography for women, such as the 2011 British novel (then 2015 American film) *Fifty Shades of Grey*, reflected the rise of female consumerism in this regard, as did the expansion of lingerie sections in High Street stores and of High Street shops specifically selling lingerie and sexual aids, such as the Ann Summers shops, the first of which opened in 1970, with seventy-three in the UK by 2022.

Self-expression was presented as part of the equation, but greater female expenditure on cosmetics suggested that a lack of self-confidence was part of it. Feminist themes were an aspect of female self-expression as in the Making Mischief season of feminist theater that was staged in 2016.

As so often, this new world was frequently slanted in its impact and benefits. It was, in particular, more pronounced and attractive for wealthier women than for their poorer counterparts, for whom the details of life and work remained harsher. There was also a powerful generational contrast in experience, one that was frequently related to tension and disputes within families. The young experienced change far more than their parents and certainly believed they did, although the young could be more conservative than their parents, as well as differently conventional.

Again, allowing for all these caveats, the pace of change was such that with time, more women experienced, or had experienced, gender relations that were very different to those of the 1930s and the late 1940s. Moreover, changes were expressed in law and institutions and were then ingrained in the fabric of much of society. The 1970 Equal Pay Act was important, although, in 1972, the National Joint Committee of Working Women's Organisation reported to the

Shadow Cabinet that it discerned no movement toward equal pay for women workers covered by national agreements or wages councils. The Act was followed by legislation on equal pay for work of equal value. The equalization of pensions was another factor in encouraging women to continue working. The state pension age has been rising from sixty for women and sixty-five for men.

Personal relationships were also affected by legal changes. In 1991, in a marked rejection of earlier conventions, the legal offense of rape was extended to victimhood within marriage. Moreover, the treatment of unmarried mothers changed, notably with improved provision of housing and benefits, and this change was linked to more liberal attitudes toward living outside marriage and toward illegitimacy.[11] In 2021, 63.1 percent of petitions for divorce in opposite sex couples were initiated by women.

Records on the proportion of women in work began in 1971, an aspect of increased interest in the subject and of the government responding. The percentage was then 52.7 whereas by the end of 2021, it had risen to 72.2 (78.8 for men), a major change that was crucial to many family economies. Linked to this change in work, there was a major shift in female activity as a whole. Cooking, baking, preserving food (notably jam making), knitting, and needlework were regarded as less important than hitherto as accomplishments, and this change was related to the decline of traditional voluntarist activities—for example, the Women's Institute—and notably so in cities. These activities remained more significant in rural communities. Most women no longer gave up work when they married or, increasingly, when they had children. As a result, the balancing of commitments, particularly home and family, became a major theme. This was true of both conversation and of advice columns.

Jobs and lifestyle became more important as aspirations for women, complementing rather than replacing home and family. The range of female activities expanded: the Women's Rugby Football Union was formed in 1983; the first Briton in space was Helen Sharman; and, in 1987, Elizabeth II amended the statutes of the most distinguished of British chivalric orders, the Order of the Garter, to permit the admission of women on terms equal to those of the Knights Companion of the Order. In 1979, Margaret Thatcher became Britain's first woman prime minister, the second, Theresa May, following in 2016, and the third, Liz Truss, following briefly in 2022. In 2016, Truss had been the first female minister of justice and lord chancellor (head of the judiciary). In 2014, Nicola Sturgeon became Scotland's first woman first minister, although Labour's members voted down two good female candidates in the contest for its new head, as did the SNP for Sturgeon's replacement in 2023. The leaders of Scotland's Conservative and Labour Parties in 2016 were also women. In 2016, Plaid Cymru and the Greens also had female leaders, while the UK

Independence Party (UKIP) briefly gained one. By April 2016, 51 percent of the judges under forty across the courts were women, as were 28 percent of all judges, a percentage that had risen from 25 percent in a year.

After considerable controversy and indecision, the first women were ordained priests in the Church of England in 1994; the Church of Scotland had women ministers from the late 1960s. English Congregationalists ordained women from 1919, and by World War II, Congregationalists were quite used to women ministers, although they were not numerous. After much controversy, the Church of England followed with women bishops in 2015. By then, there were sufficient women priests to provide an impressive talent pool for promotion. Characteristically, the Catholics remained rigidly unyielding, and, despite repeated speculation, the possibility of their union with the Church of England was implausible for this and other reasons.

The decline in personal service (servants), a decline that was notable in the 1940s and thereafter, was particularly significant for women, as most of those called servants were women. This was true both of living-in servants and of those who lived out. Conversely, although butlers, cooks, parlor maids, footmen, and chauffeurs in private households became far less numerous, service, subsequently, especially from the 1980s, became more important in other forms, notably as nannies, cleaners, and care workers. Indeed, according to *Which* magazine, 38 percent of households in 1998 employed domestic "help," and the size of the domestic industry was the same as in 1939. Most of the "help" were women, and the work was generally undervalued and poorly paid. In the late 1940s, there was scant interest among women in employment in this sector, and in the 1950s and 1960s, offices and shops appeared preferable as employment. This situation helped to ensure an interest on the part of householders in domestic appliances, such as vacuum cleaners.[12] The less attractive jobs, such as cleaners and care workers, were usually poorly paid and many were taken by immigrants. At the same time, social norms played a role, as Eastern European women, especially Poles, proved far readier to seek this work than religious Muslims. Domestic "help" became more prominent from the late twentieth century, in part due to the increase in disposable wealth, notably in the 1980s, and in part due to the greater need for help from an increasingly elderly population. In this, there was an overlap with employment in sheltered housing. Women are more prominent than men in the health, social work, and education sectors.

More generally, male employment, at a percentage of 79 at the end of 2022, remained higher than that of women (72), and more female employment was part-time: 38 percent at the end of 2021, compared to 13 percent in men. In this and other trends, broad and long-term social changes interacted with the impact of more specific policy decisions. The attempts to equalize the pension age of men and women, and to change single-parent benefits, were both significant in increasing female employment, the former helping to lead in the 2010s to a major increase in employment among women over fifty. There was still, however, a significant pay gap between men and women, at 15.4 percent in April 2020, in large part due to more women being employed part-time, while for full-time employees, hourly pay (excluding overtime) was 7.9 percent more for men.

Ironically, a social consequence of changing opportunities in a complex matrix of class and gender was that working-class men largely lost educational and job opportunities and also cultural norms to the benefit of women and, more particularly, middle-class women. This loss was very much the case with access to universities. Part of the feminization of society was that few wanted to note this change. Nevertheless, by 2016, it was so blatant that the Cameron government called for action and May referred to it in her list of social ills when taking office. Moreover, the issue recurred in discussion over policy for secondary education and debate over university admissions.

More generally, "positive discrimination" in favor of hiring and promoting women from the 1980s worked most to the benefit of middle-class women. Moreover, the practice of endogamy (marriage within the clan, i.e., of members of similar social groups) may have ensured that social differences were reinforced: male doctors increasingly tended to marry female doctors, rather than female nurses. The end of the link between sex and marriage encouraged this process: male doctors could readily have sex with female nurses without marrying them. The major expansion of higher education for women was part of the equation of social change. It helped ensure that by 2019, women made up 48 percent of all licensed doctors.

The impact of change on the role of the family proved a matter of contention, with conservative commentators, such as the *Daily Mail*, regularly painting a dire picture, notably of the consequences of women working. In practice, there was a social/class dimension. The female family anchor now faces greater challenges, and this has led to great strain the further down the "social ladder" the situation is considered. For those in more advanced employment, two adults who want to work can do so and can afford childcare. For the less well placed, the situation is less easy. At the same time, the need for increased income has become blended with consumerism for those whose lifestyles can be greatly improved by both spouses working. However, childcare is a major problem. Family control and self-discipline have been put under strain as a result or, more positively, have had to adapt.

As a different point, the collection and analysis of data by gender had an impact on statistics and on the response to them. For example, by 2014, the prevalence of smoking in men was 20.4 percent and in women 17.2 percent, according to the ONS reporting in 2016. The difference was minor, but the figures revealed more interesting trends, with the male percentage being the lowest ever recorded, while that of women rose, due to an increase in the sixteen-to-thirty-four group. Greater female longevity continued to be a factor, with the ONS also revealing, in 2016, that the average British woman lived to eighty-nine, compared to eighty-six for a man. Ironically, this longevity exposed women to greater risk of diseases linked to age, notably Alzheimer's disease and dementia.

Meanwhile, the change in gender norms was very much seen not only in the case of gender stereotypes but also in sexual behavior. The law on homosexual sex was liberalized in 1967, with the first British openly homosexual play, that by Colin Spencer, following a year later. Alongside homosexual activism came its lesbian counterpart. On BBC television, in 1974, James Robson's *Girl* provided the first lesbian kiss on British television. The public nature of relationships came to the fore with marriages. In 2013, after a bitter fight within the Conservative Party, the Marriage (Same Sex) Bill was passed by Parliament, with the first same-sex marriages following in March 2014. This provides an equality not offered by civil partnerships and was to be described by Cameron as probably the greatest achievement of his premiership. In 2016, Ruth Davidson, the Scottish Conservative leader, announced her engagement to her partner, Jen Wilson, with the Scottish Labour leader following suit, while Justine Greening became the first Cabinet minister to come out as a lesbian, and was promoted subsequently to become secretary of state for education in 2016. The Scottish UKIP leader and the co-convenor of the Scottish Green Party were both gay. Separately, changing attitudes to masculinity were seen in the response to the comedy *The Full Monty* (1997), a film about unemployed men in Sheffield who become strippers in order to get money. The film was a success, although few raised the obvious suggestion that the characters could have left Sheffield in search of work.

As a very different issue, but one also very much reflecting the determination to define and assert identities, the transgender issue became more prominent in the 2010s, not least with the 2011 government report *Advancing Transgender Equality: A Plan for Action*.

Statistics certainly vary. In 2013, the Integrated Household Survey, the largest social data collection other than the census, found that only 1.6 percent of adults described themselves as gay, lesbian, or bisexual, which is regarded by many commentators as an underestimate. In 2016, the ONS reported that the number of people in the UK openly identified as bisexual had risen from 230,000 in 2012 to 334,000 in 2015, with 1.8 percent of sixteen- to twenty-five-year-olds in 2015 describing themselves as bisexual and 1.5 percent as gay or lesbian. In 2015, the *Times* reported that half of young people and nearly a quarter of the population overall defined themselves as something other than 100 percent heterosexual. In 2016, the *Oxford English Dictionary* added the words *gender fluid* to describe a person who does not identify with a single fixed gender, a term first recorded in 1987; as well as *moobs*, a term for unusually prominent breasts on a man, a term first appearing in 2001.

The gender dimension to politics was important. A long-standing female preference for the Conservatives had been important to the electoral success of the latter, but this preference declined in the Blair years hitting the Conservatives in successive elections, and this decline continued thereafter. Indeed, in the the 2010s, the Conservatives were challenged by the prospect that they would do worse with female voters. In the 2016 European referendum, both males and females backed Brexit by 52 to 48 percent.

The extent to which women were Members of Parliament (MPs) became a more significant issue from the 1990s: Labour had a higher percentage than the Conservatives. To address the issue, the Conservative Central Office advocated all-women selection shortlists but met much resistance from constituency associations who did not want to be dictated to. Commentators moved on to consider the percentage of women who were ministers and shadow ministers, and, if so, which posts they held. In 2015, this issue became significant in discussion of both the new Conservative ministry and the new Labour shadow ministry, with charges of misogyny directed within Labour over the choice of party leader, Jeremy Corbyn, over his selection of senior colleagues, and in 2015–16, over attitudes to female MPs that dissented from Corbyn's views. In 2016, Theresa May emphasized that she was bringing forward female ministers, which she did, including to key posts, notably her successor as home secretary, although the majority in the Cabinet remained male.

YOUTH

The rise of youth society and culture was another aspect of the period. Again, this was not distinctive to Britain, yet alone unique to it, but it was an important change on past patterns of behavior and earlier assumptions. Whereas the practice had been of the next generation following the beliefs and lifestyles of their parents, now the young increasingly came to make their own choices. This was another important solvent to earlier hierarchies that gave cohesion and continuity to society. Now neither goal was judged significant, and this posed the challenge of how to provide both other than through consumerism and populism. The authority of age and experience was overthrown and, in their place, came an emphasis on youth and novelty. This was seen in politics with the lowering of the voting age from twenty-one to eighteen by Labour under legislation in 1969 and in Scotland , with the Independence Referendum Act of 2013, to sixteen. The distinctive nature of youth was seen in the 2016 European referendum, as the voters most opposed to Brexit were the youngest. At the same time, they were the group that voted least.

The rise of youth society was especially pronounced from the 1950s, with the 1960s, again, attracting particular attention. Popular music and drug use received considerable coverage,[13] as did sex before marriage. The role of technology and government were both significant. In the former case, amplifiers and transistor radios affected popular music, while the contraceptive pill and abortions were both very important to the increased fashion for premarital sex, a fashion that very much affected intergenerational attitudes. A former student noted of his return to university in the 1960s: "Wardens . . . , particularly women wardens, thought nothing of bursting into bedrooms [in the late 1950s] to see whether any sexual activity was taking place. . . . I returned . . . to find that the place had changed. Students were richer, were free to enjoy sex."[14] The latter has very much continued to be the pattern.

Drug use increased from the 1960s, in part linked to student protest and the counterculture, both of which were, in practice, middle class, whatever their pretensions, although there were also working-class drug users. The government accepted a situation in which cannabis use remained an offence but with far fewer drug users sent to prison, and this remains the current situation.[15] The use of "hard drugs" in theory and, to a degree, in practice is treated more firmly. At the same time, a fall in youth drinking played a major role in the decline of the average annual adult consumption of alcoholic beverage, from 173 liters in 2005 to 135 in 2014. This decline was linked to the falling number of nightclubs and other nighttime venues in the 2010s, a trend in which inner-city gentrification also played a major role.

More generally, the young were affected by the crisis of the family and its values, without, for many, a replacement existing, and by the decline of the established churches. Their lives altered as the years spent in education increased. Moreover, the character of the education provided changed. In particular, Labour and Conservative "Butskellism" (see chapter 5) replaced the previous ability-related secondary school system of grammar schools and secondary modern schools, with "comprehensive education," an inclusive system that, in practice, failed to live up to many of the hopes placed in it, not least because the ability to counter social differences in attitudes was limited. Selective education, however, remained the system in Northern Ireland.

AGE

Alongside the cult of youth, rising life expectancy for both men and women has ensured that the average age has risen, a process accentuated by the extent to which the birth rate has not comparably increased. Linked to this, the pattern of disease changed. In 2013, there were, according to the Alzheimer's Society the following year, 815,827 people with dementia in the UK. Dementia and other conditions have encouraged anxiety and fear about aging. Moreover, concern about loneliness is an issue. The charity Age UK estimated in 2014 that two million over-75s live alone in England and that two-fifths of older people said they relied on televisions for company. However, the English Longitudinal Study of Ageing suggests that the percentage of the elderly complaining of significant loneliness has not altered significantly since World War II. Fear of aging also encouraged the elderly to stay in work, although the impact of low interest rates on savings as well as a later state pension age also played a part. By 2016, about one in ten pensioners were either in full- or part-time work, a factor that may have affected opportunities for the young. Thanks also to the protection of benefits, the elderly saw their average income rise after the 2008 financial crisis. This process was encouraged by the furor over the small pension increase announced in 1999, even though that was in line with inflation. In contrast, those aged between twenty-two and thirty had a 7 percent lower average income in 2014–15 than in 2007–8. This contrast was repeated in the early 2020s.

A number of personal, emotional, social, and legal responses and remedies have resulted as a consequence of concern about aging. For example, the number of applications for "living wills," or lasting powers of attorney that set out wishes in the event that mental capacity is lost, doubled, in 2014–15, to reach half a million in 2015. Assisted dying remains illegal for those who assist, although suicide is not. High-profile legal cases have arisen from those helping relatives or friends who had serious health problems to commit suicide. The merits of such action forms a major topic of conversation, as, more generally, does the issue of aging. This is a sphere in which public unease has grown. Because of the contrast between suicide which is legal and helping people to commit suicide which is illegal, the fate of helpless people who wish to kill themselves but are unable to do so, has been put into prominence. Novelists repeatedly turned to the issue, as in *Sweet Caress* (2015), when William Boyd had his heroine-protagonist, Amory Clay, observe, just before attempting suicide, "it should be available to anyone who wants it as a matter of civil liberty, of human rights and human dignity . . . you're given your bottle of pills."[16]

Rising life expectancy has affected the pattern of society. The elderly have become more significant as consumers, not least as, although very much in average terms, their real wealth and disposable income have risen. This has an impact across society. For example, assisted living and other housing for the elderly has become more important, although less so than in the United States.

Rising life expectancy has also influenced the content of politics, especially with the emphasis placed in the 2010s on supporting the interests of pensioners, an emphasis that greatly affected fiscal policy, helped explain the prominence of the NHS, and generally benefited the Conservatives electorally, although with constraints on their behavior, arising accordingly. It is difficult for the Conservatives, or indeed any political movement, to encourage a rational discussion about the cost of the NHS. In 2016, the Labour leadership contest saw Owen Smith, the unsuccessful challenger to Jeremy Corbyn, having to defend himself against groundless charges that his support for the NHS was limited.

SOCIAL POLICY

The role of government in social policy was highly varied. It included the legalization of abortion, a measure achieved with less contention than in the United States, although in 1967 a degree of controversy continues in the UK. Less contentiously, the abolition of national service (conscription) in 1957–63 was also highly significant. It altered the relationship between the state and the young and also between the young and earlier generations that had served in the military, while also being linked to a change in defense expenditure by type and a fall in the percentage of gross domestic product (GDP) spent on defense.[17]

In addition, smoking was limited by legislation, notably being banned in 2007 inside public places such as clubs, pubs, cinemas, and restaurants.[18] In this, social policy interacted with broader changes in society, as with altering assumptions about the place of smoking and the decline of the male working class, the core smoking group. Litigation and the risk of costs arising also played a role, particularly increased sensitivity to passive smoking in the shape of the risk of legal action by workers exposed to cigarette smoke.

So also with divorce. Divorce rose markedly from 1945, in part due to the difficulties of coping with the disruption of World War II, with a major spike in England and Wales in 1949. This rise was followed by a fall in the divorce rate in the relatively conservative 1950s, albeit to a rate considerably above the prewar rate. In the 1960s, the rate began to rise again, a process eased by an emphasis on female satisfaction and self-expression, and the Divorce Reform Act in 1971 reflected this, and encouraged a further increase. Most divorces were initiated by women. From 74,437 divorces in England and Wales in 1971, the figures rose to a record high of 165,018 in 1993, before falling to 147,735 in 2002 and 113,505 in 2021. In 2021, fewer than one-fifth of marriages were ending in divorce by the tenth wedding anniversary, compared to a quarter in 1995. The latter, however, was still high not least because it was on a smaller base of marriages. These figures concealed significant variations, notably the growing trend for divorce later in life, which reflected rising expectations about happiness, as well as new technology in the shape of links through social media and dating websites, and the availability of Viagra. There were also significant variations between ethnic, religious, and social groups.

Family structure changed as a consequence of increased divorce. Due in large part to divorce, the percentage of single-parent, female-headed, households increased, from 8.3 percent of households with children in 1971 to 12.1 percent in 1980. In 2014, Lord Wilson of Culworth, a judge, declared that the traditional nuclear family had been replaced with the "blended family," with divorce ensuring many "stepfamilies of the half-blood." Politicians who came from broken homes and were brought up by one parent were referred to in positive terms: for example, the prominent Conservatives David Davies and Stephen Crabb, both of whom were Cabinet members in the 2010s and each of whom had sought the party leadership. Being divorced did not prevent the rise of politicians, as with Amber Rudd, the new home secretary in 2016, who was a single mother. Lower marriage rates among the young were also a factor in changing family structure.

Priorities in the discussion of social policy are difficult to establish. Abortion affected both women and the men who made them pregnant, and conscription the men who served and their female relatives who had to cope with their absence; women were not conscripted. Today, abortion appears more significant than conscription, but if chronological order or the perception of the population directly affected are to be the basis of selection, then the abolition of conscription should come first.

The combined effect was that of more freedom for the young, and this was linked to their sense that they should be free. "Free love" was a particular call in the late 1960s, and there was an assault on what was termed middle-class conventions. Ironically, many of those who decried such conventions can best be classified as middle class. Such views have continued to affect assumptions and have become more significant as the young of yesterday, in turn, become middle aged, middle class, and differently complacent and conventional.

SOCIAL CONTEXT

Housing was the key context for social relationships and interaction. It affected the dynamics of family space, the nature of privacy, and relations within and between families. Housing also revealed the impact of a range of factors including government policy. A postwar rise in the birth rate after demobilization was a key factor in affecting the need for new housing, as was the expectation, as a result of the war, of a better life. Thus, better housing was a counterpart to the foundation of the NHS. Moreover, much of the housing stock, notably in London and Liverpool but also in many other cities, had been badly damaged by German bombing, while there had been no building during the war. Due to the bombing, one in six Londoners was homeless. Another forty thousand people were to be left homeless after coastal floods in 1953.

However, a severe shortage of resources in the postwar economy, as well as the priority given to industrial reconstruction, affected provision. As a consequence, many lived in prefabricated temporary accommodation or with older family members who had accommodation. Thus, the wartime situation, in which extended families had played a major part in providing housing, continued, albeit in a very different context. This continuation fed family tensions.

In contrast, there was a major focus on housing provision in the 1950s. Many of the new houses provided people with their first bathrooms and inside toilets, a major enhancement to their quality of life; and nuclear families were able to free themselves from having to live with parents. Nevertheless, aside from the social disruption of the compulsory move to new locations linked to slum clearance, a disruption particularly felt by those who had never previously moved, many of the new neighborhoods were poorly planned and (separately) unpopular with their occupants. Some working-class council estates, notably those with high employment and linked to good schools, worked,[19] a factor that is often downplayed. Nevertheless, other new neighborhoods tended to lack community amenities and means of identification, such as adequate local shops and pubs.

The social fabric that had helped families cope with strain, as well as to maintain social cohesion and conformity, was sundered. Families were separated from relatives, hitting the support systems crucial for childcare and for looking after the elderly. On the new housing estates, there was a decline in the three-generation extended family, and a move toward the nuclear family, which hit traditional communities and patterns of care. Grandparents were more socially and geographically isolated as a result of these changes, and many old people found the new housing estates alien, if not frightening. Furthermore, the interconnection of work and tightly packed terrace housing seen in many prewar neighborhoods was not re-created in this rebuilding. For example, in dockland areas, instead of trying to preserve close communities, or implement utilitarian notions linked to port activities, generalized notions of supposedly progressive town planning were applied, without reference to local experience or historical associations. This was an aspect of the failure to use planning in order to help economic growth, a failure that was particularly notable at the local level. New estates were often built at a distance from work, which created journey-to-work problems (encouraging the purchase of cars) and exacerbated the issues of childcare. Individual estates varied greatly in their character, reflecting the extent to which council housing was far from homogeneous. Instead, it was linked to subtle contrasts in social geography, as in the percentage of high-grade white-collar workers in certain Newcastle estates.

The movement of people was a result not only of government policy but also of market pressures linked to land values. These played a particularly pernicious role in the late 1950s and early 1960s in what was known as Rachmanism: supposedly using intimidation or violence to remove controlled tenants of properties too lowly rated to have their rents increased under the 1957 Rent Act, so that, as a result of this removal, the properties could be newly let at a higher rent, especially to West Indian immigrants. Intimidation was sometimes part of the process. The 1957 Rent Act would not allow the removal of controlled-rent tenants from low-rated properties.

Further, rent controls, the response of the Labour government elected in 1964, hit landlords' profits, led to the replacement of private landlords by owner-occupiers, and resulted in a decline in the amount of property available for rent. This decline reduced the flexibility of the housing market and put greater pressure on the government, both local and national. Labour believed that it should be possible to replace private renting with its public counterpart. The problems of landlords did not attract sympathetic review, unlike those of tenants, and this contrast contributed to the direction of politics and policy toward Labour solutions. These put control in the hands of local government and reduced flexibility, notably for those seeking to move area in search of employment.

In turn, flexibility was increased by the 1988 Housing Act, passed by the Thatcher government, and the resulting revival of private renting and was helped later by "buy-to-let" policies and the development of financial packages to facilitate mortgages for this end. Housing provision, however, not only continued to be inadequate but became increasingly so. Funding for new housing and, indeed, for maintenance was affected by successive fiscal crises in the 1960s and 1970s, as well as by the instability of the latter linked to poor, if not anarchic, labor relations. In the 1980s, the Thatcher government's drive for the sale of council housing was made far more serious by the failure at the same time, earlier or subsequently, to increase the provision of new rented housing. The 1988 Housing Act allowed Housing Associations to borrow privately (as opposed to relying on government loans), which led to a rapid expansion of Housing Association Provision with more than £70 billion in borrowing to the present. Unfortunately, there was an even greater decline in local authority provision. Local authorities saw their housing stock decline over a thirty-year period from a peak of 4.99 million to 1.726 million in 2012. In contrast, Housing Association numbers increased from 281,000 to 2.4 million during the same period. Particular housing shortages developed for poor families, not least as inner-city regeneration and new inner-city housing focused on flats for single people, for childless couples, or for students. New housing provision remained inadequate in the 1990s, 2000s, 2010s, and 2020s, and despite the frequent promises of politicians, there is no sign of this situation changing.

Alongside inadequacy, there was the issue of cost. In 1986, the average first-time buyer paid just under £30,000 for a new home, whereas in 2015 the figure was over £150,000 for England and £330,000 in London. The combined impact was a fall in homeownership. Homeownership in England, having peaked at 71 percent in April 2003, fell steadily to 64 percent in 2022, compared to 63.5 percent in 1986. The recent fall has been more pronounced among younger age groups, although the number of owner-occupiers then was lower as the population was lower, and 57 percent in 1980. In the UK as a whole, the percentage dropped from 73.3 percent in 2007 to 63 percent in 2018.

The housing crisis was seen not only in London, the place that overly dominates the news, with Outer London seeing a drop of 13.5 percent in homeownership, from a peak of 71.4 in October 2000 to 57.8 in February 2016, but also elsewhere. For example, in Greater Manchester, homeownership peaked in 2003 at 72.4 percent but fallen by 2016 to 57.9 percent, the biggest drop in the UK. The percentage falls in the West Midlands was 11.2, in West Yorkshire 10.6, in Northern Ireland 10.5, and in Merseyside 9.1. There were sharp falls in Leeds and Sheffield. In February 2022, ONS figures indicated that whereas London had 50.9 percent home ownership, the rate in every other one of the nine English regions was between 60.8 percent (North East) and 69.4 percent

(East Midlands), with seven of them above 65 percent. At that stage the average house price in the UK according to the Land Registry for the end of 2021 was £274,712, a 10.8 percent increase on the previous year, with London at £521,146, the East Midlands at £235,004 and the North East at £196,877. The mismatch of high house-price increases, well above those in incomes, was crucial as it made the large deposits required to purchase a new home increasingly unaffordable and that despite government efforts to help. In 2002, the median house price in England was around 5.1 times higher than the median annual earnings of a full-time worker, but by 2019 the figure was 7.8 and in London 12.8. As a result, renting came to the fore, but very high rents in the private sector made it impossible for many to save for a deposit. The percentage renting privately in England rose from 11 percent in 2003 to 19 percent in 2015, with that in Greater Manchester rising from 6 percent to 20 percent, and both Outer London and West Yorkshire also seeing the percentage rise by more than 10 percent. In 2016, addressing the developing situation, the new May government set out to focus on improving rental provision rather than the owner occupation that had been the center of attention for previous Conservative governments.

A long-term rise in the price of housing led, in the early twenty-first century, to an increase in intergenerational living, which was part of a global trend. The number of twenty- to thirty-four-year-olds living with their parents rose from 1.9 million in 2000 and 2.8 million, just under a quarter, in 2015. Financial necessity was a key element in this situation, including saving to buy houses as well as the common reasons of inability to afford rent and the need for help with childcare. Although this trend seemed unusual and disturbing to some British commentators, the percentage in the rest of the EU was 48 percent and in the United States 32 percent.

The class character of living arrangements emerged clearly, with the poor more likely to live with their parents, although most did not. The "bank of Mum and Dad," a term that became common from 2012, referred to the parental support increasingly necessary if young adults were to get into the housing market or, indeed, enjoy university without running up considerable debts. However, there was no such "bank" for much of the population. There was also pressure related to the handover of assets by grandparents and related issues of care for the elderly and the rate of death duties. Tension between the now older baby boomers and younger millennials became a major theme.

Separately, changes in the way of life and the pattern of expenditure helped create pressures for millennials, not least the amount spent on vacations and on eating out.

Another factor in intergenerational living was provided by the number of grown-up children moving back home because their marriage or relationship had broken up. Childcare by grandparents provided another element. A 2015 survey by Gransnet suggested that its annual worth was £17 billion.

CRIME

A sense of rising crime was an issue in the late twentieth century. An increase in criminality, especially in contrast to the 1950s, was related to a widespread breakdown in the socialization of the young, especially of young males. The numbers and percentage of young men with criminal records rose, and there was also an increase for young women. Although crime was not limited to these areas, crime hit most in run-down neighborhoods, further desocializing life there and encouraging outward movement by those who could afford it. This situation led to a greater measure of social segregation and was linked to the appeal of the suburbs. Although blamed by many commentators on Conservative governments between 1979 and 1997 and their economic policies, crime had, in fact, increased from the 1950s, and for much of the period, unemployment rates were low and the standard of living of the poor rose. Indeed, robberies in London rose by 105 percent between 1991 and 2002, a period of falling unemployment. Many commentators, however, found it easier to blame Thatcher, the Conservatives, "the system," or racism. Similarly, in 2011 and 2016, disorder in London took place in a city with very high rates of employment.

In practice, an economic explanation of rising crime, in London and elsewhere, appears less pertinent than one that focuses on social dislocation, especially family breakdown. In addition, detailed variations chronologically owed much to changing age profiles, in the shape of the number of adolescent males, a group that was more likely to commit crime. Knife crime became more prominent in London from the 2000s, in part because large numbers of young men began to carry knives in order to give themselves a sense of protection. The resulting killings led to a change in the age profile of violent death among males. However, the murder rate (11.7 per million in England and Wales between April 2021 and end of March 2022) was low by global standards, and certainly compared to the United States, and that despite the fact that the country was relatively crowded, while imprisonment was less common than in the United States. The low rate of gun ownership, and notably of the legal ownership of guns, was an important factor in keeping the murder rate low, although there were notable issues in specific communities, and "black-on-black" killings among young men in London, often with guns, caused concern. As so often in Britain, the weather played a role. In 2016, disturbances in London occurred on the hottest day of the year so far, with temperatures peaking at 33.5°C. Conversely, when temperatures rose even more later that summer, there were no riots.

There were also issues about the wider reporting of crime and of low conviction rates. Reporting issues led to dissension about real crime rates, notably for robbery. In particular, it was claimed that downward trends in police figures for many crimes were misleading. Low conviction rates were especially the case for rape, and notably of young women as contrasted with older ones: linked to these low rates for rape came a critique of the policing and legal systems, a critique that was justified, although issues of proof played a significant role. The questions of innocence until proven guilty also arose, as did those of anonymity for alleged victims and the ease of making accusations. There were also very low conviction rates for robbery and burglary. So also for drug use. Surveys indicate that in 2018–19, 9.4 percent of adults between the ages of 16 to 59 had taken an illegal drug, and 20.3 percent of those aged 10 to 24. The worst areas for drug abuse and related crimes were Cleveland, West Yorkshire, and Greater Manchester.

There were major moral panics, especially about pedophilia in the 2000s and 2010s and about the large-scale exploitation of girls, particularly girls in local authority care, in the 2010s. The term *moral panic* is frequently employed by academics as a distancing one that implies that the situation has been exaggerated in order to make moral or political points. In practice, both pedophilia and the "grooming" of children for sexual exploitation were later revealed as major problems. They were linked to new technology, in the shape of child pornography on the Internet. Ethnic tension also played a major role, with young white girls in care in certain Northern cities—notably Rotherham— but also elsewhere in the country—for example, Derby and Oxford—being exploited and mostly by Asian Muslim men who used intimidation, "grooming," rape, and getting young women addicted to drugs. Gang rape was part of the process. Trial testimony suggested that the accused regarded white women as inherently sluttish and therefore ripe for brutal exploitation.

For long, commentators would not refer to these issues for fear of being labeled racist, and the same factor appears to have affected the police. As a result, the scandal when the stories broke in the 2010s, and many cities were revealed to have such gangs, reflected on the major problems Britain faced in looking at the nature of its society. The official report on Rotherham suggested that fourteen hundred girls, aged about 11 to 16, had been exploited there—an astonishing number. Persistent failures to act on the part of local authorities and the police caused justified outrage, although, possibly, not the level of public anger and action that would have been seen in some countries.

Alongside crime, the massive spread of CCTV (closed-circuit television), notably in cities, ensured that life was literally under supervision as well as being more regulated, for the poor and wealthy alike. Greater regulation left less space for autonomy or independence, unless permitted by government or, indeed, criminal. This was a situation that impoverished the range and dynamism of activity that are so important to the vitality of society. Popular television series, such as *Only Fools and Horses* and *Minder*, depicted a world of semilegal expedients as a residue of the entrepreneurial spirit. At the same time, justified concern about terrorism from the 2000s led to growing pressure, notably from government, for surveillance and for extended policing practices. However, government attempts to introduce identity cards failed.

SOCIAL STRUCTURES

The changes outlined so far, notably with gender, age, ethnicity, and religion, raise the question of how far social structures linked to traditional assumptions relating to employment and income were still relevant. In practice, these assumptions and structures remained important, not least for government statistical evaluations and for consumer research. The relationship between these structures and new social practices, however, was complex. In particular, older patterns of explanation were seen as overly limited. For example, the idea that the social condition of a household or family was set by the adult male, thus defining the unit, appeared increasingly anachronistic. In particular, the resulting presentation and treatment of women and children was often flawed. So also with the idea that individuals had a fixed social position throughout their life, as opposed to having different social positions at various stages of it. Whereas the bone-weakening condition of infant rickets used to be associated with poverty, by the 2010s, it was discussed in terms of vitamin D deficiency linked to lack of exposure to the sun, notably through indoor lifestyles and a lack of outdoor exercise.

The net effect of criticism was to introduce a fluidity to social analysis—for example, on the role of class dynamics in causing and sustaining poverty.[20] However, this was a fluidity that itself was a matter for political dispute. Labour and Conservative views of society could overlap but, in general, were very different and were usually understood in this light. Alongside its progressive, liberal aspirations, the Labour Party was, in practice, inherently traditionalist in many of its social assumptions. This was notably so on its trade union side. Labour was most inclined to emphasize collectivist notions and solutions and, in particular, class consciousness and identities and, therefore, divisions. In contrast, the Conservative Party was more inclined to stress individualist notions, as well as a national big society or, as it was termed for the 2010 election, "big tent." The latter was an aspect of what was termed one-nation Conservatism. In her opening remarks as prime minister in 2016, Theresa May referred to "One Nation Government... social justice" and "a union between all of our citizens."

These distinctions between Labour and Conservative views, distinctions that were far from fixed, helped frame discussions over a range of topics, especially access to housing, educational opportunity, health, and income support. In practice, however, it was implicit assumptions about social issues and values that were more potent than supposedly objective analyses. This remains the case, but also poses a challenge to historians. At the same time, values could change greatly or apparently so. Most significantly, Tony Blair, Labour Party leader from 1994 to 2007 and the prime minister from 1997 to 2007, sought to temper (as he would have seen it) traditional Labour policies in pursuit of a middle, or "third," way that discarded socialism, nationalization, and trade union dominance (see chapter 8), although, in government, Blair increased government power in some respects by regulation. Blair sought to incorporate the legacy of Thatcherism in devising a new form of social democracy. As shadow (opposition) home secretary in 1992–94, Blair promised toughness on crime, a policy not hitherto associated with Labour, and one that helped regain the initiative for the party. In 1994, as the new young leader, Blair spoke to the party conference about his goals: a society "rich in economic prosperity, secure in social justice, confident in political change" and offered the linkage "New Labour, New Britain." Under Blair, the emphasis was on a democratization, notably of opportunity, health, and consumption, one that would seek to encompass the bulk of society.

Yet there were unavoidable elements of class that both the Conservatives and New Labour tended to underplay, and these elements encouraged criticism of both movements by commentators and radicals. Thus, consumption of fresh fruit and vegetables and fresh (as opposed to fried) fish is higher among affluent groups, while the poor tend to have less variety and fewer fresh ingredients in their diet and less opportunity to take exercise. This was an important aspect of a more general crisis of obesity, with 28 percent of the English population rated as obese in 2019 and 36 percent as overweight, percentages that are rising. Linked to this, heart disease rates and diabetes are high by EU standards.

Poverty, meanwhile, was a persistent feature of British life. The high rate of deindustrialization in the 1970s had led to a major rise in unemployment, which was repeated at a strong rate in the early 1980s and at a more modest rate in the early 1990s. Payday lending was a key element in the shifts and expedients that was the life of many of the working poor.

There were also those who, in the 1990s, were increasingly termed the underclass. Large numbers of beggars appeared on the streets, and sleeping rough became more common. The closure of mental hospitals created a serious problem, as the alternative policy of "care in the community" proved inadequate. More generally, class mortality differences widened from the late 1950s, at least in relative terms. In addition, 2010 figures indicated that children eligible for free school meals because of family poverty were four times more likely to receive a permanent exclusion from school due to bad behavior and thus to lose out on significant life chances.

The poverty rate, based on the number of people whose income after tax is less than 60 percent of the national average (equivalent in 2014 to £20,907 for a family of two adults and two children) was, in 2014, 16.8 percent of the UK population, which was the twelfth largest rate out of the twenty-eight EU countries. However, this is a relative measure of poverty, not an absolute measure. Indeed, one indication of poverty that is employed is the inability to afford a subscription to Sky Television. Furthermore, because it was easy in Britain's fluid labor market, to leave, as well as enter, poverty, Britain in 2014 had the third lowest rate (6.5 percent) of those remaining in persistent poverty over three years or more. This percentage was still equivalent to 3.9 million people but was the lowest rate since comparable figures were introduced in 2008. At the same time, nearly a third of people in the UK had fallen into poverty at least once in 2011–14, with women more likely to do so than men. In 2018, the UN Special Rapporteur assessed a fifth of the population as living in poverty including 1.5 million as destitute. The COVID pandemic led to a significant increase in poverty, including turning to emergency food parcels. As another index of poverty, a study found in 2010 that 25 percent of London primary schools were in areas that exceeded air pollution limits, and nearly 85 percent of those polluted schools were deprived, which underlined the range of deprivation, as well as its interactions. In 2016, Sadiq Khan, the new Labour mayor of London, made air quality a policy and political issue.

One unattractive consequence of class distinctiveness was in the social impact of medical attention. A survey by the Royal College of Surgeons, reported in 2016, noted that 34 percent of NHS clinical commissioning groups in England contravened national clinical guidance by restricting access to routine surgery such as hip and knee replacements until patients stopped smoking or lost weight.[21] This underlined the tension between planning and equality: what might appear fully justified on functional grounds was not necessarily equitable. Possibly linked to this, the social position of doctors and their very good pay and pension provision insulated many of them from social pressures. These incomes and pensions were paid by the taxpayers, most of whom earned far less than them, as well as by taxes on cigarettes and alcohol. Similarly, proposed action against sugary drinks, while necessary for all, will hit hardest on the poor who consume them disproportionately. In 2016, there were conflicting signs as to whether the new government, which was subject to contrary lobbying, would implement such action. At the same time, widespread behavioral changes, notably the reduction of smoking, ensured that absolute inequalities in mortality declined, even as relative ones remained significant. In 2016, Theresa May claimed that the "poor die on average nine years earlier."

Class distinctions fired radical commentators to anger. However, in the 1990s, class-based criteria became less prominent in public discussion while governmental support for wider homeownership bore fruit. At that stage, the core description of the majority of the British was of a capitalist, consumerist, individualistic, mobile, predominantly secular and urban, property-owning democrat. The views of this cohort were very important to the politics of those and subsequent years, not least to the character of Blair's Britain. From the 2000s, the situation changed as homeownership declined. In part, this was due to a supply mismatch for a larger population and, in part, to a rise in the rental sector linked to the cost of house purchase and to investment by the wealthy in buy-to-rent property, investment that rested on rising property values and on the growing rental market. That offers an appropriate class-based analysis. So also with the overwhelming percentage of the working class, notably of boys, that does not obtain adequate school results, a result attributed by some commentators to them hearing fewer words from their parents in their early years. White working-class boys are 50 percent more likely than the average pupil to begin secondary school with a poor standard of mathematics, reading, and writing, and less than a third of them gain five General Certificates of Education (GCSEs) at grades A–C, a worse performance than any other group. In 2016, David Hoare, the chairman of Ofsted, the schools-inspection body, referred to the Isle of Wight as characterized by white ghettos with low educational standards, crime, and drugs. This was a serious exaggeration, but there was also a kernel of truth.

There were elements of social change that were not class based. One in particular, one that was unwelcome to trade unions, was the increased percentage of the workforce taken by the self-employed. This was a long-term consequence of the privatizations and labor-market changes of the 1980s, such that by the mid-2010s, the number of the self-employed was close to those of public servants.[22]

Meanwhile, social images continued to change. Alongside the long-term decline in the concepts of the gentlemen, the lady, of "nice" behavior, and of "politeness" came that of the once-established landscape of social positioning, a positioning that was based on easy identifiers. These had been well grounded in the social elite in the 1950s as in "an outsider would have thought him the average sort of fellow with good background, good public school, good university: dependable, but not very ambitious."[23] There had been similar conventions of placing throughout society, but there was already change due to a variety of factors including the impact of World War II and of high postwar taxation. In 1953, Agatha Christie reflected on "vast houses nowadays. No one would buy them to live in. It would be pulled down, perhaps, and the whole estate built over. . . . Would it be turned into an hotel, or an institute?"[24]

Social conventions had been greatly mixed up and subverted from the 1960s, and the process continued thereafter. Generational change, however, helps explain why the 1960s was less transformative than sometimes thought. Instead, it represented an accentuation of changes seen in the 1950s, but one that in part was brought to fruition in the 1980s and 1990s. In many senses, this was a more disruptive period than the 1960s, not simply because of the impact of neoliberalism, but also because those who were young in the 1960s, many of them believers in change, were now in positions of authority. Although it led to a situation of overlap, this lapse factor, in experience, assumptions, policies, and implementation, was of great importance as a result of differences between the generations. In addition, there was the perception of these differences as being strong, a perception that played a major role in the characterization and story line of sitcoms such as Ab Fab (Absolutely Fabulous, 1992–2012). On the whole, the critique was one by the young of the old and an accompanying demand for the rejection of established practices. Having gathered and then deepened, change had suddenly become normative. What had hitherto appeared "unmentionable," such as gay lifestyles, was now not only taken for granted but also advertised as positively good.

However, there was also a critique by the old of the young. Such intergenerational tensions had always existed, being seen, for example, in the 1920s, but they were more pronounced from the 1950s and, even more, 1960s. In turn, these tensions ebbed with the spread of "'60s values" across the generations. Nevertheless, the tensions continued to play a role and helped explain why social analysis in terms of family units had its disadvantages irrespective of the misleading assumption of social homogeneity. Polls in 2016 suggested that the young were more conservative than their parents in attitudes to work and in some social attitudes, although less so in sexual behavior and matters of race.

Observing changes in the past, including in classification, raises the question of how the present situation will be assessed, and how far circumstances and analysis will alter in the future. The most likely outcome will be one in which attempts are made to link values and structures, but that approach risks a reductionism and determinism that are inappropriate and that may lead to criticism. There is a particular danger of a determinism in terms of values being allegedly caused by structures or, at least, dependent on them. Moreover, it is unclear how far the combination of a movement for change and a generation willing to endorse change may occur in the future. This combination was seen in the 1960s and, very differently, in the 1980s.

Inevitably, the consideration of social change in the past is linked to the sense of the present, and to anticipations about the future. At present, the possible revival of class consciousness is an element. This is being highlighted by the question of property, not only the ownership of property assets but also the costs of property, in mortgages, rents, taxation, and benefits forgone. Very high as they are, these costs were contained in the early 2010s by the quantitative easing and political, monetary, and fiscal measures that helped keep interest rates extremely low for a very sustained period, before a major rise in 2022–23. Near-zero interest rates encouraged asset prices to surge, while average real wages fell by about 10 percent between 2007 and 2015, although they rose in 2016.

This contrast greatly widened regional, class, and generational disparities. The ONS estimated in June 2016 that just under a million households were worth almost £700,000 excluding property assets, while, including them, more than two million households were worth more than £1 million. Conversely, the Institute for Fiscal Studies reported in July 2016 that due to low wages, the gap between the poorest households and those on median incomes had fallen to the lowest level for twenty years, with many middle-income working families dependent on benefits, which is partly due to the expansion of welfare benefits under the Blair and Brown governments. Whereas household wealth in Britain rose by 14 percent between 2006 and 2014, it declined in the North East and Midlands and rose above 20 percent only in the South, while in London the increase was 47 percent, both due to higher house prices and thanks to greater savings. In contrast, net national disposable income was in 2015 still 3.1 percent below its pre-crisis peak.

It was hit anew in the early 2020s. The rise in interest rates in 2022–23 highlighted the potential costs of owning property (if on a mortgage) and also, indeed, albeit less seriously, of paying rents. Such a development made the property issue even more significant. If such, there might be a move away from classification linked to the recent agenda of gender, sexuality, and ethnicity, or, at least, a lessening of attention devoted to those factors. However, the considerable institutional intellectual capital and political interest invested in this agenda may well make such a reconceptualization contentious and not least because it may challenge the position and positioning of some of the commentators involved. Again, international factors are crucial, for Britain is unlikely to adopt a unique system of social classification and understanding, a point clearly seen with the Black Lives Matter movement in the early 2020s.

A revitalization of concepts of class dynamics might well affect the languages of cultural and political identification and contention. As yet, that is not certain, but it looks increasingly likely. The 2016 EU referendum suggested such an outcome, for alongside backing from the majority of voting homeowners who did not owe mortgages, principally the wealthy elderly, although also much of the agricultural community, the Brexit vote owed much to support from the poor, and notably a working class that had lost out from globalization and felt vulnerable accordingly. This element was more significant in the voting than issues of gender, sexuality, or ethnicity. For example, Slough, a working-class town with a large ethnic population, notably from South Asia, voted for Brexit. The betting companies lost on Brexit because they "followed the money." This was dominated by the large bets laid out for "Remain," but there was a longtail of small bets on Brexit that better reflected voter decisions. Nonprofessionals voted 64 percent to 36 percent for Brexit.

The recovery of class as an interpretative structure will affect not only the understanding of Britain in the 2010s and 2020s but also that throughout the period from 1945. At the same time, values were, and are, important, and this is the case irrespective of social status. An emphasis on values encourages us to consider culture in the broadest terms, as in the next chapter.

4

CHANGING CULTURE

As with environmental, economic, and social circumstances and developments, cultural counterparts showed a mixture of international trends and of distinctive national ones. As also with these other factors, there was a lessening of the distinctive national ones and a degree of homogenization at the international level. Whether described or discussed as Americanization or as globalization, and both indeed were at play, the homogenization can readily be seen as value laden. It was an aspect of the consumerism that was central to both Americanization and globalization.

Advertising played a major role in this consumerism, but advertising was not the only element. There was also the more subliminal imagery of desirable life presented by television programs and with the lavish color photography in Sunday color newspaper supplements that began in 1962 with the first *Sunday Times* color supplement, an issue entitled "A Sharp Look at the Mood of Britain," that depicted a new sense of national purpose and classlessness. Such supplements provided a way for newspapers to raise revenue through advertising and thus to counter the competition of television. Beginning with the "quality" press, supplements were subsequently introduced by lower-price popular newspapers, enhancing the magazine-type character of the press.

To use the terms *Americanization* or *globalization* was (and is) itself to make a choice about the source and direction of international influence. In addition, the use of *Americanization* was generally as a pejorative term. It was an aspect of culture as politics in the broadest sense, which indeed was, and is, one way to approach culture, although not the sole one. The same, for some, is true of the word *globalization* which frequently serves as a description of international capitalism.

The impact of international links and models, of contents and forms, in Britain interacted with transformations in identity and behavior that contributed, in the broadest of forms, to the culture as well as politics of the period. Moreover, they were aspects of the incessant nature of change, and of unprecedented changes; with the extent, rate, and persistence of change leading, for many, to a strong sense of discontinuity and disruption, but, for others, to a welcome excitement.

In addition to altering, and more assertive, gender and youth expectations and roles, there were other broad currents that helped to give a character to the age. The decline of formality in all its respects was a major one. Informality in means of address and conversation became far more pronounced. Informality in dress, which was an aspect of personality through spending on particular fashions and items, also became commonplace. The visual identifiers of class, position, and status were abandoned or became less common. Moreover, they were also mocked or caricatured, although the significance of this process for discarding the identifiers is unclear. Male hats were a classic instance: the bowler hat, let alone the top hat, of the upper class and the flat cap of the working class all became very uncommon. So too with women wearing hats and gloves at social occasions, which had been the norm, with a major effort being put into having a matching outfit. Indeed, the covered-up nature of Muslim women took on greater significance as it was so much at variance with the far more uncovered nature of clothes for "white women." The signifiers that were lost included those of particular appearances for unmarried and married women and for widows. Means of address, both verbally and in correspondence, also changed with the decline of "Miss" (for an unmarried woman) and "Sir" (for an older man), and the rise of "Ms.," a form of address for women that removed attention from their married state. There was an increased use of first names—for example, toward hospital patients. Writing conventions altered greatly as letters were replaced by electronic communications: Facebook, Twitter, and other formats proved particularly significant.

The nature of clothing changed in many respects. In place of clothes that were altered, adapted, darned, and mended by the owners, by friends, or by tailors and seamstresses, of shoes repaired by cobblers, and of coats reproofed against the weather, came "disposable items." Older women and men wore more casual clothes and shoes than in the past. Men ceased to wear ties and wore open shirts instead. The principal changes were as far as the young were concerned, and notably so from the 1960s when fashions changed greatly with the miniskirt and with brightly colored pants and shirts. The fashion among young women in the 2010s for pants with holes, and increasingly large holes, in them was a clear example of a nonfunctional choice that appeared almost willfully negligent, at the individual level, of environmental considerations of staying warm and not wasting resources. Young men wore sneakers on their feet.

Previous conventions in hairstyles and makeup were abandoned, as were restraints on tattoos, piercings, and unusual jewelry in the shape of studs and chains. Noses, tongues, eyelids, belly buttons, breasts, and genitals were among the parts of the body embellished with studs, rings, and other objects. Men were part of the process—for example, with their earlobes thus decorated. Indeed, at the same time that fashion helped set the tone for appearance and behavior, so both were deliberately unconventional in their content and presentation. In 2016, it was estimated that one in five people and one in three young adults had tattoos.

Class and gender stereotypes were rapidly surmounted, and, if notably so from the 2000s, they had already changed greatly from the 1960s. Paradoxically, at the same time as these changes, there was a degree of continued and new division within national culture, not least in response to Britain becoming an increasingly multiethnic society. One description of this combined situation was multiculturalism.

Tensions and divisions were also diachronic or across time. Indeed, there was a major breach in continuity, a breach that focused on the 1960s, although being prefigured in the 1950s. The earlier situation was outlined in *Death at the President's Lodging*, a detective novel by J. I. M. Stewart published in 1936. Of one character, he wrote that he reflected an epoch "of English life. Dodd, heavy, slow, simply bred, and speaking with such a dialectical purity that a philologist might have named the parish in which he was born, suggested an England fundamentally rural still."[1] To Stewart, this situation was already changing in the 1930s, as, indeed, was the case, in part due to the major impact of internal migration, the motorcar, the radio, and mass education.

However, essentially in the 1960s, a set of values and practices that had provided cohesion and continuity, at least since the mid-nineteenth century, and often for far longer, was much challenged or, in part, collapsed. Respect for the monarchy, the Church of England, Parliament, the legal system, the military, the nation's past, unwavering support for the union in Scotland, for the landed Protestant ascendancy in Northern Ireland, and for much else, including the rural railways destroyed after the Beeching Report, were all eroded. This erosion occurred in response to shifts in the understanding of gender, youth, class, place, nation, and race. This challenge greatly affected the content and reception of culture, both new culture and the cultural past that was presented, revived (or not), and reviewed (or not).

It would be readily possible to move, in a chapter on culture, after an initial introduction, to a discussion of particular cultural forms, with so many words on theater or on poetry. However, to do so would be to underplay common themes and also to overemphasize the autonomy of these individual forms. In practice, the trends that were most apparent across the world of culture were the rise of a television society and the complex interaction of government, the market, and consumers. That world does not make the discussion of individual forms and specific arts less consequential, but a focus on trends puts this discussion and these forms in context.

In practice, *contexts* is the correct term, not *context*, because there are many that affected and reflected cultural life. Particularly important ones related to the means of transmission and reception of cultural forms and opinion. This was even more the case if sport and other leisure activities are also understood as forms of culture, rather than being separated from it. This very classification is a matter of controversy but rests on a rejection of elite definitions of culture, a rejection that became increasingly important in this period and, indeed, was an aspect of its cultural history. There is also, and repeatedly so, the question of the very meanings of words, one captured in her first Prime Minister's Questions on July 20, 2016, when Theresa May responded to the Labour leader, Jeremy Corbyn, "He uses the language of austerity—I call it living within our means." Culture was similarly a matter of linguistic debate, or, rather, disagreement, as well as its conceptual counterpart.

TELEVISION

The rise of television culture was dramatically present in increased television ownership, longer broadcasting hours, more channels, and rising viewer numbers, each of which altered greatly from 1945 to the present. These trends were interlinked and interdependent. As a result, individual television programs, as well as the very process of watching the television, could acquire an iconic force within society, expressing values, and encouraging a sharing of experience. The sharing was particularly pronounced when there were relatively few channels. For both families and individuals, mealtimes were organized round the television.

Initially, television was very much a state concern. Established in the 1920s, the BBC (British Broadcasting Corporation) was a public monopoly supported by a license fee charged on every household with a television. It had an exalted, self-referential, and self-congratulatory sense of its mission for public enlightenment. There were no advertisements. A culture already developed by the BBC for radio was applied to television, which was a more challenging and expensive medium. However, at that stage, there was only one channel, only limited transmission hours, including no daytime or late broadcasts, and only black-and-white images. For much of the day, only the unchanging test card was shown on the television, thus proving that it worked.

This situation did not alter until 1955 when the BBC monopoly was deliberately breached as the Conservative government allowed the foundation of ITV (Independent Television) which first broadcast on September 22, 1955. This was a national channel based on a federation of new independent regional companies, which both produced and transmitted material, while the central organization provided the ITN news. ITV, which received none of the license fee, was funded by advertisements and provided a more consumerist account of life, and one that was focused on viewer interests. The companies, which had potentially highly profitable franchises, sought to make money, and advertisers favored and pushed for programs with high viewing figures. The terms on which the franchises were awarded (and later renewed) aroused controversy, appearing to some as aspects of a "crony capitalism." Had more been known about the process then, this perception would have been stronger, but there was little public clarification. Also in 1955, an increase in television viewing time from forty-one to fifty hours a week was authorized.

Reflecting a reaction against the state planning and control of the late 1940s, ITV helped usher in a profound change in the national psyche, one of mass consumerism, although, looked at differently, a desire for the latter was the basis for the success of ITV. I once heard the veteran far-left-wing politician Tony Benn claim that ITV had made true socialism impossible in Britain. The obvious parallel is between the iconic role of the BBC and that of the NHS which, in a very different context, did not have to accept any equivalent to ITV: private health provision remained the choice of a minority, less than 10 percent of the population.

Ownership of goods, as pushed by advertising, was matched by the "soap operas" that ITV carried, with actors depicted as surrounded by material goods and, in part, defined by them. Indeed, such goods became a major aspect of conversation, with gender norms coming into play. Men were expected to talk about cars, women about shopping and washing machines. Ownership was linked to the acquisition of novelty and to one-upmanship toward neighbors. It granted status, as when neighbors and relatives who lacked televisions were invited over for "television suppers"—meals in front of the television—or to see programs.

Like the liberalization of borrowing by means of "hire purchase," ITV was important to the spread of car culture in the 1950s, and also to the increased vogue for "white goods," such as washing machines and, later, dishwashers. American soaps, such as *I Love Lucy*, were significant in ITV's schedules, as were American-style advertisements. The soaps and the schedules helped make particular aspects of British life appear anachronistic and unattractive. This was the case, for example, with the use of coal fires, with living in terraces (row housing), and with a degree of internal twilight due to poor lighting. Beards and moustaches seemed out of place in the 1950s given the clean-shaven men on American programs. Instead, ITV's "soaps" encouraged the preference for electricity and for living on modern estates of detached or semidetached houses with a car parked in the driveway outside the house. The emphasis was very much on nuclear families. Thus, ITV was part of the enormous American contribution to British life and culture. This was particularly apparent with films, music, television, fashions, consumer objects, and the idea of the teenager. Without American influence and participation, life in the UK, at least up to 1960, would have been dreadfully boring.

By August 1959, 80 percent of the population could receive ITV, and its network was completed in 1962. To respond to ITV, BBC had to adapt, and, in a chase for ratings, it increasingly adopted a populist approach, both on television and on radio, one that did not reflect its founding principles and long-held precepts and that some commentators decried. The BBC, which also launched BBC2 in 1964, produced its own soaps, some of which were indistinguishable from their ITV counterparts, and this was more generally true of much of the production of the two rival systems. Television hit cinema audiences in the late 1950s. They fell from more than 900 million in 1954 to 450 million in 1959, which ensured that financing was a problem, fewer films were made, and most were on safe topics such as *The Colditz Story* (1955) and *The Battle of the River Plate* (1956), both war epics.

The tension between the BBC and ITV was an aspect of a more general tension between state provision of culture and popular interests. It was seen, for example, with the contrast between, on the one hand, patronage by the Arts Council, a government body, and the activities it subsidized, and, on the other hand, the desires of much of the public for a more populist tone and content to culture. This tension became more pointed with time and remains significant at present. Arts programing and commentary on the BBC, both television and radio, provides a particular instance. There is a marked tendency to focus on the avant-garde or critically fashionable, and, in contrast, not on the popular, still less the populist. The popular press takes a very different approach.

Television was important in other respects as well, creating a shared context in which experiences were received and common experiences developed. Families were encouraged to sit down together to watch "*the* television," for at this stage it was very rare to have more than one per household. Popular programs became common experiences as they were watched by more than 50 percent of television viewers. They were true, for example, of the *Morecambe and Wise Show*, and phrases or jokes from such shows entered the national vocabulary of the period. This process was accentuated because Britain is only on one time zone. The impact was varied. ITV took to broadcasting the first television showing of James Bond films on Christmas Day at 3:05 p.m. and the pressure on the National Grid and its system of electricity provision of people switching on their electric kettles during the intermissions was such that a large stand-by capacity had to be made available. Color television introduced in 1967, and fully operational across all three channels in 1969, dramatized a sense of change: everything before now appeared gray, unattractive, dull, and redundant.[2] Moreover, color made television far more attractive. Living in Northwest London, the fictional Chen household in Timothy Mo's (1983) novel *Sour Sweet* had added no furniture to that purchased from a previous tenant "bar a gigantic television."[3]

Television viewing (like reading in the eighteenth century) was to move from an intensive experience to an extensive one. Television provided a "TV culture," with common points of reference. In contrast, in the channel boom and format proliferation that gathered pace from the 1980s, that shared culture was lost and was replaced by a fragmented, extensive media culture. The same has happened since with social media. Under the Broadcasting Act of 1980, Channel 4 was launched in 1982, followed by TV-AM in 1983: a second independent (non-BBC) channel had been anticipated by the Conservative government in 1963, but Labour had not been supportive.[4] Although largely commercially self-funded, Channel 4 is ultimately publicly owned. Originally a subsidiary of the Independent Broadcasting Authority, the station is now owned and operated by Channel Four Television Corporation, a public corporation of the Department for Culture, Media, and Sport.

By 2015, the average commercial channel viewing on a TV set had increased to two hours twenty-four minutes daily. Attempts to re-create common memories by revivals—for example, in 2016 of *Are You Being Served?*, *Porridge*, and *Cold Feet*—suggested a lack of confidence in the ability to create convincing new inclusive programs. Lazy stereotypes of class differences continued to be produced as in the BBC sitcom *From Home* (2014).

Television is changing fast. Terrestrial television has already been diminished in importance by satellite and cable services. These are all now being diminished in importance by streaming services such as Netflix and by YouTube and social media. The rapid rise of the last is of importance in its influence on politics, and not just in the changes that it has made in the social interaction of the young.

COSMOPOLITANISM AND NATIONALISM

The tension between cosmopolitanism and xenophobia became more acute with time. The forms of this tension varied. In some respects, there was not so much tension as a positive synergy. This was most clearly the case with food. The impact of foreign cuisine was linked to the deficiencies of British food culture, as there was no level below which British food could not drop. For many, food that actually tasted of something became a new experience. British cuisine was totally reconceptualized as a result of the popularity and, to a degree, Anglicization of foreign foods. Initially, this was a matter of Italian restaurants, which, as with Italian ice cream, spread after 1945, in part as many Italian prisoners of war sought to stay in Britain. The end of food rationing was also important.

Particular dishes entered the British diet and vocabulary. Thus, from Italy, "spag bol," or spaghetti bolognese, became a British staple, as did lasagna, veal escalope, and tiramisu. Some of these dishes, notably spaghetti, lent themselves to convenience foods and were canned and sold accordingly. Chili con carne was spaghetti bolognese's Mexican counterpart. There was singularly little resistance on the part of the defenders of more traditional food— for example, mutton, sheep's cheeks, eel pies, and offal. The eating of kidneys declined markedly, let alone of hearts, although the cooked "English breakfast" of bacon and egg continued to hold its sway at the start of the day. In practice, much of the bacon came from Denmark.

From the 1960s, the Anglicization of foreign food was notably in the form of Chinese and Indian cuisine. Particular adaptations served the British market, while, conversely, many elements of Chinese and Indian cuisine did not translate: a more meat-based choice was offered to British consumers, and less in the form of vegetarian food. In addition, it took a while for the more delicate South Indian dishes to join the North Indian tandoori dishes and strong curries that British restaurant-goers liked to consume.

Chinese and Indian restaurants are not just common in areas with concentrations of immigrants but are found across the country, including Elgin in distant northern Scotland when I visited it in 1975. Their cuisines are also extensively stocked in supermarkets. The National Catering Inquiry published in 1966 indicated that 11 percent of Londoners had visited an Indian restaurant at some point. The percentage subsequently increased sharply, with newly affluent young males playing a key role, and, accordingly, drinking a lot of lager and eating strong curries, notably vindaloo, which accordingly entered the vocabulary. This was very much an Anglicization of Indian food and eating, in part indeed a translation to Britain of developments in India under British rule, which had ended in 1947.

Other national cuisines broke into the British restaurant world and into supermarket cuisine. This was true, in particular, of Thai and Mexican food. Like Chinese food, these cuisines did not have the former imperial link seen with the British popularity of Indian food and the Dutch and French popularity of Indonesian and Vietnamese food, respectively. Japanese and, then, Korean food entered the British restaurant world, although with less of a penetration than Thai or Mexican, let alone Indian or Chinese restaurants. By the 2000s, London had replaced New York as the restaurant capital of the world, in part due to the cosmopolitan nature of the city (whether permanent residents, part-year counterparts, or transients), which included large numbers of American, Arab, French, Japanese, Portuguese, and Russian residents.

The international tendency was less pronounced in other cities. For example, Itsu, the profitable and expanding British-owned Asian fast-food chain, had sixty-nine stores by July 2016, of which fifty-eight were in London. Nevertheless, across the country, Thai green curry or lasagna became commonplace pub dishes alongside the established fish and chips. There were also separate restaurants. In Exeter where I live, a city of about 134,000 people, there are Chinese, French, Indian, Italian, Lebanese, Japanese, Moroccan, Nepalese, Palestinian, Spanish, Thai, Turkish, and Vietnamese restaurants or cafés. The situation was very different when I arrived in 1996.

In contrast, Afro-Caribbean cuisine and restaurants have had scant impact, either on the "white" British diet or that of the other ethnic groups, which is in marked contrast to the strong Afro-Caribbean impact on popular music. Contrasts in part reflect the availability of investment capital and of entrepreneurial networks in the restaurant trade, as well as opportunities at the local level.

Cookery programs on the television were increasingly devoted to producing foreign dishes. For example, *The Great British Bake-Off*, a highly popular competition BBC television program that was launched in 2010, saw contestants instructed to produce foreign cakes and pastries, as well as their British counterparts. In 2015, Nadiya Hussein, a Muslim woman, won the competition using baking that brilliantly reflected her heritage, a result applauded by David Cameron, the prime minister, whose wife went on to win a related celebrity competition in 2016. In 2016, the first episode of series seven drew a record audience of ten million, nearly half the total viewing public that night. There was controversy when the series was sold to Channel Four. Of the other popular television competition programs, dance programs, which became very popular in the 2010s, notably with *Strictly Come Dancing* on BBC1's prime Saturday night slot, saw foreign dances, such as the Argentinean tango. At the level of members of the public, salsa classes became common.

Cookery books also devoted attention to foreign dishes. The French staples of foreign cooking were challenged. Italian cooking was the first addition. In 1979, Marks and Spencer, a leading department store, published an all-color *Italian Cooking*. In the introduction to *Jamie's Italy* (2005), a book of a television series, Jamie Oliver regretted not being Italian: "Why, oh why, was I born in Southend-on-Sea?"[5] Subsequently, the geographical repertoire widened greatly. First published in 1948, and selling more than two million copies by 2014, the *Good Housekeeping Cookery Book*, in the new edition published that year, included recipes for Béarnaise sauce, beurre blanc, borscht, prawns fried in garlic, mixed Italian bruschetta, fritto misto di mare, poussins with pancetta, artichoke and potato salad, risotto Milanese, Spanish omelet, among a large number of dishes that originated abroad.

However, constrained by the climate, gardening programs were far more "national" in their tone and content. There was attention to introducing foreign plants, as there had been for centuries, but the center of attention was on the already-established range of what, therefore, was presented as British plants. Radio and television programs that catered to gardeners—for example, *Gardeners' Question Time* on the radio—enjoyed significant listening and viewing figures. Their presenters, for example, Alan Titchmarsh and Monty Don, became celebrities. So also with celebrity chefs. Whereas Fanny Cradock, the most prominent early television chef, had focused on helping housewives to cook more adventurously in the years after rationing, her successors in the 2010s, such as Rick Stein, took off with the television cameras around the world, in his case to India.

The great growth in British tourism to foreign countries from the 1960s proved particularly significant in encouraging interest in foreign lifestyles, not least in the form of food and drink—for example, Spanish tapas, which became increasingly important as restaurant food from the 2000s. The numbers taking vacations abroad rose, from 4.2 million in 1971 to 32.3 million in 1998. If many traveled abroad to resorts such as Benidorm in Spain, in order to find aspects of little Britain, and ate quintessential British dishes there, such as fish and chips, and drank British beer, this was less the case for other tourists. Jet aircraft, all-inclusive vacation packages, television advertising, and the search for the sun all encouraged foreign tourism, and, while many did not travel abroad, domestic tourism became relatively less important. Moreover, domestic routes were abandoned—for example, the ferries taking South Wales workers across the Bristol Channel to resorts in the West Country, notably Ilfracombe and Minehead.

In the 2000s and 2010s, the numbers going abroad rose again, due to the expansion of inexpensive flights, including from more regional airports, and the development of direct train services to the Continent via Eurotunnel. Booking online was an aspect of the situation. Entrepreneurial companies, notably EasyJet, Ryanair, and Flybe, played a key role in creating, defining, and satisfying demand or producing grievances about their terms and conditions. This process was linked to the ownership of second homes abroad and to the wider practice of self-organized (nontour) vacations. As a result, travel companies, a feature of the late twentieth century, both those that provided vacations and the travel agencies that sold them, were hit badly.

Trends, in turn, were affected by more immediate circumstances, and notably so in 2016 as sterling fell significantly after the Brexit vote, and then even more in 2020–21 due to the COVID pandemic.

However, a trend for more vacations at home had already developed prior to Brexit. In 2015, as a result of tourism from abroad and at home, 43.7 million overnight vacations were taken in England, with spending of £10.7 billion, both figures up 7 percent. Although London topped the list, coastal towns, essentially catering for British tourists, also did well, notably Scarborough, Blackpool, Skegness, Torbay, Whitley Bay, Brighton, Margate, and Llandudno in Wales. This again underlined social division as the affluent, and also Londoners, proved much keener to go abroad than other British travelers.

A very different foreign or cultural influence was offered by foreign films and books. American ones were of great influence. In addition, there were vogues for particular genres that were made available in translation—for example, Scandinavian crime stories in the 2000s and, even more, 2010s. A greater openness to foreign influence was increasingly apparent. The key foreign influence was the United States, most obviously through cinema, popular music, and, from the 1950s, the increasingly ubiquitous television. At the same time, mainstream culture could reflect hostility toward Americans, as in the critical treatment of an abusive visiting president by a British prime minister in the romantic film *Love Actually* (2003).

There were also important Continental European cultural influences. From World War II, French plays, especially by Sartre and Anouilh, were frequently performed in translation. From the mid-1950s, Brecht had a significant impact, and major productions of his works were staged in the National Theatre in the 1960s. The "theater of the absurd," a term applied in 1961 to nonrealistic modern drama, such as Samuel Beckett's *Waiting for Godot*, was centered on Paris but was influential in Britain, notably with the playwright Harold Pinter who produced plays such as *The Caretaker* that pleased critics more than mass audiences. In concert halls, the works of the Russian composer Dmitri Shostakovich were frequently performed in the 1950s and 1960s and in the 1960s and 1970s those of Luciano Berio, Pierre Boulez, and Witold Lutosławski.

1945–55

To look at chronological changes with more attention, the late 1940s and 1950s saw a revival of prewar patterns and as part of a society that very much sought such continuity after the trauma of war. The ruralism of much 1930s' culture was revived, as in continued interest in landscapes,[6] and the appearance in 1950 of Vaughan Williams's *Folk Songs for the Four Seasons*. The classics were celebrated, notably on film, as in David Lean's 1946 version of Charles Dickens's novel *Great Expectations*.

In addition, however, there was more of an engagement with the urban experience under the 1945–51 Labour governments, and notably with the welcome to modernity seen in the 1951 Festival of Britain, which was centered on buildings constructed on a site on the war-bombed South Bank of the Thames in London. The architect Basil Spence made his name with the Sea and Ships Pavilion there, as well as with his prize-winning design for Coventry Cathedral. Offering a Labour vision of progress, the festival, which was visited by close to 8.5 million people, and that included exhibitions outside London, reflected confidence, or at least interest, in new solutions.[7] The rocket-like, cable-tensioned Skylon presided over the site. Boldness was designed to replace the drab dullness of the 1940s. Nevertheless, most people were less confident than at the time of the Great Exhibition in London in 1851. Modernism was also seen in projects and buildings that were aspects of a planned environment, a key theme in the politics and public culture of the period.[8] More bluntly, W. H. Auden began his poem "The Chimeras" with the line "Absence of heart—as in public buildings."

The theme of modernity proved weak, as well as challenging—for example, in the film *Seven Days to Noon* (1951), which deals with a scientist threatening to set off an atomic bomb in London as a warning about the dangers of nuclear destruction. In 1952, Churchill, a critic of the Festival of Britain as Socialist, had the Skylon taken down. Instead, it was continuity that was apparent. This was clearly seen in the theater, with the production of new or revived plays by established playwrights such as Terence Rattigan and Noel Coward. Agatha Christie's *Mousetrap*, a play very much located in a world of conventional social distinctions, was first produced in 1952. It, unexpectedly, became the world's longest-running play and is still running. In contrast, the works of avant-garde playwrights, such as Samuel Beckett, scarcely appeared. There was also more continuity in music, alongside an engagement with difficult works such as the operas of Benjamin Britten and the music of Michael Tippett and Harrison Birtwistle.

In books, there was also much continuity with interwar authorship, notably with Christie in detective fiction and P. G. Wodehouse in light satire continuing to publish as if there had been no change in British society. Popular genres did not alter, notably the detective novel as with Christie. *Casino Royale*, the first of Ian Fleming's James Bond novels, was published in 1953 and depicted a hero who was a comfortably off gentleman, unworried about his income, and at home in Continental casinos and eating pâté de foie gras. Like most heroes in British fiction and films of the period, he had had a "good war," as indeed had Fleming. The war helped define that generation of British males, as World War I had defined their predecessors.

In the real world, clothes in the early 1950s were more similar to the 1930s than the 1970s, and reflected hierarchies of class, gender, and age. They could do as clothes rationing had ended in 1949. In addition, this was very much the "New Elizabethan Age," that, referring back to Elizabeth I of England (r. 1558–1603), which was forecast at the time of the accession of Elizabeth II in 1952 and her coronation in 1953. The latter was a highly traditional occasion, albeit with the addition of a deferential television coverage, broadcast live and watched by just over twenty million people, 56 percent of the population. Christianity and the pinnacles of the class system were much in evidence in the ceremony. Moreover, the Christianity of the period was mostly establishment in tone, as well as being very much a matter of old, white men telling others what to do. A standard heading or subheading in the popular press, notably in the *News of the World*, a Sunday shocker, was "Bishop speaks out," usually in response to reported moral outrages that challenged the established moral code.

1956–63

Change gathered pace in the late 1950s with the "angry young men" and "kitchen-sink drama." This saw an engagement with difficult issues and in a difficult tone. John Osborne, Harold Pinter, Alan Sillitoe, Arnold Wesker, and other playwrights of "kitchen-sink drama" deliberately rejected earlier conventions in a determined effort to shock, as with Osborne's (1956) bitter *Look Back in Anger*. This was an aspect both of the 1950s as a decade of change and of the 1950s as the anticipation of the 1960s, each elements that it is overly easy to neglect due to the focus on the 1960s as the decade of change, a focus that directs attention on the young of that period who now comprise many of the commentators.

This aspect of the 1950s was seen in the popularity of American rock 'n' roll music, which very much was a rejection of established British popular entertainment and also in the degree to which the women in the James Bond novels did not seek matrimony or motherhood. With rock 'n' roll, Bill Haley and the Comets proved popular in Britain, as did Buddy Holly. Bob Dylan first performed in London in 1962. As an aspect of protectionism, the Musicians Union opposed the entry of American pop stars.[9]

"Kitchen-sink drama," however, was different as it had a clear social and, often, regional placing. These were not plays depicting the lives and mores of the social elite, as with the plays of Coward and Rattigan. Instead, "kitchen-sink drama" sought to be socially gritty; to deal with people in difficulties, and in commonplace milieu, as with Wesker's *The Kitchen* (1957); and to focus on the North of England, which was understood as a tough environment, or on the world of London bedsits. The net effect was a new "condition of England" literature, one that looked back to the interwar writing of George Orwell. In fiction, Colin MacInnes focused on the West Indian community in London and on race relations in his novel *City of Spades* (1957), going on, in *Absolute Beginners* (1959), not only to discuss youth culture but also the antiblack Notting Hill race riot of 1958 in London. The content, tone, and language were scarcely conventional: "his chief exploit . . . had been to wreck the Classic cinema in the Ladbroke basin, and, with some of his four hundred, drop the law's coach-and-four into a bomb site, while others engaged the cowboys [police] in pitched battle with milk bottles and dustbin lids."[10]

"Kitchen-sink drama" and its equivalent spanned the late 1950s and early 1960s. It was often iconoclastic in tone and it sought to question, even subvert, existing genres. For example, in spy fiction, Fleming's James Bond was joined by Len Deighton's Harry Palmer, a working-class spy who had to cope with betrayal from within the Secret Service by a social and professional "superior." This was certainly not a Bond theme but was an aspect of the real history of the postwar Secret Service, notably with the spy Kim Philby, an establishment figure who was revealed as a Soviet spy. In a less iconoclastic fashion, Alan Hunter, in his 1957 novel *Landed Gently*, referred to jingoism as doomed alongside other aspects of the Old World, especially the satanic mills and social injustice, the former a reference to traditional factories.

Change in a very different form came with the Mini, designed in 1959 for the British Motor Corporation by Alec Issigonis. This was a car very different in design to those earlier in the decade, and it reflected an inventive engagement with the possibilities of the new. Indeed, design was to become an important theme and language, one that deliberately focused on new and newly presented products.

There were also major developments in architecture. Completed in 1963, the Engineering Building at Leicester University, which was designed by the Scottish architects James Gowan and James Stirling, was deliberately futurist, and was proclaimed as Britain's first postmodernist piece of architecture. The Engineering Building was actually rather a bolder modernism than that of Le Corbusier, and was influential in using industrially produced materials. The auditoriums in the building were topped by protruding cuboid skylights.

Bold architectural schemes responded to the cult of the new, leading to much "New Brutalism" in architecture. Seven green-field, plate-glass universities were opened, beginning with Sussex in 1961 (for which Spence did much of the architectural work) and ending with Kent and Warwick in 1965. The new universities offered new initiatives in teaching and organization, notably with interdisciplinary curricula. Meeting in 1961–63, the Committee on Higher Education chaired by Lord Robbins recommended a marked increase in the number of students. The thesis of the committee report, which was presented to Parliament by Harold Macmillan, the prime minister, in October 1963, was that every child with the potential for higher education should receive it, and, if not at state expense, then with a significant state subsidy.

The political placing of cultural change was significant but also difficult. In the latter case, focusing on traditional assumptions of social structure, Marxist New Left thinkers failed to engage with youth or the variety of working-class culture.[11] Nevertheless, there was a relationship between cultural changes and the rise of Labour to power in 1964. This relationship was indirect but significant. A sense that a distinct and anachronistic "old order" existed and needed replacing by a new meritocracy able to use planning[12] provided a clear way to stir up opposition to the Conservatives as well, less prominently but also significantly, as to encourage the latter to show increased interest in reform policies. These themes were very much part of the public culture of these years.

They helped fuel the "satire boom" that became significant in the early 1960s, with clubs, such as The Establishment Club in London, live shows, and radio and television programs. Programs, such as *That Was the Week That Was* (1962–63) on television, and the new satirical periodical *Private Eye* (published in London from 1961), made existing class distinctions and social conventions appear ridiculous as well as dated. Failure in government, economy, and society could thus be traced to the alleged incompetence of British arrangements. The satirists were largely well-educated young men and were scarcely representative of society as a whole, but that did not lessen the force of the charge. There were particularly strong attacks on the last years of the Macmillan government and on its aristocratic character.

At the same time, it is instructive to note popular interest. The commercially most successful film of 1959 in Britain was the smutty comedy *Carry on Nurse*, part of a long-running sequence of *Carry On* films that remained successful until the 1970s. The commercially most successful film of 1962 was the Cliff Richard musical *The Young Ones*, a vehicle for a very conventional English type of pop singer.

1964–70

The 1960s were already offering less establishment and more radical models in novels and on the stage before what is generally understood as "the sixties" began, a process variously dated to 1963–66. The sense of the sixties owed much to the impact of popular music. This was an impact that emanated from every transistor radio, thus linking culture, technological provision, and entrepreneurial ability. Initially, the key change was the response to the Beatles, a Northern popular group who, with their debut single "Love Me Do," released in October 1962, set the "Mersey beat" (Liverpool, their home city, was on the River Mersey), and who offered working-class experiences prominence and sound.[13] Pop music challenged the "received pronunciation" of the English language, providing a regional difference that was taken up by the BBC where the importance of conformity in diction, style, and tone declined from the 1960s. The film director Guy Hamilton later noted:

> The combination of angry young men, Michael Caine and the Beatles killed the leading men who all spoke with Oxford accents. . . . Unless you had a Brummy [Birmingham] accent, forget it. I think the Beatles and the pop scene in general had a major influence on the cinema at this time.[14]

Other groups and performers also came from Liverpool including Cilla Black. Indeed, popular music lent itself to female as well as male performers. If the bands, with their emphasis on electric guitars, were very much male preserves, many singers were women. This was very different to the alternative Liverpool cult: football. Interest in Liverpool was also shown by the popularity of *The Liver Birds*, a television sitcom set there that began in 1969.

In practice, in the context of "Beatlemania" in 1963–64, the Beatles went south, to London, and became a global as well as a national product. It set the sound of the sixties. Their broadcast of "All You Need Is Love" in 1967, transmitted to twenty-six countries, was seen by about four hundred million people. Thanks largely to the Beatles, popular music became a British industry, replacing the American rock 'n' roll of the 1950s. This was to be a major export industry.

The Beatles contributed powerfully to the idea of a "New Britain," an idea that was very powerful in the mid-1960s. This idea was linked to the policies advocated by the Labour Party, which governed the country from 1964 to 1970 and which entitled its 1964 general election manifesto "The New Britain." Labour introduced a range of social legislation. This idea was related to a variety of cultural and product developments, including the new clothes fashions pioneered in Carnaby Street in London and the modern design themes often related to new technology, such as the supersonic Concorde aircraft (1969–2003) and the Post Office Tower in London (1964). Harold Wilson, a northerner who cultivated his image as a northerner, and also went south, ensured that the Beatles were given honors, although this proved controversial.

Appearances changed in the mid- and late 1960s. Male hair became longer, while the dress code changed from shirt, tie, and sports jacket for males to jeans and sweaters. Women wore miniskirts, showing an expanse of flesh that would have amazed their predecessors; corsets were out; tights replaced stockings, suspenders and garter belts; and birth control was transformed with the contraceptive pill, its ready availability, and the sexual revolution. Working-class talent provided a powerful infusion of energy in a world in which pop stars, hairdressers, and photographers were celebrities. In a different fashion to "kitchen-sink drama," the working class emerged into the light of day.

Beat music drove the rhythm. The mid-1960s saw a cycle of "Swinging London" films, including *Darling* (1965) and *Blow-Up* (1965), both of which examined the morals and mores of a permissive society in which the role of family values and of the churches were largely redundant. For Alfie in the 1966 film of that name set in London, women, clothes, and cars were commodities that proved one could get on in the world without the privileges of birth and education. Supermarkets provided new, anonymous, shopping experiences and spaces.

Change accelerated. By 1967, the Beatles had become hippies and drugs were in the air. The Beatles changed music in a number of respects. With *Sergeant Pepper's Lonely Heart Club Band*, the lyrics were printed on the back of the album for the first time, and the meaning was a long way from their earlier "She Loves You, Yeah, Yeah, Yeah." Half a million people attended an open-air pop festival on the Isle of Wight.

The young were not the only ones to the fore. A focus on change also affected the built environment, with much torn down in the 1960s by a well-meaning but often misguided and sometimes corrupt combination of developers, planners, and city councils, who were convinced that the past should be discarded. They embarked on a rebuilding that was very different in style and tone. As a result, cities such as Newcastle saw major damage to their centers. The needs of road transport played a central role, with major roads driven through the cityscape, as with London (with the Westway), Birmingham, Exeter, Glasgow, Newcastle, and Wolverhampton.

Modernist functionalism drove the pace of architectural development, as with Richard Seifert's uncompromising slab-like Centre Point (1967) skyscraper in central London. This modernism was seen in hospitals, schools, and other buildings, as well as housing. Ironically, it was often far from functional, not least due to a misguided preference for flat roofs, a mistaken design in a rainy climate. Concrete cladding also frequently proved a problem. Erno Goldfinger, after whom Fleming named a villain, was responsible for modernist horrors including Trellick Tower in West London.

At the same time, there was resistance to, or, at least, criticism of, many of the cultural changes of the period. For example, alongside novels pressing for new experiences and for the experience of the new came the antisixties novel, such as A. S. Byatt's *The Game* (1967) and Kingsley Amis's *I Want It Now* (1968).[15] The *Carry On* films continued with classics such as *Carry On Screaming* (1966), a spoof on horror films.

1970–79

Youth and novelty, key elements in the 1960s changes, continued to be significant in the 1970s. However, optimism was shadowed by the economic recession and political tension that gathered pace from 1973 (see chapter 6), and this shadowing affected the arts. A darker tone was evident in some spheres. The television police drama *The Sweeney* (1975–78) brought to an abrupt end the cozy image of the kindhearted London policeman that had been built up carefully in *Dixon of Dock Green* (1955–76), a comforting popular television series that was much at variance with the world of London crime and policing in the 1960s, a world that had included police corruption. Similarly, *Taggart* (1983–2010) provided a bleak view of Glasgow crime and policing.

Novels repeatedly registered problems. The "social revolution" became for some novelists self-deception, adultery, and confusion, as in Iris Murdoch's *The Sacred and Profane Love Machine* (1974).[16] Complaining about a decline in radicalism, Melissa Todoroff, a self-obsessed character in Malcolm Bradbury's mordant satirical novel *The History Man* (1975), says, "There was action. People really felt something. . . . They just don't feel any more. . . . Who's authentic any more?"[17]

A darker tone was more generally apparent with the fracturing of the sixties, which, in practice, had always been a diverse experience, let alone a movement lacking unity and coherence. The "look" of the age was highly diverse. David Bowie, one of the leading pop singers of the period, relished the role-playing of his androgynous look.[18] His albums, such as *Ziggy Stardust*, tested established boundaries. So also with enthusiasm for the reggae of Bob Marley.

Some themes continued, not least the role of popular music in introducing working-class language and values into mainstream culture. This, however, proved less easy a process than in the 1960s. The violence of the rebellious punk aesthetic, as in the Sex Pistols' debut single "Anarchy in the UK," released on November 26, 1976, and their album *Never Mind the Bollocks, Here's the Sex Pistols* (1977), was mirrored by "Oi!" music, that of skinheads, mostly working-class Londoners, which was often racist and misogynist.

At the same time, regional, local, and social differences were to the fore. In 1976, Johnny Rotten and the Sex Pistols made their first appearance outside London, playing in a nightclub in Northallerton, a small, quiet Yorkshire town. The noise and lyrics did not go down well, and much of the audience promptly left. The Sex Pistols became a sensation, and there was criticism in the popular press, not least for their song "God Save the Queen" which attacked Elizabeth II as head of a "Fascist regime" and claimed "There is no future in England's dreaming." This and "Anarchy in the UK" were banned by the BBC.

Such differences were more generally present. If, for example, the 1960s was a period of pop concerts and drugs, it also saw a burst of Christian evangelism, notably centered on the American Billy Graham and his revivalist missions to Britain, while trainspotting and making jam remained popular hobbies, and the 1970s began with the election of Edward Heath, a Conservative prime minister, just as the United States had seen the election of Richard Nixon in 1968 and France that of Georges Pompidou in 1969. In 1975, the commercially most successful British film was the soft-core pornographic *Confessions of a Window Cleaner*. For an older generation to the Sex Pistols, dyspeptic novels, such as Kingsley Amis's *Jake's Thing* (1978), included much criticism of the new cityscape and of fashionable social mores. Drugs and self-indulgence did not produce attractive images of behavior.

1979–90

This situation of tension was more apparent in the 1980s with the arts far more of a political battleground during the Thatcher years. These saw a degree of countercultural reaction. Thatcher openly attacked what she termed the "progressive consensus" and called for a return to older norms, telling the *Times* on October 10, 1987, that children "needed to be taught to respect traditional moral values." The radical world of universities, once potent models for an apparently improvable future, was criticized in a series of television series.[19] More-specific policy failures contributed to the countercultural reaction, notably those of the high-rise public housing projects that had represented a civic culture focused on planning and technocratic solutions, rather than on the views of individual consumers.[20] This housing all too often became a matter of "slums in the sky." Lifts (elevators) that did not work, the use of stairways as urinals, issues with noise, and criminal activity, especially drug dealing, all helped make many high rises undesirable and dangerous, and they tended to be praised by those who did not live in them. Similarly, public transport was often advocated by those who found a reason why they still needed cars.

Architectural style played a part in the debate. Modernism was increasingly criticized by conservation movements and on aesthetic grounds. Buildings such as Denys Lasdun's National Theatre (1965–76) and the Institute of Education (1970–78) had already been attacked as instances of a "New Brutalism," lacking a human scale and feel. This criticism was popularized by Prince Charles (Charles III from 2022) from the 1980s, perhaps most memorably with his description of the initial plans for the extension to the National Gallery as a "monstrous carbuncle," with his unsuccessful condemnation of the plans for the new British Library, and with his successful criticism in the 2000s of redevelopment plans for Chelsea Barracks. By the 1980s, modernism in architecture was being challenged by a neoclassical revival pioneered by Quinlan Terry.[21]

There was, however, a determined effort by many artists to use their work as part of an assault on Thatcherism. This was particularly apparent on the stage, as with the plays of David Hare—for example, *Plenty* (1978). An attack on Thatcherism was seen in art, popular music, poetry, and cultural commentary. Films of the period, such as *Mona Lisa* (1986), showed Britain, or, at least, London, as patterned by crime, with class, sex, and race suffused by themes of individualism that some critics linked to Thatcherism. *Bread*, a television series that ran for more than seventy episodes from 1986, and whose audience grew to more than twenty million, sympathetically depicted a Liverpool family whose younger members were mostly unemployed and ready to cheat the social security system. It was to be followed by *The Royle Family*, a sitcom about a television-fixated family living in a Manchester council house, which ran from 1998 to 2000.

In turn, there was criticism by the government of the automatic assumptions of public financial support made by the arts establishment. This criticism was well justified, but that did not make it popular. Particular tension shrouded the BBC, not least with reporting of security matters and of the IRA. To contain IRA propaganda, their statements when reported on the BBC had to be read by actors.

Differences between the Thatcher government and the arts were not driven to the point of breakdown (whatever that would mean), not least because the government continued to provide much patronage for culture, while there was no united artistic bloc. However, there was a degree of tension not seen in the 1970s, and one, moreover, that prefigured much of the self-conscious politicking over art seen in the 1990s.

1990–

In the 1990s, politicization in culture continued to be a theme, but, despite this, the impact of consumerism and internationalism on the arts were more significant. Elected in 1997, "New Labour" sought to have a cultural impact comparable to that of Labour in the 1960s but did not do so. Nevertheless, there were developments, including the foundation of museums, notably outside London, and the attempt, with the 2000 Millennium Dome, to stage a revival of the 1951 Festival of Britain. The theme was one of taking culture to the people. Ultimately, however, New Labour and its language of "core values" and so forth proved very superficial as a cultural movement and was increasingly seen in that light.

Continuity was provided by a financial model in which public provision, while significant, notably with the central taxation that paid for BBC and museums—providing free entry to all permanent exhibitions in national museums—was also limited, obliging many institutions to seek commercial sponsorship. This situation was an aspect of Britain as a hybrid society, one that can be compared with another hybrid in the shape of the relationship between cosmopolitan tendencies and national perspectives.

The nature of the national perspective was of particular significance, as rising nationalism in Scotland encouraged a distinctive cultural voice there with particular institutional expression in Edinburgh and Glasgow. The Edinburgh Festival, founded in 1947, was joined by numerous initiatives, including national arts bodies in Scotland in the 1960s. Glasgow in 2016 has the highest concentration of museums and visitors outside London. In Cardiff, more active cultural life, and notably more governmental expenditure, followed devolution in 1998. This was a pointed instance of a more general grounding of culture away from London. This grounding was seen in England with a range of regional initiatives and experiences, most notably the greater cultural consequence of Manchester and Birmingham, as well as similar, but less prominent, developments in a number of smaller provincial cities, especially Bristol and Newcastle/Gateshead. Thus, the cultural dimension replicated the developments, tensions, and alignments seen in other aspects of British life.

This process is likely to gather pace as the regional devolution of government functions within England becomes of greater consequence. The tendency to search for identity for new governmental entities will encourage the funding of regional arts, and the emphasis will probably be on distinctiveness, rather than on regional voices of British or English nationalism.

At the same time, cultural variations between social groups remained, although frequently underplayed. A YouGov poll in 2014 revealed that, on television, Labour voters preferred urban and unexalted settings, especially *Phoenix Nights, Coronation Street, The Office,* and *The Royle Family,* while Conservative voters preferred costume dramas and rural settings, as with *Downton Abbey, Foyle's War,* and *To the Manor Born.* Labour voters particularly favored accounts of working-class life. This group had been largely ignored by television up to the 1960s, but then attention became more prominent, as with the creation of the memorable character of the bigoted working-class Conservative Alf Garnett in *Till Death Us Do Part* (1965–75) and, also, the gritty and highly popular soap opera *Eastenders* (1985–), another series set in East London, and one that has depicted topics such as rape, homosexuality, child abuse, violence, and murder.

There was a more general change in plots. In 2016, the leading radio soap, *The Archers,* for long regarded by those who did not listen to it as somewhat conventional in its subject matter, covered a controlling husband driving his distraught wife to stab him, and outlined the legal and psychological issues involved, including advising women being controlled in this fashion on how best to seek help. This BBC soap, which produces a new episode on six days of the week, had earlier moved a long way from its conventional origins. From the late 1970s, it portrayed social division more frequently and it subsequently engaged with a range of challenging topics, or ones that would have surprised its early listeners, including divorce, homelessness, homosexual marriage, and dementia.

Concern about the content and morality of modern culture was a recurrent theme among some commentators, but this concern had very different manifestations. From the late 1980s, much of the criticism focused on the conceptual "BritArt" that became increasingly influential, passing rapidly from its antiestablishment origins in 1998 to become an affluent new establishment. The presentation of animal parts, fixed in formaldehyde, by Damien Hirst, including *The Physical Impossibility of Death in the Mind of Someone Living* (a dead tiger shark), *Away from the Flock* (a dead sheep), and *A Thousand Years* (the head of a slaughtered cow being assailed by flies), and *House of Ghostly Memory*, the concrete cast of a house by Rachel Whiteread, did not strike everyone as art. Striving for immediacy, these artists drew on punk and pop culture and deliberately set out to shock with their works and provocative lifestyle, presenting this shock as enhancing their relevance. In response, some commentators, who were willing to accept these works as art, did not see them as good art, and were unimpressed by the glamorous freakiness that was readily apparent as an element in Hirst's work.

Criticism of artistic fashionability reached a height with the "Sensation" show at the Royal Academy in London in 1997, which led to unprecedented media attention being devoted to British art. Hirst's animals were on display, but much of the controversy related to Marcus Harvey's large portrait of Myra Hindley, a sadistic murderess of children. Painted in 1995 with the template of a child's hand, this painting led to controversy, with ink and eggs thrown at the painting and the resignation of some academicians. The range of printed opinion over the exhibition indicated the ability of the arts to focus discussion, including about social developments. There was the clash between individualism and social convention and also the sense of a continuous rhythm of cultural change. Value and values appeared to be in conflict. For some, BritArt was a critical comment on Blairism; for others, a critical comment on capitalism; and for still others, an instance of the cult of celebrity and its questionable value. Subsequently, the graffiti art of Banksy also led to controversy.

The debate over fashionable art was given an annual outing in the popular media with the award of prizes to faddish works that did not strike most of the population as art. This was especially so with the Turner Prize, which was won in 1993 by Whiteread's *House of Ghostly Memory* and in 2001 by a light installation. Each year, the judges threw the modern to the fore and tested popular assumptions about what was art. In 2016, the Charles Wollaston Award for the work judged the most significant of the Royal Academy's summer exhibition went to David Nash for "Big Black," a large standing section of redwood, charred by Nash in a fire pit and then painted black. In 2002, Ivan Massow was made to resign as chairman of the Institute of Contemporary Art, after he described most conceptual art as "pretentious, self-indulgent, craftless tat." He was particularly unimpressed by the work of Tracey Emin, a leading figure in BritArt. This included displaying her unmade bed in an exhibition.

The 1990s were also the decade of "Britpop" in which the band Blur played the leading role. Blair sought to associate himself with this music and to appeal to the young through his links with musicians, whom he invited to No. 10. His success in doing so was limited and ephemeral.

The modish arts overlapped. For example, Hirst's works and those of Emin were among the modern British art collected by the leading pop singer David Bowie. Such patronage drove prices up.

Plays that attracted controversy also increasingly attracted picketing or complaints. *Behtzi Behtzi*, a play by Gurpeet Kaur Bhatti which featured rape, abuse, and murder among fellow Sikhs, was greeted by a riot when it opened at the Birmingham Rep in 2004. The police were unable to maintain order, and the play was rapidly canceled. In 2009, there were demonstrations when the National Theatre staged Richard Bean's play *England People Very Nice*, claiming that its account of immigration in London was critical of Bangladeshis.

Most art, however, was far less controversial, by intent or response than the "Sensation" show. Harvey's painting of Hindley said less about the 1990s than Howard Hodgkin's explorations of color and its use to depict emotion. In addition, David Hockney's luminous depiction of British landscape had a great impact in the 2010s, as did his successful exploration of the possibilities of producing art on screen, notably on iPhones, which he found "a luminous medium and very good for luminous subjects. I began to draw the sunrise seen from my bed on the east coast of England. . . . It was the luminosity of the screen that connected me to it."[22] In the biggest exhibition of 2012 in Britain, 600,989 people visited the Royal Academy to see *A Bigger Picture* with his paintings of the Yorkshire Wolds where he lives, providing, as was accurately noted, "an extraordinarily moving and cheering homecoming," one in which "he paints the passing moment, but does not mourn its passing."[23] This was painting in which trees in different seasons were to the fore. In 2016, at the Royal Academy, Hockney followed up with portraiture in the Royal Academy exhibition *82 Portraits and 1 Still Life*.

In addition, the popularity of art classes, and of lectures on art, saw a focus on traditional means and themes. Watercolor painting was most popular for art classes, and the standard subjects were landscapes and flowers. For lectures, it was the grand tradition of famous painters that engaged most attention. Far more people went to lectures on Dutch masters or the impressionists than to those on BritArt. The choice of lectures at the National Association of Decorative and Fine Art Societies (NADFAS, founded 1968) branches was instructive, as were the attendance figures for particular lectures.

Yet, a less optimistic note can be struck. For, alongside cultural change and continuity, there was the structural fissure between elite and popular cultural forms, or what were referred to as "high-" and "low-brow" works. This fissure in cultural politics frequently overlapped with social assumptions. There were overlaps, and some were very striking, as in the popularity of J. R. R. Tolkien's somewhat arcane *Lord of the Rings* trilogy, or the ability of

Harrison Birtwistle (1934–2022), a producer of characteristic modern music, also to write *Grimethorpe Aria* (1973), a first-rate piece of brass band music. Many cultural figures, however, failed to show, or even to seek to show, this range, a situation that readily paralleled that in politics. A lack of engagement with the experiences of the bulk of the population was frequently to the fore. An example of cultural discontinuity was provided by the decision of English Heritage in 1998 to list five housing blocks on the Alton Estate in Roehampton as an architectural masterpiece, which made their replacement or alteration less likely, a decision widely deplored by the tenants.

In new architecture, a continued determination to embrace modern shapes and materials and to focus on functionalism was seen in important works such as Nicholas Grimshaw's Eurostar rail terminal at Waterloo (1994) and the Serpentine Gallery designed in 2000 by Zaha Hadid. Moreover, far from being seen as a redundant form, skyscrapers were built and projected, notably in London where successive mayors encouraged them. Work that was far removed from neoclassicism included Norman Foster's Swiss Re Tower (2002) and his egg-shaped Greater London Authority building (2002), and Richard Rogers's Tate Modern (1999) and Millennium Dome (2000). Such buildings, followed by the rebuilt Charing Cross station, the MI6 building, and the Shard, provided the background for tourist perceptions of Britain, for, as in previous centuries, London was the most visited site there and for many tourists the only site. In 2015, around nineteen million foreign tourists visited London. This made it the most visited city in Europe and the second most visited in the world after Hong Kong. London surpassed Britain, which, in 2014, was the sixth country most visited by international tourists, after France, the United States, Spain, Turkey, and Germany, with 32.6 million, and its average annual growth rate in this category in 2010–14 being 3.6 percent, which was lower than these others bar France.

However, Rogers's unimaginative 2008 plans for the redevelopment of the Chelsea Barracks site to produce a new crowded barracks of high buildings providing expensive residential property indicated that, at least in this major case, little had been learned about reconciling the profit motive to the needs of the livable environment, let alone to aesthetic considerations. Architecture, indeed, was scarcely the most popular form of culture. It greatly affected the built environment in which most people lived and worked, and many doubted the aesthetic or utilitarian contribution of new buildings. Such themes resonated strongly in the background to fiction as novelists set the scene. Thus, in *The Body on the Beach*, Simon Brett (2000), who lived in the south coast region he depicted, wrote:

The architect who'd designed the new supermarket (assuming such a person existed and the plans hadn't been scribbled on the back of an envelope by a builder who'd once seen a shoebox) had placed two wide roof-supporting pillars just in front of the main tills. Whether he'd done this out of vindictiveness or . . . incompetence was unknowable.[24]

The issues remain, while the forms change.

SPORT

Other forms of culture were also crucial to public experience. In particular, sport was a major public activity and preoccupation of the people, one that benefited greatly from its transmission by television. The expansion of organized sport, notably football (soccer), profited from the finance available from television rights, from major global interest in English football, and from the increase in the average real earnings of the working population and the reduction in their working hours. In 2016, Football League clubs spent more than £1 billion in the transfer season, spending part of the over £5 billion made from the latest TV rights. In the same year, a corruption scandal led to the departure of the newly appointed manager of the England team and to wide-ranging claims about corrupt practices in English football.

Major events, such as the underdog team Leicester City winning the FA League Championship in 2016, engaged much of the nation. So did international results, both triumphs, notably victory for England in the 1966 World Cup, which was held in England, and humiliations, such as the 1950 World Cup exit as a result of defeat by the United States and the Euro 2016 defeat of England at the hands of Iceland. Wales did better, reaching the semifinals in 2016.

Football, a game developed in Britain in the nineteenth century, provided parallels with other aspects of British life. Globalization and money were related themes. In place of the 1950s' teams of local players, managers, owners, and sponsorship came international players, managers, owners, and sponsorship. This was particularly true of leading teams. There was sometimes opposition on the part of the supporters' clubs to the policies of foreign owners—for example, in Liverpool in the early 2010s to American owners—but, in general, this opposition was speedily overcome. Moreover, the prices charged to see football matches rose rapidly, not least because stadiums became all-seating. As a result, what had originally been a working-class sport very much became a middle-class one, with others having to watch on television.

Other sports also had major public followings and showed the impact of globalization and money, notably cricket, rugby, and tennis. These sports could attract the attention of the arts as with L. S. Lowry's football painting *Going to the Match* (1953) and his *Lancashire League Cricket Match* (1964–69). They certainly received large-scale television coverage. So also with the Olympics where, in 2016, Britain had the second highest number of medals and in 2020 the fourth, a result that owed a lot to support organized by UK Sport and financed by the National Lottery in a policy introduced by John Major when he was prime minister.

Aside from sport, other aspects of public life and experience also engaged much of the nation. The doings of television stars, such as Jeremy Clarkson on *Top Gear* or Simon Cowell on *The X Factor*, of the judges and contestants on *Strictly Come Dancing*, of the objects in *Antiques Roadshow*, or of the plots in *Call the Midwife*, or the accuracy of *Downton Abbey* played a key role in public discussion, as measured by entries on social media in the 2010s. Allowing viewers at home to vote, as in *Strictly Come Dancing*, enhanced public interest.

So also with the doings of sportspeople. The media very much supported the personality-driven account of sport. Television programs such as "Sports Personality of the Year" attracted large viewing figures. Celebrity was very much a function of the media and the latter, accordingly, defined a national hierarchy of attention. The context and content of culture was different to that of 1945, and this transformation was more generally reflective of a changing society.

5

THE AFTER-ECHOES OF WAR, 1945–60

BEFORE WAR WITH Japan ended in 1945, Britain had already elected a new government, returning the first majority Labour administration, with Clement Attlee as prime minister.[1] Winston Churchill, the wartime prime minister from 1940, and the Conservative Party he had led from then, were rejected. This result was in line with Gallup poll results from 1942 onward. It was a reaction against the 1930s and against the Conservatives as the party of privilege and prewar division. This was ironic as Churchill had been in the political wilderness during that period. The result was also an endorsement of the role of the state and of collectivism, which were championed by Labour, with its promises of social welfare from 1940. The war led to praise for collectivism. Labour had been part of a wartime coalition government, with Attlee the deputy prime minister from 1942, but, in 1945, to Churchill's disappointment, it chose, after the defeat of Germany, to end the coalition and to return to party politics.

Held on July 5, the election saw a 10 percent swing to Labour, which gained an overall majority of 146 MPs, becoming the first Labour government with a majority in the House of Commons. There were widespread successes, including in Manchester, Birmingham, Glasgow, the London suburbs, and the south coast towns. As in the Labour landslide of 1966 and, even more, 1997, a significant portion of the middle class voted Labour, while it also moved from being a unionized working-class party, able to carry steel, rail, and coal towns and constituencies, to a party supported by much of the working class.

Just winning reelection in 1950, this Labour administration remained in power until defeated in the next election, which was held in 1951. British governments could choose when to hold elections as long as they were held within five years, until, under legislation passed in 2011, fixed five-year terms were introduced by the coalition government elected in 2010 in order to give stability to that coalition. As a result, the following election was held in 2015, and the next one is due in 2020.

The Labour government proved to be very influential for postwar British history. It consciously set out to remodel British society and the economy and to a considerable extent did so. Labour also moved the parameters of British political debate, such that the Conservative administration of 1951–64 substantially maintained many of its policies. There was only to be significant alteration in the late 1970s and 1980s, as financial crisis and, then, Thatcherism led to a major change in tone and policy. Even so, many of the changes brought in by Labour, notably the establishment of the NHS in 1948, were not reversed, and, indeed, remain highly significant today. This helps ensure that 1945 was a year of transition and has been very much seen in this light, as it still is; however, to do so risks underrating significant continuities in attitudes, circumstances, and institutions from the 1930s.

The end of World War II was also a fundamental transition for many European countries. In Britain, in practice, the constitution did not change in 1945 or the late 1940s, as it did in France (with the establishment of the Fourth Republic), Italy (with the move to a republic), the countries of Eastern Europe bar Greece and Finland (with the establishment of communism), West Germany (with the establishment of democracy), and Eire (the Republic of Ireland), with the full constitutional break from Britain). There were also fundamental changes in China (communism), India (independence), and Japan (democratization). In contrast, the victorious states, the United States, the Soviet Union, Britain, Australia, Canada, and New Zealand, did not have to make changes. Nevertheless, alongside key continuities, including the monarchy, described by Churchill in Parliament on May 15, 1945, as "the most serviceable" and secure in the world, there were also important changes in Britain.

There was an intense desire for change, much of which had no particular ideological dimension. The major contribution of the Labour Party was to concentrate that desire for change on themselves, and thus save Britain from the threat of postwar communism. The Labour government of 1945–51 drew on a number of traditions and ideologies, including socialism, Protestant nonconformity, and trade union collectivism, thus ensuring it was a national party. The uneasy interaction of these tendencies, however, meant that there was no one consistent template for Labour, let alone for left-wing reform, a situation that has continued to the present, helping cause the serious divisions in the party that have been consistently apparent from the 1970s.

The religious background to Labour was significant, and notably the Protestant nonconformist rejection of the ascendancy of episcopalism. In addition, alongside the growth of religious tolerance, the nineteenth century was very much a period of religious evangelicalism, which was by no means confined to the middle class, and this evangelicalism encouraged a sense of national distinctiveness and mission. This sense remained pertinent into the mid-twentieth century, contributing to collectivist solutions to social welfare but then falling victim to the rising role of the state, as well as the social liberalism of the 1960s.

Despite the variety of tendencies involved, there was a general theme to the Attlee government and one not simply arising from the need to cope with the aftermath of a destructive and bankrupting war. This theme was that of the state as the solution to social ills and the controller of the economy and of a suspicion of private enterprise. Moreover, with the state presented as the mobilizer of society, the emphasis was on the central government: power was deployed from London and answerable to it, and consistency in regulation was a clear means. These were aspects of a subordination of society to the state and to its ideology that was also seen in high and unprecedented rates of taxation. Much of the preparatory work on Labour's major reforms was done during the war years when Labour leaders learned something of government, in a context in which it had emergency war powers, and were prominent in administrative departments dealing with social policy, such as education, health, and planning.

Nationalization, the state takeover of much of the economy, could be explained on practical grounds—for example, providing investment in a country damaged by war and short of liquidity. Rather than Socialist dogma, a pragmatic drive for efficiency encouraged Attlee and Herbert Morrison to support nationalization, and even Churchill backed that of the Bank of England. The nationalization of the coal mines was seen as a way to secure industrial peace there. In practice, however, it was ideology that was crucial to nationalization. The fault lines of the Attlee government exist to today— namely, the artificial structure of the Labour Party with its basic combination of well-meaning liberal intellectuals with the more Socialistic and the trade unions. This was a socialism very much affected by collectivist principles and convinced that public ownership of the means of production, and of much else, was crucial to social well-being and economic success. Moreover, themes of equality were highly important. Thus, the social welfarism introduced by the Liberal government of the late 1900s, notably old age pensions and national insurance, was greatly extended. Planning was a key theme.[2] Looked at less positively, state control of the economy, public ownership, and control over people's lives were aspects of a socialism that overlapped with communism.

The creation of the NHS in 1948 represented an opportunity to improve medical services as well as make them free at the point of delivery, which was perceived as a reward to the public for winning the war. The NHS encouraged a strong sense of new beginnings but also marked a tremendous extension of state control and direction and of centralized control in particular. Moreover, it is far from clear that health provision benefited greatly from the new administrative system. Free at the point of delivery meant that the taxpayer paid for the system, which posed a major tax issue. That the NHS was not "free" because it was paid for by taxation and by state borrowing, was a point neglected by much of the population, as it still is. Bar the NHS, however, the welfare state was fairly conservative, with the social security system initially intended to impose Victorian ideas of thrift, although that is not the case now.

Opposition to Labour's policies was overcome. In 1947, the government was obstructed by the House of Lords in nationalizing the steel industry. As a result, Attlee passed the Parliament Act of 1949 which reduced the number of occasions on which the Lords, in which the Conservatives were strong, could block legislation passed by the Commons before it became law from three to two, and reduced the delaying period of the Lords from two years to one. This looked toward the removal of most of the hereditary peerage from the Lords under Blair.

It is possible to offer pragmatic reasons alongside ideological ones when assessing Labour policies under Attlee. In particular, in the combination of economic modernization and social justice, there was a wish to counter possible revolutionary tendencies among the working class, a wish that stemmed from the struggle between communism and socialism on the Left and the anxiety that discontent could be exploited by the Soviet Union. Thus, in part, Labour's domestic policies can be understood in the context of the Cold War that became increasingly significant to its foreign and military policies. The overthrow of Socialists in Eastern Europe in the late 1940s encouraged Labour hostility to communism, although this hostility was already well established. The Cold War also played a major role in the response to trade unions. Troops were used to contain strikes, which were illegal until 1951. The Labour government, which was determined to keep Communists away from influence and from Labour politics,[3] claimed that Communist conspiracies were behind the strikes, most prominently the London dock strike of 1949. Alongside the Cold War and other pragmatic reasons for collectivism, however, it is necessary to note that there was a strong ideological commitment to universal health provision under state control and to other associated policies.

The evaluation of the postwar Labour government has varied greatly with time. Prior to the Thatcher years (1979–90), it was widely positive, but the attempt then to roll back the boundaries of the state led to criticism of the policies of the Attlee administration and of their very practicality. In turn, "New Labour" (in the 1990s and 2000s), while strongly rejecting the state ownership seen under Attlee, applauded the social welfarism of the postwar government. Its policies have also tended to find favor with historians, most of whom adopt a progressive position. Attlee, moreover, is widely admired for his diligence, his modesty, his common sense, and his unflappable style of leadership, not least in firmly holding together some very determined individuals. He had been leader from 1935.[4]

Given contradictory views, the historian should tread with care, although that approach can lead to an anodyne tone. What is possibly less contentious is the point that the administration proved overambitious, both in domestic and in foreign policy, and that its policies had already run into serious difficulties by its last years. The rearmament introduced in these years, notably as a response to Communist expansionism, which was very apparent from 1948, proved a major fiscal strain. This strain affected social programs, and particularly the principle hitherto of their freedom at the point of delivery. This issue led in 1951 to a rift over health and defense expenditure between Aneurin Bevan, the left-wing minister of labour, who had earlier established the NHS, and Hugh Gaitskell, the chancellor of the exchequer. Attlee finally came down behind Gaitskell, and Bevan and Harold Wilson, the president of the Board of Trade, resigned in April 1951 rather than commit, as Attlee expected, to Cabinet consensus. There was an earlier compromise in pensions, with the 1946 National Insurance Act establishing the contributory principle, as opposed to the flat-rate pensions paid for, essentially, through taxation, the method under the Liberals' Old Age Pensions Act of 1908.[5] There had also been a division over iron and steel nationalization with Herbert Morrison, a leading Labour figure, urging a focus on making efficient what had already been nationalized rather than on nationalizing more.

These were not the sole flaws and problems in Labour policy or its implementation. In addition, while proclaiming modernity, Labour conspicuously failed to reform trade union practices, in large part due to its political and financial dependence on the unions and to the role of major trade union figures in the ministry, notably Ernest Bevin, the foreign secretary. In this, Labour matched the situation as far as aspects of left-wing politics were concerned on the Continent. The Labour government realized many of the unions' political aims, including nationalization of much of industry (the miners wanted the coal mines nationalized), universal statutory social services, and the goal of full employment. Britain, indeed, was run by the government in a corporatist fashion in accordance with Socialist views and with taxation increased and directed accordingly. A wages policy was maintained until 1950, but the unions' refusal to continue the wages policy helped Labour lose the 1951 general election.

As a serious, long-term problem, Labour's emphasis on state planning and centralization and its focus on central government led to a general downgrading of local autonomy and initiatives, notably in health provision. This weakened local government and meant, in particular, that the voluntary sector was neglected, which increased the pressure on the NHS and on the social services run by the local government. This neglect had detrimental long-term consequences for the fabric of British society. The weakening of the local government looked toward subsequent attacks on its autonomy and role under Conservative governments, especially reorganization in the early 1970s, a range of Thatcherite policies in the 1980s, and serious expenditure cuts in the 2010s. Nationalization also asset-stripped Scottish and Welsh control of Scottish coal and steel production, centralizing it on London.

Labour's popularity continued relatively high, in part because of its success in persuading the electorate that the sole alternative was the Conservative Party of the Depression years of the 1930s, which was a misleading contrast. In addition, Labour benefited from the strong desire for something new and from the potent rhetoric of a fairer society that the war had encouraged. Economic recovery was significant as, by 1951, was an increase in prosperity.

At the same time, the government direction of the period and its association with austerity and bureaucracy angered many. This was linked to a degree of polarization, as the Conservatives attacked these elements and the ethos and practice of redistribution. The Labour government found, like its successors, that the people did not live up to its expectations, expectations that were mocked in the case of Communists in terms of "low rations, the long working hours, and the general absence of pampering."[6] Building on the public solidarity seen during the war, the government regarded the nation as mobilized to act for progress and to make sacrifices accordingly. The news was manipulated accordingly as with government-produced films that sought to offer the public facts in order to maintain mobilization. In practice, it found not a mobilized nation but a democratic citizenry willing to make its own choices about goals and conditions, choices that frequently did not match Labour suppositions.[7]

Idealized by some, planning became a dirty word to many. This was an instance of the process by which words had varied meanings, but, more significantly, these meanings had an impact in the wider political culture within which assumptions developed and responses to policies were formulated. In 1947, Churchill, who continued to lead the Conservative Party until 1955, called for the government to "set the people free," freedom proving an emotive term and a rallying call.

Introduced during the war, rationing enforced the call for restricting consumer demand, but public discontent with rationing, which was unprecedented in peacetime, rose and notably from 1947. It was a signal failure of the Attlee government that their policies kept the economy repressed for so long after the war that rationing was felt necessary. Gasoline rationing continued until 1950. There were also serious shortages of coal, the basic source of energy and fuel, especially in 1947. People were often cold, a situation that was accentuated by unusually harsh weather. The cities continued to show bomb damage, with extensive bomb sites, which were captured in films of the period such as *Passport to Pimlico* (1949), and that provided many parking spaces. The attempt to introduce an egalitarian collective politics was unpopular with many, and black market activities became more commonplace.

Yet, the Conservatives found it difficult to translate Labour's unpopularity into the necessary votes. Indeed, although Labour's majority was considerably reduced in 1950, it held on to power, keeping the Conservatives at bay. The Communists lost the two seats they held. In the 1951 election, held on October 23, Labour was exhausted and disunited and had few policy ideas, which, indeed, had been the case in domestic policy since 1948, by when most of the party's program had been introduced. They still polled more votes than the Conservatives. However, the Conservatives won more seats and, with a majority of seventeen, formed a new government. The Liberals, the governing party in the late 1900s and early 1910s, only won six seats in 1951 and appeared to be on the eve of dissolution. They suffered from the takeover of reform and the Left by Labour and from the consolidation of the non- and anti-Labour vote by the Conservatives.

1951–60

The Conservatives were to be continually in office until 1964, winning reelection in 1955 and 1959 by very convincing majorities. They had four leaders in this period: Winston Churchill, the party leader since 1940, until poor health led to his resignation in 1955; followed by Anthony Eden, until failure in the Suez Crisis led to his fall in 1957; Macmillan, until illness led to his resignation in 1963; and Alec Douglas-Home, until he was narrowly defeated by Labour in the 1964 general election.

The Conservative Party's position varied with leaders and circumstances, notably international relations, economic fortunes, electoral successses, and internal tensions. There has since been a tendency to smooth out all these factors and to refer to the period in terms of "Butskellism," a reference to the Conservative chancellor of the exchequer (finance minister) from 1951 to 1955, Rab Butler, and his Labour predecessor from 1950 to 1951, Hugh Gaitskell. More specifically, this term captures particular continuities. There was the major exception of steel in 1953, but the Conservatives did not reverse most of the nationalizations under Labour. Nor, despite Labour predictions in 1951 that the welfare state would be destroyed by a Conservative government, and, indeed, further NHS cuts in 1952, was the welfare state created under Labour dismantled. In addition, Labour's failure to tackle excessive trade union power was not reversed.

In large part, this situation reflected a move to the Left by the Conservatives in part in response to their view that the 1945 election defeat was due to society moving to the Left. In addition, many of the more traditional strands of the Conservative Party had supported the politicians replaced and superseded by Churchill in 1940, notably Neville Chamberlain, the prime minister from 1937. Conciliatory attitudes toward the trade unions were adopted by the Conservatives, in part in response to paternalistic views, but also because the Conservatives lacked an alternative answer to egalitarian policy. A committee chaired by Butler, the key figure in devising new policies, and one criticized by more traditional figures, argued, in *The Industrial Charter* (1947), that the Conservative Party was in favor of trade unionism. In practice, the Conservatives were too soft on emerging Socialist ways. They were trying to be modern, postimperial, and socially progressive, as with the birth of the One Nation Group. With hindsight, however, Butskellism was a great mistake as it meant that major problems were not addressed.[8]

These, and other continuities and similarities between Labour and Conservative government, were to be more apparent with the benefit of hindsight, and notably in contrast with Labour's attempted progressivism in the 1960s and the Conservative rejection under Thatcher, from 1975, of what had come before in terms of failed decades. A pragmatic consensus on the role of government was accompanied by the dominance of both Labour and the

Conservatives by their moderate wings, with more radical ministers leaving office in 1951 and 1958, respectively.

However, that approach underplays significant contrasts between the Conservatives and Labour in 1951–64. Moreover, it is mistaken to extrapolate from an essential similarity in foreign and defense policy, in terms of support for the North Atlantic Treaty Organization (NATO) and the retention of the nuclear bomb, opposition to the Soviet Union and backing for managed change in the maintenance of empire, to the situation in domestic policy. In practice, there were major differences in the tone, content, and direction of policy. These were not least seen in the ending of Labour government for thirteen years, an ending that cut short the prospect of developing the record of the 1945–51 government and adopting second-stage policies. The latter might have taken Britain in a Social Democratic direction similar to that which the West German Socialists were to take, albeit in opposition to the government of the Christian Democrats. Yet, in Britain, there were few signs of the realism necessary if such a policy was to be adopted and especially so on the part of the trade union leadership. Indeed, Labour was not, and never have been, a Social Democratic Party as such, with all the talent such a denomination would have brought them.

Although constrained by assumptions about popular views from some of their plans to roll back the state, the Conservatives dismantled much of the controlled, state-directed environment that a combination of war and socialism had left. Rationing, which had continued after the war, was brought to an end in a context of greater consumerism. The rationing of chocolate and sweets ended just before Christmas 1953. In his fantasy novel *Nineteen Eighty-Four* (1949), George Orwell had captured the devastating nature of such rationing for family relationships.[9]

Politics was increasingly focused on satisfying the consumer, and both deliberately and publicly so, as with the inflationary tax cuts before the 1955 election. Looked at differently, these cuts meant that the state took less of people's money. The establishment in 1955 of independent television with its advertising (see chapter 4) was part of the process. The Churchill government both sought the popularity of consumer politics and failed to take on vested interests, notably the trade unions. This reflected not lethargy but a commitment to inclusive, middle-of-the-road politics that Churchill supported. He was not enamored of "market forces."[10] Looked at more positively, there was a principled rejection of proto-Thatcherism and an attempt, unlike under Thatcher, to adapt Conservatism to a rapidly changing economy and society. Yet, to take this a stage forward, the corporatism Churchill accepted and Thatcher rejected was poorly suited for such adaptation.

Although the home secretary, Sir David Maxwell Fyfe, pressed for the enforcement of the law against homosexual sex between consenting adults, which he referred to as "this plague," the Conservatives tended to favor individual liberty and, certainly, low taxation. Labour, in contrast, preferred collectivist solutions and was therefore happier to advocate a leading, controlling role for the state.[11] Neither party invested adequately in infrastructure, although this only became readily apparent later.

The governments of Churchill (1951–55) and his protégé, Eden (1955–57) devoted much of their attention to trying to keep Britain a major power and more particularly to preserving the empire as a dynamic force. To that end, there was an emphasis on inherited assets in the shape of imperial and Commonwealth links and a special relationship with the United States, rather than on any focus on European integration.[12] Churchill, seventy-seven years old when he regained power in 1951, very much sought to preserve empire, and the government adopted a firm and forceful response to Communist insurgency in Malaya and nationalist insurgency in Kenya. Although suffering a stroke in 1953, he continued to hold power, which was a mistake. He was poor at directing government, concentrating only on matters that interested him, personalizing issues, and proving a poor chairman of meetings.

Eden, a landed, Eton-educated[13] baronet (hereditary knight; he was Sir Anthony Eden), had been a decorated officer in World War I and a highly active foreign secretary in 1935–38, 1940–45, and 1951–55. The emphasis on preserving empire culminated in 1956 in the Suez Crisis, the humiliatingly unsuccessful, as well as duplicitous attempt to overthrow Colonel Nasser, the populist dictator of Egypt, who threatened Britain's interests in the Middle East as well as those of France and Israel.[14] The crisis led in January 1957 to the resignation of the demoralized and ill Eden, who had lacked the personality to succeed as prime minister, notably the necessary persistent determination.

Harold Macmillan, chancellor of the exchequer at the time of Suez, brilliantly succeeded in avoiding blame for the Suez Crisis even though he had been involved in the planning for it. Like Eden, Macmillan had shown great bravery in World War I. Although his lineage was far less exalted than that of Eden, such that his snobbishness could seem somewhat fake, his background had become prosperous and upper class. The Eton-educated Macmillan married the daughter of a duke. Like Eden, Macmillan was a Churchill protégé. Replacing Eden, Macmillan, a consummate stylist, proved astute in his handling of internal party divisions as well as in sensing the mood of public opinion.[15]

This mood appeared of greater significance due to the development of market research. Indeed, politics, society, culture, and the economy all moved in a similar direction in this respect. This was not a development unique to Britain, or indeed to the capitalist world. There was a greater concern with consumerism also in Eastern Europe. Satisfying the workers was regarded as more significant there after the shift in economic priorities that followed the death of Stalin in 1953. To explain developments in Britain therefore simply in national terms, and notably by reference to the policies of the Macmillan government, is of limited value. Instead, the wider context within which it operated was crucial.

Macmillan was helped by the spread of consumerism and, directly played into this, by his argument that rising living standards were largely due to government policies. However, the loose money policies that made it easier to borrow and spend were (correctly) regarded by critics as inflationary, and this situation led to a major rift within the government. The politically adept Macmillan overcame his opponents, notably Peter Thorneycroft, the chancellor of the exchequer, and Enoch Powell, in 1958 when they sought to cut government expenditure in the shape of the welfare state in order to improve the public finances and contain inflation. However, their views were important to the eventual genesis of Thatcherism; Thorneycroft was to be close to Thatcher.

Differences among Conservatives in judging the legacy of Macmillan were to be linked to Thatcherism. These differences were compounded when, in 1983, he criticized Thatcher's policy of privatization as "selling off the family silver." Macmillan saw himself as a "one-nation Tory," a Conservative for the entire people and not simply for Conservative core groups. He regarded corporatism as an aspect of the inclusive society that Conservatives ought to pursue as a freer and more liberal alternative both to socialism and to free-market capitalism.

Macmillan indeed looked, notably in the early 1960s, to corporatism and a state role in the economy in a way that the Thatcherites were to criticize. Macmillan, and he was far from alone, was struck by the degree to which British economic growth rates were lower than those of France and Germany. He also regarded it as necessary to find an alternative to the imperial economic and political links that were dissolving as Britain's imperial age came to an end.

Economic growth was politically necessary. The 1959 general election was the high point for the 1951–64 Conservative era and an election that captured the combination of prosperity and popularity. GDP per capita rose by 40 percent between 1950 and 1966. Purchase tax on consumer durables had been cut from two-thirds to half in 1953, as the Conservatives replaced Labour austerity with affluence and consumer demand. Thanks to the state provision of free or subsidized health care, education, council housing, pensions, and unemployment pay, rising real incomes fed through into consumption. This became a golden age for many later commentators who disliked subsequent developments, including "the '60s." Indeed, in the 2010s, UKIP (the United Kingdom Independence Party; see chapter 10) was to be accused of trying to return Britain to the mid-1950s, notably 1957. The percentage of households owning a washing machine rose from 25 in 1958 to 50 in 1964; with the relevant dates for cars being 1956 and 1965 and for fridges, 1962 and 1968. This was a rapid rate of change.

Associated with rationing, Labour appeared dated. In the 1950s, Labour lost middle-class support, as that group grew. In 1959, the Conservative billboards proclaimed "Life's better with the Conservatives. Don't let Labour ruin it." "Most of our people have never had it so good," a phrase Macmillan had employed in a speech on July 20, 1957, made in a football stadium, was much used during the 1959 campaign. However much intended by some as ironic and critical, the epithet's "Supermac" and "The Actor Manager" would never have been applied to Eden. The novelist John Mortimer was to write of England entering into the 1960s: "In the Hartscombe Conservative Association there was a general feeling that Mr Macmillan was in his heaven and all was more or less right with the world."[16]

Although unwilling to tackle inflation or poor economic fundamentals, the Conservatives understood that the management of affluence also meant coming to grips with the legacy, positive and negative, of the welfare state created in the late 1940s. In contrast, Labour was still associated with the unpopular subordination of affluence to planning. Compared to Macmillan and the Conservatives, Gaitskell and Labour appeared dreary and symbolized wartime conditions.[17] Indeed, concern about planning and control played a role in consideration of changes in social policy and notably in response to libertarianism. Under the Conservatives, there were liberalizing measures, over, for example, betting, the sale of alcohol, and television, but also a concern about wider questions of social responsibility and moral values.[18] Despite pressure for changes in the law, capital punishment (hanging) was maintained, as, despite the 1957 report of the official committee chaired by Lord Wolfenden cautiously recommending a change in the law, was the ban on consensual sex among adult homosexuals. Hanging was not only a punishment available for cases of murder (as well as treason and arson in the royal dockyards) but was one that was employed. The balance over liberalization was to be different under Labour.

The number of Conservative seats in Parliament had risen from 1951 to 1955 (321 to 345 seats) and, in 1959, rose to 365. This compared to 258 for

Labour (277 in 1955). Even though their percentage of the vote rose, the Liberals failed to gain effective traction. In 1959, the Conservatives had a majority over Labour of more than one hundred. This was a society that was changing socially and culturally but without a comparable transformation in its political leadership, although there was one in political style. Indeed, in 1959, the Conservatives made use of new techniques of media electioneering, including hiring a public relations firm.

There is not necessarily a discontinuity between these elements of social, cultural, and political change. In practice, the political dominance of the Conservatives was not that of a party or government unable to accept or respond to change. Instead, the Conservatives sought to stand for the brave new world ahead. That view became a Labour narrative in 1964, one used in order to criticize the Conservatives of the time and the legacy of their government, and this criticism might appear substantiated by comparison with the 1964–70 Labour governments. However, the subsequent context is not the best basis for looking at the situation in the 1950s or Conservative plans then and subsequently. Instead, what the 1959 election revealed was an electorate largely satisfied with the rate of change that was occurring and with the balance between change and continuity.

6

THE POLITICS OF CRISIS, 1961–79

THE 1950S WERE a decade of prosperity after the postwar gloom, and, as a result, a period of reasonable optimism as far as the bulk of the population was concerned. One index was a relatively high birth rate that, in combination with the response to peace and demobilization in 1945, produced the postwar baby boomers. The 1960s and 1970s was far more mixed. For the young, these years, and especially 1968, might be one of optimism focused on personal liberation and a sense of social progress, and the period was subsequently to be celebrated in these terms. This was especially the case when cultural icons died, as with the pop singer David Bowie in 2016.

Much of the population at the time, however, was confronted, and notably in the 1970s, with the consequences of economic decline and serious political failure. These were brought dramatically home with the power cuts experienced during the miners' strikes and those of the power workers. A public that got used (as I did) to periods of no heating, to shopping and living by candlelight, to bathing in the dark, and to going to bed early was not a public readily persuaded that things were getting better. The increased use of electricity, as opposed to coal fires, made power cuts more serious than in the past for individuals could store coal but not electricity. There was a literal metaphorical gloom.

The period had not begun like this. With an echo of the situation in 1945, there was a sense in the early 1960s of a need for new beginnings but also of a belief that such a beginning was possible and that Britain could, and would, benefit. As discussed in chapter 10, the Conservatives sought to pursue this by means of joining the European Economic Community (EEC). Doing so was presented as a key means to modernization, an argument that at the time linked leaders with most party members.[1] The bolt from empire under Macmillan made Britain's attempt to stand apart from the EEC prove less credible, as did the extent to which neither the United States nor the Commonwealth were ready to pursue relations with Britain that would be as close as the British government wanted.

The application to join the EEC, however, failed. The French veto of January 1963 made Macmillan appear irrelevant as well as unsuccessful. In practice, the other five members of the EEC supported British entry, but the French attitude proved crucial.

Moreover, as with John Major in 1992 (see chapter 8), the Conservatives proved unable to maintain their record for effective economic management. Macmillan came to show an interest in government economic direction. He called for a "new approach," including more planning and better labor relations, which was designed to put him ahead of the curve of change and thus both relevant and crucial. A Cabinet committee on modernization was established in 1962. A supporter of "one nation" Conservatism, Macmillan adopted views on social welfare accordingly, notably that of universal benefits. However, the National Incomes Commission, which Macmillan saw as the arbitrator of incomes policy, was boycotted by the unions, who had scant interest in helping the Conservatives nor in planning or policies that were not in their interests. This attitude of the unions was a key problem with planning in Britain, one that Labour as a party or government never satisfactorily addressed. "Neddy," the National Economic Development Council, was established in 1962, with an independent research think tank to back it up. Neddy had the task of creating a national economic plan, and its membership was drawn from employers, unions, and government but had little real effect on policy or developments.[2] It was a classic instance of the practice, seen in all countries, of drawing up policies and pressing buttons at the center, only to discover that little actually happened as a consequence and notably so in the regions.

Macmillan strengthened the welfare state in the face of efforts by the Treasury and the Conservative Research Department to roll it back in order to block upward pressure on taxation in response to more children needing education, there being more of the elderly, and the higher expectations from welfare expected by a more affluent population. There was discussion of fees for school education, of education vouchers, of loans for university students, of the means testing of pensions, of the privatization of dentistry and eye testing, of charges in hospitals and for going to the doctors, and for the financing of the NHS by insurance, not taxation; but none of these happened. There had been some liberalization in policy in Macmillan's early years as prime minister, with the Housing Act of 1958 reducing rent control and the 1959 Town and Country Planning Act backing a free market in land. Earlier, in 1956, subsidies for building council houses for ordinary people had been scrapped. Moreover, in 1961, prescription charges were increased, as were the contributions for insurance charges for the NHS.

However, the direction of policy was very different. By 1957, everyone was entitled to a full pension, and in 1959, graduated pensions were introduced, offering a standard beyond subsistence.[3] There was no privatization of the NHS, no new charges, and, instead, in 1961–62, a plan to have a modern district hospital in every area was introduced, with an estimated expenditure of £500 million over ten years. No state school fees, loans, or vouchers were introduced in education. Instead, money was spent on secondary modern schools to give them parity of esteem with grammar schools. There was also, unlike under Labour, an active regional policy focused on trying to improve supply-side economics. Demand management was improved with public works in 1958 and 1962 to counter problems in depressed regions such as North-East England. The Industrial Training Act, to tackle skill shortages, was joined by a Redundancy Payments Act, and every permanent worker was given a contract of employment. In social welfare, the principles of the Victorian Poor Law were replaced by the idea of relative poverty, notably in terms of an inability to take part in ordinary life. The provisions of the 1959 Town and Country Planning Act were superseded in order to protect the environment, and in 1962, subsidies for building council houses were restored, as the market was seen as not working adequately to this end. The Offices and Shops Act of 1963 improved working conditions.

Macmillan fired one-third of his Cabinet in March 1962 but was not alone in his views about modernization and a Tory commitment to the welfare state. In 1963, when the up-and-coming Edward Heath became secretary of state for industry, trade, and regional development, a new combination of responsibilities that reflected his interests, he sought to use the ministry in order to regenerate industry and the economy. Heath very much supported government interventionism in the economy.[4] In March 1964, he also pushed through the end of resale price maintenance (RPM), the practice by which manufacturers could fix prices and therefore prevent price cutting by supermarkets. By restricting competition and keeping prices up, this was very much a practice that protected small shopkeepers, a traditional Tory group. Many

Conservative MPs opposed the end of RPM, but it was driven through by the government.

The abolition, however, helped cost the Conservatives the next election, which was very finely balanced. Moreover, the end of RPM hit independent shopkeepers hard, and this helped ensure a different townscape to that in Continental cities, one dominated by multiples. By removing a substantial degree of initiative and independence from the local economy, this development also weakened local identity and power.

Also, at the local level, a change that had even greater impact was the dramatic cuts in the rail network following the implementation of the Beeching Report of 1963. Freight and passenger services were greatly curtailed, the workforce cut, lines taken up, and many stations were converted to other uses. One of the major "public spaces" of Britain, the railway, a major legacy from the Victorian era, was thus greatly diminished in favor of the more "individual" car. This was also a dramatic reconceptualization of rural and small-town Britain, with the railways that had integrated it into an urban-centered network dramatically and finally removed. Replacement bus services proved limited. In addition, towns that had been served by rail lost their links, as did many that had been junctions. For example, the Exe Valley line to Tiverton was closed, as were the other lines to Tiverton, and Tiverton was served thereafter by Tiverton Junction, a distant stop on the main line reached by car or bus.

The move from steam to diesel was part of the process of change for the railways, one that encouraged the idea of concentrating on a core network. The Beeching Report, indeed, did not only lead to the loss of facilities and identities. It was also a means of addressing the failure of the earlier private railway companies (prenationalization) to establish an efficient and productive network. There were, however, also suggestions that, in implementing the cuts, the minister for transport, Ernest Marples, was influenced by his personal links with roadbuilding.

The more general point was one also seen with the "urban renewal" that had followed the war, notably a conviction that modernity required change and, in particular, a deliberate break with much of the legacy of the past. It is possible, and relevant, to point to particular factors in individual aspects of this process, as also, for example, with developments in the position of the Church of England. What was more significant was the general trend and the ideology it focused and encouraged.

In the early 1960s, Labour offered a specific strategy of modernization, one centered on technological modernity and talk of a society open to talent, rather than what was presented as the policies of the Macmillan government.

In 1960, at the party conference, Gaitskell sought to discard the Socialist legacy and to move Labour toward a broader democratic agenda. He failed, leading to an emphasis under Wilson on a modernized socialism.

The theme for both political parties was change, but the key element was
the tone of change, which ultimately came to the fore in 1962–64 as the Conservatives were presented by Labour as anachronistic and class dominated and
as unable to confront the need for change. These views helped ensure that
Heath won the party leadership in August 1965 by a ballot of MPs, the first
time that method had been used. In contrast, "Rab," R. A. Butler, the deputy
prime minister in 1962–63, Quintin Hailsham, Reginald Maudling, and Ian
Macleod, had been unsuccessful in 1963 when hoping to succeed Macmillan,
who felt obliged to resign due to health problems. The undemocratic process that was adopted by Macmillan in advising the Queen on the choice led
Macleod and Enoch Powell to refuse to serve under the new prime minister.

Macmillan's choice, Alec Douglas-Home, was an old Etonian aristocrat
who, like Macmillan, was unable to appear as a technocrat. He admitted to
using matchsticks in order to understand economics. The 14th Earl of Home,
and the first and only prime minister drawn from the House of Lords since the
3rd Marquess of Salisbury in 1895–1902, Douglas-Home had estates of 96,000
acres. He disclaimed his peerage and was elected an MP. The Labour candidate as prime minister in 1964, Harold Wilson, proved particularly able to
mount the charge of class domination and notably at the expense of Home.
That the election was between a privately educated aristocrat and a North of
England grammar school boy set off many echoes. The dead hand of privilege
appeared to be at stake.

It is possible that had Butler been leader, then Wilson would have lost.
That represents a different view to that which focuses on the abolition of RPM.
This difference serves to underline the variety of explanations that can be
offered for particular developments or specific events, and, therefore, the need
for caution in adopting too definite and uncompromising an explanation. In
this case, the key contrast is between policies and leadership. As a reminder
of contingencies, Wilson only became Labour leader in 1963 after the unexpected death of Gaitskell, a Londoner who, like Home, had attended a major
private school (in his case, Winchester) and, who, therefore contrasted heavily
with Wilson. Gaitskell, the lover of Ian Fleming's wife, Ann, died suddenly
after taking tea at the Soviet embassy which led to rumors that he had been
poisoned to make way for the more left-wing and pro-Soviet Wilson. This was
very unlikely. His cause of death was the rare disease lupus erythematosus.

At the same time, the degree to which there was a diversity of views in
Britain in the early and mid-1960s is underplayed if the emphasis is simply

on Labour victory and the factors that apparently led inevitably to it, because the results of the general election held on October 11, 1964, were actually very close and much more so than had appeared likely a year earlier, which was a testimony to Douglas-Home's electoral appeal. Labour's percentage of the vote rose from 43.9 in 1959 to 44.1 in 1964, a very small increase. In contrast, the Conservative percentage of the vote fell from 49.3 to 43.4, in part because of a strong increase in the Liberal vote, which drew both on traditional political support, especially in parts of Cornwall, Scotland, and Wales, and on the protest vote. The Liberals were able to win antimetropolitan support, while also seeming progressive to some of their supporters. They proved the key element.

The Conservatives had been hit by a series of scandals that encouraged a sense of their being out of touch, notably the Profumo Affair, a sex-and-deceit scandal involving the minister for defense, his sharing his lover with a Soviet defense attaché, and his lying about this. At the same time, the Conservatives had failed to respond adequately to sociocultural shifts and, in that context, to benefit from the marked trend of rising real wealth and for the bulk of the population. As a result, they lost 1.75 million votes. In terms of representation in the House of Commons, Labour took 317 seats to the Conservatives' 304 and the Liberals' 9. This was both a close result and one markedly more pro-Labour than the Conservative landslide in 1959, although Labour's share of the poll was marginally down from that of 1951. A richer working class had not deserted Labour. That an election could be interpreted in very different fashions, or in both together, serves as a readily accessible instance of a more general issue, namely the need to offer accounts and explanations with care and to be aware of alternative narratives and analysis.

Labour came to power in 1964 under Wilson with high hopes, including plans to use economic planning to improve economic performance, harness new technology, and end what was presented as the "stop-go" cycle of economic bust and boom that was held to characterize Conservative government from the mid-1950s. To these ends, a Department of Economic Affairs (DEA) was created in 1964, as an alternative to Treasury control, and put under George Brown, the deputy prime minister, and a man of talent as well as someone who could not hold his drink. In 1965, the DEA produced the National Plan, an optimistic blueprint for growth. A National Board for Prices and Incomes was also created in 1965, while a Ministry of Technology was designed to encourage new industrial processes. Prices and incomes policies were joined by active policies for regional regeneration, with the establishment of a Regional Development Fund. It was hoped that growth would fuel improved social welfare, and pensions were increased.

As with the increasingly conspicuous failure to ground foreign policy on realistic assessments,[5] Labour's policies lacked a sound economic basis, but, in political terms, the show was all. Hamstrung by his small parliamentary majority, Wilson sought an opportunity for a new election. In this, he benefited from being an adept opportunist and also from the public's sense that he had not yet had a chance to prove himself. In the general election, held on March 31, 1966, to strengthen its parliamentary position, Labour's share of the vote went up from 44.1 percent in 1964 to 48 percent, a significant increase in an already-strong position, and the Conservatives down from 43.4 percent to 41.9 percent, a marked widening of the popular vote between the two parties. Heath had failed to enthuse or persuade the voters. The shift in seats from 317 to 364 for Labour, compared with 304 to 253 for the Conservatives, was much more dramatic. With a majority of nearly a hundred, Wilson had a parliamentary position that left him with fewer excuses for subsequent mistakes. He was no longer at the mercy of maverick Labour MPs as he had been in 1964–65, especially over steel nationalization. This was 1945 renewed or, at least, seemed to be.

The general election had been held then to take advantage of apparently favorable circumstances. However, the economy rapidly reasserted itself, first with a seamen's strike, which Wilson blamed on left-wing agitators, and then with the serious sterling crisis of July 1966 which led to the ditching of the National Plan as deflation was imposed in order to support sterling. Anxious about Britain's international situation, about inflationary consequences, and about his political position within Britain, Wilson was overly concerned to avoid a recurrence of the devaluation of sterling in 1949. This was a period of fixed exchange rates. However, British industrial productivity was lower than that of other leading industrial powers, and an overvalued currency helped price exports out of markets as well as make imports more attractive.

As a result, despite Wilson's attempts to defy reality and the inevitable, the pound was devalued by 14.3 percent in November 1967. His promise to the public, that "the pound in your pocket" was worth no less, reassured few. Indeed, devaluation contributed to the inflation that increasingly became a more pronounced feature of the social experience as well as of the economy, an inflation that helped fuel labor disputes. The devaluation wrecked any attempt to use the pound as an effective reserve currency, and, instead, encouraged the focus on the dollar. Wilson saw devaluation as a national humiliation and it gave the Conservatives a sense that the tide had turned. Britain's lessened status was shown, moreover, by the rejection of a second application to join the EEC, by the failure of Wilson's inherently implausible attempt to mediate in the Vietnam War, by the cancellation in 1966 of the plan for a through-deck carrier, by the decision in 1968 that Britain would withdraw its forces from east of Suez, and by Wilson's inability to produce a solution to the Rhodesian crisis (see chapter 10).

Devaluation did not end serious questions about economic management, while, more generally, Wilson came to be regarded as stronger on image than on substance, a reasonable view albeit one that is more widely true of prime ministers including Blair and Cameron. The great expectations raised by Wilson ensured that the abject failure of his government, outside of social reforms, hit hard. In particular, the failure of Wilson's attempt, termed "In Place of Strife," to improve industrial relations and reform the trade unions in 1969, by giving government powers to demand strike ballots or impose cooling-off periods, encouraged a sense of broken hopes. This failure owed much to divisions within the government, including the opposition of James Callaghan, the home secretary, and most of the Cabinet, as well as an irresponsibly unhelpful stance on the part of the trade union leadership, and entryism into the unions by Trotskyites. The failure also presaged the crises that were to face Heath in 1974 and Callaghan in 1979.

More generally, Wilson's pragmatic efforts to keep the party united and a party of government led to claims of duplicity and Machiavellian opportunism, while his populist gestures did not commend him to all. He appeared superficial and a master of the short term. Serious divisions within the Labour Party (always in practice a coalition) were also significant, leading to attempts to replace Wilson, as in 1968.[6] The very intractability of the tasks facing him was also crucial.

Wilson at least had a droll sense of humor. When a senior colleague, Barbara Castle, asked him what he would do about the Abortion Bill, meaning the proposed legalization to legalize abortion, a divisive major piece of legislation, Wilson quipped that he would pay it when it came, a play on the idea of an abortion bill. The married Wilson himself was widely believed to have had a long-standing affair with his secretary, Marcia Falkender, to whom he was certainly in thrall. In a particular abuse of government patronage, he permitted her to exercise undue influence and had her ennobled as Lady Falkender.[7]

The years 1964–70 did not lead to economic reform but were certainly a time of social and cultural change and were understood in that light. The Wilson government captured, shaped, and encouraged a mood of the time for progressive change. Without the support of the government, and notably that of the home secretary, Roy Jenkins (for Wilson was more reluctant), a number of key legislative moves would not have taken place. Liberalization of the laws concerning abortion, homosexuality, capital punishment, censorship, and divorce and the passage of the Race Relations Act in 1965, which crimi-nalized racial discrimination and banned the incitement of racial hatred, were intended to transform Britain into a more tolerant and civilized society. Access to birth control, a governmental issue due to the NHS, was extended and totally detached from marital status.[8]

There were important reforms in the education system in England, Wales, and Northern Ireland, notably the changeover to mixed-ability com-prehensive schools, rather than, as under the previous system, the separation of pupils after the 11 Plus examination into grammar schools and secondary moderns. The establishment of the Open University was innovative. In addi-tion, the deep-seated concern for such disadvantaged groups as the elderly and the handicapped revealed a government guided by a genuine humanitarian imperative. Increased pensions and reform of the Rent Act made a major dif-ference to much of the population. The age of majority was lowered from 21 to 18 in 1969, which increased the size of the electorate. In its social policy, Labour was developing liberal social democratic tendencies at variance with the trade union, left-wing interest in the party. However, the latter became more pow-erful after the 1970 election defeat, and the tendencies did not reemerge in Labour until "New Labour" in the 1990s.[9]

At the same time, there could be a theme of continued or stronger govern-ment control, as in the Gaming Act (1968), which addressed gambling. More-over, in some areas of public provision seen elsewhere in Europe, for example childcare, there was scant development in Britain where the welfare state remained both expensive and incomplete. The introduction of comprehensive schools worked in some cases, but there was also an erosion of educational standards, and the attack on grammar schools removed an important means for upward social mobility by bright working-class pupils. Some counties retained such schools, and right-wing commentators continued to press for their reintroduction, including in the mid-2010s when the new prime minister favored the policy.

Comprehensives offered a theme of inclusion. However, they also played an important role in the detailed local world of difference between, and within, communities and in creating new differences in terms of the catchment areas from where individual comprehensives drew pupils. The price of houses in areas with good comprehensives rose strongly, which greatly lessened inclu-siveness. This was a classic instance of the mismatches between policy and implementation, and between ideology and practice.

Alongside the reform strand, there was also a root conservatism among much of the electorate, even if there was no issue, symbol, or individual around which conservative forces could rally. Due to the winner-takes-all system of British elections, it is easy to neglect the Conservatives in the 1960s. However, in the general elections of 1964 and 1966, they polled more than 40 percent of the votes, a greater percentage than for any political party in 2015, the latest general election, including for the winning party in 2015, the Conservatives.

Moreover, on June 18, 1970, the Conservatives unexpectedly defeated Labour. The failure of Labour to inspire its own supporters in 1970 was important. On a low turnout, the voters turned against Wilson, who was widely distrusted, rather than toward the unpopular Heath, who had already been defeated in 1966, and there were few signs in 1970 of a widespread rejection of Labour ideas and policies. Instead, Labour management appeared flawed, which was to prove a weak basis for Conservative government during what was to be a difficult period. The Labour percentage of the vote fell from 48 in 1966 to 43 in 1970, the lowest since 1935, while the Conservative rose from 41.9 to 46.4, the highest since 1959. The Scottish Nationalists won 11 percent of the vote in Scotland, an unprecedented figure for them. Labour won 287 seats; the Conservatives won 330 seats and an overall majority of 30. The pollsters got this election badly wrong, as they were also to do with the 2015 election and the 2016 EU referendum.

In line with his policies in government earlier in the 1960s, Heath eagerly pushed through change in what he saw and presented, as an attempt to modernize and reform Britain. The structure of government and of the NHS was reorganized and a Central Policy Review Staff was established. Decided on long before the general election, the decimalization of the currency in 1971 discarded centuries of usage and, despite promises that this would not be the case, contributed to inflation.

The Local Government Act of 1972 drastically altered the historic territorial boundaries of local government. This formed a major contrast with the United States where the role of the individual states (historically, but not in practice, the equivalent, on a different scale, of British counties) offered, and still offers, a continuance of older English roots. The changes in local government included the ending of historic counties, such as Huntingdonshire, and of the ridings (divisions) of Yorkshire, the creation of new ones, such as Avon (Bristol and Bath) and Tyne and Wear, and the movement of areas between counties, all amid much controversy. The movement of areas helped alter the character of counties. For example, Durham lost urban areas, notably Gateshead and Sunderland, and gained rural ones, from North Yorkshire. New urban counties linked areas with scant mutual interest, notably the rival cities of Newcastle and Sunderland in Tyne and Wear. Local government units were transformed to an even greater extent in Wales and Scotland. The theory was that of rationalization so as to provide areas that could support services, but, in practice, it was the contempt for traditional identities and values and for local opinion that emerged most clearly. Far from this being separate to other aspects of Heath's policy, it was very characteristic of the tone as well as content of his politics.

Joining the EEC (see chapter 10) was central to Heath's plan to modernize Britain. However problematic this accession proved to be, Heath was able to achieve this objective. He was less successful elsewhere. When he came to office, Heath had outlined an economic policy different from that of Wilson, one, set out at a meeting at Selsdon Park in 1970, that was more prudent and business friendly and far less ready to intervene in the economy, notably with a refusal to subsidize inefficient industries. Income tax was to be cut alongside public spending in order to help Britain compete effectively within the EEC. Industrial relations were to be reformed with government interventionism ended, and there was to be more selectivity in welfare. These policies prefigured those of Heath's successor as party leader, Thatcher. "Lame ducks," companies that were unable to compete or maintain profitability, were to be let go, and the Mersey Docks and Harbour Board was allowed to go into liquidation, an end to the docks of Liverpool, the prime port of empire.

However, under strong pressure from the unions, who, from a national point of view, behaved in an increasingly irresponsible fashion, and notably responded with strikes and sit-ins, this policy was not sustained in 1971. This policy change contributed to a growing, and deserved, sense of weak government. Heath proved inconsistent and unable to convey a sense of being able to overcome crisis. Unable to relax and socialize, Heath proved unattractive to the people and could not therefore be a strong prime minister in the modern age. He gave in because he could not carry the day and also because he had a liberal streak and hated social division.

Moreover, both wage and price inflation rose significantly, making British goods uncompetitive and putting great pressure on the balance of payments. Unemployment rose to over a million, a shock after three decades when it had been low, and tax revenues fell. This world financial system was already in severe difficulties due to the weakness of the dollar from the 1960s both as the US economy was put under pressure by the growth of those of West Germany and Japan and because of the use of borrowing to pay for US government expenditure including the Vietnam War. Differential growth rates put mounting pressure on the system of fixed convertibility for international currencies that had been established under the Bretton Woods Agreement, the system that had made devaluation a matter of government policy. Britain was in a vulnerable positon to deal with the resultant turmoil when this system weakened and then collapsed. The remedies that President Nixon pursued in the United States, notably wage and price controls, and the difficulties he encountered, serve as a reminder that Heath was scarcely alone in being under pressure.

In Britain, inflation further surged as the government changed direction in 1972, as Mrs. Thatcher was to refuse to do in the early 1980s when she presided over high unemployment. Heath sought to reflate the economy by easing the money supply: the provision of money and credit. Attempts to limit wage and price rises, never easy or convincingly successful in this period, were largely so once a compulsory incomes policy was adopted. However, they were blown apart by the National Union of Miners (NUM). In 1972, the NUM staged the first national coal strike since its failed attempt in 1926, and won a 32 percent wage increase. This settlement set the scene for a crisis of governability in the face of the excesses of trade union power. The NUM caused a renewed and more serious crisis in winter 1973–74, when the government was also hit by the oil price rise and economic crisis that followed the outbreak of the Yom Kippur War, the war between Israel and Egypt-Syria. There was no equivalent to the position of the NUM in the United States, Japan, or West Germany. Thus, domestic conflict and international problems combined for Britain. The crisis was felt by most people in the form of power cuts and the imposition of a three-day working week in order to save power, an enforced idleness in winter gloom that did nothing for the mood of the nation.

Heath called a general election to bolster his position and try to overawe the miners. It was intended as a vote of confidence. Held on February 28, 1974, the election left the Conservatives with the biggest percentage of the popular vote (37.9 to 37.1 for Labour), but with fewer MPs (297 to 301), and with the Liberals (19.3 percent and 14 MPs) under Jeremy Thorpe holding the balance of power. Heath tried to hang on to power, but, in protest against Heath's policy in Northern Ireland, notably the attempt to impose power sharing, including for the Catholic Social Democrat and Labour Party, the Ulster Unionists, now under the hardline Ian Paisley, refused to back the Conservatives. The Liberals, whose share of the vote had greatly increased, rejected Heath's offer of a coalition, and Wilson returned to power. He did not form a coalition government with them.

Wilson reversed much of the legislation of the Heath years. Having failed to deal with the trade union issue in 1969, Labour had proved bitterly opposed to Heath's efforts to tackle the same problem. Labour's attitude was to help lead to the wasted 1970s and to the advent of Thatcher which might otherwise have been unnecessary. In the manifesto for the general election of February 1974, there was a "proud" declaration of "Socialist" aims and a commitment to "a fundamental and irreversible shift in the balance of power and wealth in favour of working people and their families." This course represented a departure from the Social Democratic path seen in Continental Western Europe and notably in West Germany. Indeed, as Labour became closer to radical trade unions, so the emphasis shifted, from the classless rhetoric of the mid-1960s, to a stress on "the workers," with the latter allegedly represented by the unions. This emphasis helped accentuate a sense of political division both between Labour and Conservatives and within Labour. Many Labour MPs were sponsored by particular unions, and union occasions, such as the Trades Union Congress (TUC) and the Durham Miners' Gala, saw a major turnout of Labour leaders. The self-employed did not count in the Labour worldview.

Labour held office until 1979. Thwarted by his lack of an overall majority after the February 1974 election, Wilson, instead, won a small overall majority of three in another general election, which was held in October 1974 after an increase in state pensions. Wilson had wanted this election held earlier, but the Queen apparently argued that to do so would be destabilizing. In the October 1974 election, there was no equivalent to the major shift toward Labour seen between the 1964 and 1966 elections. Indeed, although the uncharismatic Heath was losing support within the Conservative Party, the latter still enjoyed the backing of much of the electorate which was wary of both Labour and Wilson.

Despite his parliamentary overall majority, which Labour was not to lose until 1977, Wilson was unable to govern effectively or with any clear sense of direction, or indeed, to keep Labour united. In 1974–76, indeed, Wilson, through mismanagement and short-termism, completed the dire process begun by Heath. An economy, state, and society that had been muddling through for decades, operating far below the level of effectiveness of other countries, but, nevertheless, at least avoiding crisis and breakdown, slid into chaos and confusion.[10]

The overall situation was very difficult. The failure of the fixed exchange rate system for currencies, as well as the inflationary pressures and economic problems arising from the oil shock, continued to affect the entire world, and Britain, as yet, was not a major producer of North Sea oil. The global recession hit British exports. The collapse of the long postwar boom had triggered, as elsewhere in the West, including the United States, "stagflation," a combination of rapid inflation and rising unemployment. This posed problems for the Keynesian policies and economists that determined Labour's macroeconomics, as an adverse relationship of inflation and unemployment had been assumed. Moreover, there was a serious failure to address problems at microeconomic levels, levels to which corporatist approaches to policy making tended to devote insufficient attention.

Britain managed the recession far less well than Japan or West Germany. In part, this was a matter of government policy and management. Wilson compounded Heath's inability to control wages by measures that let them rip. At the same time, controls were placed on prices and dividends. As a result, alongside very high inflation, company profits collapsed, there was a massive fall on the stock market that hit liquidity in the economy as well as many family incomes and pensions, and there was no incentive to invest. In addition, there was a financial crisis. The end of the fixed exchange rate had seen sterling float against the dollar from June 1972. Moreover, in 1971, controls on bank lending were relaxed, leading to an increase in liquidity and the start of a property lending boom, only for a fall in liquidity and property prices in 1973–74 to hit secondary banks, producing a banking crisis in 1974.

As a consequence of the economic illiteracy of Wilson's policies, 1974–76 was the closest that Britain has yet come to the fall of capitalism, and notably in the shape of failures of liquidity and profitability. Amid rising anxiety, social and industrial cohesion appeared threatened, and there was widespread concern about rising crime levels, as well as fears that Britain was broken and finished, which led to lurid talk of the need for extraparliamentary solutions. Indeed, a number of senior figures discussed the possibility of a military takeover, although none was planned or attempted. Rumors about this possibility encouraged a febrile atmosphere. This was one to which the washover of conspiracy and violence from "the Troubles" in Northern Ireland (see chapter 9) contributed. The use of force there to maintain government control encouraged some to speculate about similar solutions in Britain.

There were also growing rumors about Thorpe, the Liberal leader from 1967 to 1976. These culminated in a bizarre trial focusing on Thorpe's one-time homosexual lover whose dog had been killed in a botched assassination/intimidation, although the pretrial committal proceedings were not held until late 1978. Thorpe was eventually acquitted in what was seen by many as an "establishment setup." More generally, Nicholas Henderson, the British ambassador in Paris, argued that the British had become obsessed with "declinism," a sense of the country and its institutions as finished. There was certainly widespread pessimism and a degree of despair.

Like Thorpe, but more seriously, Wilson had become a fixer who could no longer fix anything. In 1974, he had repealed the Conservatives' Industrial Relations Act and the legal sanctions on pay bargaining. In its place, Wilson announced a "social contract" with the TUC, including regulated wage bargaining, an extension of welfare benefits, and redistributive taxation. However, that agreement could not contain a massive wage explosion that began with buying off the miners. Other unions sought to follow the lead, driving up wage inflation with that, in turn, encouraging price inflation and being encouraged by it. Union leaders themselves were under pressure from their members as plant bargainers gained power within the unions. They tended to be much more radical, as was also true of many Labour backbenchers. Strikes were the key means to apply pressure and were often intimidatory.

Keen to avoid governmental wage controls and the disputes to which these would lead, Wilson focused on restraint. The voluntary agreement on wage restraint offered by the TUC in 1975, which helped lower inflation to below 10 percent (still a very high percentage) in 1978, however, enjoyed scant support from union members. On their part, there was a widespread refusal to face up to economic realities, and this contributed to an appalling failure of leadership by the trade union leadership and the Labour Party. This was a part of what appeared to be a lack of statecraft and even an inability of government. Both France, under President Valéry Giscard d'Estaing (1974–81), and the United States, under President Jimmy Carter (1977–81), came out of recession with fewer economic and political problems than Britain.

Prefiguring the situation in the late 2010s, both the trade unions and Labour were greatly affected by far-left "entryism," and there was only limited attempt to disguise the process. The Communist Party played a role in the union movement, and, with it, the Soviet Union. In addition, Labour MPs who were judged right-wing (in Labour terms) were destabilized and, if possible, deselected by activists—for example, Militant Tendency, which, in practice, was the Revolutionary Socialist League. Many activists were Marxists seeking class struggle. Deselection helped move Labour to the Left and to terrorize those who did not agree. Failing to lead, Wilson did not help. He did little to address, let alone stop, "entryism."[11]

Moreover, by keeping most of his Cabinet in the dark and relying on unofficial channels for information and on a "kitchen cabinet," Wilson contributed to distrust at, and about, the center of government. An able man, he proved a poor prime minister, and all for the sake of a party divided and ill-constituted that he sought to keep together. Wilson offered no new solutions, and, indeed, none that worked.[12]

Alongside Heath's serious failure as a leader, both in government and in opposition, these developments encouraged the Conservatives to move toward the Right. In a bitter leadership contest in 1975, Margaret Thatcher, a former secretary of state for education, who had been willing to challenge Heath, benefited from doing so while other critics were more cautious. She won the leadership on the second ballot of February 11, with 146 votes among the Conservative MPs, after the outnumbered Heath had pulled out following the first in which he won 119 against 130 votes for Thatcher. Five candidates stood in the second ballot, dividing the opposition to Thatcher. The second-ranking, William Whitelaw, won 79 votes. A former party chairman, he also had more ministerial experience but was overly identified with Heath.

Thatcher's success was to be crucial for the 1980s, but, at the time, her victory did not seem fundamental. The first woman to lead a British political party, she was not at the time regarded as a figure of much political consequence. Heath, indeed, found it difficult to accept his defeat and sulked for the remainder of his career and life, a tedious and undignified course that tarnished his reputation. Henry Kissinger observed in 1975, "I don't think Margaret Thatcher will last."

Probably fearing the onset of mental illness but also affected by government defeats in the Commons, Wilson unexpectedly resigned in March 1976 and was succeeded by "Sunny Jim," James Callaghan, the foreign secretary, who, while not an ideologue, was not particularly imaginative. An MP since 1945, he had great experience, being the sole prime minister to have been chancellor of the exchequer (1964–67), home secretary (1967–70), and foreign secretary (1974–76). Nevertheless, his grasp of economics, in what was a very difficult situation, was limited. Callaghan opposed the policy of state socialism offered by Labour's Left, led by Michael Foot and Tony Benn, with its call for import controls, further nationalizations and yet higher taxation.

Instead, Callaghan and Denis Healey, the chancellor of the exchequer, advocated pragmatism and were willing to rethink the Keynesian prescriptions of the previous thirty-five years. Heavy spending cuts were introduced by the government. It had to turn, in September 1976, to the IMF for a loan, the resort usually of far weaker states. In turn, the IMF demanded further cuts, which were accepted after a political battle within the Cabinet in which left-wing ministers were defeated. As a result, the pound rose.[13]

Having lost by-elections, always a measure of government popularity, and (alongside resignations) the parliamentary majority in 1977, Callaghan was obliged to rely on a pact with the Liberals from spring 1977 until July 1978. Fearing defeat, he did not feel able to seek reelection through a general election. At the same time, he was conducting a bitter struggle with "entry-ism" within Labour.

Meanwhile, industrial disputes remained a serious problem, discouraging domestic and foreign investment. In 1977, violent mass picketing in support of a union-recognition strike at the Grunwick film processing factory in London raised serious issues about the possibility of maintaining public order. At the same time, the Grunwick dispute appeared to many as an example of a legitimate union activity against an exploitative company that had treated Asian women workers especially badly.

Industrial disputes caused a particular crisis in the public sector, which culminated in the "winter of discontent" of 1978–79. In this, the government's norm of 5 percent in wage increases was challenged by a series of strikes, including by hospital ancillary staff and trash collectors. Hospitals were picketed, and, in some areas, the dead unburied (much to Callaghan's shock) and troops called in to shoot rats swarming around accumulated garbage. The large number of simultaneous strikes; the violence and mean-mindedness of the picketing, including the turning away of ambulances from hospitals; and the lack of interest by the strikers in the public discredited the rhetoric and practice of trade unionism for much of the public.

Callaghan might have been more successful had he held the general election due in 1979 before winter 1978–79, as it was reported he would do in the pro-Labour *Mirror*. He appears to have thought that he would have won (and Labour was ahead in the polls), but possibly without the overall majority necessary to secure effective government. In the event, he could not deliver the latter in the meantime.[14] As a result, the *Sun* was able to talk about a "winter of discontent," a Shakespearean term that stuck and, with his "Crisis? What crisis?," to suggest that Callaghan, who had been to an international conference in the Caribbean, was underplaying the crisis. In part, the political struggle was also one between newspapers, in particular between the *Sun* and the *Mirror*, both competing for the leading position in mass readership. The *Sun's* phrase stuck and became totemic for the Conservatives when criticizing Labour.

An inability to manage parliamentary arithmetic in the aftermath of the Scottish and Welsh devolution referenda (see chapter 9) on March 1, 1979, led Labour, amid high political drama, to lose a parliamentary motion of no confidence in March. One of the crucial votes in a division, where the government's downfall was secured by a single vote, was that of Reg Prentice, a former Labour Cabinet minister who, feeling threatened by deselection by left-wing constituency activists, had defected to the Conservatives in 1977. The impact of Scottish nationalism offered a reprise of the role of Northern Ireland in Heath's failure in February 1974. Yet again, British questions came to bite political leaders' hands.

The no-confidence vote opened the way for a Conservative victory with a majority of forty-three seats in a general election held on May 3, 1979. The national swing of 5.2 percent from Labour to the Conservatives reflected widespread frustration with Labour, while Labour itself seemed to be drifting and without any appreciable message or purpose other than hanging on. This appeared to be a politics of managing decline, a decline that, at best, would be eased by compromises with unwilling trade unionists and reluctant minority parties. This prospectus did not work against the more attractive message or techniques of the Conservatives in 1979. More energetic and focused than Callaghan, Thatcher proved adept at photo opportunities and slogans and made good use of advertising agencies. The Conservative manifesto in 1979, moreover, was not one to "frighten the horses," to use a British image that was increasingly without much direct meaning in a country where there were few horses. Legislation against picketing and the closed shop (the requirement for workers to belong to a trade union) were on offer in the manifesto but not the wholesale changes that were to follow under Thatcher's government.

Looking back on the 1970s, it is clear that the political system had held and social peace been maintained. The EEC was joined in 1973 with no violent political disruption. Scotland (which had voted for one) and Wales (which had not) failed in 1979 to gain devolved assemblies, again with no violent political disruption. Governmental change occurred peacefully in 1970, 1974, and 1979, although the situation was far less favorable in Northern Ireland. This might appear a somewhat bland and complacent conclusion. There were major features that should have created alarm. In particular, the takeover of sections of the Labour Party by entryist Trotskyist groups, such as Militant, contributed to the difficulty in facing the trade unions, notably when the Transport and General Workers Union made the strike by road haulage and oil tank drivers official, and when the secondary picketing of other employers spread.

In many respects, the situation in Britain was more serious than that in countries that had a violent revolutionary movement, notably Italy with the Red Brigade and West Germany with the Baader-Meinhof Gang. In Britain, there were such movements: the Angry Brigade on the mainland and the IRA in Northern Ireland. The second proved a major threat and also conducted operations on the mainland, but its separatist character meant that it could not become a wider movement. IRA attempts to assuage Scottish and Welsh opinion by focusing mainland attacks on England did not lead to an alliance with the Scottish and Welsh nationalists. The Angry Brigade tried its hand at terrorism but was small scale and highly ineffective. Nevertheless, the situation was more serious because the trade unions proved far more able to challenge the governability of Britain than their counterparts elsewhere.

There is a possible narrative of developments into the 1980s that sees the secret services and others linked to them as playing an important role in politics in the broadest sense, culminating in the rise of Thatcher. There had been serious concerns about Wilson. His surprise resignation in 1976 may have been due to fears about Alzheimer's disease or to defeats in the House of Commons, but there were also persistent reports about pro-Soviet links, about bugs in his office revealing the sale of honors, and so on. Unproven is the verdict on these charges, but it was certainly the case that the secret services were suspicious of Wilson. Concerned about possible KGB links and about his relations with businessmen from Eastern Europe, MI5 maintained a file on him throughout his period of office. Wilson, in turn, was worried about attempts to destabilize his position. He did not help his reputation by drawing up a resignation honors list that included Rudy Sternberg, who was probably a Soviet spy, as well as at least two fraudsters. Moreover, the KGB had a link in Wilson's Cabinet and among the trade union leadership. Thatcher had supporters with links to the Secret Service.

These issues indicate the difficulties involved in writing the political history of the period. So much focuses on an established narrative, but many of the factors and individuals possibly involved are shrouded in a degree of mystery, one that the archives scarcely clarify. This can make the true significance of events and the nature of causes difficult to establish. At any rate, in 1979, what the new government would bring was unclear.

7

THATCHERISM, 1979-90

THE DEATH OF Margaret Thatcher in 2013 underlined the contentious nature of her legacy. The death also demonstrated the changing character of British society, being greeted with more division than that of any former prime minister. A state funeral in St Paul's Cathedral attended, most unusually, by the Queen in a very public show of respect, contrasted with the vocal abuse circulating in, and from, some circles. This difference captured the ambiguities of Thatcher's government and legacy, each of which bulk especially large in foreign attention. These ambiguities also relate to very different histories of Britain, and these histories focus on Thatcher's intentions and impact.

Coming to power determined to reverse what she saw as Britain's decline and to overthrow what she presented as the causes, Thatcher presented herself, not as a restorer, as Churchill had done when replacing Labour in 1951, but as a radical reformer and an opponent of big government, whose reforms were intended to change as much as to restore. Churchill had focused on foreign policy and defense, but, while doing so, the hyperactive Thatcher was also determined to change Britain from within, as Churchill had not sought to do. Her agenda was greatly shaped by a response to what had happened earlier in her life, including her upbringing as the daughter of a devout Methodist self-made grocer in small-town England, which was a background very much outside the usual circles of Conservative privilege. World War II was also important. However, coming from outside the circles of privilege did not entail any obvious political trajectory as both experiences had also been true of Heath and Powell and were to be true of Major and May. A key element in all these cases (bar Major) was a lack of "clubability" and, notably, of the upper-class clubability of shared assumptions and background that was true of the social elite from which the Conservative leaders of the 1950s had come.

Thatcher's agenda, and, even more, the language with which she expressed it, challenged not only those she believed needed challenging but also many of those who provided her with electoral and political support. Seeing herself as a radical reformer, Thatcher sought to transform not only the country and its politics but also the Conservative Party, believing that the last was necessary to the former. In her mind, politics was a necessary and moral struggle, and doubt had to be overcome.

It never was. Indeed, it was one of the great ironies of her career that, having won three elections in a row (1979, 1983, 1987), at that point an unprecedented triumph under the mass franchise (Blair was to repeat it in 1997, 2001, and 2005; Wilson had won four but not in a row), Thatcher was overthrown in 1990 by a rebellion within her own parliamentary party, although not one by the party members in the country; Blair, in contrast, had become unpopular with the latter. Whereas her two Conservative predecessors since Macmillan in 1963 (who resigned due to poor health), Douglas-Home and Heath, had been defeated in the polls, in 1964, 1966, and 1974 (twice), Thatcher never was. This was the source of much of her mythology.

In part, this success increased the anger of those who deplored her. "Thatcherite" became a term of abuse to a degree that "Heathite" could never match, though, on the part of her supporters, "wet" did to a degree. The values and locations of many of her supporters, notably the suburbs, also aroused ire. Not all the anti-Thatcherite Conservatives were wealthy patricians in background and/or manner, but many of the more prominent—for example, Sir Ian Gilmour[1] and Francis Pym—were. Moreover, their "one nation" paternalism was often linked to a somewhat static view of society and to a condescending view of social mobility. One patrician remarked of another Member of Parliament (MP), Michael Heseltine, who had made a large fortune, that he had had to buy his furniture. That Heseltine had therefore not inherited it but had earned it, supposedly made him less impressive.

Thatcher, in her turn, had contempt for those who, from 1980, she called the "wets" and a dislike for a tradition, ethos, and practice of compromise and consensus that she felt had contributed greatly to Britain's decline and led to a destructive permissiveness. Indeed, Thatcher's right-wing radicalism entailed a break with a more traditional paternalist and complacent Conservatism that centered its role on the national fabric. She was essentially an outsider, in social and political terms, to the more Tory side of the Conservative Party, which had created its traditions and more paternalist ways.

Instead, Thatcher not only broke with the centrist, fashionable, consensual soup of accepted beliefs, but she also became critical of leading national institutions, including the Church of England leadership, local government, and the universities. Macmillan complained that there were more Estonians than Etonians in her Cabinet, a toxic anti-Semitic response to her willingness to look for more talent. A Conservative MP, John Biffen, referred to "Tory Maoism," and Thatcher, an economic liberal and a modernizer, could certainly be radical.[2] She did not face up to the problem that allegedly, "the free market destroys tradition and culture,"[3] although the alternative of Socialist control can be a very effective destroyer of tradition and culture. Thatcher's radical stance as well as her policies made others uneasy and made her unpopular. In 1985, the academics of her old university, Oxford, very publicly voted down the proposal to give her an honorary doctorate. They had no such problems with far more unworthy candidates.

She was apt to refer to "our people." Indeed, Thatcher had a sharp eye for the partisan nature of society. I had one long conversation with Thatcher when she was leader. She started by telling me that she had recently come back from an official visit to a hospital in Barrow-in-Furness, Cumbria. The doctor who had shown her round, and she strongly emphasized to me that he had worn a red tie, the color of Labour, had complained about the state of the NHS and yet, she angrily pointed out to me, this was a new hospital, and there was no new hospital in her suburban London constituency. Opened on October 14, 1984, the Furness General Hospital was visited by Thatcher on September 3, 1986. Some NHS staff protested, but there was also a gathering of supporters. Thatcher also said that she was going to get rid of academic tenure. The content and tone of her remarks were characteristically clear. Her eye for detail was unusual for a politician. Lunching, later in the decade while on a tour of the North-East, at Durham University where I taught, Thatcher sent a hand-written thank-you letter in which she commented on her pleasure that the mineral water on the table was British, not French.

Pleased to be known as "The Iron Lady" and promising strong leadership and no "U-turns" in the face of opposition, Thatcher publicly relished her determination to weather the storm. This endowed her politics with a sense of virtuous struggle and ensured that Thatcherism was just as much a moral as an economic creed, or, at least, in her eyes, those of her supporters and those of her critics. She associated "U-turns" with Heath, and this association was widely understood. While ready to explain her views, she was not given to debate and, instead, self-consciously sought to implement an ideology. On revision, that judgment appears in need of qualification. Thatcher was more ready to debate than Tony Blair and Gordon Brown, the Labour prime ministers between 1997 and 2010. Indeed, she could delight in an argument. It would be more accurate to suggest that, in public, she was not inclined to equivocate, and, in private, less so than other politicians.

Thatcher's determination to bring change involved a rewriting of recent history in an attempt to secure the present and ensure the future. Post-1945 economic management and 1960s' social policies were both criticized by the Thatcherites. In the former case, Keynesian economics, providing more liquidity by increasing the money supply in order to maintain economic activity and employment, were condemned for a willingness to accept dangerous levels of inflation. Inflation itself was seen not only as damaging for the economy but also as socially disruptive, as well as a threat to core Conservative constituencies, such as the elderly, and to the value of "sound money." In controlling the money supply as a key aspect of the monetarism she espoused, and thus pursuing the very opposite to the Keynesian "quantitative easing" that was to be followed anew in the United States and Britain in response to the 2008 recession, Thatcher offered a clear and apparently straightforward solution to Britain's economic problems, and at a time when other politicians appeared lacking in both insight and determination. In practice, Callaghan had already broken with aspects of Keynesianism, by putting the reduction of inflation above that of unemployment and by addressing government expenditure, but, influenced by monetarist thinkers, notably Friedrich Hayek and Milton Friedman, Thatcher did so with more clarity.

Thatcher used successive electoral victories in 1979, 1983, and 1987, albeit victories without any particular rise in support, to push through major changes. In this process, she shattered much of the "moral economy" of postwar corporatist society, especially in its 1970s' form. In doing so, she challenged a range of interests, from trade unions to the traditional structure of the City of London, in part in order to provide supply-side remedies to economic difficulties but also to offer what she saw as freedom. Indeed, a "freedom" agenda was much discussed in circles close to Thatcher. This was an agenda that bridged the Atlantic. British and US conservatives developed close personal links, although there were major contrasts in practice between Reaganite and Thatcherite policies. In particular, Reagan greatly increased the budget deficit, whereas Thatcher sought to pursue a fiscal prudence of cutting government expenditure and reducing borrowing in order to finance tax cuts. As Conservative chancellor of the exchequer in 2010–16, George Osborne was to adopt similar priorities, not least in the distribution of the burden of taxes and in spending priorities, although government debt increased.

Thatcher was able to introduce change in part because the "moral economy" had already faced a crisis in the divided 1970s, a decade in which confidence in established practices declined. Thatcher's critics failed, and still very much fail, to appreciate the degree to which the "moral economy," and the corporatism to which it was linked, did not appear credible to many commentators or much of the public. Subsequent romanticization of groups such as the miners, who went on strike against Thatcher in 1984–85, many of them using intimidation if not violence, is highly misleading. So possibly, however, were aspects of the use of language by which Thatcherites reordered or sought to change the understanding of Britain.

Thatcher, herself, tapped into broader currents of disenchantment. The excesses of trade union disruption in the 1970s, and notably in the "winter of discontent" of 1978–79 (a phrase frequently repeated), made it easy for her to argue that both Conservative and Labour governments had failed to restrain union power. In addition, Thatcher benefited from the extent to which the views toward poverty and the poor that had contributed to the welfare state created in the late 1940s were insecurely rooted. In particular, support for the welfare state, or rather of specific aspects of it, were affected by concern about the tax implications, and notably so as inflation was taking more people into higher tax brackets. Criticism of unmarried mothers was especially noticeable. There was a parallel to similar developments in the United States, although without the racial dimension frequently seen there.

Thatcher therefore drew on wider political and social developments, and both undermined class politics and benefited from their decline, especially in southern England, in the sense that she profited from the decline in a separate working-class political consciousness, one organized by trade unions and committed to Labour. Thatcher also pursued a particular agenda of getting inflation under control and trying to ensure that it did not recur. Inflationary structures and expectations were confronted, and this confrontation encouraged rhetorical and practical struggle with the trade unions. It also encouraged the employment of interest rates in order to control the money supply and its consequences. "Sound money" became a goal and a means, although many experienced these as factory closures and mass unemployment.

Indeed, the arguments for Thatcherite economics were challenged as a result. That her policies were denounced by the majority of (although not all) academic economists appears to have given her a degree of pleasure. The economists, in turn, had scant understanding of microeconomic factors and, in some cases, their macroeconomic counterparts. The challenge to Thatcherite economics was both highly reasonable and yet also based on the misleading premise that many companies that were scarcely competitive and plants that were obsolete would have survived but for government policies and their consequences. Some, indeed, would have done so, and thus have maintained employment, but the British economy was under great pressure due not only to trade union power but also to competition within the European Community from West Germany, as well as thanks to the rise of Japan. That of China was still distant.

The government could not run deficits comparable to Reagan in the United States because the economy was far weaker than that of the United States, while the dollar, not the pound, was the international reserve currency. However, Thatcher, anyway, was in favor of her concept of "sound money," which she saw as crucial to a free-market capitalism. Ironically, the deregulation of finance she encouraged was to introduce elements of unsound money, elements that were to cause very serious problems for both her and for her successors, problems that continue to the present. This was not a point Thatcher dwelled on as she did not focus on problems. Indeed, she expected her ministers to bring her solutions, not problems, and favored those who did so. There were certainly parameters within which she had to operate. She could not be a Reagan. Nor, given her views and the attitudes of many of the trade unions, could Thatcher resort to the alternative of a German-style social democracy.[4]

In practice, as with all politicians, there was much compromise; in fact, Thatcher was not the most Thatcherite. Indeed, there was to be criticism that her rhetoric of "rolling back the state," while true of the privatization of most state industries, was misleading in other respects, and that government expenditure did not fall as anticipated. In one respect this was an aspect of the extent that neoliberalism had to be absorbed and championed by political actors.[5]

More generally, the possibilities for restructuring offered by the fortuitous combination of North Sea oil revenues and three election victories (1979, 1983, 1987) were not fully grasped, and, in some ways, the baleful consequences have continued to the present. In particular, the entitlement society continued to find government all too receptive, and notably so as far as the NHS was concerned. Thatcher's lack of radicalism might prove her most harmful legacy, but it is not clear that the Cabinet or the parliamentary party, or the electorate, would have accepted more radical measures. Nor is this a conclusion that conforms to the presuppositions of most historians.

Thatcher's stated determination to persist in the face of economic and political adversity, a clear contrast with Heath, was different in degree and style from that of her predecessors. This difference aroused both widespread hostility to Thatcher and genuine doubt about her. Both also owed much to the particular policies and problems of the first years of the government. The tone was rapidly set in 1979, in the first budget, launched on June 12, when public expenditure and direct taxation were cut, which helped establish the new value system. I can recall a left-wing friend bursting into tears.

Rising prosperity and more widespread taxation had ensured that 80 percent of households were paying direct taxation by 1975. As a result, taxation levels, and notably of income tax, became more common in public awareness and public debate and were the principal factor in the response of many throughout society to government policy and claims. Income tax was cut by three pence in the pound in the first budget.

Lower tax rates, however, released purchasing power, helping to push up inflation which rose to 21.4 percent in 1980. Amid considerable confusion in government and among the monetarists themselves, the Medium Term Financial Strategy launched in March 1980 led to a rapid rise in money supply and a tightening of monetary policy that, in practice, made the recession very much worse.[6] Interest rates rose greatly to cope with inflation and, alongside the export of North Sea oil, this increase led to a marked rise in the value of sterling. This rise hit export industries hard, and much of the economy became uncompetitive as far as providing exports and competing with imports were concerned. It also became easier to export capital for investment. Company bankruptcies rapidly pushed up unemployment and, thus, social security payments. In response, in a key budget, that of March 10, 1981, the government cut its expenditure anew, instead of reflating. Unemployment, 1.3 million in 1979, rose further, to reach, by January 1982, the unprecedented postwar (i.e., post-1945) figure of 3.07 million, a figure that was disproportionately urban-centered and older. The shrinking of the economy hit manufacturing industry, especially in traditional industrial tasks, very hard. Furthermore, many factories that were closed were crucial to entire communities, as with the steel works at Consett in County Durham and Corby in Northamptonshire, and with coal mines.

To critics, fiscal and economic policies had failed, and the government had to change direction; however, Thatcher's response defined her government for good and ill. "The lady's not for turning," she told the 1980 party conference, with her typical habit of speaking in the third person. The delegates applauded, much to the discomfort of some of Thatcher's Cabinet colleagues and the fury of liberal commentators. Television news carried the speech and the response around the country.

She remained adamant in 1981, despite widespread, albeit small-scale, disturbances that July. Crowds rioted, looted, and fought with the police, notably in London and Liverpool. That sounds dramatic, but, in practice, only relatively small parts of these cities were affected by rioting, particularly Brixton in London and Toxteth in Liverpool, both run-down "inner-city" areas. So also with the St Pauls area of Bristol. There were also small-scale disturbances in a number of cities, including Derby and High Wycombe. Several cities that experienced acute economic problems, such as Sunderland, did not see rioting.

Instead, poor relations between black youth and the police were a key element in the riots. The Scarman Inquiry that was set up after the riots focused on "racial disadvantage." Inner-city discontent was not simply a matter of racial issues, however, but, in part, a consequence of the economic transformation caused by the decline of manufacturing. The results included the loss of unskilled and semiskilled work, and the development of an economy of shifts and expedients, which led to an openness, on the part of some, to criminal behavior such as drug dealing. In turn, this behavior increased tension with the police. The Broadwater Farm Estate riots that followed in London in October 1985 saw a policeman murdered. Broadwater Farm itself was a supposedly model estate that had rapidly become a classic instance of the social failure of some of these environments. The "inner cities" became a topic of analysis and concern; inner-city rioting on this scale was certainly a new phenomenon for the twentieth century.

On September 14, 1981, Thatcher used a reshuffle to impose her authority on a Cabinet, many of whose members were opposed to further public expenditure cuts. However, in the face of rising unemployment, difficult public finances, and riots, it was widely assumed in the early 1980s that Thatcher would be removed by the electorate in the next general election, which was due by 1984 at the latest. In the event, she benefited greatly from the division of Labour, and thus of the opposition as a whole. Disenchanted with Labour's growing extremism as the party moved to the Left, a portion departed to form a new Social Democratic Party (SDP) in 1981. Those leaders leaving in the "Gang of Four" included a former Labour home secretary (Roy Jenkins) and a former foreign secretary (David Owen), neither of whom were Socialists. The narrow election of Michael Foot as the party leader in November 1980 after a bitter election suggested that the party would do little to stop MPs from being deselected, and thus Labour moving further to the Left. With the SDP untested, many electors found Thatcher a more attractive option.

Moreover, eventual victory in the 1982 Falklands War over Argentina (April 2–June 14), strengthened Thatcher's position, not least, but not only, with Conservative Party activists. Indeed, Thatcher's successful defense of Britain's interests in that war struck a chord across party boundaries. Conservative criticism of Thatcher over the war had been muted, whereas Labour had not been able to offer a united position on the war and had anyway suffered from the news focusing on the war.

That the conflict for long appeared to hang in the balance made Thatcher's resolve and determination appear more impressive. The war defined her premiership and showed off her leadership qualities for all to see. She gambled and won in a contest in which defeat would have been catastrophic. The war, in which she personally wrote to the families of all servicemen killed, was certainly a personal strain for Thatcher, as well as a make-or-break issue. Having in her eyes, begun to thwart the decline of Britain at the hands of trade unions, was she to be brought down for failing to defend one of Britain's few remaining possessions, one, moreover, where the population wished to stay with Britain? Politicians do, indeed must gamble, and this one came off and how. A sense of "us" versus "them" was captured in Thatcher's critical response to the eventual thanksgiving service at St Paul's Cathedral. Robert Runcie, the archbishop of Canterbury, and a veteran of World War II decorated for his bravery, aroused her anger by praying for the Argentinean combatants (of whom 650 had died) as well as the British (255 died). Thatcher's patriotism was somewhat more uncomplicated and unsubtle, as in her "Rejoice" response to the recapture of the island of South Georgia, the first territory regained.

A measure of recovery in the economy in 1982–83 also helped create a sense of achievement. Falling unemployment figures suggested a measure of success and a positive trend that appeared to vindicate Thatcher's policies. In practice, she could be criticized for having made both the recession and her policies harsher in their consequences than they need have been. This is a reasonable assessment. At the same time, the attempt in France under the Socialist leader François Mitterrand, who became president in 1981, to follow reflationary policies failed and had to be abandoned. As a separate criticism, she failed to invest adequately in the national infrastructure and notably in the rail system.

Thatcher responded to improving political and economic circumstances by calling a general election for June 9, 1983, instead of waiting until 1984. Having won 339 seats in 1979, to gain a clear but modest majority, the Conservatives now won 397, while Labour's number of seats fell from 269 to 209, giving Thatcher a working majority of 144, the biggest since 1945. This success was especially strongly marked in London and southern England. Yet, at 42.4, the Conservative percentage of the vote was the lowest since 1922. There was no Thatcherite tide, but, like Blair later, Thatcher benefited from the particular weaknesses of the opposition parties, as she had already done in 1979 and was to do again in 1987.

In 1983, it was the division of the opposition that was crucial: Labour, under the ineffective Michael Foot, endorsing extreme policies and offering a manifesto that Gerald Kaufman, one of its MPs, described as "the longest suicide note in history," gained 27.6 percent and the alliance of the Liberals and the SDP 25.4 percent, even though the latter won few seats due to the first-past-the-post electoral system, which was crucial to the result of elections. With a bit more success, they would have broken through and might then have swept the country whenever the opportunity arose.

More positively, the Conservative vote represented the rejection of two alternatives: Labour and the Alliance. In this context, the perception of success that was obtained was impressive, not least due to the high rate of unemployment. The need to stress the relatively low Conservative percentage of the vote, and the fact that it was won at the expense of two opponents, as well as thanks to there being two opponents, exemplifies the challenge facing the historian. It is all too easy to offer only one interpretation, and notably so when space is limited. At the same time, offering more than one does not help answer the question of assessing where to place the weight, and in both exposition and analysis. The division of the opposition vote was probably the key element.

Having won the election, Thatcher faced, from March 1984, a bitter fight with the National Union of Mineworkers (NUM), which, under a far-left leadership, was determined to resist the closure of uneconomic pits. Moreover, although many of his supporters sought only to circumvent the election result, the NUM's general secretary, Arthur Scargill, was resolved to overthrow it by inflicting a fatal defeat on the government. He saw capitalism as in crisis and the working class as requiring mobilization and direction. In practice, the NUM was heavily divided, and Scargill refused to hold a national strike ballot. This ensured that miners who wanted to work but had been denied the chance to vote were picketed. Indeed, the mass, often violent, picketing the union leadership organized was directed as much against working miners, notably in the vital Nottinghamshire-Derbyshire coalfield, as against attempts to move coal to the power stations. In addition, open-cast pits were vandalized by NUM activists—for example, in County Durham.

Eager to bring down a union that she saw as dangerous, keen to show she could break with Heath's example, and unsympathetic to the working-class culture of the coalfields,[7] Thatcher focused the government's resources on defeating the strike. However, the response was not unlimited. In particular, it was the police, not the army, that was used to maintain coal movements and to enable working miners to continue to work. On June 18, 1984, in a key confrontation, the police deployed six thousand officers to stop about five thousand pickets shutting down the coking plant at Orgreave near Sheffield. The police, some of whom were on horseback, were seen by the miners as Thatcher's militia. The NUM was seeking to repeat a similar clash at Saltley Gate in 1972 in which overwhelmed police units were unable to stop pickets from closing a coking plant. Thatcher was determined not to let this happen. The strike, in part, was an aspect of the Cold War, for the NUM received financial support from the Communist bloc, including Libya, which also backed the IRA. The latter had sought to kill her in 1984, by placing a bomb in her hotel suite during the party conference which was held that year in Brighton. The miners' cause also lacked popularity, a poll in July 1984 revealing that only 15 percent approved of their tactics, while 79 percent disapproved. Thatcher's statement, "The rule of law must prevail over the rule of the mob," resonated. A mere industrial dispute had become a question of who ruled the country, and Thatcher defined it as such in order to rally support for her determined stand.

The strike collapsed in March 1985 as poverty and weakness in the face of the power of the state sapped support among the striking miners, while the move into summer, with its lesser need for power, was significant. The failure to move to a more general strike was important to this collapse. So also was the ability to receive electricity by a recently opened power line from France. Thus, the NUM's defeat owed much to the large coal stockpile built up in anticipation of the strike and to the electricity generated by French nuclear power stations and supplied by a Socialist government under Mitterrand that had no love for the Communists. Oil and natural gas from the North Sea were also important to the energy situation in Britain.

Subsequently, pit closures were pushed through, and the defeated NUM remained divided. As a result of the strike's complete failure, Thatcher's recasting of labor away from the traditional heroisms, and toward new industries in which the workforce had different social and political values, had been taken a long way forward. The collapse of the coal industry reflected international economic trends, including growing trade in energy and the range of energy sources now available, but her deliberate marginalization of the industry left many former pit communities bereft. Not only were pit communities hit. On September 16, 1987, Thatcher visited the Thornaby bank of the River Tees in the North-East, an area of industrial closures, and was photographed in what was described as a "walk in the wilderness" of industrial decay. She was persuaded to open a university college in the area, although it failed to realize the hopes placed on it. In 1985, when Thatcher visited the North-East, she described her critics as "moaning minnies."

More positively, the defeat of the strike contributed greatly to a decline in trade union militancy and in related hopes on the far-left for a collapse of the Thatcher government. Following on from the Falklands War, Thatcher's determined stance against the striking miners was important in permitting a recovery of grip after the chaos of much of the 1970s. This won her international and domestic plaudits from some surprising sources on the Left, as well as some more obvious sources on the Right, and this response has continued to the present.

Instead of trade unions, nationalized industries, and council houses, Thatcher wanted a property-owning democracy in which corporatism was weak and capital supreme. This was a British version of globalization. Institutions and opinions that resisted were marginalized, and one vocal center of opposition, the Labour-controlled and left-wing Greater London Council (GLC), under its radical leader Ken Livingstone, was abolished in 1986. This was part of a wider process of centralization that took place under Thatcher: some fifty Acts of Parliament were passed transferring power from local government to Westminster and Whitehall. For example, the Rate Act of 1984 allowed the government to put a ceiling on rates (local property taxes) and thereby to control local authority finances and protect (as well as reward) supporters by keeping the rates low. Yet again, the nature and the cost of a property-owning democracy were key issues.

At the same time as centralization at the national level, there was also a driving back of public powers at the local level. The extension of compulsory competitive tendering to a wide range of local government services in 1988 was designed to challenge the role of council workers and the influence of their unions. It led to the entrance of private-sector contractors into public-service work—for example, refuse collection. In theory, services became more efficient and costs were cut. Trade union power and patronage were cut. This certainly happened in some councils, such as that of Wandsworth in London, which attracted much attention, but not in all of them. More generally, trade union reforms included making strike ballots mandatory (as opposed to the previous emphasis on shows of hands at meetings) and the banning of secondary picketing.

Nationalized industries and council houses alike were sold, the latter to tenants. The sale of council houses was a key Thatcherite policy that was defended as an assault on council fiefdoms and, instead, an empowerment of individuals, most of whom were expected to vote Conservative. The long-term fall in the size of the private rental market, in large part as a result of Labour governments making it less attractive to landlords, had encouraged demand for owner-occupation. The council houses were sold to their tenants at a heavy discount, under the "right to buy" Housing Act of 1980, and many of the former tenants rewarded Thatcher by supporting her in the 1983 and 1987 general elections. In the latter, the Conservative advance was greatest in Greater London and the outer metropolitan area, the combination of which provided nearly a quarter of the British electorate. As an indicator of activity in this region, the M25 around London, completed in 1986, became the busiest route in the country. Outer London also favored Thatcher for abolishing the GLC because that was perceived by many as a redistributive system that ensured that London's suburbia financed the inner city and notably Livingstone's policy of fixing public transport fares.

Council house sales contributed to growing social separation, as well as to spatial differentiation between socioeconomic groups. In contrast to the skilled manual workers who bought council houses, helping ensure their upward mobility and, therefore, that the lower middle classes grew, welfare dependents did not, and the poor were therefore further isolated. They did not switch to the Conservatives, but this did not hit the party hard as the electoral turnout of these dependents was low. The sales of council houses did not cut the overall number of houses. The houses still existed, and the new owners of council houses not only acquired a capital asset but also gained an economic freedom and a reduction in the influence of government on their lives. These owners spent heavily on do-it-yourself home improvements, which led to a major expansion in that branch of the economy, the stores of which, such as B&Q, tended to be located on out-of-town shopping areas. Privatized council homes also became key areas for the satellite dishes that enabled much of the public to follow Sky Television and notably its transmission of sporting events. The provision of social housing is only too low if one considers that there is some inalienable percentage of dwellings that should be state subsidized.

More generally, taxes were cut under Thatcher, while personal pension plans were launched, allowing large numbers without company pensions to gain tax relief on retirement savings. This measure was designed to increase share ownership. Share and home ownership were presented as key elements of the new property-owning democracy. The highly publicized sale of the nationalized industries, notably British Telecom in 1984 and British Gas in 1986, as well as of state shareholding in other companies, represented a very marked shift in ownership, with state control of assets and working in state industries both falling greatly. In order to encourage the purchase of the shares, and Thatcher's hope of a popular capitalism, they were priced very favorably for the purchasers. The other side was that state assets were sold at a discount, and an unnecessarily high one, and the purchasers were in effect bribed to support the process. There were also accusations that financial institutions close to the government—for example, the merchant bank Lazard—were rewarded by being allowed to handle privatizations at great profit to themselves. This was one aspect of the "property-owning democracy." The money raised helped finance tax cuts rather than infrastructure. More generally, there has been a serious failure across the period of this book to maintain and invest in public transport.[8]

Under Thatcher, economic growth, tax changes, and privatizations came to contribute to a strong feel-good factor, at least among many of those with assets and jobs. Indeed, average British disposable income rose by 37 percent between 1982 and 1992. So, too, did income differentials. The real income of the bottom 10 percent increased by 10 percent in 1973–91, but the top 10 percent gained 55 percent. The ownership of goods increased, notably of telephones, washing machines, dishwashers, cars, and video recorders. By 1996, nearly 90 percent of households had a deep freezer, and 20 percent had a dishwasher. The increased flow of oil from the North Sea contributed to this feel-good sense and helped push sterling up, which made foreign vacations far less expensive and also made it easier to purchase second homes abroad.

On June 11, 1987, Thatcher held another general election. The Conservative percentage of the vote declined very marginally to 42.3 from 42.4, but the number of MPs fell from 397 to 376, in large part because the opposition was not as evenly divided as in 1983. Labour won its percentage increase (27.6 percent, 209 MPs, to 30.8 percent, 229 MPs) essentially at the expense of the Alliance. The Alliance of the Liberals and the SDP had been seen as an opportunity to break the mold of politics, profiting from the extent to which both Labour and the Conservatives had vacated the political center ground.

However, the resilience of Labour, which began to recover, combined with Alliance divisions and poor leadership, closed this opportunity. The notoriously difficult David Owen, the SDP leader, alienated David Steel, the Liberal leader, and the other Liberals, quite effortlessly. Moreover, both Labour and the Conservatives had extensive areas of core support, both social and geographical. The Conservatives continued to do very well in London and southern England, but Labour was far more successful in Scotland and Wales as well as over most of northern England. Electoral distinctions became more marked in this election. The Conservatives still had a very large majority (of 102), not least because they were able to win key marginal seats in the

Midlands. Industry there was not the highly unionized heavy industry seen in South Wales, the Central Belt of Scotland, and North-East England.

Having won, Thatcher, who was increasingly determined to end socialism and to entrench her changes, characteristically avoided all temptation to consolidate and, instead, became more urgent and strident. The Education Reform Act of 1988 sought to lessen the control of local government, while a core curriculum, supported by regular testing, reduced the autonomy of teachers. The Criminal Justice Act of 1988 sought to standardize sentencing, and in 1989, the NHS was restructured as an internal market so as to create competition. Income tax was cut further, by the March 11, 1988 budget, to a basic rate of 25 percent and a top rate of 40 percent, which compared to 33 percent and 83 percent when she took office. Combined with easier credit, seen in the ease with which credit cards could be obtained, this cut encouraged a consumer boom, which was helped by a lack of regulations over consumer lending. The consumer boom, which contrasted with the poverty of parts of the state sector, pressed on an economy that had lost much of its "excess capacity" in the recession of the early 1980s. As a result, domestic production could not rise to match increased demand. Inflation and imports, therefore, shot up, leading to a record balance of payments deficit of £20 billion in 1989. Increased imports were encouraged by the strength of sterling.

The Conservatives deservedly lost their reputation for economic competence, and a marked sense of malaise developed. Criticism of Thatcher from within the Conservative Party increased, although she still benefited greatly from the maladroit public leadership of Labour by Neil Kinnock who, repeatedly, proved both verbose and poorly prepared in parliamentary debates. His capacity to win over floating voters, let alone exploit Conservative dissent, was limited.

In 1989, as the financial crisis escalated, the political position of the government was under acute pressure, with the poll tax, introduced in Scotland in 1988 and elsewhere in 1989, one of the most unpopular pieces of legislation passed since 1945, although the essentially law-abiding nature of the population ensured that most people paid it. In place of funding local government by a property tax charged on property owners, "the rates," the government proposed a "community charge" from every adult, with all those in a given council area paying the same amount. This so-called poll tax was designed to forge a link between expenditure and revenue. However, the tax was poorly handled and was presented as one in which millionaires only had to pay the same as everyone else. That was also true of the levy through which the BBC was supported, but that less expensive measure did not attract opposition.

Growing public criticism of the poll tax, notably a mass demonstration in London in 1989 involving two hundred thousand people, a small minority of whom rioted in Trafalgar Square, encouraged restless Conservative MPs to feel that Thatcher had lost the ability to respond to the popular mood. Many of the MPs were vulnerable to any fall in government support in a future election, and they were worried by bad by-election results for the Conservatives. Preparing the way for Blair's "New Labour," Kinnock's 1987–89 "policy review" was shedding the more unpopular aspects of Labour policies.[9]

Thatcher was now less popular than the government and certainly with a growing number of her colleagues. Characteristically, unlike her popularity with the Conservative rank and file in the country, she had never spent much time wooing the support of her colleagues, but then, this was true of most prime ministers, including Blair, Cameron, and May. More seriously, she failed to have her allies devote sufficient attention to the issue.

Caricatures and the television puppet program *Spitting Image* presented Thatcher as bullying her colleagues and that was certainly how many of them perceived the situation. Giles, the cartoonist for the *Daily Express*, a paper that backed Thatcher, depicted her on June 14, 1983, as a presence in the sitting room of a Conservative MP in the form of a portrait depicting her as a public executioner. A *Spitting Image* sketch had the Cabinet going out to dinner, and the maître d' asking Thatcher what she would like. She replied, "Steak." He asked, "And the vegetables?" to receive the reply, "They will have steak as well."[10] The fall of Thatcher had been steadily building up. After 1987, she became visibly imperious and arrogant. She was surrounded by advisers who were not up to changing circumstances and lost touch with her backbench MPs. She ignored advice given to her and the warning offered in December 1989 by a leadership challenge from Sir Anthony Meyer, a minor figure who still won a reasonable amount of support.

Thatcher's views about the political situation, "fostered by rhetorical excess," did not convince increasing numbers of her colleagues.[11] Tensions within the government over leadership and over future European integration (see chapter 10) led to a major challenge to Thatcher for the leadership of the Conservative Party, a challenge mounted by senior figures in the party. A crisis was well under way and organization was in place by November 1990. The trigger to the challenge was serious public criticism of Thatcher in the House of Commons on November 13 by Geoffrey Howe, formerly chancellor of the exchequer and then deputy prime minister. He accused her of not listening. Howe disapproved strongly of Thatcher's opposition to further European integration. Thatcher had also broken with Howe's successor, Nigel Lawson, in

1988, over his policy of shadowing the deutschemark, and in October 1989 he resigned because he objected to her seeking contrary advice from elsewhere. Lawson was also opposed to the poll tax.[12] Moreover, she had irritated colleagues by being reluctant to join the Exchange Rate Mechanism of European currencies, although she eventually did so under pressure from colleagues, notably Douglas Hurd, the foreign secretary, and John Major, Lawson's successor.

Opposition to Thatcher in the parliamentary party triggered a bitter contest for the leadership. The first ballot, on November 20, 1990, gave Thatcher, whose campaign had been poorly managed while she focused on European diplomacy, 204 votes, to Michael Heseltine's 152. This was not a wide-enough margin, by four votes, to prevent a second ballot, and raised the prospect of Heseltine gaining sufficient momentum to win, as Thatcher herself had done when replacing Heath in 1975. The public watched *House of Cards*, a fictional television drama series about murderous goings on as a Conservative succession was being contested, a series later transposed by Kevin Spacey to the United States. In fact, in 1990, the real party leaders plotted, Major himself making public reference to *House of Cards*. Thatcher was made aware that much of her Cabinet was unwilling to support her automatically on a second ballot. Determined to block Heseltine, a persistent critic of hers, and the candidate of the left of the party, but now aware she might not be able to do so on a second ballot, Thatcher stood down as prime minister and leader of the Conservative Party on November 22. For her successor, she supported the relatively inexperienced chancellor of the exchequer, Major, and on November 27, on the second ballot, he won, defeating Heseltine and Hurd.[13] The 1980s were over.

The long-term impact of Thatcher and Thatcherism is less clear. It is misleading to exaggerate the impact of government and, indeed, of a particular period of government by one party, or one strand within a party, and, accordingly, to attribute all or most change in a period to state initiatives or policies. Successive public opinion polls in the 1980s and early 1990s in practice revealed limited support for much of the agenda of the "New Right," with its emphasis on self-reliance and a limited role for the state. Instead, there was clear popular backing for the welfare state, especially the NHS, the latter a persistent theme. Similarly, the recessions of the early 1980s and early 1990s did not lead to a revival of left-wing radicalism. The hard core of the Communist Party who refused to accept reconfiguration into Democratic Left put up four candidates in the general election of 1992, only for them to win an average of 150 votes.

Nevertheless, whatever the limits, there were major developments under Thatcher in the nature of public policy and in the character of state and society. The privatization of many nationalized industries was important, as was the preference for market mechanisms as opposed to planning and state pricing. Under Thatcher, there was a thorough and widespread assault on trade unionism in order to further her goals of economic growth and individual freedom: picketing and secondary strike action were greatly limited, preentry closed shops largely abolished, and unions forced to ballot members by post before strikes were called. Fixed-term contracts for employees became more common. In the late 1980s, trade union militancy, which had been a very serious problem, became less common, and the level of industrial action (strikes) continued to fall in the early 1990s. By 1990, only 48 percent of employees were union members and the number covered by closed-shop agreements had fallen to 0.5 million, compared with 4.5 million a decade earlier. Trades Union Congress membership, more than 13 million in 1979, fell to 7.3 million by January 1994, although this was not the total trade union membership, which remained well over 8 million. Although membership displayed a considerable degree of resilience in the old heartlands of unionism, the unions failed to capture sufficient new members in the growth sectors and growth regions of the 1980s.[14] Far more wage negotiations were at a local level by 1990, there were fewer demarcation disputes, and the spread of "single-union agreements" eased industrial tension. Thanks to privatization in the 1980s and early 1990s, fewer trade unionists, moreover, were the employees of state-owned companies.

After Thatcher's death, Tony Blair commented, "I think the trade union framework, the privatisation of certain industries, and some of the things that she did in relation to tax and spending, this is part of the common political consensus now."[15] On balance, Thatcher was historically necessary and deserves praise and thanks for much that she did. She divided, but she certainly ruled. Not all agreed, as the trend in Labour politics in the 2010s, and very much from 2015, made clear. The consequences of Thatcher are still bitterly debated. However, contemporaries and commentators, whether supportive or not, and whether British or not, were, and are, certain that Britain in 1990, whatever the continuities,[16] was different to the situation in 1979. Serious issues and weaknesses remained, but the country no longer appeared ungovernable.

8

CHANGING DIRECTIONS, 1990–

INITIALLY SEEN AS a stop-gap until a likely Labour victory at the general election due in 1992 at the latest, John Major, a politician who had come through the middle to win the leadership, proved both more and less successful than might have been expected. More because he was prime minister for six and a half years, winning the 1992 general election and also seeing off challenges from within the Conservative Party. In the event, Major was prime minister for longer than Heath or Callaghan, or, indeed Eden, Douglas-Home, and (later) Brown, Cameron, May, Johnson, and Truss. He held on to power as Douglas-Home, having replaced Macmillan, had not been able to do in 1964. Moreover, in 1995, Major faced down opposition by resigning as party leader and, on July 4, winning reelection in a contest with John Redwood, the candidate of the Euroskeptic Right, whereas May, Johnson, and Truss all fell in the face of opposition from within the party.

Less successful, however, because Major's years in office witnessed serious blows to governmental policy, a disunited ministry that seriously lost public confidence, and a party that was increasingly divided and tarnished in its public reputation. In addition, having clung on to office for five years after the election, Major was very heavily defeated by Labour under Tony Blair in the general election in 1997, resigning the day after. This defeat was much heavier than those suffered by Douglas-Home in 1964 or Heath in 1974 or to be suffered by Brown in 2010 and May in 2017.

Major came from a very different background than his 1990 rivals for the leadership, Heseltine and Hurd. The son of a circus artiste and a garden-gnome maker, Major had faced a youth that was far from affluent, left school at sixteen, did not go to university, and later had a period of unemployment. In his opening campaign statement, Major came out strongly for a classless society and made a positive impact, as Theresa May was to do in 2016.

Once elected leader, the pleasant, thoughtful but uncharismatic[1] and thin-skinned Major was less able to control developments than most prime ministers and, crucially, unable to create a sense that he was in control. From this, flowed many of his difficulties with his colleagues, party, and the public. He lacked any distinctive ideas or policies with which to find favor with the electorate and was very readily contrasted with Thatcher. In part, Major continued the direction of Thatcherite policies, privatizing the railways in 1991, but without her drive, charisma, or, from 1992, parliamentary strength.

When Major did attempt to strike a new note, as with his call in 1993 for a return to basic values, the private lives of some of his ministers led to accusations of hypocrisy, although that would have been the case with all prime ministers. Even more so would it have been the case had it been known that the married Major had had an affair, while a minister, with Edwina Currie, a married ministerial colleague. This gave rise to the repeat of one of the more memorable political lines of the period. When the affair was subsequently revealed, Major said that he was deeply embarrassed, to which Currie responded, "That was not what he said at the time." That Major was able to keep the affair secret while in office reflected the degree to which press intrusion could be held at bay.

Major can be blamed for fatuous ideas such as "the Citizen's Charter," the "quality of life" debate, and, more positively, in part held responsible for Ofsted (the intrusive but valuable schools inspectorate). More seriously in the 1990s, the European issue gravely and publicly divided the Conservative Party, inside and outside Parliament (see chapter 10). As a result, Major was hit hard, and he also left his successors as party leaders with a difficult legacy. In addition, the economy faced serious problems, with the recession of the early 1990s leading to unemployment rising, inflation in double figures, and high levels of individual debt. These problems were also seen elsewhere around the world, but those in Britain were widely blamed on the Conservative government.

Labour victory was widely anticipated in the election held on April 9, 1992, but its leader, the verbose and conceited Neil Kinnock, often referred to as a "Welsh windbag," was widely disliked and there was a strong suspicion that taxes would rise sharply if Labour gained power. Labour was not able to win over many Conservative voters or those of the Liberal Democrats. Ditching Thatcher had enabled the Conservatives to shed some of the unpopular legacy of the 1980s, and, in a preelection budget, Major offered attractive tax cuts. Indeed, tax was a key issue in this election. Major was also strongly supported by the *Sun* newspaper, which suggested that a Kinnock victory might lead to mass emigration (indeed, everyone leaving the country). In 1991, Tony Benn, from the Labour Left, had remarked, "I think the culture of subservience in Britain is the real characteristic of our society. . . . I think it is time we took off our caps and straightened our forelocks and decided to do something about it."[2] The electorate was not interested. The Conservatives promised a significant increase in public spending as part of their election manifesto, which was to put major pressure on public borrowing.

The election took place in the aftermath of a war, the first Gulf War against Saddam Hussein of Iraq, fought in 1991. In this war, Britain had played a significant role as part of an American-led coalition supporting a UN resolution to drive Iraq from Kuwait. Victory was rapidly achieved, and the costs to Britain were far lower than those encountered in defeating Argentina in the Falklands War. Major, however, did not really benefit electorally. Conversely, his reputation did not suffer as that of Blair was to do seriously and lastingly from the second Gulf War in 2003 and its aftermath, notably suggestions that he had lied.

The Conservatives did well in percentage terms in the 1992 election. However, their overall majority, of only twenty-one, was small because of tactical voting by Labour and Liberal opponents. The alignment of the non-Conservative majority as an anti-Conservative majority was to be even more significant in the election of 1997 but was not to recur in 2010, 2015, or 2019, although there were signs of it in 2017. As a different aspect of the election, over 20 percent of 18- to 25-year-olds had not registered to vote in 1992. This suggested a wider disenchantment with politics, one also seen with a low youth vote in the 2016 EU referendum.

His small majority gravely hamstrung Major in the face of serious party differences over Europe, as he was therefore highly vulnerable to rebellions from within the parliamentary party. Moreover, the government's failure on September 16, 1992, Black Wednesday, despite major efforts, to keep sterling in the Exchange Rate Mechanism (ERM) for European currencies, which entailed an agreed currency exchange band, proved a humiliating defeat for economic policy. On September 16, interest rates were raised from 10 percent, first to 12 percent and then 15 percent. Moreover, a large amount of the reserves were spent in an attempt to prop up sterling. The failure to stay in the ERM led to a collapse in public confidence in the government as a whole. Major sacrificed a close ally, Norman Lamont, chancellor of the exchequer, in May 1993 (as Truss was also to do with Kwasi Kwarteng in 2022), but this did not rescue the political situation (see chapter 10). In December 1994, there was a particularly sharp drop in consumer confidence. There was not to be a sharper drop until immediately after the Brexit vote in 2016.

Divisions, notably over Britain's position in the EU, seriously sapped Conservative unity, purpose, and popularity even when the economy markedly recovered from the mid-1990s, with inflation falling to 1.3 percent in May 1993. Rebound played a role, but so too did a rapid and aggressive cutting of interest rates to 6 percent, as well as two tax-raising budgets that limited domestic consumer spending, while lower interest rates and a pound that fell by 15 percent stimulated exports and investments. The economic recovery, however, brought less of a feel-good factor than in the recoveries of the 1980s, in part because property prices did not rise. Strongly hostile in successive local (notably May 5, 1994, and May 4, 1995) a contrast to the situation in the early 2010s prior to the 2015 election, and by-elections (notably July 29, 1993; June 9, 1994; December 17, 1994; May 25, 1995; and July 27, 1995), the electorate was not inclined to reward the increasingly exhausted government.

A strongly hostile media did not help. It made much of "Tory sleaze," which became a significant story from 1994, although the extent of the corruption involved was very small by international standards. Indeed, compared to France, India, Italy, Japan, or the United States, Britain remained singularly uncorrupt. Nevertheless, that helped to ensure high standards that a number of Conservative parliamentarians could not meet and clearly had no intention of trying to meet. A key issue was that of MPs asking parliamentary questions in return for payments. This was seen, and certainly presented, as unacceptable influence peddling and served to taint the entire parliamentary party, although most MPs were not involved.[3] So also with the deceit seen under the Johnson government of 2019–22.

Staying in office as long as he could, Major limped on until the 1997 election, held on May 1, but, against a backdrop of consistently bad results in local elections, its result surprised few. The Conservatives lost heavily in England, while a collapse of their support cost them all their seats in Scotland and Wales. Labour, with 418 seats, won a big overall majority of 179 seats. The Labour vote had not really risen, but rather, that of the Conservatives had fallen greatly compared to the 1992 results, thus ensuring that the Labour share of the vote rose by 10.8 percent on the 1992 figure. Many Conservatives did not vote for anyone, ensuring that the number of electors who voted overall in the general election fell. Some Conservatives voted for the new Referendum Party as a protest against Major's European policy, a situation that was to recur with UKIP in the 2015 election. The Referendum Party, which demanded a referendum on whether Britain should be "part of a federal Europe," did not win any seats, but it appeared to cost the Conservatives several of theirs. The Conservatives had not lost so many seats in any election since their rout by the Liberals in 1906, after which they had not formed a majority government until 1922.

The victorious and youthful Tony Blair, Labour's leader since the death of John Smith in 1994, fought on the platform of "New Labour." In particular, there was a move by Blair away from collectivist solutions based on state planning and toward, instead, aspects of Thatcherism, not least the role of the marketplace and modest rates of taxation.[4] There were still important differences between the parties, but, as with Butskellism in the 1950s and the absence of socialism from the minority Labour governments of the 1920s, and later with the Sunak–Starmer leaderships of 2022–23, the similarities were also striking, and, indeed, more notable than on these earlier occasions. In economic and ideological terms, nationalization of the means of production was rejected as a goal, with the dropping in 1995, as Hugh Gaitskell had not succeeded in doing in 1960, of the traditional clause four of the historic Labour constitution. With that, the *Marxisant* strand in Labour was discarded and as part of a wider Labour loss of early sources of inspiration.[5]

Compared by some to Thatcherism without tears, or as a clone of the US Democratic Party, Labour now appropriated the rhetoric of "one nation" Conservatism in all but name: "New Labour" appeared to offer a more appealing vision of life in post-Thatcher Britain, by championing a society in which the dominance of the marketplace was not to be allowed to undermine social cohesion. Moral purpose was affirmed, and, more specifically, one that Blair saw as more appropriate for the condition of the country than that of Thatcher. Indeed, it was a new, modern corporatism that was on offer, one open to global capitalism but seeing this as a means to community, idealism, and even equality. Terms such as *comrade* ceased to be part of the lexicon of the party, and links with the trade unions were downplayed or cut, and certainly so compared with earlier times.[6]

This trend in Labour ideas and language also had a symbolic aspect. Although its subsequent failure led the Labour government to seek to distance itself from the Millennium Dome, the project was earlier seen as an affirmation of the government's determination to modernize Britain. It was deliberately decided to exclude any section on national history from the dome's contents. Blair also condemned the weight of the past when decrying sectarianism in

Northern Ireland and former Yugoslavia. In December 1999, Blair rounded on critics of the dome project whom, he claimed, with no evidence, "despise anything modern," and stated, instead, that the dome was a "triumph of confidence over cynicism, boldness over blandness, excellence over mediocrity." The opening ceremony was similarly used to affirm an image of modernity, although, in the event, the entire project revealed the folly of the government's claims and the tackiness of the scheme. It did not compare well with the Great Exhibition of 1851 or the Festival of Britain of 1951.

"Modernization" of the country became a focus of government activity, and this modernization led to large-scale constitutional change. Key points were the establishment of a Scottish Parliament and a Welsh Assembly and the removal of most of the hereditary peerage from the House of Lords, although there was no significant reform of the appointment of other peers. Moreover, under the Greater London Authority Act of 1999, the Greater London Council (GLC) was in large part restored, although in a different form. Referenda in Scotland and Wales played a role in this process, but there were no referenda in Britain as a whole. The criticism of referenda as un-British in the 2010s, on the grounds that Britain was a parliamentary democracy, and not a plebiscitary one, looks somewhat surprising given the referenda of 1975, 1979, and 1997, and so also with the high level of constitutional change. As another break with the past, a law was passed in 1998 that stopped the creation of new grammar schools in England beyond the current 163.

The economic growth that had followed the recovery from the recession of the early 1990s and the abandonment of the European ERM, benefited the Blair, not the Major, government, as rising tax revenues served to support its social programs across the country. Indeed, the financial sector was cited as an equivalent to North Sea oil and was treated with a similar lightness of regulation and with a comparably favorable tax regime. Financiers, and the architects they sponsored, referred to London as Manhattan-on-Thames. It provided the key setting for Labour's pursuit, at once nervy in manner and complacent in practice, of an image of "Cool Britannia." In certain respects, this was another version of Wilson's image in the 1960s. The money made helped fund the purchase of BritArt (see chapter 4).

The ban on fox hunting with hounds (see chapter 1) was an aspect of modernization, as well as a move aimed against conservative rural society. Ironically, this led to one of the biggest demonstrations of the period: a quarter of a million people took part when the newly formed Countryside Alliance staged a demonstration in London in 1998 against the measure. Blair no more paid attention than he did to the even larger demonstration in London in 2003 against taking military action against Iraq.

Meanwhile, in control of both Cabinet and Parliament, and, for both, to an unprecedented extent for a Labour prime minister (although not of his chancellor of the exchequer, Gordon Brown), and making obsessive, bullying, and generally highly successful efforts at news management, Blair was castigated for being presidential. The notion of an "elective dictatorship," which had been advanced as a criticism of the Labour government in the 1970s and of Thatcher, appeared to have been adopted as a means of government from the outset by the autocratic Blair. Cabinet meetings were frequently short, and Blair limited the number of occasions on which he appeared in Parliament and thus could be questioned there. His informal and personal style was described as "sofa government," and he preferred those of Cameron and Johnson. Blair was more autocratic than Thatcher but avoided being pilloried for this. Alistair Campbell, his news manager, proved brutally successful in preventing or limiting criticism. The dysfunctional nature of the government, however, contributed greatly to the nature of decision making in the run-up to the invasion of Iraq in 2003. The Chilcot Inquiry, published in 2016, revealed major flaws, not least arising from Blair's ability to circumvent critical ministers.

Blair easily won the general election held in 2001. Standing on a manifesto similar to that in 1997, he benefited from his continuation of the Conservative policy on keeping income tax low and from the economic growth of the late 1990s. Inflation, interest rates, and unemployment were all low. Moreover, the Conservatives continued to lack traction under Major's successor, William Hague, a talented leader who could not identify a plausible program and who was unfairly stigmatized as overly populist by an unsympathetic media. Hague had beaten the more experienced Ken Clarke for the leadership in 1997 because the latter advocated Britain joining the eurozone. Blair was far smoother than Hague in his presentation. As a result of a modest recovery in the Conservative vote, the 2001 election left Labour with a smaller share of the vote but with a still-commanding majority of 167.

Nevertheless, confidence in Labour's intentions, integrity, and competence had already been hit by its years in office. A series of controversies linked to corruption by figures close to Blair did not help. This corruption began from the outset, with the donation of a large sum of money to Labour by Bernie Ecclestone, the leading figure in motor racing, being linked by critics to the government changing policy to his benefit. Blair's Svengali, Peter Mandelson, was involved in scandals over his purchase of a house and over intervening to gain citizenship for two Indian businessmen who gave money to the party. Subsequently, David Blunkett, the blind home secretary, had a somewhat implausible affair with a Conservative journalist, and John Prescott, the Labour deputy leader, was involved in another sex scandal. There was a major "cash for honors" scandal in 2006 with Blair interviewed three times by the police as part of a criminal investigation, although no charges were brought against him. The press, however, did not investigate as hard as they had done for the Tory "sleaze" in the early 1960s and mid-1990s. Indeed, the contrast suggested wider questions about bias.

This was also true of the failure to devote due attention to the serious rivalry at the center of government between Blair and the chancellor of the exchequer, Gordon Brown. Bitter about not becoming party leader in 1994 and thus prime minister in 1997, Brown continually intrigued against Blair and the Blairites. Brown built up a following among trade union–linked MPs, and among the Scottish MPs and many of the North of England ones. He claimed to be a modernizer but was, in practice, psychologically opposed to the metropolitan, southern ambience of politics associated with Blair. This rivalry gravely weakened the purpose of government by introducing a fundamental division.

More seriously under Blair, and despite rising expenditure, notably on the NHS, there was concern about the ability to improve public services. Labour increasingly appeared corporatist, with the bold rhetoric of the first term, of supposedly thinking the unthinkable in social policy, replaced by an absence of fundamental reform and, instead, by a commitment to a cultural and complacent approach to public service, as in a quasi-mystical positive presentation of the NHS. Partisanship and cronyism were also very much to the fore. This was apparent in the establishment and use of regulatory bodies. Under Major, regulation had been devised for privatized quasi-monopolies (e.g., Ofwat for the water suppliers), in order to prevent them from exploiting their economic power. This was done with reasonable objectivity, by mechanisms such as the permitted return on regulatory capital employed.

In contrast, Blair and Brown extended the agenda and, to a degree, wanted the regulators to be agencies of transformation, notably the social change that their government sought. John Prescott, Labour's deputy leader, told the Labour conference in 1998 that he was going to have a "spring clean of the regulators," and this was followed by a politicized approach to selecting the heads of the regulators and a politicized approach to the stance adopted by the regulators. New bodies included the Food Standards Agency (2001), Ofcom (2001), the Financial Services Agency (2001), the Pensions Regulator (2004), and the

Equality and Human Rights Commission (2006). Aspects of financial regulation, such as the Financial Services Ombudsman, became more concerned with championing consumers than acting as objective regulators.

Far less attention was devoted to securing the economic growth able to pay for government ambitions and commitments, including the inefficient and centralist system of the NHS. Indeed, structural economic problems such as low productivity became more serious. Thus, domestic demand outgrew the economy, fueling imports. As an instance of the selective nature of public expenditure, the NHS and rapidly rising social welfare payments took precedence over the provision of housing or investment in the energy and transport systems. Indeed, a serious charge against the Blair government was not so much that it spent too much on the public sector but that it spent with deeply flawed priorities, and notably as far as economic growth was concerned. The consequences were readily apparent in the economy in the 2010s and 2020s and notably as far as the infrastructure was concerned.

Another charge against Blair related to the inability, in a benign politico-economic period of solid parliamentary majorities, economic growth, and rising tax revenues, to improve the situation so that the UK would be able to cope with adverse circumstances more easily than was to turn out to be the case from the late 2000s. A key problem was that of the failure to cut or alter government expenditure and to influence public assumptions accordingly. Instead, the economy was left to Brown, the chancellor of the exchequer, who proved far less able than he and others claimed then and subsequently, while Blair devoted too much attention to imagery, foreign policy, and, arguably, Northern Ireland. These faults became very apparent in hindsight, although, at the time, perceptive commentators noted all of these points. By 2000, "Cool Britannia" was ebbing, and the rhetoric of Blairism appeared increasingly ridiculous, although the Conservatives were stuck electorally and in a bitter struggle between "modernizers" and their opponents.

Meanwhile, the al-Qaeda attacks on the United States in 2001 led to new and acute concern about the nature of British multiculturalism. A failure to control Islamic extremists had already resulted in French antiterrorist police referring to Londonistan. This term became more common, not least because of the inability of the government to prevent radical Muslim preaching that stirred up hatred against the host society.

Deadly suicide bomb attacks on the London Tube and bus system on July 7, 2005, lent fresh point to these concerns, which were exacerbated by the hunt for other would-be bombers. The febrile atmosphere of July 2005 highlighted worries that Britain's traditional tolerance, and especially the openness to immigrants and multiculturalism, might be sowing the seeds for mass destruction or at least large-scale murder. Being very close to the site of one of the 2005 bombings that morning, I can testify to the shock that day in Central London. Subsequently, walking back to Paddington Station (the Tube was shut), it was the quiet of the city that struck me. A Londoner by birth and upbringing, I had never known it that quiet, a quiet somewhat mocked by the brightness of the sunshine.

Thanks again to Conservative unpopularity under a new leader, Michael Howard, whose appeal outside the party core was weak, Blair had easily won the 2005 election, with 356 seats to the 198 won by the Conservatives. The Conservatives remained largely a party of the south of England. At this rate of improvement in results (from 1997 to 2001 and 2001 to 2005), it appeared that the Conservatives would never pass Labour, and hubristic commentators and others talked of the death of Conservative Britain. The other political parties remained minor, although both the Liberal Democrats and the Scottish National Party (SNP) were each becoming more prominent in electoral terms.

Nevertheless, the decision to support the United States in the attack on Iraq in 2003 greatly compromised Blair's popularity, especially within Labour. A number of prominent Labour figures, notably the former foreign secretary, Robin Cook, criticized the attack. It also proved unpopular at the constituency level, in part because of distrust of President George W. Bush and suspicion of Blair's intentions and probity. The scale of subsequent violence in Iraq kept it in the news. Alongside serious divisions within the government, the Gulf War led to his resignation in 2007. His failure to criticize Israel for the bombing of Lebanon in 2006 proved especially divisive as his government came to a close. Blair's wider popularity had also been shredded. In particular, the flair for presentation so readily apparent earlier was perceived as spin, and particularly so as far as his claims to integrity were concerned. He had also stayed in office for too long.

The Conservatives, meanwhile, in 2005 elected David Cameron as their leader, their sixth since summer 1990. Defeating David Davis, a right-wing rival, in the poll of party members, Cameron apparently represented a victory for modernization, although it was not clear what this was to mean. He was certainly a triumph of and for glibness.

Blair's lackluster Labour replacement, Gordon Brown, chancellor of the exchequer from 1997 to 2007 and prime minister from 2007 to 2010, proved an extraordinarily poor manager of the nation's finances. His taxation policies on dividends gravely weakened private pension schemes, challenging the interests of both employers and workers. That should be rephrased to private-sector employers and workers. Brown was far more prone to consider the interests of the public sector, and a contrast between its better pension provision and the deteriorating situation for most private-sector workers was a legacy of the Brown years. So also was an overemphasis on the already strong British practice of investing in property.

Moreover, Brown's policies contributed greatly, despite his repeated claims to the contrary, to Britain facing the worldwide fiscal crisis and economic recession that began in 2008 in a worse condition than other major countries. Brown's inadequate regulation of the financial sector had played a role in the development of excessive and risky liabilities on the part of the banks and in their serious exposure to adverse international developments. This situation produced a banking crisis, a drying-up of credit, and the triggering of a recession that owed much to a failure not only of the fiscal system but also of both government and people to live within their means. In a major shock, the economy shrank by 6.4 percent between the first quarter of 2008 and the fourth quarter of 2009. Unemployment rose to 7.2 percent in June 2009, which put serious additional burdens on public expenditure, underlining Brown's failure in the good years to tackle this problem. In response to the downturn, the Bank of England's benchmark interest rate was cut to 0.5 percent in 2009, a major blow to savers, and subsequently fell to 0.25 percent in 2016. However, there was a limit in what monetary policy could achieve, in part because the global recession reduced the options for export-led growth.

At the same time, there were, as on previous occasions, pronounced regional and local variations in economic circumstances. For example, to take the situation within a region, the June 2009 unemployment rates in London varied from 1.8 percent in the prosperous areas of Chelsea and Wimbledon to 7.4 percent in far poorer Hackney South and Shoreditch. Similarly, in the north, the cities of Manchester, Newcastle, Preston, and Wakefield did better in the early 2010s than those of Blackburn, Burnley, Hull, and Sunderland. However, the prime contrast was between the regions, notably between the north and south. Whereas, for example, Liverpool had employment rates in July 2009 to June 2010 of 62.7 percent and Sunderland of 64.9 percent, those for the southern cities of Milton Keynes and Bristol were 72.5 and 74.2 percent, respectively.

Partly as a result of economic problems, the expensive social democracy advocated by New Labour appeared unaffordable, although there was a widespread failure to accept this point. Britain ended up with a large budget deficit, a large public debt that was growing at a fast rate, and a large private debt, as well as a weak economy and inflation that was overtarget. Brown, who had publicly prided himself on his economic competence, appeared increasingly adrift, indeed incompetent. He was unwilling to confront the size of the public debt, and his grim public profile and serious temper tantrums suggested, to some observers, psychological issues. Brown was also guilty of humbug. Like other politicians, notably but not only Labour ones, he disguised his love for high living. Wilson liked smoking cigars but presented himself as a pipe smoker. Brown, who liked champagne, presented himself as a beer drinker.

On May 6, 2010, the unpopular and unengaging Brown lost the general election, which, like Major in 1997, he had delayed holding until the last possible moment. Labour won 29 percent of the vote and 258 seats, compared with 36.1 percent and 307 for the Conservatives, and 23.0 percent and 57 for the Liberal Democrats. The UK Independence Party (UKIP) gained 3.1 percent, the extremist Right British National Party (BNP) 1.9 percent, the SNP 1.7 percent, and the Greens 1.0 percent. Labour had 98 seats fewer than in 2005 and the Conservatives, who had started from a low base, 110 more (they had also won seats from the Liberals).

This result did not give the Conservatives sufficient seats for a majority, and over the following days, a tense series of negotiations saw Labour try to cling to power while the Liberal Democrats sought to play off both Conservatives and Labour. The possibility of Labour being kept in power by the Liberal Democrats, in a "popular front" of the Left, however, angered a number of Labour leaders who distrusted the Liberal Democrats. Moreover, in coalition negotiations, the Conservatives proved willing to offer the Liberal Democrats good terms, in part because they were overly convinced that such a "popular front" was a prospect. Chance played a major role, notably that Nick Clegg was the Liberal Democrat leader. Other prominent Liberal Democrats would have been less willing to join the Conservatives. At the same time, keeping the largest party, the Conservatives, from government at a time when Brown had been widely rejected, appeared wrong to many and would have created both a government with a weak parliamentary majority and an image of the Liberal Democrats as willing to thwart the public rejection of Brown.

In the end, the Conservatives and the Liberal Democrats formed a coalition, bringing to an end thirteen years of Labour government. David Cameron, the young Conservative leader since 2005, became prime minister and Clegg, deputy prime minister with them promising to work together for the sake of the economy for a fixed term of five years. There was little peacetime experience of coalition government, and the resulting agreement—notably Clegg abandoning a pledge to end university fees—led to a considerable amount of uninformed criticism, as neither Conservative nor Liberal supporters, especially the latter, appreciated the compromises involved. The Liberal

Democrats successfully insisted on a fixed-term, five-year Parliament, on a referendum on proportional representation, on reforming the House of Lords, and on raising the income tax threshold but had to abandon pledges to end nuclear power and the nuclear deterrent. The Conservatives lost out on inheritance tax, the replacement of the Human Rights Act, and an end to the West Lothian question: the ability, since Scottish devolution in 1989, for Scottish MPs to vote on English domestic matters but not vice versa. There was suspicion on the part of those on the Right of the Conservative Party that Cameron, a self-styled modernizer, preferred a coalition as it gave him an opportunity both not to depend on the Right and to abandon unwelcome pledges. There was also disappointment that Cameron had not won an absolute majority. In practice, the coalition government, which enjoyed a substantial parliamentary majority, proved viable and reasonably stable. Cameron was widely perceived as charming and was reasonably effective in the House of Commons, although the "chumocracy" that greatly characterized his Blairite handling of patronage alienated many Conservative MPs, and he displayed very poor judgment in some cases, notably in his handling of press links.

The parlous state of the nation's finances in the aftermath of the 2008–9 recession, and the fact that the government spent about half of the national income, notably on the NHS and on social welfare, led Cameron to emphasize public expenditure cuts, alongside his earlier vague plans for a "big society" in which public activism and noblesse oblige replaced or supplemented some of the social welfare functions of government. The latter were certainly caught short, most prominently with the closure of public restrooms, over 1,700 of which closed in the UK from the mid-2000s to the mid-2010s. Moreover, some local authorities, including Newcastle and Merthyr Tydfil, had none by 2016, while Manchester had only one. A different form of public deprivation was provided by the decline in average travel speeds, notably for buses, as a result of the increase in the number of minicabs and of delivery vans moving Internet shopping. By the end of 2015, the average speed of traffic on all local roads had fallen to 23.4 miles per hour in the morning rush hour.

At the same time, the coalition government struggled with a range of problems, especially an overambitious and costly military intervention in Afghanistan begun under Blair and the difficulties of funding pensions in the state sector. Economic problems, and notably the weak nature of the recovery, hit government finances, and in 2011, the budget deficit was about 8.8 percent of GDP. A convinced and overt Keynesian who emphasized the value of reflationary spending, Brown had not responded in 2008–10 by limiting government expenditure or public expectations, or facing up to the difficulties posed, and this inadequate response left the coalition with a very difficult legacy as it sought to impose austerity in order to cut the debt without exacerbating economic problems.

The possibility of public discontent was indicated by riots in London in August 2011, riots in which anger with the police and looting for consumer goods both played a role. The number of rioters was relatively small, but a delayed response exacerbated the situation and the rioters made good use of social media in order to organize and to thwart the police. Moreover, violence spread to Birmingham and then to Manchester, Merseyside, and Nottingham. Ultimately, after five people had been killed in the riots, order was restored by concentrating police from across England in London, which, however, provided opportunities for criminals elsewhere. More than three thousand people were arrested in the riots. Combined with the later comments by the chief constable of Nottinghamshire that he doubted whether the county police force could maintain order adequately, there were signs of a possible future crisis in public order.

An important index of social strain was provided by the rising use of food banks. In 2015, the Trussell Trust, which runs more than 420 food bank, gave out 1.1 million three-day emergency food packages. The Food Foundation suggested that more than eight million people in Britain lived in households that cannot always afford enough to eat. The burdens of divorce and debt played a major role in creating the widespread need for food banks, as did the rising cost of rent.

At a different level of debt, Osborne made winning Chinese investment a major goal. In 2015, Britain agreed to support the China-led Asian Infrastructure Bank, much to the irritation of the United States, and he sought large-scale Chinese investment for Britain's energy and rail systems. In 2000–15, China provided more direct investment in Britain than in any other EU state.

A degree of recovery from the economic and fiscal crisis of the late 2000s, from early 2013, and a rise in the housing market helped the Conservatives to victory in the 2015 general election. They also benefited from winning the 2014 referendum on Scottish independence (see chapter 9), and, even more, from the unpopularity of the Liberal Democrats, their former coalition partner who wanted to fight the election separately. Already, in May 2011, the Liberal Democrats had done very differently in the local council elections, losing 748 seats, as well as seeing the proportional representation they had backed defeated in a referendum by 67.9 percent to 32.1 percent on a turnout of 42.2 percent.

The inability of Labour to achieve an electoral breakthrough was also important in 2015. Its leader from 2010, Ed Miliband, struck many as unlikely to prove a good prime minister and as overly left wing. Labour's economic management and understanding of the market economy were not trusted. These flaws were admitted to in the memoirs of Ed Balls, the Labour shadow chancellor from 2010 to 2015, which were published in 2016. Both Balls and Miliband were former aides of Brown. Balls was very critical of Miliband's failure to face realities. In addition, there was widespread opposition in England to the idea of a Labour government dependent on support from the SNP, which was correctly seen as likely to do very well.

In the voting, Labour's share rose but only from 29 percent in 2010 to 30.4 percent. A modest swing from the Conservatives to Labour in England won Labour seats, notably in London, but Labour lost all bar one of its Scottish seats to the SNP, while the Liberal Democrat collapse to only eight seats benefited the Conservatives, particularly, but not only, in South West England and especially in Cornwall. Given the choice of how best to vote against Labour, there was more support for the Conservatives than the Liberal Democrats. With 7.9 percent of the votes, Liberal Democrats suffered very badly electorally from having been in coalition between 2010 and 2015, which is the usual risk for smaller parties in coalition government. Cameron and Clegg between them had greatly weakened the Liberal Democrats. Overall, Labour won 30.4 percent and the Conservatives 36.9 percent.

Moreover, the anti-EU UKIP, under its showman leader Nigel Farage, although only winning one parliamentary seat, gained 12.6 percent of the vote (and over 14 percent in England), 3.8 million votes in total, taking more votes from Labour than had been anticipated. About one million voters deserted Labour for UKIP in 2015, which prefigured the Conservative success in 2019. Instead of winning essentially discontented Conservative votes in the South, as had been anticipated, UKIP showed that it had considerable traction in Labour's working-class strongholds in the North and the Midlands, although not in Scotland. UKIP success ensured that the Conservatives had a far higher percentage of the vote than Labour. Plaid Cymru did not achieve a breakthrough in Wales comparable to that of the SNP, and, although winning more votes, the Greens failed to gain more seats than the one they already held. However, the effect of the percentages won by UKIP, the SNP (4.7 percent), the Liberal Democrats, the Greens (3.8 percent), and Plaid Cymru was to ensure that the joint Conservative and Labour share was the lowest since 1945.

Many Conservative leaders were surprised by the result. They had assumed that they would defeat Labour anew to be the largest party but that they would again lack an overall majority and need to enter into a coalition agreement with the Liberal Democrats. In line with the public opinion polls, neither did the leaders (nor indeed the betting market) assume an overall Conservative majority, and the results caused much surprise among commentators and raised questions about the accuracy of polls.

Once victorious, however, the Conservatives dissipated their advantage, notably by dividing very publicly and bitterly over Europe in 2016, as a referendum on continued membership of the EU drove out other issues. Having failed to convince either his party supporters or the country, Cameron resigned in 2016 immediately after his EU referendum failure on June 23. In addition, the uneasiness of much of the public with the condition of the country affected support for the government. In particular, there was only limited backing for further austerity. Indeed, the backing, such as it was, did not extend to the NHS, while, in the face of opposition within the parliamentary party and Cabinet, the government failed in early 2016 in its attempt to stop the marked rise in disability payments. Despite his call at the 2015 party conference for a "one nation" government and for social reform, Cameron was increasingly perceived as out of touch and complacent, both charges that had always been pertinent.

However, as Labour moved leftward from 2015, becoming very much the product of a particular type of activist, it also failed to convince. This created a considerable political opportunity for Cameron, one he lost by holding the referendum. Miliband resigned after the 2015 election. The subsequent Labour leadership election was won by none of the experienced candidates but by Jeremy Corbyn, a left-wing maverick who benefited from a decision to allow anyone to vote in the election in return for a nominal £3 subscription as an associate party member. Corbyn's success and subsequent performance led to serious dissension, with much of the parliamentary party unwilling to follow his lead leftward and many unwilling to serve in the Shadow Cabinet. They argued that Corbyn's policies were not shaped to the electorate, nor, necessarily, to Britain's first-past-the-post electoral system. Meanwhile, Corbyn's supporters sought to use their position to drive moderates from their position in the party. This included a measure of intimidation and some violence.

The local elections of May 2016 revealed little public enthusiasm for politicians or the political parties. In particular, there was a marked cultural disconnect across much of Britain between the fashionably radical middle-class Labour activists and the concerns of much of the working class.[7] Benefiting from ethnic-minority votes, Labour won the London mayoralty from the Conservatives but did not enjoy comparable success elsewhere. This encouraged the sense of Labour as metropolitan if not different. Meanwhile, in 2016, the Conservatives, at least under Cameron, did not engage with the working class either.

To add to this sense of political dysfunctionality, the new Liberal Democrat leader lacked traction, UKIP under Farage provided an object lesson in infantile backstabbing before he finally stood down to be rapidly followed by his successor, the Greens ditched their unsuccessful leader, and the SNP lost its majority in the Scottish Parliament. The background to the referendum on continued EU membership was one of a political world presided over by seriously limited individuals, some of whom appeared to have become party leaders by mistake or, more accurately, the failures of others.

At the same time, there was a broader dissatisfaction with politics and government. This took a variety of forms, from anger with specific policies to a more general hostility toward being told what to do. A lack of "civic engagement" or interest was clearly displayed in the decline in the percentage of the population that voted in general elections. Even the EU referendum had a turnout of only 72 percent, with younger voters, the group who most supported staying in the EU, being particularly disinclined to vote.

This decline was separate to that of confidence in the idea of nationhood, but a variety of indications suggested that such confidence was lacking among many. They identified with subsectors—for example, place, ethnicity, religion, or football team—but often found it hard or very difficult to link this to Britishness other than in a somewhat vague fashion.

More specific hostility toward being told what to do was focused on environmental changes that apparently threatened long-established practices. Thus, public opinion polls revealed the persistence of long-standing popular opposition to genetically modified crops and foods, even though they require less artificial fertilizer. So also in the 2010s with hostility to fracking for shale gas. In 2016, North Yorkshire Council received 4,800 representations on a proposed fracking site at Kirby Misperton, with the overwhelming majority opposed.

As a result of the political crisis and chaos that followed the EU referendum, by late summer 2016 the future of Britain's place in the world, of the UK as a united country, and of the political system, all appeared unclear to many commentators. Despite the generally positive response to the capable, moderate, and reassuring Theresa May when she succeeded Cameron as Conservative leader and prime minister in July, and the likelihood that she would dominate a political scene further emptied by Labour's bitter civil war, optimism about new beginnings was very much in short supply. It was widely assumed that May would not be able to negotiate an agreement with the EU. In the event, she did, but agreement proved impossible for a divided Conservative party. In order to strengthen her position, May had held a general election on June 8, 2017, but the campaigning was over-lengthy and the Conservatives lost control of the dynamic of electioneering, not least as the result of controversy over social care reforms. The Conservative share of the vote rose from 36.9 in 2015 to 42.3, its highest since 1983, and Labour's from 30.4 to 40.0, its highest since 2001, with UKIP seeing its percentage fall from 12.6 to 1.8. The Conservatives lost 13 seats, the SNP 21, and UKIP its only seat, while Labour added 30 and the Liberal Democrats 4. The Conservatives lost their working majority and continued in office with support from the Democratic Unionist Party. From then on, May was in a weak position. In December 2018 she won a vote of confidence in her leadership of the Conservative party, and a parliamentary vote of confidence the following January, but was thrice defeated by substantial majorities on the EU withdrawal deal in January–March 2019. These were comprised of the opposition and a minority of Conservative MPs. In the face of growing opposition within the party, May resigned as party leader on June 7.

Her successor, Boris Johnson, had been Mayor of London (2008–16) and Foreign Secretary (2016–19) and a prominent campaigner for Brexit. Winning the leadership election in July 2019, Johnson controversially prorogued Parliament that September in order to hold off parliamentary criticism of the Brexit negotiations. A revised withdrawal agreement hit parliamentary problems. Criticism and a wish to win through the deadlock led Johnson to call an election on December 12, 2019.

Jeremy Corbyn won the election, but for the Conservatives. On many doorsteps, he was the issue. The Conservative vote percentage increased to 43.6 (365 seats; plus 48), and Labour's fell to 32.1 (202; minus 60), with the SNP gaining 48 seats (plus 13) and the Liberal Democrats 11 (minus one, on 11.6 percent). The Conservative victory included many in long-held Labour seats, called "the red wall," which had voted for Brexit, for example Ashfield, Bassetlaw, Bishop Auckland, Blyth Valley, Bolsover, Sedgefield, and Workington. Johnson pressed on to implement Brexit on January 31, 2020. Labour still had a strong presence in the North, notably the Northeast and Merseyside, as well as South Wales. It was also strongly backed in London and by university cities, such as Cambridge, Canterbury, Exeter, Oxford, and Plymouth.

Johnson's triumph was short-lived. After having to respond to floods in northern England, Johnson's government was swamped by the COVID-19 pandemic. Initially, the government sought to avoid lockdown, but in March 2020 a lockdown throughout the UK was imposed, while soon after Johnson tested positive for COVID-19 and in April spent several days in intensive care. The lockdown and programs of financial support placed heavy burdens on the public finances. In October 2020, a second national program was imposed, a third following in January 2021. Meanwhile, infighting in the government saw the dismissal of Johnson's chief adviser, Dominic Cummings, in November 2020. In turn, Cummings publicly challenged Johnson's judgment and integrity from April 2021, helping begin a longstanding crisis over Johnson's conduct and honesty. Johnson survived a vote of confidence in June 2022 but by-election defeats and fresh criticism of Johnson's judgment and favoritism forced him to resign in July 2022. Like May, he had been leader for less time than Corbyn who had resigned after the 2019 election.

The subsequent leadership campaign was won by Liz Truss who set out for a new record in brevity, announcing her resignation in October 2022 on her forty-fifth day in office. Gaining Cabinet office under Cameron, May, and Johnson, Truss favored growth through financial pump-priming, but this was harshly received by the financial markets, who opposed tax cuts and greater borrowing. Political and public confidence had always been somewhat limited, and the budget acted as the lightning rod for the sense of crisis that forced her resignation.

In turn becoming Prime Minister in October 2022, Rishi Sunak was a product of a different society to that into which he had been born in 1980, and, even more, that when his parents of Indian descent immigrated from East Africa to Southampton in the 1960s. The first British Asian and Hindu to become Prime Minister, he had been beaten by Truss, only to replace her. He came to office facing a formidably difficult political situation, most clearly due to the nature of the fiscal crisis. Moreover, the public opinion polls were highly unfavorable, Labour leading 47 percent to 30 percent at the start of November 2022. At that stage, the possibility of Sunak winning the next election appeared remote. This was even more the case by July 2023 when the percentages were 47 and 22.

9

BRITISH ISSUES, 1945–

BRITAIN HAS CHANGED in many ways since 1945, but especially so in the British dimension of politics and public identity. In 1945, the nation was very much Britain, and the only significant institutional division occurred at the level of the United Kingdom. That title rested on the union between Ireland and Great Britain (or Britain for short). Northern Ireland, that section of Ireland that had remained with Britain and not followed the rest into the Irish Free State in 1922 (later Eire, the Republic of Ireland), had a separate Parliament in Belfast—Stormont—as well as a separate government. There was no equivalent for Wales, Scotland, or for the English regions, the last the element of British issues that tends to be forgotten.

SCOTLAND AND WALES

There were Welsh and Scottish separatists in 1945, but they enjoyed very limited popular support, and there was no equivalent to the strong tradition of Irish separatism prior to the Irish War of Independence that had been the prelude for Irish independence. Nor, within the British political system, was there much allowance for separate government. A Scottish Office had been created in 1934, but it had only limited power. A Council for Wales and Monmouthshire was established in 1949, but it had no more independent power than the Ministry for Welsh Affairs created in 1951, although a Welsh Office and Secretary of State for Wales followed in 1964. Macmillan had refused to establish them in 1957, but Labour brought in these innovations, while also seeing them as of limited significance.

Formed in 1925, Plaid Cymru, the Welsh Nationalist Party, won only 61,000 votes in the 1966 general election: 4.3 percent of the Welsh vote. The bold nature of the party's appeal was illustrated by the adoption speech made by Gwynfor Evans in launching his parliamentary campaign in 1959:

> There is a great awakening in Merioneth [a county in Wales] and through-out Wales—the sound of chains and fetters breaking. Wales is experiencing an awareness of its nationhood, becoming proud of its ancestry, and gaining mental and spiritual freedom which will inevitably lead to national freedom.

The rhetoric did not work and he came bottom of the poll. Indeed, Plaid did not win a seat until the 1966 general election, rising to three (out of thirty-six seats for Wales) in that of October 1974. Plaid's long identification with the cause of the Welsh language ensured that its support was strongest in areas where the language use was strongest, notably North West Wales and Cardiganshire. In the latter, the Free Welsh Army was created in 1965, but it remained a very small activist body. However, only a small minority of the population spoke Welsh, and, for long, the language issue cost Plaid Cymru support in South Wales where the use of English was most pronounced and very few spoke Welsh. This was by far the most populous part of Wales. For example, the 2011 census revealed that in the Bridgend Local Authority, 90.50 percent of the population could not speak Welsh, and 83.09 had "no knowledge" of Wales. In Blaenau-Gwent, the comparable percentages were 92.39 and 83.09, and this despite Wales being a compulsory element taking at least 5 percent of the National Curriculum for Wales for schoolchildren. Plaid was also hit by strong support for Labour and, in particular counties, the Liberals.

Politics in Wales was often very local, with antipathy among neighboring communities. There were also strong political and economic links between Wales and England. Welsh Labour politicians sat for English seats, and the English James Callaghan, Labour prime minister from 1976 to 1979, sat for a Welsh seat. So did the Welsh Neil Kinnock, the party leader from 1983 to 1992. Significant economic links with England reflected the west-east nature of communication links rather than the north-south ones within Wales. As a result, North Wales was linked to Merseyside, Mid Wales to Herefordshire and Shropshire, and South Wales to Bristol across the new Severn Bridge.

In Scotland, which was electorally more important as there were more parliamentary seats, the Scottish National Party (SNP) was more significant than Plaid in Wales. After the victory of Winifred Ewing in a by-election in

Hamilton in 1967, the SNP rose in prominence in 1967–70, winning 11 percent of the Scottish votes cast in the general election of 1970. Moreover, the chaos in Northern Ireland from 1968, as fighting over its future escalated, resulted in concern about threats to the future stability of both Scotland and Wales. This led Labour to establish a royal commission on the constitution in 1969 and then to support the idea of elected assemblies for both. In October 1974, the SNP achieved a breakthrough, taking 30 percent of the Scottish votes cast, winning eleven seats. Moreover, the discovery of North Sea oil and in large quantities appeared to make Scottish independence credible, and it certainly did in the eyes of the SNP.

The Conservative Party, which had won half the Scottish vote in 1955 and had a Scottish prime minister in 1963–64 with Alec Douglas-Home, began a period of serious long-term decline in Scotland from the late 1960s. This decline hit the unionism it represented and was also reflected by its decline. Unionism referred to the parliamentary unions of England and Scotland and of Britain and Ireland. Working-class Scottish conservatism/unionism was particularly badly hit. Thus, Britishness in Scotland was put under pressure with the crisis of empire and the loss of pride in being British. Meanwhile, a sense of a distinctive Scottish viewpoint frequently opposed to that of London was encouraged by the activities of Scottish independent television companies. The alternative in Scotland increasingly appeared to be Labour or the SNP. The latter was not circumscribed by the language issue and thus had a potential that Plaid Cymru lacked. So also with the greater size and potential of the Scottish economy.

Activism culminated with pressure for the devolution of power from London. A Scotland and Wales Bill, introduced in 1976, proposed an assembly for each with control over health, social services, education, development, and local government but with no taxation power and with the Westminster Parliament retaining the veto over legislation. The Bill met opposition from nationalists, who felt that it did not go far enough, but, more substantially, from Conservatives and from some Labour politicians who were opposed to nationalist aspirations. In February 1978, separate Bills were passed by Parliament for Scotland and Wales. To secure the legislation, however, the Labour government conceded referenda in Scotland and Wales. Held on March 1, 1979, the referenda required the support of 40 percent of the electorate, not simply, as was the norm, the majority of votes cast, a limiting provision that cost the Labour government nationalist support in Westminster. This threshold was not obtained in Scotland, although the majority of votes cast there was favorable to devolution (52 percent). In contrast, devolution was heavily defeated in Wales by 79 percent to twenty-one of the votes cast.

Thereafter, the nationalist issue interacted with the response to the Conservative government in 1979–97. Election results in Scotland were repeatedly very different from the Conservative triumphs in England. The Conservative Party's historic claim to be the Unionist Party, for long its official title, was fatally undermined during the Thatcher years, as the parliamentary party became predominantly representative of the more affluent parts of southern England and was certainly seen in that light in Scotland where, under the first-past-the-post system, its parliamentary representation collapsed even though a minority of Scots continued to vote Conservative. Moreover, older patterns of class identity as well as established views of civil society proved particularly strong in Scotland where Thatcher was very unpopular. The SNP went into decline in the 1980s as Labour dominated Scotland and was able to present itself as the voice of Scotland against the Conservative national government.

Conservative weakness became especially marked in the late 1980s, in large part because, in response to requests from the Scottish middle class concerned about local property taxes, the "poll tax" was introduced in Scotland in 1988, a year earlier than elsewhere in the UK. In response, "Can't Pay, Won't Pay" proved a critical campaign in rallying opposition. This introduction was repeatedly used as a nationalist charge against Thatcher and government from London. Meanwhile, Scottish Conservatives were deserting their party, and as the SNP, originally a single-issue party, adopted a relatively centrist opposition on the economy, it began to attract Conservative support.

It was Labour, not the nationalists, that was to be instrumental in changing the situation. The Labour victory in 1997 was even more a Conservative disaster, notably in Scotland and Wales where they won no seats, an outcome that attracted much attention. The new Labour government had such a powerful position in Parliament that it had no need to consider nationalist moves there. However, Labour had decided to support devolution, as a means, it hoped, to assuage nationalist sentiment, prevent the growth of separatism, and thus help maintain Labour's long-term position in Westminster which depended heavily on Scottish and Welsh seats. The legacy of devolution helping cause the fall of the Labour government in 1979 was potent.

Alongside this opportunism and history, devolution also sat easily with New Labour's drive to create a new Britain with modernized institutions, and to replace what was presented as the overcentralized character of the British constitution and government. In September 1997, referenda provided support for an assembly in Cardiff and a parliament in Edinburgh, with the latter wielding powers of taxation. Only 50.3 percent of those who voted supported devolution in Wales, but that narrow victory sufficed, while, far more convincingly, 74.9 percent did so in Scotland where the election was held first in order to influence the Welsh. Without that, the majority in Wales might have been against devolution. Defeated in the recent general election, the Conservatives were in no position to organize effective opposition to the referenda or in the subsequent first elections for the assembly and the parliament which first met in 1999. These elections left Labour as the largest party in each, with the nationalists as the official opposition party, and the Conservatives in a weak position. In Scotland, Blair aimed to outflank the SNP by providing devolution.

In Wales, Labour proved able to maintain its dominance, helped by Plaid Cymru's problems in winning support across Wales and notably in its populous South-East, although Plaid won occasional victories there. In contrast, Labour's position in Scotland was eventually taken by the SNP. Labour's embrace of devolution had caused dissension and disunity in its ranks. The leading Scottish Labour politicians decided, almost en masse, to retain their Westminster seats rather than stand for the assembly. Moreover, the regionalist agenda of the EU suggested a Europe in which existing nation-states might be reconceptualized. The SNP formed, first, a minority government in 2007 and then a majority one in 2011. In Scotland, SNP, which won the elections to the Scottish Assembly in 2011, provided a viable alternative both to the unpopular Blair and Brown governments and to the Conservatives, neither of whom made a strong case for the union. Although strong in particular regions, the Liberal Democrats failed to do so.

Trends, however, are generally complex and interrupted by events. After the 2016 elections, the SNP reverted to forming a minority government, but, to considerable surprise, Labour was pushed into third position in this election by the Conservatives. More crucially, the SNP, however, had failed on September 18, 2014, when the Scottish electorate rejected independence in a referendum it had sponsored. Nevertheless, winning over 40 percent of the votes cast in the referendum was impressive, and the referendum, which was seen as in the balance for a while, appeared to threaten the breakup of the UK.[1] It is unclear, however, whether the eventual support for remaining in the UK was consistently underestimated by some polls during the campaign or whether the result was swayed by last-minute campaigning and promises. Both the UK coalition government and the Labour opposition campaigned against Scottish independence.

So also with the 2016 EU referendum, as victory on the UK scale for departure led to a revived attempt by the Scottish government to talk about independence from the UK. Indeed, the Scottish political establishment as a whole supported continued EU membership. The potential value of independence, however, was called into question by the consequences of EU membership.

For example, in 2016, the attempt by the Scottish government to introduce minimum alcohol pricing in order to tackle alcoholism and its health consequences was challenged by the decision at the European level that the measure was in breach of EU laws against restricting trade. In 2016, 62 percent of the Scots who voted opted to remain in the EU. Yet the viability of an independent Scotland is unclear, and this is linked to the question of whether the EU would accept Scotland as an independent member as the SNP suggests and on terms the SNP wants, notably not joining the euro.

In part, this is a matter of economics. In the long term, the Scottish economy has been hit by the decline of heavy industry and in the short term by the collapse in the price of oil and natural gas in the mid-2010s and the related decommissioning of drilling rigs in the North Sea, not least as supplies run down. The impact on the finances of what would be an independent Scotland was harsh, not least because of heavy social welfare costs. Thus, Scotland could be a burden on the EU. The political argument may be different, as there would be a strong inducement for the EU to see the breakup of an independent UK, although Spain was concerned about the example that might be offered to separatist Catalonia.

By 2014, there were, as a result of the policies of the devolved Scottish and Welsh assemblies, different governmental solutions to those in the remainder of the UK. For example, Wales abolished prescription charges. The banning of genetically modified (GM) crop development by the Scottish government in 2015 was in part to protect salmon exports, as salmon feed was a key element in GM research and the quasi-organic reputation of Scottish—even farmed— salmon was one that had to be protected. In 2016, the Scottish Parliament banned fracking at the same time that it was moving ahead in England. In the 2017 general election, the Conservative share of the Scottish vote rose to 29 percent, while the SNP took 37 percent (a loss of 13 percent) and Labour 27 percent. This led Sturgeon to postpone a proposed second referendum. In contrast, in the 2019 general election, the SNP won 45 percent of the vote and 80 percent of the Scottish seats. The 2021 Scottish Parliament election saw a fourth consecutive victory for the SNP, leading to renewed interest in an independence referendum, but, due to poor policies and financial scandal, the party's popularity fell greatly in 2023.

ENGLISH REGIONS

In contrast, to Scottish and Welsh devolution, attempts to create autonomous English regions have as yet been unsuccessful. That appears a minor point that can be rushed past as an inconsequential nonevent. In practice, this was highly significant, not least as it meant that England was out of line with most of Western Europe. Moreover, the lack of English regionalism highlighted the absence of national, as well as regional, institutions for England to match those for Scotland, Wales, and Northern Ireland, and, as a linked point, what was termed the West Lothian issue: the ability of MPs from those three to vote on arrangements affecting England despite the relevant arrangements in these three being under the control of devolved assemblies and thus not affected by English MPs and Westminster legislation. In 1977, in a warning against devolution, Tam Dayell, the Labour MP for West Lothian asked, "For how long will English constituencies and English Honourable Members tolerate . . . at least 119 Honourable Members from Scotland, Wales and Northern Ireland exercising an important and probably often decisive effect on English politics while they themselves have no say in the same matters in Scotland, Wales and Northern Ireland?"

The lack of English representation particularly troubled Conservative MPs in the 2010s, but they were unable to do anything about it. Cameron had wished to do so in 2014 as part of a constitutional settlement linked to keeping Scotland in the UK, but he was dissuaded; looked at differently, this was one of the many passing enthusiasms he did not sustain.

Unwilling to address the issue of an English Parliament, the Blair government sought to introduce regional government but found what was seen as the most likely test case, the North-East, vote it down in a referendum, in part due to local political rivalries, notably hostility toward Newcastle, and in part to an unwillingness to create a new level of government, which was presented as likely to be a cause of expenditure. Under the 2010–15 coalition government, the Liberal Democrats were instrumental in the creation of local crime commissioners, who proved of limited value as overseers of the police. The 2016 Conservative government sought to have elected mayors introduced across all regions of England as part of a new structure of local government that included powers for economic planning.

Northern Ireland

Changes in Northern Ireland also occurred in the 1990s, although as the outcome of a violent process. By the end of 1992, more than three thousand people had been killed in the "Troubles" that had begun in the late 1960s as Catholic demands for civil rights, notably in housing allocation, took a violent turn. This was a hard-edged aspect of the 1960s, one in which political activism met a hostile response not seen in mainland Britain. The Protestant-dominated government of Northern Ireland resisted pressure for change, and disorder increased as the situation was radicalized.

Britain deployed troops from 1969 onward in order to try to stabilize the situation, notably to provide a nonpartisan system of control, one that would guarantee Catholic rights in the face of the paramilitary police of the government of Stormont (that of Northern Ireland); the Labour Party had scant sympathy for this government. However, the decision not to suspend the Stormont government at that point was a mistake. It meant that the resurgent Provisional IRA could cast the British army as pawns of Stormont and work to provoke hostilities between the Catholic population and the army. Indeed, opposition to the British presence and to British policy, especially from Catholic separatists, grew in a highly partisan environment. The resulting violence from the Provisional IRA,[2] a violent radical anti-British and anti-Protestant separatist group based in the Catholic community (although many Catholics were opposed to the IRA), led the British government to take greater power, reducing that of local (Protestant) politicians: the position of secretary of state for Northern Ireland was accordingly created as the suspension of Stormont in March 1972 brought direct government or "rule" from London. Alongside the hostility of the Catholic separatists for the British government, there was tension between the Northern Irish Protestants and that government. Indeed, an "Ulster Workers' Strike" by Protestants in May 1974 was designed to challenge direct rule and the plan for a power-sharing executive between the constitutional parties, that is, including Catholics.

Military deployment was successful at one level, with troops, in Operation Motorman, in 1972, moving into "no-go areas" of Londonderry and Belfast hitherto controlled by the Provisional IRA. Having driven the police away, the IRA installed their own "law" and saw these areas as a stage in the Maoist theory of revolutionary warfare, but the army ended this attempted trajectory.[3] The success of Motorman, which made it easier to arrest terrorist suspects, led the IRA, instead, to follow the course of terrorism, rather than that of waging guerrilla warfare. Terrorism, notably through sniping and bombings, proved far more difficult to overcome.

The British army was handicapped by the extent to which terrorists could take shelter in the neighboring Republic of Ireland, where there were many sympathizers, as well as by the encouragement of the Soviet Union, Libya, and US backers for the terrorists, support that provided weaponry and funds. In 1988, an Irish-American friend took me to a bar in New York where money was openly being collected for the IRA. These IRA terrorists also launched attacks in mainland Britain, notably the bombing of two pubs in Birmingham in 1974 that killed 21 people and left 182 others injured. These and other killings, including in pub bombings elsewhere, remain contentious to this day, not least due to recent IRA refusals to condemn past atrocities in what is presented, instead, as a just cause. Given the extraordinary support many Irish Americans still show to this cause, it is worth noting the comments in 2016 of the sister of one of the Birmingham victims about an IRA apologist:

> I wonder if one of his own kids was killed beyond description, where all their skin has literally been stripped off their body, they have got no legs and no arms and you cannot recognise them by their face because their injuries are such that they have already been partially cremated.[4]

Terrorism on the British mainland included attacks on the Conservative Party conference in 1984 and the Cabinet in 1991 and led to the murder of three Conservative MPs, including two key advisers of Margaret Thatcher, notably Airey Neave in 1979. His murder at Parliament, by a car bomb, deprived her of crucial help, particularly sound advice.

As a result of changing circumstances—namely, the IRA focus on terrorism, not guerrilla warfare—the army was principally in place in Northern Ireland from the mid-1970s to support the police. The Special Branch of the Royal Ulster Constabulary (police) focused on intelligence-led operations, but the army continued to play an important role. This was notably so on the extensive border with the Republic of Ireland. The army made much use of helicopters to supply fortified posts (as roads were vulnerable to mines) and employed intelligence gathering in order to strike at terrorists and to thwart their operations. With the exception of the 1982 Falklands War, military history is not generally given much of a role in accounts of post-1945 British history, but that is mistaken. Aside from the significance of the military for developments in Northern Ireland, it is instructive to consider what might have happened in mainland Britain had there been a total military failure in Northern Ireland, possibly comparable to what had affected France in Algeria in the early 1960s. All comparisons, however, are problematic, as the Protestants, a majority in Northern Ireland, had been there since the early seventeenth century, which was more akin to that of European Americans in North America than to the French in Algeria, who had been there from only 1830.

There was a limit to what could be achieved by the government. At the same time, the terrorists were unable to overthrow policing or to drive the army out of Northern Ireland.[5] The situation, however, was made more difficult by police and army security tactics that alienated many Catholics, as well as by the rogue behavior seen when some troops shot at nationalist demonstrators in Londonderry on Bloody Sunday on January 30, 1972, killing thirteen.[6] The situation was also complicated when Protestant "loyalist" movements developed. They were determined that Northern Ireland should remain part of the UK, but also committed to sectarian violence against Catholics.

As the IRA struck at the Unionist Protestant community, as well as the British military, while the "loyalists" attacked Catholics and also thwarted the policies of the Westminster government, the situation drifted from crisis toward chaos. The attritional character of terrorism and counterterrorist operations was apparent. The police and army had to maintain a semblance of order sufficient to demonstrate to the IRA that they could not win and also to encourage intransigent Catholic and Protestant politicians eventually to see that there was no alternative to talking to each other. Northern Ireland placed a major strain on the British army's manpower and morale. IRA terrorism made it difficult for the army to fraternize with the population, while the IRA continued to find shelter in the Republic of Ireland, and it proved impossible to control the long border. The difficulties of ending terrorism in the absence of widespread civilian support from part of the community became readily apparent in Northern Ireland.

British military and governmental policy would probably have been different had there been a conscript army. Conscripts might have been unwilling to serve in Northern Ireland, and the deployment and tactics employed might have placed a greater emphasis on avoiding casualties. Conscription, however, had been phased out by the Conservatives in the late 1950s and 1960s, in large part because the expenditure involved did not seem merited in the context of competing high technology possibilities, notably submarine-launched ballistic missiles. This phasing-out was important to the distinctive character of British society. It represented a reversion to the usual peacetime pattern of the British military, one that contrasted with the general system across Europe. As a consequence, it was not possible, or necessary, to rely on conscripts in Northern Ireland.

In the event, the professional infantry, who bore most of the commitment, proved resilient, training adjusted to the particular challenges of the task, and the army acquired considerable experience in antiterrorist policing. Military proficiency was measured in traditional infantry skills, such as patrolling and the use of cover, while intelligence success was a key element, and the IRA was penetrated at a high level, with several of its leading figures providing information for the British. This is an aspect of the role of the secret services and intelligence operations in British history.

There was considerable confusion as to whether this was a counterinsurgency or a law-and-order situation. Eventually, the latter view prevailed as part of a strategy to end the crisis by political means.[7] The army and police contained the situation sufficiently to allow negotiations that produced a peace settlement in 1998. In a major success for counterinsurgency, terrorism had clearly failed by then. The lack of foreign armed intervention on behalf of the

IRA, as opposed to the provision of arms supplies by the Soviet bloc, was a significant factor. So also was Britain not being at war, with the exception of the short-lived Falklands War in 1982. The British would have found the Northern Ireland crisis far more difficult had it coincided with the Kenya, Malaya, and Cyprus crises of the 1950s or those in Borneo and Aden in the 1960s. That had certainly been a major issue for the British army when faced with the earlier nationalist uprising in Ireland in 1919–21: at that stage, the army had major commitments in Germany, Russia, the Middle East, and India.

Given the difficulties of its task, the British army, with the exception of Bloody Sunday, maintained a high level of professionalism. That conduct did not protect them from criticism from many, in Britain and, even more, abroad, who appeared less willing to condemn the deliberate terrorist policy of the murder of civilians repeatedly employed by the IRA.

In the early 1990s, the bloody disintegration of Yugoslavia and the development of "ethnic cleansing" there led to new fears about the future of Northern Ireland. Fresh dynamism for peace talks, which had already led to the November 1985 Anglo-Irish Agreement, which, to Thatcher's disapproval, gave the Republic of Ireland a formal role in Northern Irish affairs, developed from late 1993. This led that December to the Downing Street Declaration, which helped encourage a paramilitary ceasefire in 1994 and talks between government officials and Sinn Féin, the political wing of the IRA. In February 1995, a consultative framework document for the future government of Northern Ireland followed. By the 1990s, the IRA was running low on supporters willing to lose their life, while large social welfare payments, funded from the British exchequer, helped lessen support for the nationalist cause.[8]

In 1996, the IRA ceasefire broke down, in large part over the decommissioning of terrorist arms, which the IRA was unwilling to accept as a precondition for talks, but also because Major was dependent on the parliamentary support of the Ulster Unionists. In 1997, however, talks resumed. The IRA had found that its terrorism broke neither the British will to remain in Northern Ireland nor that of the majority of the people of Northern Ireland to remain British. This led to a settlement of differences with the Good Friday Agreement of 1998, an agreement that Major and Blair had played a key role in securing, as had the Irish taoiseach Albert Reynolds and President Bill Clinton.

The Good Friday Agreement laid the basis for the resumption of provincial self-government, a decision endorsed in May 1998 by a referendum in Northern Ireland. An assembly and an executive were both created. The subsequent years were to be difficult, but a power-sharing executive that brought together the Unionists and Sinn Féin from 2007 was an outcome that would have amazed observers in the 1960s. So also would have been Sinn Féin denouncing Catholic terrorists, notably the Continuity IRA, who rejected the new agreement and continued to stage murderous terrorist attacks, particularly one in Armagh that, ironically, killed more Catholic than Protestant civilians. The long-term viability of the settlement is unclear, both because of the continued prominence of sectarian differences, notably in education, and because of the heavy dependence of employment and social welfare in Northern Ireland on the transfer of funds from Britain.

CONCLUSIONS

The future trajectory of the UK is unclear. To many Scots, accustomed to the expression of grievances and the demand that spending be rightly focused on Scotland, Great Britain has become an English-dominated Little Britain, a Great Britain that the English want to own but not want to be. Other Scots, however, as the referendum in 2014 and the elections in 2016 showed, are enthusiastic for a maintenance of the union. This is even more the case in Wales despite the effort of Plaid Cymru to ape the SNP. The Welsh flags enthusiastically waved in Cardiff in 2016 when the team did very well in the European football competition and the repeated talk then of the "Welsh nation" did not mean the end of Britain.

The extent to which this situation will be reshaped by Brexit is unclear. Strains in that relationship arising from a separatism that is strongest in England and Wales, leading to Brexit majorities in 2016, strongly threatens Scottish support for remaining part of Britain. Looked at differently, these are different nationalisms and each is on the rise. In Northern Ireland, there is also opposition to being in a separate economic zone to the Republic of Ireland, and a majority of 54.8 percent voted for "Remain" in 2016, including a clear majority of Catholics, who were proportionately growing. Sinn Féin then voiced the possibility of a referendum for the reunion of the island of Ireland, although this was rejected by the secretary of state for Northern Ireland. The complexity of Ireland being separated by a boundary that was also that between the EU and the non-EU excited attention.

The question of the strength of separatist nationalism in Scotland and Wales is more generally unclear. In particular, it is difficult to understand how far it will be possible to reconcile British nationalism, let alone a British identity, with Scottish and Welsh identity. The popularity of Queen Elizabeth II, one amply indicated when she celebrated her ninetieth birthday in 2016, supported a Britishness that may be less apparent in the future. An independent Scotland and an independent Wales could, however, retain the monarch as the head of state, on the pattern of Australia and some other Commonwealth countries.

If few are confident about the future, it is not clear that this will necessarily lead to long-term animosity. Norway and Sweden in 1905 and the Czech Republic and Slovakia in 1994 are instances of successful separations. Such a comparison or possible future would have surprised most British people in 1945 or 1970. That the situation is now very different shows how far the years have brought change and have made further transformation or, rather, transformations, a possibility.

10

EUROPEAN AND WORLD QUESTIONS

IN 1945, BRITAIN was a world power able to support Western European unity but not to see its destiny in those terms. By 2016, there were overseas possessions, including the Falkland Islands, Ascension Island, and Saint Helena, but there was no empire. Moreover, Britain was an extremely uneasy member of the EU having voted to leave it. From the global perspective, the change from 1945 was the most significant aspect of British history in this period and notably the abandonment of empire. In 1945, this empire had included what is now India, Pakistan, Bangladesh, Sri Lanka, Myanmar, Malaysia, Singapore, Hong Kong, Fiji, Tonga, Israel, Kenya, Tanzania, Uganda, Malawi, Nigeria, Ghana, Gambia, Sierra Leone, Zambia, Zimbabwe, Swaziland, Botswana, Guyana, Jamaica, Barbados, Belize, Antigua, Cyprus, Malta, Gibraltar, the Falkland Islands, parts of modern Somalia (British Somaliland), and Yemen (Aden) and a number of other islands, notably in the West Indies and South Pacific. Protectorate status gave Britain effective control of the Persian Gulf, Jordan, and Brunei. Former territories of the empire, by 1945 self-governing dominions, Australia, Canada, Ireland, Newfoundland, New Zealand, and South Africa, were all parts, to a varying extent, of the British system. Britain was also the occupying power in parts of the former Italian empire (Libya and Somalia) and in large parts of Germany and Austria.

The weakening and abandonment of empire was a process largely carried out between 1947 and 1964, although with important anticipations and a long sequel. The longer term impact of decolonization on Britain has been significant, in terms of Britain's relations with the rest of the world but also with reference to Britain itself.

END OF EMPIRE

The loss of empire reflected a marked change in attitudes within Britain and led to such a change about Britain. In particular, the sense of Britain's distance from, and difference to, the Continent was eroded by the retreat from empire. Control over India, the most populous colony, was crucial to the image of British Empire and to the British idea of their role and destiny. Labour was committed to Indian independence, and this was achieved in 1947, although at the cost of partition into the new states of India and Pakistan and of large numbers of deaths in related Hindu-Muslim clashes. There are no precise figures, but more than one million people were killed. The loss of India was crucial because it had provided the military manpower for the British Empire in Asia, the Middle East, and East Africa. Moreover, the future of India had been the main issue in discussions about empire in the 1930s.

Despite Indian independence, that of Burma and Ceylon (1948), and the ending of the Palestine mandate in 1948, Britain, however, was still a major imperial power, and imperial rule was not regarded as anachronistic. Instead, it was seen as a progressive force designed to develop colonies and to bring them to independence in a commonwealth of nations, united across racial boundaries, that Britain would lead. There was, nevertheless, tension due to increased demands in some colonies for independence as well as uneasiness in Britain about immigration.[1] That France, the Netherlands, Portugal, and Spain were also imperial powers helped make British rule seem normal.

The Labour government, especially its foreign secretary, Ernest Bevin (1945–51), had high hopes of using imperial resources, particularly those of Africa, to strengthen the British economy and to make Britain a less unequal partner in the Anglo-American partnership. To help provide the necessary military strength, wartime conscription was continued in Britain. Bevin acted in a lordly fashion in the Middle East, but empire ran out in the sands of rising Arab nationalism and a lack of British resources. The latter led to a succession of crises, starting with that in 1947 over sterling convertibility. In defending empire, the British faced a number of serious imperial problems in the early 1950s, including the Malayan Emergency (a Communist uprising in Malaya, which was eventually tackled successfully) and the Mau Mau Uprising in Kenya.

However, it was the Suez Crisis of 1956, an attempt to destabilize the aggressive Arab nationalist regime of Gamal Abdul Nasser in Egypt, that clearly exposed British weakness not least in contrast with earlier British interventions in Egypt. Just as echoes of the appeasement of dictators in the 1930s were initially to be voiced when the Argentineans invaded the Falklands in 1982, and it was misleadingly thought that the British government would not respond, so, in 1956, the prime minister, Anthony Eden (1955–57), who had resigned as foreign secretary in 1938 ostensibly in protest at appeasement, was determined not to repeat its mistakes and to accept Nasser's nationalization of the Suez Canal, the key maritime route of the empire. Secretly acting in concert with France and Israel, Eden sent British forces to occupy the Canal Zone. The invasion was poorly planned and unwisely delayed but was initially militarily successful. Nevertheless, American opposition and its impact on sterling were crucial to weakening British resolve and thus leading to a humiliating withdrawal. British political and public opinion was deeply divided about the intervention. Whether, in hindsight, those over the last fifteen years in Iraq, Afghanistan, and Libya were not far more problematic is open to discussion.

As with the Dutch and French empires, a lack of US support has been seen by some historians as a major problem for the empire ever since World War II. In 1956, US anger made Britain's dependent status obvious and made British prime ministers determined to stay on good terms with the United States. The Americans sought to persuade Arab, Asian, and African opinion that the United States was anti-imperialist in order to reduce the dangers posed by Soviet exploitation of the Suez Crisis and by further Afro-Asian alienation from the West.

However, in a separate narrative, once the Cold War with the Soviet Union began, and, more particularly, in the 1960s, the Americans also sought to sustain Britain's role as a world power. They were interested in preserving many of Britain's overseas bases, either to maintain Britain's utility as an ally, or to have them ready for American use. Nor did the Americans want premature decolonization to result in chaos and, perhaps, communism. As a result, the Americans supported the continued British military presence east of Suez in the 1960s, notably in Aden, the Persian Gulf, and Malaysia, and in the Suez Crisis itself had seen themselves as rescuing a friend from a fit of madness.

The fourteen years after the Suez Crisis witnessed the rapid loss, in the sense of departure from, of most of the rest of the British Empire. Attitudes within Britain proved crucial. The British people might not have been European-minded after 1950, but neither were they particularly imperial-minded. After Suez, some leading Conservatives, especially Iain Macleod, the colonial secretary, became deeply disillusioned with the empire and ready to dismantle it. Macmillan took a pragmatic approach aimed at safeguarding British power in the longer run. He probably did not quite know what he was letting himself in for when he appointed Macleod; indeed, Macmillan had wanted the much harder-line Lennox-Boyd to stay on. The "Future Policy" paper of 1959, followed by Macmillan's 1960 "Wind of Change" speech, announced British withdrawal from Africa. However, decolonization was bitterly criticized by some right-wing Conservatives. Moreover, anticolonialism was also a minority view. Empire, nevertheless, was proving too expensive, too troublesome, and too provocative of other powers.

Decolonization, indeed, was hastened by a strong upsurge in colonial nationalist movements, particularly in Ghana and Cyprus. Policy makers did not know how to confront these movements, as, while willing to use force, they sought to rest imperial rule on consent, not force. The US government encouraged decolonization, while the logic of Britain's self-proclaimed imperial mission—bringing civilization to backward areas of the globe—ensured that the granting of self-government could be presented as the inevitable terminus of empire. Independence was granted to most colonies, notably Ghana and Malaya in 1957, Nigeria and Cyprus in 1960, Sierra Leone and Tanganyika (most of modern Tanzania) in 1961, Jamaica and Uganda in 1962, and Kenya in 1963. That for Cyprus was especially significant as it had been assumed that it was too small for independence.

Empire had been presented as a stage to a process of linked development, a civilizational model that ultimately looked back to the idea of Britain as a modern Rome. Under Macmillan, there was initially an attempt to convert the empire into the Commonwealth, as most of the former empire that had already gained independence had become, as a key means of maintaining British influence on the world stage while trying to juggle with the United States and Europe as well. Subsequently, however, this abandonment of empire was accompanied by a view that the Commonwealth, would not, in practice, be able to meet, or, indeed, contribute greatly to, Britain's economic, political, or security needs, a view that was to be fully justified by subsequent events. Thus, parting with empire was seen as an aspect of the modernization that was to be linked to joining the European Economic Community (EEC) and to economic planning within Britain.

Some traditional Conservative interests, such as the military and those linked to white settlers in the colonies, notably in Kenya and Southern Rhodesia (now Zimbabwe), were concerned about the maintenance of empire. However, this concern was less the case with much of the party's middle-class support, and the latter was increasingly prominent in constituency associations and at party conferences. Leaders such as Edward Heath and Reginald Maudling, neither of whom came from the traditional ruling group, felt little commitment to the empire. The same was true for R. A. Butler, party chairman from 1959 to 1961, and of his successor Iain Macleod from 1961 to 1963. Established by the Conservatives in 1906, the Junior Imperial League was succeeded by the Young Conservatives in 1945. Further to the Right, The League of Empire Loyalists was founded in 1954 by A. K. Chesterton, cousin of the novelist G. K. Chesterton and formerly one of Sir Oswald Mosley's lieutenants in the British Union of Fascists. The league never had many members, and the four candidates it ran in parliamentary elections in 1957–64 all did very badly.

The balance between the generations was also important, with the young not experiencing the sense of discontinuity from the loss of empire felt by their elders. Generational shifts also related to specific points—for example, attitudes to British settlers in Africa. Differences between the generations encouraged and reflected a contrast between their historical memory and imagination. The empire served as a foil for defining the British national character. Commitment to empire was increasingly perceived as the antithesis of what it meant to be "modern," as an obstacle to economic reform, an emblem of outdated social values, and a view out of kilter with "democratic" political values. It appeared redundant, and imperial withdrawal seemed necessary. This view was an aspect of the Americanization of British culture.

In contrast, the discontinuity between imperial past and the present was far greater in the former colonies, especially, but not only, if violence was involved in gaining independence and/or as a consequence of independence. There was fighting in some cases, as nationalist movements clashed with the imperial state. For example, in Aden in the 1960s, the air power and compulsory resettlement policies used by the British in Malaya in the 1950s were deployed again, not least with punitive tactics against resistance, but the National Liberation Front's inroads forced an abandonment of the interior in early summer 1967. Once the British were clearly on the way out, they found it hard to obtain accurate intelligence, and this made mounting operations difficult. Reduced to holding on to the port city of Aden, where the garrison itself had to be protected, the only initiative left was to abandon the position, which was done in December 1967, bringing to a humiliating end a rule that had begun in 1839.[2] Field Marshal Montgomery observed that when a force was reduced largely to protecting its own position, its presence had become largely redundant. Aden was important to Britain's presence in the Indian Ocean and the Middle East and a key position on the Suez Canal route.

In most colonies, notably Africa, with the exception of Kenya, and the West Indies, the degree of violence involved in the loss of empire was limited. In addition the loss appeared inexorable. Although, in 1964, Wilson, newly elected as prime minister, bombastically and foolishly declared, "We are a world power and a world influence or we are nothing," by 1969 none of Africa remained under British rule, and the "East of Suez" defense policy, supported by both Labour and the Conservatives, had fallen victim to fiscal problems and to the consequences of the devaluation of sterling in 1967. Against the wishes of the US government, Wilson made the situation to abandon positions "East of Suez," the following year. British forces withdrew from Aden and the Simon's Town naval base in South Africa in 1967, the Persian Gulf in 1971, and Singapore in 1974 (most had left in 1971).

Independence continued to be granted to colonies, including to Gambia and the Maldives in 1965; Bechuanaland, Basutoland, and Barbados in 1966; Aden in 1967; and Nauru, Mauritius, and Swaziland in 1969. This decolonization was largely peaceful. In practice, indeed, decolonization proved less traumatic than was the case for the Dutch, French, Belgian, and Portuguese empires. Moreover, Britain rapidly found itself coming to the assistance of former colonies, notably in the Malaysian Confrontation of 1963–66, which involved the protection of Malaysia from Indonesian aggression. In 1964, British forces were deployed to help the former East African colonies against military revolts. In 1967–70, Britain provided arms to Nigeria as it overcame Biafran separatism which was backed by France. In the early 1970s, troops were also sent to help Oman, a former protectorate, overcome Soviet-backed separatism in Dhofar.

Central Africa proved a more difficult issue. Britain had sought to bring stability and to secure continued influence by grouping the colonies of Northern Rhodesia (now Zambia), Southern Rhodesia (now Zimbabwe), and Nyasaland (now Malawi) into a regional federation, which was the policy also followed in Southeast Asia (with Malaysia), the Persian Gulf, and the West Indies. This solution, however, fell apart in Central Africa under the pressure of both black and white nationalism, while it also failed in the West Indies and, in 1965, Singapore quit Malaysia.

There was a large white minority in Southern Rhodesia and, in 1965, it declared independence, which created a major issue for British foreign policy. Britain refused to recognize this independence, but its efforts to apply pressure, notably economic pressure, in order to bring it to a close failed. To many former colonies, Britain was insufficiently forceful, both in this case and with reference to the apartheid (white supremacist) regime in South Africa, although economic and strategic considerations were significant in the latter case.[3] The issue created serious strains in the Commonwealth until the introduction of black majority rule in Southern Rhodesia (Zimbabwe) in 1980 and South Africa in 1994 and, focused on the Cold War, Mrs. Thatcher made herself unpopular by being unwilling to go along with the views of most Commonwealth leaders. Indeed, there was support among sections of the Conservative Party for the white regimes, although this support failed to determine policy. As an aspect of the political significance of military issues, it is unclear how far the army would have welcomed orders to act against Southern Rhodesia, but the range of other commitments did not make this a viable prospect.

THE COLD WAR

Struggles over the end of empire and its aftermath were intertwined with the Cold War. Britain had played a major role in opposing communism from the outset, taking a prominent part in the Russian Civil War in 1919–20. Communism was regarded as a threat to the European order and the British Empire. Hostility to Soviet expansion became a leading issue anew from the late 1940s, as the Labour government came to appreciate the threats posed by Soviet expansionism, notably in Eastern Europe, Greece, Turkey, and Iran. From 1944, Britain played a major role in supporting the Greek government against Communist insurrection.

Combined with the apparent weaknesses of Western Europe, these threats led to a determined effort to anchor the United States in an international order resolved to thwart Soviet expansionism. This effort entailed Britain committing itself, as the United States, to the North Atlantic Treaty Organization (NATO), which was founded in 1949, and to a long-term military presence in West Germany,[4] and also led Britain to play a significant role in resisting Communist expansionism in the Korean War (1950–53).

As a result, military expenditure rose greatly at the close of the 1940s, which affected the funds available for social welfare. Britain's role as a "warfare state" was readily apparent in the 1950s, with military modernization linked to the deployment of nuclear and then hydrogen warheads. Initially to be dropped as bombs by aircraft, they were, from the 1960s, to be fired as missiles from submarines. Confrontation with the Soviet Union remained a key theme in British foreign policy until the end of the Cold War at the close of the 1980s. It also played a part in the struggles over the end of empire.

Britain never had the same interest in opposing China, and that policy helped lead to low-level tension with the United States. The key point was that in the Cold War, Britain was the United States' leading military ally. At the same time, despite strong pressure from President Johnson, Wilson refused to commit British forces in the Vietnam War. This contrasted with the position taken by both Australia and New Zealand, ensuring that, for the first time, Britain, Australia, and New Zealand were not allies in war. There were persistent reports that British Special Forces were sent to Vietnam, but, if so, the commitment was small and not a public one. When pressed by Johnson in 1964 to help in Vietnam and send a token troop deployment, Wilson argued that Britain already had a major regional military commitment against Indonesia and that the Labour Party was opposed to involvement. Wilson tried to remain a supportive ally but felt Britain could best do so as a peace broker. Johnson did not respect Wilson's advice, while Wilson in 1966 publicly dissented from the bombing of North Vietnamese cities.

Tensions with the United States continued under Heath (prime minister 1970–74) and President Nixon, but relations improved thereafter, not least because the United States regarded France and West Germany as more problematic allies. Britain was more determined than they were to focus on opposition to Soviet expansionism and, with the loss of empire, increasingly configured its forces accordingly. Both James Callaghan (prime minister 1976–79) and Margaret Thatcher (1979–90) were committed to alliance with the United States, and the relationship saw alliance in two wars with Iraq, in 1991 and 2003.[5]

RELATIONS IN EUROPE

Initially after World War II, British governments were very wary about attempts to develop nonmilitary cooperative systems in Western Europe. The European Coal and Steel Community was regarded by the postwar Labour government (1945–51) as a threat to their new nationalized control over the British industries and also as a challenge to their powerful trade union allies. Both Labour and Conservatives favored West European integration but with Britain remaining outside, in large part due to its US, Commonwealth, and imperial links, and the relations and interests arising as a result. The focus on empire remained significant into the late 1950s.

Britain therefore was not involved in the new organization, the EEC, encompassing France, West Germany, Italy, Belgium, the Netherlands, and Luxembourg, established on January 1, 1958, as a result of the Treaty of Rome of 1957. Joining the EEC subsequently gained more support in British political circles, as it became clear that the organization would be more than a short-term flurry—indeed, that it would be a success in terms of the level of economic growth enjoyed by the member states. In 1961, Macmillan applied to join the EEC, fearing that otherwise he would have less influence with the United States and, therefore, be less able to win US support for British interests. It was also hoped that Britain would enjoy economic growth within the EEC.

In 1963, Charles de Gaulle, the French president, vetoed the British application. He had argued that Britain was too close to the United States and told a press conference, "England is insular . . . the nature and structure and economic context of England differs profoundly from those of the other states of the Continent." The other five members of the EEC had supported the application.

The French veto dampened the debate within Britain. There was a degree of opposition to the application among Conservatives, but it was Labour, then in opposition, that was more ambivalent about membership. This ambivalence reflected economic protectionism, and a fear that Continental workers would accept lower levels of welfare and thus price British workers out of work. This fear prefigured British working-class anxieties in the 2010s about large-scale immigration within the then EU. There was also in the early 1960s a sense of national identity under threat, which was memorably captured by Hugh Gaitskell, the leader of the Labour Party, who declared, in a television interview, on September 21, 1962, that entry into the EEC "means the end of Britain as an independent nation; we become no more than Texas or California in the United States of Europe. It means the end of a thousand years of history." For Gaitskell, wartime memories of the Commonwealth supporting Britain meant a lot. It was significant of the new politics that Gaitskell made these remarks on television.

After Labour, under Gaitskell's successor (from 1963), Harold Wilson, came to power in October 1964, there was an attempt to maintain Britain as an international power (while also using planning to transform the economy). This attempt indicated a strong confidence in national remedies. However, economic failure forced the government to abandon its political and military prospectus and encouraged a focus, instead, on Europe. This focus took a number of forms. Balance-of-payment crises led to growing concern in London that the "confrontation" with Indonesia in which Britain supported Malaysia in 1963–66 could not be sustained. In the event, Indonesian generals aligned with the United States overthrew the populist left-leaning dictator Sukarno in 1965, which led to the end of the "confrontation." Plans to build new aircraft carriers were abandoned in 1966, while remaining "East of Suez" imperial commitments, commitments that had a strong resonance in British history back into the eighteenth century, were discarded from 1968. Instead, defense priorities were focused on deterring a Soviet invasion of Western Europe. David Bruce, the US ambassador, reflected, "The truth is, we have been witnessing the gradual, now accelerated, decline of a formerly great power." Dean Rusk, the secretary of state, remarked, "For God's sake act like Britain."[6]

In May 1967, Wilson launched a new bid to join the EEC. Like Macmillan, Wilson was driven by a sense of the need to redress declining British international influence. He was also motivated by the higher growth rates in the

EEC. The policy was supported by Heath, the Conservative leader. The populist nationalism that was to be offered and defined anew by Enoch Powell when he began to attack the consequences of immigration in 1968 was unacceptable to Heath, who was no populist. In November 1967, de Gaulle again blocked entry, emphasizing what he presented as the underlying weakness of the British economy. More broadly, de Gaulle declared that the British people

> doubtless see more and more clearly that in the face of the great movements which are now sweeping the world—the huge power of the United States, the growing power of the Soviet Union, the renascent power of the Continental countries of Europe, the newly emerging power of China—its own structures, its traditions, its activities and even its national character are from now on all at risk. This is brought home to her, day after day, by the grave economic, financial and currency problems with which she is currently contending. This is why she feels the profound need to find some sort of framework, even a European one if need be, which would enable her to safeguard her own identity, to play a leading role, and at the same time, to lighten some of her burden.

This geopolitical approach reflected a continent-based spatial imagination that downplayed the value of maritime links and oceanic identities, particularly the North Atlantic, as well as underplaying the real and potential roles of the flow of trade and capital. As such, the approach was in line with the dominant historical strand in French strategic culture, one that was different to that of Britain.

When negotiations resumed, there was a different president in France. De Gaulle's resignation in 1969, after the French government had lost a referendum on constitutional changes, was a necessary prelude to the invitation by the European Community (EC)[7] in 1970 to four applicants—Britain, Ireland, Denmark, and Norway—to resume negotiations, Britain being the key negotiating partner. De Gaulle's successor, Georges Pompidou, president from 1969 until his early death in 1974, was concerned about growing West German strength and the need to balance it, and not, as de Gaulle had been, by the challenge from Anglo-American links, which, anyway, appeared weaker. Pompidou was also more committed to the EC than de Gaulle had been and therefore more willing to respond to his partners' pressure for enlargement.

By the time serious negotiations resumed, at the end of June 1970, Heath had replaced Wilson: the latter lost office on June 18 in a surprise general election result, twelve days before the beginning of negotiations. The work done by the Wilson government, however, was important, not least because its team of officials, negotiating briefs, and timetable, were all used by its successor. This instance of continuity underlines the danger of assuming that party distinctions are necessarily always the key element and, accordingly, that politics should be judged and achievements assessed in terms of separate administrations. The same point can be made about economic policy, social welfare, and, even more, defense.

A keen European, Heath had been the chief negotiator in the application vetoed in 1963 and had made his name through this role. As prime minister, pushing hard for membership, which he saw as crucial to the modernization of Britain, Heath was also keen on a new geopolitical alignment. He was not eager for close cooperation with the United States, particularly under President Nixon, whose policies had led to US intervention in Cambodia in 1970. Furthermore, Heath was determined not to be branded as the US spokesman in Europe. To Heath, Europe represented a welcome alternative to the United States and a way to defend British interests and exert influence. He was later to be hostile to Thatcher's focus on Anglo-American links.[8]

Meanwhile, other aspects of Wilson's foreign policy were also pursued. The Conservative opposition had criticized the Wilson government's announcement in 1968 that it was abandoning Britain's military position "East of Suez," but, in office, Heath found it impossible to reverse the policy of withdrawal and implemented it. The Americans took over the British presence, with an aircraft carrier entering the Persian Gulf in 1974.

Heath saw EC membership as crucial to the revival of Britain's economic fortunes. Specifically, he regarded membership as likely to lead to an economic competition that would ensure reform and greater efficiency in Britain. This approach prefigured the view that John Major was to take when pressing, as chancellor of the exchequer, for joining the Exchange Rate Mechanism (ERM) for European currencies, as Britain did in October 1990, even at a disadvantageous rate. In both cases, this was to be foolish economics and bad politics, prefiguring the situation many EU states were to find within the eurozone. Heath's views on the economic benefits of membership accorded with his emphasis on, and view of, modernization, the theme he pushed in the 1970 election campaign. However, joining the EC would be far more disruptive for Britain than it was for the original member states because their trade was overwhelmingly Eurocentric, while, in contrast, less than half of Britain's trade was within Europe, although that trade was increasing.

As with Macmillan (eventually) and Wilson (eventually), a lack of confidence in national solutions led to modernization being focused on the EC. To Heath, Europe was the modern alternative to an anachronistic emphasis on global influence and to a naïve confidence in the Commonwealth. Instead, he saw both prosperity and security as answered by European cooperation. The pooling of sovereignty and the creation of supranational European institutions did not worry Heath because he felt that a reformed and revitalized Britain would be able to play a major role in leading the EC and shaping its policy, a view that was repeatedly to be proved naïve. Indeed, Heath and many other Conservatives denied that the country would compromise its independence or sovereignty by joining the EC.

The negotiations were relatively easy for two reasons. First, Heath was prepared to surrender much in order to obtain membership. As a state seeking membership in an established organization, Britain anyway negotiated from weakness, but Heath seriously accentuated this, badly neglecting national interests. Although he had scant choice, Heath surrendered Britain's fishing grounds and accepted the EC's expensive, inefficient, and protectionist Common Agricultural Policy (CAP), despite the fact that it had little to offer Britain. The CAP has ensured that the financial consequences of membership have repeatedly not served British interests. Indeed, Thatcher's subsequent obduracy over the rebate on the British contribution to the EC was forced on her by Heath, who, characteristically, did not offer her any support over the issue.

The resulting agricultural subsidies and higher food costs of the CAP replaced cheap food imports from the Commonwealth, particularly of New Zealand lamb. They, indeed, had to be excluded to maintain the market for Continental products, while rising food prices fed through into the already-serious problem of inflation within Britain. Moreover, although the UK had a 78 percent peak of homegrown food production in 1984, the percentage fell to 60 percent in 2015. Entry into the EC also led to a loss of national control over nearby fishing grounds, an issue that was of great importance to the fishing communities concerned, and that certainly would have played a role in traditional Conservative assumptions. The fishing industry was to be largely destroyed, with serious consequences for many coastal communities.

Negotiations were successfully concluded in July 1971. Ignoring difficulties raised by ministers, Heath pushed membership hard on its economic merits, arguing that it opened up markets, and the white paper claimed that Britain would be able to influence policy from being in the center of Europe. In contrast, Heath said little about possible political consequences. He claimed in the House of Commons that there would be no lessening of "national identity or an erosion of essential national sovereignty" and on television that "a country's vital interest cannot be overruled." Heath ignored well-founded warnings to the contrary.

Second, negotiations were relatively easy because there was only limited opposition within the Conservative Party, still less the government. The

House of Commons voted in favor of entry by 356 MPs to 244 on October 28, 1971. Heath had reluctantly conceded a free vote, the course he had initially rejected, but that was urged by his chief Whip, Francis Pym, in order to help win over Labour support, which was less than it had been under the Wilson government. Entry was criticized most strongly by the powerful left wing of the Labour Party.[9] This opposition helped lead Wilson to declare that, while he was unwilling to reject British entry in principle, he opposed entry on the terms that Heath had negotiated. Wilson was critical of the CAP, which he saw, correctly, as a serious burden for Britain.

Labour supporters of EC entry, led by Roy Jenkins, however, were willing to defy a three-line whip, and to vote with the government, thus providing a secure parliamentary majority for entry, and one able to overcome both the bulk of the Labour Party and the role of any Conservative rebels. Although thirty-nine Conservative MPs voted against, sixty-nine Labour MPs were willing to vote in favor, while twenty abstained. The Common Market Membership Treaty was signed in Brussels on January 22, 1972, and on January 1, 1973, it took effect. Britain became a full member of the EEC, the European Atomic Energy Community, and the European Coal and Steel Community. Denmark and Ireland joined on the same day, but Norway found the Common Fisheries Policy unacceptable and has remained outside. The Norwegian public twice rejected membership in referenda.

Large majorities against entry in public opinion polls in Britain were ignored, as were the referenda in four constituencies held in August 1971. This was, more generally, a pattern in the politics of the period. There was a hostility among Conservatives to "referenda"-style government and also a hostility on the part of Labour.

EC membership was reexamined after Labour returned to power under Wilson in February 1974, in large part in an effort to quieten vocal critics on the Labour Left. Far from displaying a principled commitment to a European cause, the divided Labour government entered into a protracted and largely cosmetic renegotiation of Britain's terms of entry, which brought some regional aid and allowed the continued import of some Commonwealth foodstuffs. The fundamentals, however, were not changed. The 1972 European Communities Act, which gave EC law primacy over British law, was not altered, the CAP was not reformed, insufficient thought was given to Britain's likely contribution level to the EC budget, and the Commonwealth trading system was irreparably weakened. The renegotiated terms were passed in the Commons on April 9, 1975. Nevertheless, the governing Labour Party was far more opposed than the Conservatives, and the support of the latter were needed in order to get the measure through. One hundred and forty-five Labour MPs and 8 Conservatives voted against the Bill, and 137 Labour and 249 Conservatives voted in favor. The division that was to be seen in the Conservatives from the late 1980s was more clearly apparent in Labour in the 1960s and 1970s.

To surmount party divisions, Wilson then launched a constitutional novelty: a referendum campaign on Britain's continued membership of the EC. So that supporters and opponents of membership could both campaign, the principle of collective Cabinet responsibility did not apply in the referendum. Held on June 5, 1975, 67.2 percent of those who voted (about 65 percent of the electorate voted, compared to 72 percent in 2016) favored membership, the only areas showing a majority against being the Shetlands and the Western Isles (of Scotland), whereas in 2016 the geographical pattern was far more mixed. The available evidence suggests that public opinion in 1975 was very volatile on the EC, implying a lack of interest and/or understanding, and that the voters tended to follow the advice of the party leaderships, all of which supported continued membership. The opposition was stigmatized as extreme, although it was from across the political spectrum, from Enoch Powell on the nationalist Right to Tony Benn on the Left. A vigil was held by Churchill's statue in Parliament Square. Britain stayed in. It had joined the EC very much on the latter's terms.[10]

As a consequence of the referendum, relations with the EC were not to become as divisive a political issue again, until they emerged in the late 1980s as the focus for the ultimately fatal split within the Thatcher government. The anti-EC movement itself largely disappeared from sight after 1975. There was no real controversy in 1979 when, fearful of the deflationary consequences of tying sterling to a strong deutschemark, the Labour government under Callaghan decided not to join the ERM, the only one of the nine EC states not to do so. This decision was symptomatic of the reluctant Europeanism of the Callaghan government (1976–79) which, in turn, reflected Callaghan's ingrained Atlanticism. In light of subsequent developments, it is ironic that Thatcher criticized the decision not to enter the ERM, which, indeed, was regarded by some as the basis for monetary and economic union. It was linked to the introduction in 1979 of the ecu (European currency unit), which would eventually turn into the euro.

Under Thatcher, Conservative leader from 1975 to 1990, and prime minister from 1979 to 1990, EC issues took no real role in the 1979, 1983, and 1987 general election campaigns; and it is possible to read accounts of them in which the EC scarcely appears.[11] For Thatcher, the United States, not Europe, was the entity that could, or would, provide the military and political requirements: security for Britain and leadership for the West.[12] Thatcher met the challenges of the passing of empire, the Cold War, Americanization, and the EC by combining an assertion of national resolve with her status as the figurehead for a market economy that had an international significance and sweep. This approach gave her a way to promoting economic modernization that was compatible both with traditional free-trade priorities and with the importance of the nation-state. The Cold War, rather than the empire, a more historic entity and traditional identity, served her as the basis for a foreign policy that still asserted a national role, in a way that her successors were unable to imitate because the context had changed.

In contrast to the EC, the 1982 Falklands War played a major role in the 1983 general election. It was a conflict with marked historical roots, both in that it related to a long-standing British territorial colony and because the government's decision to fight against the Argentine invasion was criticized by some as anachronistic. This claim was advanced at the time, with a correspondent in the *Times* inquiring whether an editorial supporting military action had been misdated by a century, and also subsequently, as in 2004, when the populist president of Argentina, Nestor Kirchner, termed the British effort "a blatant exercise in nineteenth-century imperialism," which more accurately described Argentinean policy. Most of the critics of the war were on the Left, but, among Conservatives, Jock Bruce-Gardyne opposed the war and lost his parliamentary seat accordingly. The conflict and its victorious outcome saw a notable rallying of national patriotism that played a role in later populist Conservative responses to European integration.

In part because European integration did not gather pace, the anti-EC movement remained weak in the 1980s, until it revived in the late 1980s. An instance of the complacency of this period is provided by the autobiography of Denis Healey, former Labour deputy leader, which was published in 1989. He devoted very little space to the 1975 referendum, described as an issue "marginal to our real problems," which, indeed, were dominated by pressing fiscal and economic issues; while, of the direct elections to the European Parliament, Healey remarked:

> Many of my colleagues feared that direct elections would give the so-called Euro-MPs the political authority to assume powers to override the British Parliament. In fact, as I predicted at the time, the Euro-MPs now have less influence on events than before. Elected by a small proportion of the electorate from very large constituencies, they lack political authority; and because they are cut off from their national parliaments they lack influence where it really matters.[13]

Matters became much more divisive during the later Thatcher years. Again, this development was linked to domestic divisions. However, this linkage had not been much in evidence earlier, as in 1984 when a rebate was secured reducing the net amount of Britain's overall subsidy to the EC through the disproportionate payments Britain was making.

A lack of acute domestic division was also the case when the European Communities (Amendment) Act approving the European Single Market was signed in 1986, and the domestic market thus joined to the EC. This act was designed to give effect to the program for an internal market launched the previous year. Such a policy of free trade seemed in accord with British views, and Thatcher had pressed for the opening of markets in order to encourage competition. She saw it as offering a distinctive British-led future for the EC. Labour MPs opposed the act, Blair and Brown both voting against it, but only seven Conservative MPs did.

The increase in EC powers required to oversee the market was more of a problem in the long term and should have been anticipated and guarded against. The act gave new powers to the European Parliament and abolished the veto rights of a single state in some major areas of decision making. However, with key bits of information deliberately withheld from Thatcher, she no more realized what would flow from this, as the momentum for the creation of a "single market" gathered pace, than she understood the consequences of her failure to retain support among Conservative backbenchers—the latter a fate that was to confront Cameron in 2016. As a politician, Thatcher was gravely weakened by her inability to appreciate the potential strength of those she despised. She did not support holding a referendum over EC membership, which she would have seen as a distraction from government policy and as an unnecessary limitation of parliamentary authority.

In enforcing open markets, the EC also proved open to political horse trading, indeed frequently corruption, that did not suit the British. Furthermore, the internal market was a major restriction of the role of individual states and thus of the position and functions of government and Parliament. In addition, the European Single Market did not anyway lead to the promised economic transformation and notably not to the promised opening-up of national markets in services.

Keen on free trade and an advocate for economic liberalization, Thatcher was critical of what she saw as a preference for economic controls and centralist planning in the EC. Both became more marked in the late 1980s as a major attempt was made to energize the EC. This attempt owed much to French Socialists, particularly Jacques Delors, president of the EC Commission from 1985 to 1994, and reflected their response to the problems of executing their policies within France itself earlier in the decade: Delors had been François Mitterrand's minister of economics and finance. During the Giscard d'Estaing presidency (1974–81), the conservative Barre government (1976–81) had pursued an economic liberalization, cutting the government's role and emphasizing market forces, that was in line with Thatcherite assumptions, not least in putting the control of inflation above the fight with unemployment. However, these policies were dramatically reversed in 1981, after the Socialist candidate, Mitterrand, won the presidential election.

In many respects, the unsuccessful policies that subsequently followed in France in 1981–83, policies with which Delors was closely associated, linked the traditional nostrums of the Left and of state control and intervention, with the aspirations for regulation and social management that underlie aspects of the modern European project. Reflation focused less on modernization than on support for traditional constituencies (coal, steel, and shipbuilding in France in the early 1980s, agriculture today), while a determined attempt was made to control manufacturing and the financial system. Taxation in France in 1981–83 was directed toward redistribution, with a wealth tax matched by an increase in the minimum wage, and by a cut in the working week.

This French experience rested in part on a refusal to accept the disciplines posed by international economic competition, and, indeed, on their rejection as alien Anglo-American concepts. Mitterrand's ambitious policies, however, had rapidly been thwarted by economic realities, with the policies reversed in 1983. To French politicians, Europe seemed, not so much an alternative, as a way to give effect to their thwarted visions. In 1985, Delors became president of the European Commission, a post he held until 1994, and he revived the policy of European integration, seeing it as a complement to the enlargement of the "nine" to the "twelve": Greece joined in 1981, and Spain and Portugal in 1986. To Delors, a stronger commission and a weaker national veto were crucial if progress was to be made; indeed, he used the commission to provide a driving force for integration. In practice, the Delors's report on competitiveness and growth aggravated structural economic problems in the EC. The energy of the French Left was strengthened in 1988 when Mitterrand was reelected as president. Alongside the ambition of the commission, this put Thatcher in a vulnerable position.

France's ambitions for the EC were accentuated when German unification (of West and East Germany) became an option after the collapse of Eastern European Communism and the fall of the Berlin Wall in 1989. Deeper European integration seemed a way to contain Germany, just as the original establishment of the EEC had been regarded as a way to anchor West

Germany in the West. Meanwhile, French ambitions for social policy helped ensure that Labour abandoned its position as an essentially anti-EC one and, instead, became the more pro-European of the two main British political parties. The decline in Labour Atlanticism played a role, but the support for the EC from successive American presidents after Reagan helped lessen tension between Atlanticist and European identities for Labour leaders and for some Conservative counterparts. In 2016, President Obama was to urge Britain to stay in the EU.

Thatcher had absolutely no time for the integrationist ambitions pushed by Delors. She correctly discerned their serious implications for Britain and, indeed, Europe. On September 20, 1988, Thatcher declared, at the opening ceremony of the thirty-ninth academic year of the College of Europe in Bruges, "We have not successfully rolled back the frontiers of the state in Britain, only to see them re-imposed at a European level, with a European super-state exercising a new dominance from Brussels." Indeed, Thatcher could point to the pursuit at the national level of her own economic policies as leading to economic revival. This was a counter to Delors's speech earlier that month at the Trades Union Congress Conference in Bournemouth arguing that the union movement could gain through Europe what it had lost with Mrs. Thatcher.

Thatcher felt closer to Ronald Reagan, the US president from 1981 to 1989, whom she had recognized as a fellow spirit when they first met in 1975, than to European leaders, such as Valéry Giscard d'Estaing, François Mitterrand, and Helmut Kohl. Their patronizing manner was not suited to managing her frenetic assertiveness. Thatcher's government was also more influenced than its Continental counterparts by the emergence of neoliberal free-market economics in the 1980s, particularly in the United States. This influence reflected not only Thatcher's Americanism, her commitment to Britain becoming an enterprising society and dynamic economy on the US model, but also the greater hostility of much of the Conservative Party to the corporatist and regulatory state, certainly as compared with the attitude of the Continental Christian Democrats, let alone their Socialist counterparts.

This situation was accentuated by the exigencies of coalition systems on the Continent, for systems of proportional representation are generally less subject to new political departures, or, if so, do so as a result of changes in which the electorate often play only a limited role. Kohl's Christian Democrats gained power in 1982 because the Free Democrats switched its alliance to them, whereas Thatcher had become prime minister in 1979 because voters' preferences had markedly changed.

Thatcher's own attitude toward the EC was more bluntly put by Nicholas Ridley, a minister close to her, who was forced to resign from the Cabinet after telling the editor of the *Spectator*, a pro-Conservative news weekly, in July 1990 that the EC was a "German racket designed to take over the whole of Europe." Bernard Ingram, formerly Thatcher's press secretary and very much "his mistress's voice," referred to the EC in 1992 as a "Franco-German ramp."[14] Thatcher's alienation became more serious as the EC developed in a more ambitious direction. She was also unhappy about the unification of Germany in 1990, fearing that this would lead to an overly powerful and assertive Germany, an attitude she anchored in her personal grasp of history and that she sought to explore in a seminar with British and American historians held at Chequers on March 24, 1990.[15]

Ironically, Thatcher's views mirrored earlier French doubts about West German *Ostpolitik*, the reaching-out toward Communist Eastern Europe in the 1970s and 1980s. To France, Germany had to be anchored in the EC, to Britain in NATO; but German unification made the latter a less potent context for German policy making. German policy makers, such as Hans-Dietrich Genscher, the foreign minister from 1974 to 1992, claimed that unification would serve the interests of Europe. The entire process was eventually put in a European framework. Thatcher was understandably uneasy about what this entailed. Much of the British government and civil service, including Douglas Hurd, who became foreign secretary in 1989, however, did not share Thatcher's doubts and, instead, actively supported German unification. Hurd thought Thatcher's use of history, notably her references to opposition to Germany in World War II, ahistorical.[16]

The Campaign Guide 1989, produced that spring by the Conservative Research Department, as a primer for that year's county council and European elections, claimed that Britain was a model for respect based on appropriate domestic policies joined to a robust international stance:

> Britain today attracts greater respect abroad, and is able to exercise more influence in the world than for many years, because of the successful Conservative policies which have revitalized our economy. Britain's revival has not simply restored her status as a major economic power, but has made this country a model which is both admired and emulated throughout the world.[17]

The defense and foreign affairs section, which was not to the fore in the guide, began, under the title "Restoring Respect for Britain Abroad" with sections on "A Model of Economic Success," "A Champion of Common Sense," "A Staunch Ally in NATO," and "Strengthening the Western European Union."

An emphasis on the national interest was also seen in the criticism of Labour, not only for a reckless hostility toward the United States, but also for a "callous disregard for the national interests of Britain" in its defense policy.[18]

However, Thatcher had already fallen out with key members of her Cabinet, including former supporters, over what, partly as a result of this falling out, became the crucial issue of Europe. She fell out with the foreign secretary, the pro-European Geoffrey Howe, over joining the ERM of the European Monetary System, which constituted stage one of a projected economic and monetary union for the EC. Thatcher was opposed because she saw the free market as more benign than fixed exchange rates, and she was also concerned about further European integration. In November 1985, she had rejected ministerial pressure, notably from Nigel Lawson, the chancellor of the exchequer, to join the ERM. Nevertheless, threats to resign by Howe and Lawson led Thatcher, at a European summit in Madrid in June 1989, to promise to join the ERM.

In July 1989, in a countermove, Howe was removed from the foreign office and made deputy prime minister but without being given power, which left him very bitter. In turn, in October 1989, Lawson resigned in large part because of disagreement with Thatcher over his support for shadowing the deutschemark, which was an indirect form of membership of the ERM, and therefore unwelcome to Thatcher. He had done so in order to deal with fiscal indiscipline. Feeling weakened, Thatcher was reluctantly prevailed on to join the ERM on October 5, 1990, in part by Major, the new chancellor of the exchequer, and by Hurd, the new foreign secretary, each of whom seriously failed to appreciate the possible political and economic costs. Labour fully supported the policy, but, as with so many oppositions, was not to bear the political price.

Thatcher, however, made it very obvious that she had no intention of accepting further integration within the EC, not least a single currency. She correctly saw that monetary union was designed to lead to political union. That path was clearly laid out by the meeting of EC leaders in the European Council in Rome in October 1990, which declared, "The European Community will have a single currency which will be an expression of its unity and identity." Thatcher firmly and publicly rejected this conclusion, and Britain was the sole state to vote against further economic and monetary union, touching off the immediate crisis that led to her fall.

Having resigned on November 1, 1990, in anger at Thatcher's clear-cut, indeed, strident, opposition to further integration, Howe attacked Thatcher in a speech in the Commons on November 13, for being unable to accept debate and for her policy on Europe. He claimed that the latter was leading to Britain becoming isolated and ineffective. Howe also encouraged a leadership bid by Michael Heseltine, another firm supporter of the EC, who had left the Cabinet in 1986 over the Westland affair when he had clashed with Thatcher over whether the Westland helicopter manufacturer should be taken over by a US company (as she wished) or by a European consortium, the goal he unsuccessfully sought. This had caused a serious, albeit short-term, political crisis with Cabinet divisions leading to a questioning of Thatcher's position.

Major, who succeeded Thatcher as prime minister in November 1990 (see chapter 7), sought to distance himself from her confrontational style and had initially spoken about his desire to place Britain "at the heart of Europe." *The Best Future for Britain*, the Conservative election manifesto for the 1992 general election, somewhat wistfully declared,

> Under the Conservatives, Britain has regained her rightful influence in the world. We have stood up for the values our country has always represented. . . . We play a central part in world affairs. . . . Britain is at the heart of Europe; a strong and respected partner. We have played a decisive part in the development of the Community over the past decade.

This, however, was a statement of aspiration, not reality. This approach linked the global role that British Conservatives largely sought and moreover demonstrated in the 1991 Gulf War, with a very different European one that most believed necessary, but without significant enthusiasm. Britain was certainly not at the heart of Europe.

Thatcher's fall was not to settle the political and fiscal relationship between Britain and its European partners, which was increasingly problematic, creating growing difficulties for the cohesion of the Conservative Party. Seeking to defend national interests, Major resisted the concentration of decision making within the EC at the level of supranational institutions. At the Maastricht conference of European leaders held in December 1991, Major obtained an opt-out clause from stage three of economic and monetary union, the single currency, and from the "social chapter," which was held likely to increase social welfare and employment costs, to threaten the competitiveness and autonomy of British industry, and therefore not to be in Britain's competitive interest. Major also ensured that the word *federal* was excluded from the Maastricht Treaty, although that was more a victory of style than substance.

Nevertheless, the greater integration agreed at Maastricht was too much for the increasingly vocal Euroskeptics in the Conservative Party. The Treaty on European Union, signed at Maastricht on February 7, 1992, created, from the EC, the European Union (EU), the new term an indication of the new prospectus. Every citizen of an EC member state was to be a citizen of this union, with certain rights in every EC country. The treaty also extended the scope and powers of the EC over its members and announced that "a common foreign and security policy is hereby established." The scope of the commission, the EC's executive branch, was expanded in the EU over more areas of policy, including transport, education, and social policy, the last a dangerously vague concept that threatened a progressive expansion of competence. In pursuit of "a high degree of convergence of economic performance," member states were required to accept the fiscal discipline demanded by the commission and the Council of Ministers. In addition, the ability of national ministers to exercise a veto on the Council of Ministers on behalf of national interests was restricted, while the powers of the European Parliament over legislation were extended. There were clear aspects of federalism in the division of powers between the EC and individual states. The criteria for planned convergence toward European Monetary Union (EMU) in 1999 were also outlined.

The role of the Euroskeptics within the Conservative Party was increased because the general election held on April 9, 1992, left Major with only a small parliamentary majority (of twenty-one). This made it difficult for him to follow a policy on Europe that was not at risk from wrecking opposition on the part of those whom he referred to as "bastards." Euroskepticism also provided a means for disaffected Thatcherites, angry at her fall, to express their fury and ensured that the issue became a key one in steadily more bitter and public dividedness within the Conservative Party. The struggle to win parliamentary endorsement for Maastricht, in the shape of the European Communities (Amendment) Bill, badly weakened the government, which had to make its passage a vote of confidence. In what Major referred to as "gruesome trench warfare," and was certainly the most serious post-1945 revolt against a government by its own MPs, the Conservative vote against the treaty eventually encompassed one-fifth of the party's backbench MPs. The paving motion designed to take the Maastricht Bill through passed on November 4, 1992, but the vote was 319 to 316, a majority of only three. The treaty became law on July 20, 1993.[19]

The crisis led to the establishment of right-wing political groups that helped result in the focusing of interest on the European issue. The United Kingdom Independence Party (UKIP) was founded in 1992 as a sequel to the Anti-Federalist League, and the European Foundation followed in 1993. This was not simply a development on the national level for, in 1992, the European Anti-Maastricht Alliance was established. However, European-level opposition to further integration proved difficult to arrange or apply, and UKIP largely acted on the national level.

Denmark, France, and Ireland all held referenda on the Maastricht Treaty, but, aware of the unpopularity of its policy (and more generally of the government), the Major Cabinet refused to do so. This refusal lacked the constitutional basis that referenda were unprecedented, as there had already been a referendum in 1975. It was also unpopular, ignoring a Maastricht Referendum Campaign that collected more than half a million signatures for its petition to Parliament. The failure to hold a referendum provided James Goldsmith, a multimillionaire financier without any background in parliamentary politics, with an issue for mobilizing discontent. Goldsmith launched the Referendum Party in late 1994 and also helped weaken the base of the Conservative government, not least by dispiriting activists. These factors contributed to Conservative failure in the subsequent, 1997, election. Moreover, the government's "wait and see" line over British participation in the projected single currency, the eventual euro, encouraged doubt and was not a way to rally support. The popular press moved against the government, a process encouraged by Labour's wooing of it and notably of Rupert Murdoch, the owner of the *Sun*.

The government's reputation for economic management had already been crippled by another aspect of European policy. On Black Wednesday, September 16, 1992, an overvalued exchange rate for sterling, the interest-rate policies of the Bundesbank, and speculators together forced sterling out of the ERM. Major had supported entry at what was an overvalued exchange rate because he believed that this would squeeze inflation out of the British economy and thus create an environment for growth. The government, however, found itself forced to respond to the financial policies of the strongest economy in the ERM, Germany, and unable to persuade the Bundesbank to reduce its interest rates. The Bundesbank put the control of German inflation, seriously threatened as a consequence of the budget deficit arising from the generous terms offered to East Germans in order to make a success of German unification in 1990, above the prospects for British growth. This preference reminded ministers of the disadvantages of close international ties. The French government had similarly hoped that competition once France joined the ERM would squeeze inflation out of the economy, but, not least with closer ties with Germany, it was in a better political position to influence the resulting situation.

Britain had joined the ERM in October 1990 at the rate of 2.95 deutschemark to the pound, and this obliged the government to raise interest rates to defend the pound when its value reached the bottom of the permitted exchange-rate band at 2.82 deutschemark. Thus raising the interest rates helped result in an economic depression and an unsustainable deficit, but the Major government felt that it had to stay in for political reasons. In turn, departure from the ERM in 1992 was a humiliating defeat for fiscal policy, and one that involved the Bank of England, in a futile effort to stay in, deploying more than £15 billion from its reserves to this end, while, on Black Wednesday, interest rates were raised to 15 percent. In the end, political will could not prevail over financial pressures.

In practice, however, the exit brought crucial benefit, enabling Britain, in economic independence from the EC, to manage its own finances and to expand its role as a leading offshore financial center, contributing to the growing importance of the City to the British economy. This independence also looked toward Britain staying out of the euro. More generally, fiscal independence helped encourage economic growth from the mid-1990s. In the 1990s, British gross domestic product rose by an annual average of 2.3 percent, which compared favorably to the leading ERM economies: 1.9 percent for France and 1.3 percent for Germany, which had to deal with the consequences of post-Communist unification.

At the time, however, the crisis created an abiding impression of inept Conservative leadership, one that was to contribute to the election defeat in 1997 (see chapter 8). Major and his chancellor of the exchequer, Norman Lamont, had both staked the credibility of the government's entire economic and counterinflationary strategy on membership of the ERM shortly before Britain was humiliatingly forced out of it. It was not that the electorate understood the ERM or the implications for British policy of coming out of it, but what they did know from the media was that it was a massive failure of Conservative policy upon which it had staked its credibility.

The result was seen in an immediate catastrophic collapse in Conservative electoral support, which was based largely on its irrevocable loss of a substantial lead over Labour in terms of perceived economic competence. Such a perception had been at the heart of the Conservative electoral victory in 1992 in the midst of a deep economic recession. As a direct result of Black Wednesday, the Conservatives went from a 13 percent lead as the party best able to manage economic problems to a Labour lead of 21 percent by November 1992. Despite a significant recovery in economic performance by 1996–97, there was to be no "feel-good factor." Helped by much of the media, Labour was able to divert attention from the extent to which, under the leadership of John Smith in 1992–94, it had backed the ERM and EMU and criticized the Conservatives for a lack of enthusiasm on these matters.

By weakening the Conservatives in the 1997 election, the Referendum Party aided Labour,[20] although the government's record over the ERM, its broken promises over taxation, and the complete collapse of electoral faith in its economic and governing competence, compounded by the manifest divisions within its ranks, had made a Labour victory inevitable. The Referendum Party won no seats but gained 812,000 votes, about 3 percent overall, while UKIP gained 106,000 votes, which indicated the growing division on the Right. This was a division in which foreign policy, in the sense of Europe, played the central role. The post-Thatcher Conservative Party had been swallowed up in the European issue in the 1990s, and the issue has remained divisive and electorally significant thereafter.

This was important as the European context was in fact far from static. Indeed, in the early and mid-2000s, as national governments came to play a more active role in the EU, pressure for integration receded, despite the ambitions of the commission. However, the international financial crisis that began in 2008 opened up new calls for integration. The British position was distinctive, as, despite the strong wishes of Blair, Britain did not take part in monetary union. On January 1, 2002, euro notes and coins replaced existing currencies in eleven countries, the intention outlined at Maastricht, but Britain was one of the few EU states that remained outside of the eurozone. The Major Cabinet had been strongly divided over joining the euro, and Major postponed the issue by pledging to hold a referendum before doing so, a pledge matched by Labour in its 1997 election manifesto. Membership was opposed not only by most of the Conservatives but also, more significantly after 1997, by Brown, the chancellor of the exchequer, who in 1997 established "tests" to assess the degree of convergence between the British and eurozone economies. These tests were economic, and, in a crucial test of strength within the government, Brown put these factors, and not the political ones favored by Blair, at the center of the debate. As a result of this decision, Britain remained at a distance from the terrible economic crisis affecting the eurozone from 2011. The British decision was influenced by a referendum in Denmark in September 2000 that rejected the euro. Nevertheless, Blair might well have prevailed over Brown had he not changed his focus after the 9/11 attacks on the United States in 2001. Britain also remained outside the Schengen area of passport-free travel within the EU.

BREXIT

This situation did not end concern in Britain about the EU's pressure for integration and unification, and this concern became more politically prominent in the 2010s. In June 2012, John Baron, a Conservative backbench MP, led a letter from a hundred colleagues demanding referendum on the EU. This was repeatedly seen during the working out of Brexit prior to the end of EU membership in 2020. As was predictable, that was only one stage in a continuing relationship with the EU, both as an institution and with reference to its constituent states. The range of issues included trade, migration, and security. In 2022, the last was pushed to the fore as Britain took a prominent role in support of Ukraine when it was invaded by Russia. Britain's close relationship with the continent was abundantly displayed. This was repeatedly seen during the working out of Brexit prior to the end of EU membership in 2020. As was predictable, that was only one stage in a continuing relationship with the EU, both as an institution and with reference to its constituent states. The range of issues included trade, migration, and security. In 2022, the last was pushed to the fore as Britain took a prominent role in support of Ukraine when it was invaded by Russia. Britain's close relationship with the continent was abundantly displayed. The challenge from UKIP and of disaffected Conservatives led David Cameron, in accordance with a promise in January 2013 (a promise made under pressure from colleagues), to go into the 2015 general election promising to renegotiate the terms of British membership in the EU and then to put continued membership to a referendum. He appears to have anticipated a continuation of the coalition with the Liberal Democrats, and having therefore (willingly) to abandon the promise as the price of a renewed coalition, as the Liberal Democrats were against any such referendum. Instead, Cameron unexpectedly won an overall majority.

An alternative explanation suggests that Cameron, from 2013, was overly concerned about the UKIP challenge and sought to stanch Tory defections to UKIP by means of the promise. Two MPs had defected to UKIP in August–September 2014 (going on to retain their seats in by-elections), giving it a parliamentary presence, and more defections were rumored or threatened. If so, this was an instance of a tactical solution that created a strategic problem. Whatever the result, it was clear that Cameron would be judged as someone who had taken a great risk, as indeed had been the case with the earlier referenda on proportional representation (2011) and on Scottish independence (2014).

Having won the election, Cameron was unable to win many concessions on the terms of British membership in the EU and certainly not those he had suggested he would obtain and that he had pursued in exhaustive negotiations. He won agreement to restrictions on benefits for new arrivals for up to seven years, concessions to the City of London, and an opt-out from "ever-closer union," but these did not amount to what much of the public wanted. More seriously, despite his strong efforts, an impression of failure was created.

Instead, Cameron found himself in an exposed position during the referendum debate, obliged to defend British membership in the face of considerable public reluctance on the issue and of a Conservative Party that was totally and very publicly divided. In place of positive arguments for continued membership, the general theme from the "Remain" side was that of the financial, economic, and political dangers of being outside the EU. A dire picture of national isolation was painted in what critics referred to as "project fear." This picture reflected a sense that the United States could not be relied on to support Britain's interests and also an awareness of a new set of international challenges different to those of the Cold War but, nevertheless, still serious.

The difficult economic and fiscal situation of the country proved a key context, as it had done throughout the postwar period. Indeed, the 2016 referendum brought up and focused many of the tensions and issues of contemporary British history. These included immigration and the British question. Popular worries about immigration played a potent role in the debate. The immigration issue was not in fact one solely about the EU, as many immigrants came from non-EU countries. Moreover, much of the public discussion was ill-informed, not least failing adequately to appreciate the value of immigrants or to address the ethical issues involved. This was seen in August 2016 when Lisa Duffy, a UKIP leadership candidate, called for a total ban on Islamic veils in public places, on Muslim faith schools, and on Sharia courts, leading to the claim that she was "chasing the bigot vote."[21]

Conversely, the sense of a disproportionate rate of change was captured, by and for, a public some of whom claimed to be "overwhelmed." Brexit campaigners predicted that continued membership would lead to an annual immigration of three hundred thousand people and would rapidly resulted in a UK population of eighty million, and drew attention to what they claimed was the risk that Turkey would join the EU. Cameron correctly argued that there was no current prospect of long-standing accession negotiations leading to such an outcome, but the immigration question, and notably over Turkey, touched all sorts of subliminal issues. That Turkey represented apparent Islamicization made it a potent issue. Less contentiously, given high unemployment rates in much of the EU and attractive minimum-wage provisions in Britain, continued inward movement at a high rate appeared likely.

The eventual result surprised most commentators, even though the polls had shown a move to leave the EU two weeks prior to the vote. In practice, a very similar move happened in the Scottish referendum at around the same stage in 2014 and also in 1975 in the EU referendum but without any eventual vote to leave. The polls on average in 2016 showed each side on percentage

support in the low to mid-forties. These numbers did not, however, as anticipated, underestimate support for "Remain." There was the difficulty for pollsters of reaching the people more likely to vote, who are the people with jobs,
active lives, and more affluence. The history of referenda suggested that unde-
cideds break two to one for the status quo whatever the question; however,
that did not happen in 2016. Studies, moreover, indicate that up to 30 percent
change their mind in referenda in the last few days and even on the day. These
points interact with a key aspect of human psychology: humans are loss averse
and tend to favor the status quo on anything when it gets to the decision point.
This helps explain why there are few one-term British governments. Studies
also show that as the vote nears and people actually have to exercise their
vote, rather than expressing an off-the-cuff point of view, they have a frightened sense of responsibility, not just to themselves but to their friends, family,
and community. That interacts with the previous point to make them nervous
and more conservative, and therefore, it was thought by many, including the
stock market and foreign exchange dealers, more likely to vote "Remain." Fear
on the economy, accordingly, it was anticipated, would probably trump anger
over immigration.

In the event, Brexit, with 17,410,742 voters, won the majority. On a high
participation rate for the UK, 72 percent of the electorate, just under 52 percent
overall, voted for Brexit, although London and Scotland voted very strongly
for "Remain," as did graduates and the young. In the North, strong support for
Brexit from white working-class areas swayed the result. The vote for Brexit
was 70 percent in Hartlepool, 68.3 percent in Barnsley, 62 percent for South
Tyneside, 61.3 percent for Sunderland, and 57.5 percent for Durham. More
affluent cities supported "Remain," notably Leeds and Newcastle, but the
majorities were slight: Newcastle voted 50.4 percent for "Remain"—producing
the first warning sign for Cameron[22]—and Leeds 50.3 percent. Brexit also
gained a majority in the industrial areas of South Wales, including 56.4 percent
for Merthyr Tydfil and 62 percent for Blaenau Gwent. At the same time, Brexit
did well across much of the South, apart from in London.

Daniel Hannan declared on June 23 "Independence Day" while Nigel
Farage of UKIP proclaimed a victory for "ordinary people." This was not the
sole view. A French academic commentator, Pierre Manent, pointed out that
"the British political class had not given its soul to the European idea as had
its French counterpart."[23] Although the general perception is that working-
class voters in the North of England were responsible for Brexit, a perception
frequently accompanied with pejorative comments (their Scottish counterparts voted Remain), the vote in the South was more important than that

in the North due to the number of voters there. In practice, on the national scale, a majority of homeowners who had no mortgage voted for Brexit, as did social and council tenants. Only a majority of private renters and of people with mortgages voted for "Remain." Polls suggested that 96 percent of UKIP voters in the 2015 general election and 58 percent of the Conservative voters voted Brexit, compared to 37 percent for Labour, 36 percent for the Scottish National Party, 30 percent for the Liberal Democrats, and 25 percent for the Greens. Although seen as right-wing by most, UKIP's economic policies were of the Left.

At a different level, the question of British cohesion came to the fore, as it was widely anticipated that a Brexit vote would trigger another Scottish referendum on independence and that despite the economic and fiscal problems created for Scotland by the fall in the price of oil. Whereas all the Scottish council areas voted for "Remain," and 55.8 percent of the Northern Irish voted for "Remain," seventeen out of the twenty-two Welsh councils remained for Brexit. Of the English vote, 53.4 percent was for Brexit, but of the Scottish vote, only 38 percent. On July 22, 2016, in the heated atmosphere after the referendum, a YouGov poll claimed that one in nine Londoners wanted independence, while a quarter favored a London parliament with powers similar to the Scottish Assembly.

There were also questions about the fabric of national life. The murder in 2016 of Jo Cox, a Labour MP campaigning for Britain to remain in the EU, allegedly by a Brexit supporter who supposedly shouted, "Britain first, keep Britain independent," created anxiety about the vulnerability of British democracy. Significantly, the alleged assassin lived in a Yorkshire constituency with a high rate of unemployment, a constituency once known for the manufacture of textiles and cars but with both having ended many years ago. From another angle, the rarity of such attacks since 1970, other than by IRA terrorists, was notable. The net effect served to underline the range of uncertainties that faced Britain at the close of our period. For example, prior to the result, a counterfactual was apparently posed by the murder of Cox—namely, what would have happened, instead, if Farage, the prominent leader of UKIP, had been murdered by a Muslim. The role of such counterfactuals had been demonstrated by the nearness of Thatcher's assassination by the IRA in the Brighton hotel bombing in 1984. Indeed, an aspect of the role of the intelligence services in British history is that provided by its opponents in the shape of terrorist groups or individuals.

In addition, uncertainties related to the wider world. A world of unprecedented population growth provided a context for the debate over migration within Europe and notably as a result of greatly increased immigration in 2015, largely from Syria, Libya, Afghanistan, Iraq, and Eritrea, and of EU attempts to redistribute immigrants. Instability in the Middle East and Russian saber-rattling threw attention on the EU's inability to work out effective defense and foreign policy arrangements. Fears over US leadership accentuated this concern. Moreover, aside from Britain, there were fundamental questions about the long-term stability and viability of the EU, questions highlighted in 2016 by the financial and economic plight of Greece, by political instability in Italy and Spain, and by serious public order issues in France.

A lack of linkage between populists, of Left and Right, and, on the other hand, the drivers of the European "project," as well as the matter of unfunded liabilities and a dysfunctional fiscal system created questions about the ability of the EU to solve its problems. This appeared the case, whether or not Britain was a member. Equally, it was readily apparent that Britain had serious political, economic, and social problems irrespective of whether it was in the EU. In part, the EU debate was a distraction from these problems, but, in part, it contributed directly to them.

Aside from the future of the EU, there is the case of the broader significance of the referendum for Britain's place in the world since 1945. This is unclear, but the referendum suggests that fundamental discontinuities can arise from particular circumstances at specific moments. How readily Britain will be able to maintain good relations with the EU and to define a viable economic, political, and strategic relationship with the remainder of the world is uncertain and a matter of contention.

11

INTO THE FUTURE

THE REFERENDUM DEBATES of 2014 and 2016, over Scottish independence and EU membership, respectively, revealed (to put it mildly) considerable division over the future of the country, division expressed in clashing uncertainties. These uncertainties comprised past, present, and future. Dissension over history was a key aspect of this uncertainty over the future, and this dissension reached to the present. Both the Labour government of Gordon Brown (2007–10), and its Conservative-dominated coalition successor under David Cameron (2010–15), sought to emphasize Britishness and to encourage the teaching of national history. However, the British national account, with its focus on freedom, liberty, law, rights, and progress, no longer appeared so obvious or well-grounded to the public, in whatever way the abstraction of the public (or indeed the national account) was to be understood. Moreover, the confidence expressed in such views appeared increasingly precarious by the 2010s. When I sat on the advisory board for the National Curriculum for History, Michael Gove, Secretary of State for Education (2010–14) told me that that subject caused the most controversy.

Social, economic, and cultural contexts are very important in explaining a lack of confidence about present and future. There was a degree of recovery from the economic and financial crisis of the late 2000s, and notably so in London property prices which were fed by foreign investment as well as the strength of the City before being hit in 2016 by the decision to leave the EU. Nevertheless, alongside such contingent developments, structural elements of change continue and, in doing so, have a major impact. These elements include the decline of manufacturing, which by 2010, represented only about 12 percent of the economy, which was half the percentage in the early 1990s. Moreover, in 2015, business investment was only about 8 percent of gross domestic product (GDP). A House of Commons Briefing Paper of August 2016 suggested the following percentages of manufacturing output as a percentage of GDP: Germany 23, Italy 15, France 12, and Britain, Canada, and the United States all 11.

In addition, much of the future had been spent. In June 2016, the ONS reported that, in May, public-sector net borrowing for the financial year had hit £76 billion, a £2 billion rise on its initial estimate, because of a worse-than-expected £9.7 billion borrowing in May. Public-sector net debt at the end of May 2016 stood at £1,606.9 billion, the equivalent to 83.7 percent of GDP and a rise on earlier figures. The current account deficit in 2015 amounted to £96.2 billion, the equivalent of 5.2 percent of GDP. The situation was to be totally wrecked by the expenditure deemed necessary during the COVID pandemic of 2020–22 and then in response to the increasing energy costs ocovering daily bills, a situtation that gathered pace in 2022.

Moreover, much of the population was affected by anxieties about their living conditions, especially the availability of housing and covering daily bills, a situtation that gathered pace in 2022. In *Broonland*, Christopher Harvie (2010) decried the end of the respectable Scottish artisan culture that was reflected in the *Sunday Post*'s long-running cartoon *The Broons*.

Relations between the generations were, and are, a key aspect of history. There was a widespread sense that children no longer had as good a prospect as their parents, the baby boom generation that had benefited from property increases and final-salary schemes and had mortgaged the future. Notably due to the difficulty of obtaining attractive, or even any, housing, this assessment of generational prospects was certainly valid for a significant percentage. Rising house prices led to a marked increase in the average age of first-time buyers, to reach near forty by 2011. In 2013, three million people aged between twenty and thirty-four were still living at home with their parents, while there were 289,000 families housing another family under their roof, often young couples living with a parent. In addition, in 2016, the housing charity Shelter claimed that 450,000 adults required assistance from their parents to keep them in their rental home.

The Conservative government promised a remedy but like its Labour and Coalition predecessors, could not provide one. In 2016, the shadow chancellor felt it opportune to promise that a future Labour government would build one hundred thousand council houses a year. This promise was of least relevance to the affluent as, indeed, was the issue as a whole because they could afford houses, which yet again, helped explain the variety of class responses to political questions.

Immigration was part of the equation. In 2016, Jeremy Corbyn, the Labour leader, who was ambivalent about the EU, noting that Britons concerned about immigration were not "Little Englanders, xenophobes, or racists," declared that communities could change "dramatically and rapidly" as a consequence.[1] The 2016 British Social Attitudes Survey revealed that almost three-quarters of Britons believed that the influx of migrants was damaging public services, including the NHS and schools, by putting them under increased pressure. In contrast, only 35 percent considered immigrants bad for the economy. Concern about immigration was strongest not necessarily where immigration was most common—for example, London—but instead, where the recent rise in immigrants was especially high—as in parts of East Anglia. Indeed, in those local authority areas where the foreign-born population had risen by more than 200 percent between 2001 and 2004, a Brexit vote followed in 94 percent of cases. Corbyn returned during the campaign to the challenge posed by mass immigration. The high rate of immigration contributed to a strong (but far from universal) sense that the balance of government and elite concern was misplaced.

This helped explain one of the most instructive aspects of the 2015 general election: namely, the extent to which the UK Independence Party (UKIP), which won an eighth of the national vote (and an even higher percentage in England), made inroads among former Labour supporters and notably in the North of England. This was unexpected and counterintuitive to many commentators as they had seen UKIP as a right-wing movement born from divisions within the Conservative Party over Europe and therefore most likely to win votes from the Conservatives. Indeed, UKIP did, helping in particular to lessen the Conservatives' hold over many traditional supporters, especially much of its working-class support and many older votes. This working-class support had proved important to Thatcher's electoral victories. Nevertheless, in 2015, UKIP took many Labour votes, squeezing Labour majorities and, indeed, coming second to Labour in many northern constituencies. It was as if the working-class vote had split, not, as under Thatcher in the elections of 1979, 1983, and 1987, between a Labour majority and an important Conservative minority, a minority still there to help Major in 1992, but now between Labour and UKIP, helping Cameron in 2015.

It is unclear how far this will become a trend, and British electoral history is littered with flawed predictions: for example, about the impact of the Social

Democratic Party in the 1980s and their apparent ability to "break the mold" of British politics.

It is uncertain whether UKIP proved not to be a harbinger of a right-wing populist movement able to span social divides, but rather flickered out, unable to confront the electoral exigencies of the "first-past-the-post" system, as well as very serious weaknesses in its leadership and organization.

British electoral history is littered with flawed predictions: for example, about the impact of the Social Democratic Party in the 1980s and their apparent ability to "break the mold" of British politics. A section on the future has to be open to contingency and repeatedly so, and each contingency offers a cascade of possible outcomes. This is very much present when successive referenda suggested possibly major transformations in the political structure and identity of the country. It is unclear whether that will make future referenda less likely, as across much of the political spectrum, the political leadership may not welcome such uncertainty, which in particular, challenges the principles and practices of parliamentary government.

More generally, there is a volatility at play that makes not only predictions difficult, if not transient, but also a sense of continuity as increasingly, at least to a degree, a matter of nostalgia. This volatility is the case not only at the national level, but also at the international one. Recent history demonstrates the significance of the latter. In some cases, there were important elements of choice. For example, Britain could have joined Canada, France, Germany, and Italy in not taking part in the 2003 Gulf War. There were also key developments that greatly affected Britain but that it had no, or very little, influence over. The collapse of Communism and the Arab Spring are obvious instances. The former in 1989 led, within two decades, to the integration of Eastern Europe into the EU and the North Atlantic Treaty Organization (NATO) and to large-scale immigration into Britain, as well as a major expansion of Britain's defense commitments. The end of Communist economics in China resulted in the entry of its workforce into international trade which had key consequences for the viability of many Western industries and for the balance of payments. The instability linked to, and resulting from, the Arab Spring helped lead to the European immigration crisis of the mid-2010s, which was a major part of the background to the anxieties focused by the Brexit vote in 2016. The nature of key future international developments, for example the possibility of rising tensions between China and America, is unclear, but again, Britain will be greatly affected.

Certain predictions appear well founded for Britain (and the world), notably that a rising population will pose many problems for institutional provision and the social fabric. In the latter case, the extent to which the young may well be the first generation who are less well-off than their predecessors poses major issues, notably of intergenerational fairness and of potential radicalism.

Moreover, economic difficulties will thwart political hopes and make the bringing of popular expectations into line with realities even more crucial but also difficult. The level of debt is such that much of the future has been spent, in the shape of heavy borrowing, and at both the individual and the government levels. This makes any downturn in economic confidence and activity, as from 2020, especially troubling, as well as the rise in interest rates in 2022. It is difficult to feel optimistic. The balance between an exuberant welcoming of expansion, diversity, and the future, and an anxious questioning of implications is often a very fine one.

So also with climate change, with global warming a key factor, not least in rising sea levels and in increasingly stormy weather. In 2003, the summer temperature rose to 38.5° C. Global warming may lead to agricultural yields rising in the north and falling in the south, but the impact on sea levels are more serious. The risk of flooding as a result of surge tides led to the construction, between 1974 and 1982, of the Thames Flood Barrier at Woolwich (a major feat of civil engineering), officially opened in May 1984. Once seen as a white elephant, the barrier has turned out to be rather useful and is frequently raised. In 1982–2012, the barrier was closed 124 times, but in 2013–14, it was closed no fewer than 50 times. This is due not so much to surge tides, such as the terrible 1953 one that left 531 dead and more than 40,000 homeless across Britain but instead, to fluvial flooding, when rainwater causes rivers to swell. The barrier closes as part of the process of managing this. It is clear that due to global warming, higher sea levels, and storm rainfall, this barrier, and the other flood defenses, offer insufficient protection, not least because higher sea levels prevent the movement of river water downstream if there are high tides. In December 2015, more than sixteen thousand homes were flooded in Cumbria after storms. In London, maps and notices on public display, warn about how possible floods will affect the underground rail system.

Pollution levels are another cause of concern and one that very much looked to the future as well as the present. In Britain, the contamination of urban air by particles, a contamination that is linked to higher levels of heart disease, strokes, and respiratory illnesses, is not as serious as it was in the 1950s because of regulation on burning fuel in cities. However, levels of mono-nitrogen oxides routinely break European guidelines on what constitutes a safe maximum exposure. Measured in micrograms per cubic meter of air (ug/m^3), the guideline is 40, but the London figure is 126; those of Leeds and

Birmingham are 70 or over; and those of Glasgow, Southampton, Tyneside (Newcastle and Gateshead), Nottingham, Middlesbrough, Belfast, and Greater Manchester between 61 and 68; followed by Stoke on Trent, Liverpool, Cardiff, Bristol, Portsmouth, Reading, and Edinburgh at 50–58. Forty-two percent of UK nitrogen dioxide admission are from vehicles, and diesel vehicles pose particular problems, although burning coal is also an issue. Such figures are unknown to the bulk of the population, but some do note that cities now smell different, while their clothes, skin, and hair experience the consequences of air pollution. In 2016, Sadiq Khan, the new Labour mayor of London, made air pollution a key policy issue, arguing that it looked toward the future of the population in the shape of the endangered health of the young. Advertisements on the London Underground popularized the theme. Britain acceded to international standards in 1995 as part of the Environment Act, but subsequent progress in air pollution is limited, in part because of a lack of government focus but, more particularly, due to the emphasis on safety and economic growth in transport policy and planning.

Environmental considerations very much read into perceptions of the future and views about the context and method in which the future should be approached. Linked to environmentalism but far from restricted to it, an absence of confidence at times appeared paranoid or an aspect of nervous exhaustion. However, such an absence also reflected a sense that the established national narrative of greatness and achievement was no longer pertinent. Where that situation would lead to was unclear. Nationalism remains a factor, as the referendum showed, but how far this nationalism will affect the direction and content of policy is uncertain. So also with the relationships between British, English, and Scottish nationalisms.

12

CONCLUSIONS

RESOLUTION, DECLINE, AND adaptability were key narratives in the accounts the British told about themselves. Initially, the theme was resolution. Germany and Japan had been defeated in a war that exhausted Britain and strained the cohesion of its empire, but a war, nevertheless, that had been won, one that underlined British accounts of their special character. The "finest hour," the "band of brothers," Britain "fighting on alone" all became key themes and were extensively repeated in the films of the late 1940s, 1950s, and early 1960s.

The hostile international environment was to continue with the threat from the Soviet Union in the Cold War. This situation provided the backdrop for Britain's decline and the collapse of its empire, although that decline was not understood by many. From the late 1950s and even more the late 1960s, however, decline was more clearly the theme, decline that was relative if not also absolute and on the world scale if not also the national. Despite frequent attempts at rallying and adaptation, notably under Macmillan, Wilson, Heath, Thatcher, Blair, and far less surely, Cameron, the British are still in that perception of decline today, and it affects greatly the way in which they look at the past, present, and future.

Linked to this decline is the loss of the former strong sense of Britain as having a historic mission or as being special, the "Land of Hope and Glory," the "Mother of the Free." The once-strong belief that Britain and the British had special God-given roles to fulfill has gone, leaving confusion and uncertainty for many. To compare modern celebratory occasions, notably the Millennium Dome at Greenwich in 2000 or the opening celebrations at the London Olympics in 2012, with the Great Exhibition of 1851, the British Empire Exhibition in London in 1924, and its Glasgow sequel in 1937 is to be aware not only of fundamental change including in Britain's role in the global community but also of a more brittle and questionable optimism about the country and its development.

Decline provided a different background to defeat. The relationship between the lack of defeat in war and the absence of a successful challenge to the political system, or at least a major transformation of it, is unclear but suggestive. Germany, Japan, France, Italy, and Austria all suffered serious defeat in World War I and II, leading to a political and institutional transformation, which has been as important for the subsequent success of most of those societies as the rebuilding of economic systems on which attention is usually focused. No such process took place in Britain. Whereas for most European countries, the history of the twentieth century was one of shame, defeat, and/ or repression, for Britain it was not. There was also fundamental constitutional, political, and ideological change between 1945 and 2022 in the Soviet Union, Eastern Europe, Spain, Portugal, Ethiopia, South Africa, and the many states round the world whose independence arose from decolonization. For long, Britain, like the United States, did not have any major change that in any way compared.

Indeed, in several respects, with the crucial exceptions of the loss of empire including much of Ireland (which had been represented in Westminster), the essential features of the political system in early 1997 were still those of before 1914. There was a hereditary monarchy with limited, essentially consultative powers, albeit one that adopted the British name of Windsor in 1917 in place of that of Saxe-Coburg and Gotha; a bicameral Parliament, with the House of Commons being the most powerful and only elected chamber; national political parties, albeit with recognizably different regional and social bases of support; a largely two-party system; an absence of proportional representation; and a centralized British state, one without regional assemblies or, still more, devolved or independent parliaments for Scotland and Wales. Britain remained in some respects an elective dictatorship, with the prime minister enjoying great power as head of both the executive and the leading party in the legislature and also as national leader of that party.

The social system was still markedly inegalitarian, and the political system, the civil service, the armed forces, the professions, the banking system, large companies, and the universities were all disproportionately dominated by those whose background cannot be described as working class. The Conservatives stressed the ordinary background of Heath, party leader from 1965 to 1975 and prime minister from 1970 to 1974, and the modest origins and difficult upbringing of Major, prime minister from 1990 to 1997. However, neither circumstance was true of the bulk of their Cabinets and parliamentary colleagues, nor of Cameron, the party leader from 2005 to 2016 and the prime minister from 2010 to 2016, nor of Johnson, prime minister from 2019 to 2022.

In contrast to the situation in 1997 when Blair gained power, there had been a transformation by 2016. This was notably so in the case of the position of Scotland and Wales but was also generally true of the acceptance of traditional institutions and established practices. There is less confidence in the benign role of the British state than in the past. It faces frequent demands to be a solution and near-constant criticism of its attempts to do so. As part of the equation, apologies for the past are frequent. There were expressions of regret for imperial episodes, such as the killing of demonstrators in Amritsar in India in 1919. There were also demands for apology and compensation from other British institutions. Thus, in 2006, the Church of England agreed to apologize to the descendants of slaves for the church's involvement in the slave trade. The idea that nobody alive was responsible and, indeed, that another age had a very different set of values, was ignored in the face of this ahistorical and convenient assertion of responsibility. So also from 2015 and especially from 2020 with student agitation in universities, notably Oxford, over the memorialization, including naming of facilities, after historical figures now considered racist, especially Cecil Rhodes, an active proponent of empire in southern Africa in the late nineteenth century and subsequently a major philanthropist. This issue was very much presented by its protagonists as a rewriting of past and present.

Contests over the past were significant in competing ideas of value. There was a major shift in the assessment of Britain. A Whiggish approach to British history was particularly dominant in the nineteenth and early twentieth centuries. Looking to the past, present, and future, this approach emphasized a Protestant identity for the nation, the growth of respect for property, the rule of law and parliamentary democracy as a means to secure liberty and order, and a nationalistic self-confidence that combined a patriotic sense of national uniqueness with a xenophobic contempt for foreigners, especially Catholics. The positive contribution of Protestantism and liberty to prosperity and social development was stressed, but a very partial account of the latter was offered, one that concentrated on the growth of a strong middle class and of a responsible and industrious working class.

In modern academic circles, Whig history, at least in this form, is apparently dead, displaced by the scholarly developments of the last sixty years. At the popular level, however, traditional history and historical images are still well liked, generally reflect Whiggish notions, and often have little to do with the academic developments that have enriched our understanding of British history and of the diversity of people in the British Isles. Biographies and narratives are at a premium at this popular level. Narrative history is especially popular. This can be seen in the interest in family genealogies and in child, adolescent, and adult reading patterns, and there is a parallel in literature. The persistent popularity of the detective novel, with its stress on the role of the individual and chance, and with a strong narrative structure, and in most cases, its strong moral element, is especially noteworthy. This is a major British fictional format that has translated well from books to television. The genre provides exciting, often exemplary, stories that are precisely what are sought by most readers of history. In combination, narrative and the Whig approach offer a readily accessible means to produce a clear account of a highly complex subject: human history.

Alongside the rejection of the Whig approach at the academic level has come the attempt, both at that level and at that of the public, to offer a new or adapted Whiggish approach, one focused on democratization and social welfare. In this account, which is focused on the twentieth century, the experience of people's war in World War II, the NHS, the BBC, and individual and family experience bulk large. There has been only scant popular criticism of this approach, and it is one that most politicians have sought to annex or, at least, utilize. Indeed, specific arguments about history have been made by politicians, often in response to particular problems and contingencies. For example, in 2014, Cameron pressed the case for teaching national values, in part in response to concerns about Muslim influence in some secondary schools.

His definition of national values was grounded in an account of British history that, however, was contested by critics who adopted a more critical approach. Cameron ordered that every pupil be taught the "British values" enshrined in the Magna Carta (Great Charter), a key constitutional document of 1215 that limited the power of King John. Cameron added that the charter's principles "paved the way for the democracy, the equality, the respect and the laws that make Britain Britain" and that he would make the eight hundredth anniversary in 2015 the centerpiece of a fight back against extremism. This account ignored the extent to which Britain did not exist in 2015: the terms of the 1215 charter did not apply in Scotland, which was then independent. Also in 2014, at the time of the Scottish rejection of independence, Cameron referred to "the strength and stability of our ancient constitution."

In discussing continuity and the past, it remains valuable to note the comments of George Orwell (1903–50), a key public intellectual of the 1940s. In his essay "The Lion and the Unicorn," which he reworked as *The English People* (1947), Orwell wrote about a world that appeared fixed, indeed in effect an English civilization: "there is something distinctive and recognisable in English civilisation. It is a culture as individual as that of Spain—it is somehow bound up with solid breakfasts and gloomy Sundays, smoky towns and winding roads, green fields and red pillar-boxes. It has a flavour of its own. Moreover, it is continuous, it stretches into the future and the past, there is something in it that persists, as in a living creature. . . . The suet puddings and the red pillar-boxes have entered into your soul."

Today, only seventy years later, these definitions do not resonate in the same way, and many seem remote. Sundays have become less gloomy as Sunday observance is far less common; diet, and notably breakfasts and puddings (desserts), have become lighter; towns less smoky; winding roads superseded by motorways; green fields by housing or oilseed rape; and many post offices have been closed with pillar boxes replaced by slits in the shops that now offer postal services. The fabric has changed as part of a lasting transformation that has left many insecure.

Each of these elements can be anatomized to see key elements of national history. Secularism was particularly significant as it affected the way in which people looked at the world. It took many forms. For example, the rate of infant baptisms per thousand births fell from 67 percent in the 1950s to 41 percent in the 1980s and 15.3 percent in the 2010s. As a more specific issue, noise-abatement orders are now served on some churches by local authorities at the behest of people no longer happy to listen to church bells. The percentage of population describing themselves as having no religion rose from 32 in 1983 to 51 in 2009, but by 2015, there had been no increase, with the percentage of those describing themselves as Christian of some kind being relatively stable from 2009.

As far as diet is concerned, there has been further diversity in the 1990s and 2000s, notably with the rise of Thai, Japanese, Vietnamese, and Moroccan restaurants and greater diversity in the existing national categories. Thus, South Indian restaurants were added to the existing North Indian ones, while the range of Chinese regional cuisines increased. There has also been a widening in the range of fruit available: avocados, passion fruit, star fruit, kiwi fruit, and mangoes, largely unknown in Britain in the 1960s, are now widely available in supermarkets. The increased consumption of convenience foods, generally reheated rapidly by microwave cookers, has provided a major market for new dishes.

Wine (the range of which has much increased) and foreign types and brands of beer have become much more important, a process that also, in part, reflects technological and retail shifts, most obviously the growing sale of canned beers and the development of supermarket sales of alcohol, which are linked to rising alcoholism. Most wine is still imported, but British production has risen, in part due to climate change. Whereas wine imports in the 1950s focused on Europe, generally looking back to long-established sources, notably of red wine from France, by the 1990s, New World wines and their Australian counterparts took much of the market.

Supermarkets, which are generally open for longer, have also been responsible for the decline in independent retail activity. High Streets have become more uniform, and outlets are increasingly dependent on a relatively small number of suppliers. As a result, large supermarket distribution centers located near major roads dot the country, creating new retail geographies. In 2016, Carol Ann Duffy, the poet laureate, recalled other aspects of change in her poem *Meters*, an ode to the old-fashioned gas and electricity meters that are to be replaced with digital ones. In the past, the meters recorded the utility of household life; in the present, they digitally mark the units of power that fuel a lifestyle "of monitored moments skyping, googling, downloading, scanning, Facebooking."[1]

Other aspects of the past that have changed, declined, or been made redundant or uneconomic included the British seaside with its piers and amusement parks, such as Margate's *Dreamland* which closed in 2005 and then, after reopening, went bankrupt in 2016. The number of pubs has fallen: in England and Wales, from 73,421 in 1951 to 64,087 in 1971 and 39,373 in 2020. On the other hand, as in Orwell's day, houses, gardens, and football continue to engage much public commitment. Aspects of the first and last are affected by politics but are not generally seen in these terms.

In addition to differences between these histories, there are the issues raised by comparisons and contrasts with other countries and within Britain. Comparisons, however, frequently lacked attention within Britain. The British might not be impressed to be told in 2016 that the Good Country Index placed the UK fourth after the Netherlands, Denmark, and Sweden because of its contribution to the "good of humanity." In this survey, it came top for its contribution to science and technology and second for that to health and wellbeing. Most British people would have been surprised to appear above France, Germany, and Japan. By 2022, the UK was fourteenth, below the first two. Within Britain, the economic growth of London, Manchester, Milton Keynes, and Swindon was not matched in Liverpool or Sunderland. In addition, in the

UK, the average price of property in June 2016 was £214,000, an increase of £17,000 (8.7 percent) in the year. Regional variations were pronounced, with London, the outer metropolitan area, the Outer South East, the South West, and East Anglia, all having higher average prices, and the other regions lower ones. In July 2022, the figure was 292,000.

A country and nation that lost direction, an empire that collapsed, an economy that declined, an elite that ignored "ordinary people," an identity that became brittle—all these descriptions are pertinent, but they are less than the complete account. Moreover, the last reminds us that as with other countries, there are histories of Britain, rather than a history. That there are histories should be readily apparent to readers as many will disagree, or be surprised by, particular arguments. The long-standing nature of different, indeed distinct, histories is readily clear in the case of geographical and sectarian viewpoints. There are differing categories for England, Scotland, Wales, and Northern Ireland, each of those categories variously defined on political, social, cultural, and more specific geographical grounds. Most clearly, the contrast between Northern Irish Unionist and Nationalist accounts are strikingly different. At the British scale, so are those between the Left and the Right, while each of these is capable of many presentations.

In addition to differing views, there are the consequences of new historical information. The revelation, each new year, of hitherto secret archival material as the period of confidentiality lapses, provides a way to reexamine the past. So also with episodic public inquiries, such as the reports of the public inquiries into the 1972 "Bloody Sunday" shootings and the 2003 decision to go to war with Iraq. The latter, the Chilcot Enquiry, which reported in 2016, offered serious criticism of Blair's methods of conducting government and, greatly and appropriately, tarnished his reputation.

Even for those who agree in their basic assumptions about national history and/or with what is written, there are questions over how to distribute relative attention to particular topics and what prioritization to adopt. Both issues are usually not addressed by authors, which leads to the implication that there is only one way to handle the topic—the author's—which is highly misleading. What is particularly difficult is to decide how much emphasis to place on developments that are distinctly British, and how much to present Britain in terms of global or regional trends, whether globalization, deindustrialization, feminism, a decline of deference, environmental concern, or any of a whole host of factors. It is unclear how far it is pertinent to search for international comparisons when considering the relationships between the British Isles, the United Kingdom, Britain, England, Wales, Scotland, or a host of regions—for example, tensions within Spain, notably Catalan separatism. More particularly, an emphasis on one or the other units can lead to particular impressions and whether they should do so can be considered. This question can be extrapolated to include the coverage of each of these questions, both in the thematic and in the chronological chapters.

The British themselves were well aware of both change and continuity. These, indeed, were a joint dynamic, one that reflected the open-ended nature of British society and its reluctance to accept attempts to impose reform and to have moral imperatives forced upon it. Differing definitions of this dynamic led to challenges, but there was, and is, an overall willingness to see tolerance as both a goal for and a means of nationhood. Alongside a sense of continuity in this respect, there is also that of change. For example, tolerance has both benefited from what can be stigmatized as political correctness and has, at times, been compromised by it. In the first case, it is encouraging to see how racial prejudice is no longer publicly acceptable.

More generally, for many, national values, or more particularly, classic stereotypes of these values, have changed, notably with a decline in the practice of restraint, the "stiff upper lip" of the past. In *Earthly Powers*, the novelist Anthony Burgess (1980) referred to the Church of England as "a club for upper-class Englishmen . . . it's a safe church. . . . It's tepid, because it knows that fire burns."[2]

However, emotionalism was increasingly to the fore, as in the public response to the tragic death in 1997 of Diana, Princess of Wales, in a car crash. Yet this response also displayed variety, as the emotional approach was most common, polls indicated, among women, homosexuals, and those under forty, and least so among working-class men, Scots, and those over sixty. This contrast undermines the attempt to present the response in unitary terms. Indeed, in Scotland very few turned out for the memorial ceremony while there were complaints about the accompanying postponement of a football match.

Social changes that are readily apparent include a degree of feminization in attitudes and a marked questioning of former occupational, gender, and sexual roles. As the majority of lawyers and doctors became women, so also with the majority of entrants to the clergy.[3] Female roles in the military and the police changed, with women becoming chief constables and also serving in the front line of the armed forces. The emancipation of women was one of the most powerful forces democratizing society and enhancing accountability. It had an impact at every level, including the Succession of the Crown Act of 2013, which determined that the firstborn child of whatever gender will now inherit the throne. In practice, William, Duke of Cambridge, the Queen's grandson, and his wife, Catherine, had, as their first child, a son, Prince George, thus ensuring that traditional roles were not challenged.

At the same time, there was an ambivalence toward the democratization of society. Hostility to democratic accountability was demonstrated, albeit in an implicit, not overt, manner, by the unwillingness of often self-defining elites, such as the judiciary or planners, to accept popular beliefs and pastimes as worthy of value and attention, and their conviction that they were best placed to manage society and to define social values. Social and cultural condescension was linked to contempt for popular views on such matters as capital punishment or immigration or, indeed, in 2016, the EU. Most institutions resisted unwelcome pressures, while political parties tempered their desire for popular support with their wish to maintain their ideological inheritance.

Yet, affluence, social fluidity, and greater independence for the young have combined and will continue to help challenge notions of cohesion and collectivism that were often ambivalent about growth and opportunity. Adaptability and change were aspects of a significant process of transformation and of profound modernization, which were developments that Britain shared with much of the West. Where this situation would lead it was less clear, and this remains the case.

NOTES

PREFACE

1. This term refers here to the United Kingdom of Great Britain (England, Scotland, and Wales) and Northern Ireland, which is generally shortened as the United Kingdom and abbreviated as the UK.

CHAPTER 1

1. T. Williamson, *The Transformation of Rural England—Farming and the Landscape 1700–1870* (Exeter, 2002).
2. Casual conversation has brought reports of three more sightings there.
3. P. J. Larkham and K. D. Lilley, *Planning the "City of Tomorrow": British Reconstruction Planning, 1939–1952* (Pickering, 2001).
4. J. Rhode, *The Lake House* (London, 1946), 32.

CHAPTER 2

1. L. Johnman and H. Murphy, *British Shipbuilding and the State since 1918: A Political Economy of Decline* (Exeter, 2002).
2. N. J. White, "'Ferry off the Mersey': The Business and the Impact of Decolonisation in Liverpool," *History* 96 (2011): 204.

CHAPTER 3

1. *Audience Research Reports of the BBC, 1937–c. 1950*, Microform Academic Publishers, 2007 (www.britishonlinearchives.co.uk).
2. B. Thomas and D. Dorling, *Identity in Britain: A Cradle-to-Grave Atlas* (Bristol, 2007).
3. C. Julios, *Contemporary British Identity: English Language, Migrants and Public Discourse* (Aldershot, 2008).
4. M. Gaskill, *Hellish Nell: Last of Britain's Witches* (London, 2001).
5. H. McLeod, *The Religious Crisis of the 1960s* (Oxford, 2007).
6. H. Carpenter, *Robert Runcie. The Reluctant Archbishop* (London, 1996), 214–20.
7. P. Catterall, "The Party and Religion," in A. Seldon and S. Ball, eds., *Conservative Century. The Conservative Party since 1900* (Oxford, 1994), 670.
8. A. Chandler and D. Hein, *Archbishop Fisher, 1945–1961: Church, State, and World* (Farnham, 2012).
9. A. Chandler, *The Church of England in the Twentieth Century. The Church Commissioners and the Politics of Reform, 1948–1998* (Woodbridge, 2006).

10. H. Cook, *The Long Sexual Revolution: English Women, Sex, and Contraception, 1800–1975* (Oxford, 2004).

11. P. Thane and T. Evans, *Sinners? Scroungers? Saints? Unmarried Motherhood in Twentieth-Century England* (Oxford, 2012).

12. L. Delap, *Knowing Their Place; Domestic Service in Twentieth-Century Britain* (Oxford, 2011).

13. D. Simonelli, *Working Class Heroes: Rock Music and British Society in the 1960s and 1970s* (Lanham, 2013).

14. J. Black, *The City on the Hill. A Life of the University of Exeter* (Exeter, 2015), 44.

15. J. Mills, *Cannabis Nation: Control and Consumption in Britain, 1928–2008* (Oxford, 2013).

16. W. Boyd, *Sweet Caress* (London, 2015), 446–47.

17. P. Hennessy, *Distilling the Frenzy. Writing the History of One's Own Times* (London, 2012), 27–30.

18. V. Berridge, *Marketing Health: Smoking and the Discourse of Public Health in Britain, 1945–2000* (Oxford, 2007).

19. M. Clapson, *Working-Class Suburb: Social Change on an English Council Estate, 1930–2010* (Manchester, 2012).

20. S. Todd, "Family, Welfare and Social Work in Post-War England, c. 1948–c. 1970," *English Historical Review* 129 (2014): 387.

21. G. Iacobucci, "Smokers and Overweight Patients Are Denied Surgery, Royal College Finds," *BMJ* (2016): 353. doi:10.1136/bjm.i.2335; summary *BMJ*, April 30, 2016: 170.

22. L. Byrne, *Dragons* (London, 2016).

23. C. Dickson, *Behind the Crimson Blind* (London, 1953), 53.

24. A. Christie, *After the Funeral* (London, 1953; 1989 ed.), 27.

CHAPTER 4

1. J. I. M. Stewart, writing as Michael Innes, *Death at the President's Lodging* (London, 1936), 4.

2. J. Williams, *Entertaining the Nation: A Social History of British Television* (Stroud, 2004).

3. T. Mo, *Sour Sweet* (London, 1983), 3.

4. P. Catterall, ed., "The Origins of Channel 4," witness seminar, *Contemporary British History* 12 (1998): 91.

5. J. Oliver, *Jamie's Italy* (London, 2005), x.

6. *Landscape in Britain 1850–1950*, Hayward Gallery, London, 1983, exhibition.

7. H. Atkinson, *The Festival of Britain: A Land and Its People* (London, 2012).

8. I. B. Whyte, ed., *Man-Made Future: Planning, Education and Design in Mid-Twentieth-Century Britain* (London, 2007).

9. S. Frith, M. Brennan, M. Cloonan, and E. Webster, *The History of Live Music in Britain. I: 1950–1967: From Dance Hall to the 100 Club* (Farnham, 2013).

10. C. MacInnes, *Absolute Beginners* in *The Colin MacInnes Omnibus* (London, 1985), 139.

11. A. Campsie, "Mass-Observation Left Intellectuals and the Politics of Everyday Life," *EHR* 131 (2016): 120.

12. G. Ortolano, *The Two Cultures Controversy: Science, Literature and Cultural Politics in Postwar Britain* (Cambridge, 2009).

13. D. McKinney, *Magic Circles: The Beatles in Dream and History* (Cambridge, MA, 2003); K. Gildart, *Images of England through Popular Music* (Basingstoke, 2013).

14. A. Turner, *Goldfinger* (London, 1998), 89.

15. S. Groes, *British Fictions of the Sixties. The Making of the Swinging Decade* (London, 2016).

16. For example, I. Murdoch, *The Sacred and Profane Love Machine* (London, 1974), 73–74, or, with a different tone, J. Mortimer, *Dunster* (London, 1992), 213.

17. M. Bradbury, *The History Man* (London, 1975), 227.

18. P. Morley, *The Age of Bowie: How David Bowie Made a World of Difference* (London, 2016).

19. W. Whyte, *Redbrick: A Social and Architectural History of Britain's Civic Universities* (Oxford, 2015).

20. P. Shapely, *The Politics of Housing: Power, Consumers and Urban Culture* (Manchester, 2007).

21. For a more positive account, A. Higgott, *Mediating Modernism: Architectural Cultures in Britain* (London, 2007).

22. *David Hockney: Fleurs fraîches. Drawings on IPhone and iPad*, Paris exhibition at Fondation Pierre Bergé-Yves Saint Laurent, 2010–11, exhibition brochure: 1.

23. M. Drabble, "The Spirit of Place: A Certain Road to Happiness," in *David Hockney: A Bigger Picture*, exhibition catalog (London, 2012), 38, 41.

24. S. Brett, *The Body on the Beach* (London, 2000), 58.

CHAPTER 5

1. J. Bew, *Citizen Clem* (London, 2016).

2. I. B. Whyte, ed., *Man-Made Future: Planning, Education and Design in Mid-Twentieth-Century Britain* (London, 2007).

3. A. Thorpe, "Locking out the Communists: The Labour Party and the Communist Party, 1939–46," *Twentieth Century British History* 25 (2014): 242–48.

4. K. Harris, *Attlee* (London, 1982); Bew, *Citizen Clem*.

5. J. Macniol, *The Politics of Retirement in Britain, 1878–1948* (Cambridge, 1998).

6. G. Orwell, *Animal Farm* (London, 1945; 1951 ed.), 118.

7. M. Moore, *The Origins of Modern Spin: Democratic Government and the Media in Britain, 1945–51* (Basingstoke, 2006).

8. P. Dorey, *British Conservatism and Trade Unionism, 1945–1964* (Farnham, 2009).

9. G. Orwell, *Nineteen Eighty Four* (London, 1949; 1954 ed.), 132–33.

10. I. S. Wood, *Churchill* (Basingstoke, 2000).

11. S. Kelly, *The Myth of Mr Butskell: The Politics of British Economic Policy, 1950–55* (Farnham, 2002).

12. A. S. Milward, *The United Kingdom and the European Community. I: The Rise and Fall of a National Strategy, 1945–1963* (London, 2003).

13. His secondary schooling was at the leading private, all-male boarding school.

14. S. Smith, ed., *Reassessing Suez 1956: New Perspectives on the Crisis and Its Aftermath* (Aldershot, 2008).

15. J. Turner, *Macmillan* (London, 1994); R. Lamb, *The Macmillan Years 1957–1963: The Emerging Truth* (London, 1995).

16. J. Mortimer, *Paradise Postponed* (London, 1985; 1986 ed.), 137.

17. L. Black and H. Pemberton, eds., *An Affluent Society? Britain's Post-War "Golden Age" Revisited* (Farnham, 2004).

18. M. Jarvis, *Conservative Governments, Morality and Social Change in Affluent Britain, 1957–64* (Manchester, 2005).

CHAPTER 6

1. N. J. Crowson, *The Conservative Party and European Integration since 1945: At the Heart of Europe?* (London, 2007).

2. P. Bridgen, "Making a Mess of Modernization: The State, Redundancy Pay and Economic Policy-Making in the Early 1960s," *Twentieth Century British History* (2000); A. Ringe and N. Rollings, "Responding to Relative Decline: The Creation of the NEDC," *Economic History Review* (2000): 331–53; J. Davis, *Prime Ministers and Whitehall, 1960–74* (London, 2007).

3. P. Brigden, "The One Nation Idea and the Welfare State: The Conservatives and Pensions in the 1950s," *Contemporary British History* (2000).

4. P. Ziegler, *Edward Heath. The Authorised Biography* (London, 2010): 143–44.

5. J. W. Young, *The Labour Governments 1964–1970. II. International Policy* (Manchester, 2003).

6. R. Pearce, ed., *Patrick Gordon Walker: Political Diaries 1932–1971* (London, 1991); K. Jefferys, *The Labour Party since 1945* (Basingstoke, 1993).

7. A. Roth, *Sir Harold Wilson: Yorkshire's Walter Mitty* (London, 1977).

8. S. Brooke, *Sexual Politics: Sexuality, Family Planning and the British Left from the 1880s to the Present Day* (Oxford, 2011).

9. S. Fielding, *The Labour Governments 1964–70, 1. Labour and Cultural Change* (Manchester, 2003).

10. E. Dell, *A Hard Pounding: Politics and Economic Crisis, 1974–76* (Oxford, 1991).

11. M. Crick, *The March of Militant* (London, 1986); M. Wickham-Jones, *Economic Strategy and the Labour Party* (London, 1996).

12. For more positive assessments, B. Lapping, *The Labour Government 1964–70* (London, 1970); J. Haines, *The Politics of Power* (London, 1977); R. McKibbin, "Homage to Wilson and Callaghan," *London Review of Books*, October 24, 1991; R. Coopey, S. Fielding, and N. Tiratsoo, eds., *The Wilson Governments 1964–1970* (London, 1993); T. Blair, "Lessons of the Wilson Years," *Independent*, May 25, 1995.

13. K. Burk and A. Cairncross, *Goodbye Great Britain: The 1976 IMF Crisis* (New Haven, CT, 1992).

14. For a more positive account, M. Artis, D. Cobham, and M. Wickham-Jones, "Social Democracy in Hard Times: The Economic Record of the Labour Government 1974–79," *Twentieth-Century British History* 3 (1992): 32–58; K. Morgan, *Callaghan: A Life* (Oxford, 1997).

CHAPTER 7

1. I. Gilmour, *Dancing with Dogma: Britain under Thatcherism* (London, 1992).

2. E. Robinson, *History, Heritage and Tradition in Contemporary British Politics: Past Politics and Present Histories* (Manchester, 2012).

3. A. W. Purdue, "Reinventing Conservatism," *The Salisbury Review* (summer 1999): 55.

4. J. Cooper, *Margaret Thatcher and Ronald Reagan: A Very Political Special Relationship* (Basingstoke, 2012).

5. B. Jackson, "Currents of Neo-Liberalism: British Political Ideologies and the New Right, c. 1955–1979," *English Historical Review* 131 (2016): 850.

6. D. Needham, *UK Monetary Policy from Devaluation to Thatcher, 1967–82* (Basingstoke, 2014).

7. J. Phillips, *Collieries, Communities and the Miners' Strike in Scotland, 1984–85* (Manchester, 2012).

8. P. Bagwell and P. Lyth, *Transport in Britain. From Canal Lock to Gridlock* (London, 2002).

9. L. Panitch and C. Leys, *The End of Parliamentary Socialism: From New Left to New Labour* (London, 1997).

10. https://www.youtube.com/watch?v=DPzzgE34YQY

11. H. Williams, *Guilty Men: Conservative Decline and Fall 1992–1997* (London, 1998), 3.

12. N. Lawson, *The View from No. 11: Memoirs of a Tory Radical* (London, 1992).

13. B. Anderson, *John Major: The Making of the Prime Minister* (London, 1991).

14. R. Martin, P. Sunley, and J. Wills, "The Geography of Trade Union Decline: Spatial Dispersal or Regional Resilience?," *Transactions of the Institute of British Geographers*, new series 18 (1993): 56.

15. Blair interview, ITN (Independent Television News), April 8, 2013.

16. D. Marquand, "The Twilight of the British State? Henry Dubb versus Sceptred Awe," *Political Quarterly* 64 (1993): 210.

CHAPTER 8

1. For the record, I met Major twice to speak with. He showed considerable charm on both occasions. In using the term *uncharismatic,* I refer to his public reputation.

2. T. Benn, "The Diary as Historical Source," *Archives* 20 (1993): 15.

3. A. Seldon, *Major: A Political Life* (London, 1997).

4. P. Mandelson and R. Liddle, *The Blair Revolution* (London, 1996).

5. E. F. Biagini, "Ideology and the Making of New Labours," *International Labor and Working-Class History* 56 (1999): 98.

6. G. Foote, *The Labour Party's Political Thought: A History,* 3rd ed. (Basingstoke, 1997).

7. T. Hunt, ed., *Labour's Identity Crisis* (London, 2016).

CHAPTER 9

1. J. Mitchell, *The Scottish Question* (Oxford, 2014).

2. Hereafter referred to as the IRA.

3. A. Sanders, "Operation Motorman (1972) and the Search for a Coherent British Counterinsurgency Strategy in Northern Ireland," *Small Wars and Insurgencies* 24 (2013): 465–92. I have benefited from the opportunity to discuss the situation with General Sir Frank Kitson.

4. J. Hambleton, quoted in the *Times,* June 2, 2016.

5. D. Hamill, *Pig in the Middle: The Army in Northern Ireland, 1969–1984* (London, 1984); C. Ryder, *The RUC: A Force under Fire* (London, 1989).

6. T. Hennessey, *The Evolution of the Troubles, 1970–72* (Dublin, 2007); D. Murray, *Bloody Sunday: Truth, Lies, and the Saville Inquiry* (London, 2012).

7. C. Townshend, *Britain's Civil Wars: Counterinsurgency in the Twentieth Century* (London, 1986); T. Leahy, "The Influence of Informers and Agents on Provisional Irish Republican Army Military Strategy and British Counter-Insurgency Strategy, 1976–94," *20th Century British History* 26 (2015): 122–46.

8. R. English, *Armed Struggle: The History of the IRA* (Basingstoke, 2003).

CHAPTER 10

1. W. Webster, *Englishness and Empire, 1939–1965* (Oxford, 2005).

2. Jonathan Walker, *Aden Insurgency: The Savage War in South Arabia 1962–67* (Staplehurst, 2005).

3. J. W. Young, "The Wilson Government and the Debate over Arms to South Africa in 1964," *Contemporary British History* 12 (1998): 62–84.

4. J. W. Young, *Britain and European Unity, 1945–1992* (Basingstoke, 1993).

5. P. Jones, *America and the British Labour Party: The Special Relationship at Work* (London, 1997).

6. G. Bennett, *Six Moments of Crisis. Inside British Foreign Policy* (Oxford, 2013), 95.

7. This was the renamed EEC, which, in turn, became the EU.

8. A. Spelling, "Edward Heath and Anglo-American Relations 1970–1974: A Reappraisal," *Diplomacy and Statecraft* 20 (2009): 638–58; D. D. O'Hare, *Britain and the Process of European Integrity. Continuity and Policy Change from Attlee to Heath* (London, 2013).

9. L. J. Robins, *The Reluctant Party: Labour and the EEC* (Ormskirk, 1979).

10. S. Wall, *The Official History of Britain and the European Community, II: From Rejection to Referendum, 1963–1975* (London, 2013).

11. I. Crewe and M. Harrop, eds., *Political Communications: The General Election Campaign of 1983* (Cambridge, 1986) and *Political Communications: The General Election Campaign of 1987* (Cambridge, 1989).

12. A. Gamble, "Europe and America," in B. Jackson and R. Saunders, eds., *Making Thatcher's Britain* (Cambridge, 2012), 232. For the contrasting approaches of Thatcher and Blair to the United States, see J. O'Sullivan, "Serving to Win," *New Criterion*, 32, no. 5 (2014): 16–22.

13. D. Healey, *The Time of My Life* (1989; 1990 ed.), 458–59.

14. *Spectator*, July 12, 1990.

15. Hugh Trevor-Roper to Max Perutz, August 15, 1990, in A. Palmer, ed., "The Letters of Hugh Trevor-Roper," *Standpoint* 59 (January/February 2014): 82–83. The article draws on R. Davenport-Hines and A. Sisman, eds., *One Hundred Letters from Hugh Trevor-Roper* (Oxford, 2014).

16. T. G. Ash, *In Europe's Name: Germany and the Divided Continent* (London, 1993); E. Pond, *Beyond the Wall. Germany's Road to Unification* (London, 1993); S. F. Szabo, *The Diplomacy of German Unification* (New York, 1993); F. Bozo, *Mitterrand, the End of the Cold War, and German Unification* (New York, 2009); P. Short, *Mitterrand: A Study in Ambiguity* (London, 2013); comments made by Douglas Hurd at conference on the Tory World held at University of Exeter, June 20–21, 2013.

17. *Campaign Guide*, 499.

18. *Campaign Guide*, 499, 521.

19. D. Baker, A. Gamble, and S. Ludlam, "The Parliamentary Siege of Maastricht 1993: Conservative Divisions and British Ratification," *Parliamentary Affairs* 47 (1994): 37–60.

20. I. McAllister and D. Studlar, "Conservative Euroscepticism and the Referendum Party in the 1997 British General Election," *Party Politics* 6 (2000): 359–71.

21. *Times*, August 9, 2016, p. 2.

22. A. Seldon and P. Snowden, *Cameron at 10: The Verdict* (London, 2016), 558.

23. M. Mosbacher and O. Wiseman, *Brexit Revolt: How the UK Left the EU* (London, 2016), 121; P. Manent, "Les gouvernants ne nous représentent plus, ils nous surveillent," *Le Figaro*, August 1, 2016, p. 19.

CHAPTER 11   /

1. Speech at Institute of Engineering and Technology, June 2, 2016.

2. N. Clegg, *Politics. Between the Extreme* (London, 2016).

CHAPTER 12

1. The entire poem, a public relations piece commissioned by Smart Energy GB, was printed in the *Daily Mail*, July 29, 2016, p. 41.

2. A. Burgess, *Earthly Powers* (London, 1981), 629.

3. A. McIvor, *Working Lives: Work in Britain since 1945* (London, 2013).

SELECTED FURTHER READING

The following is necessarily a selective list, concentrating on recent books. Other books and articles can be traced through the bibliographies in these books.

Addison, P., and H. Jones, eds. *A Companion to Contemporary Britain, 1939–2000*. Oxford: Blackwell, 2005.

Anderson, P., and N. Mann. *Safety First: The Making of New Labour*. London: Granta, 1997.

Ball, S. *The Conservative Party since 1945*. Manchester: Manchester University Press, 1998.

Brooke, S. *Reform and Reconstruction: Britain after the War, 1945–51*. Manchester: Manchester University Press, 1995.

Brown, C. *Religion and Society in Twentieth-Century Britain*. Harlow: Longman, 2006.

Burk, K., ed. *The British Isles since 1945*. Oxford: Oxford University Press, 2003.

Carpenter, H. *Robert Runcie: The Reluctant Archbishop*. London: Hodder and Stoughton, 1996.

Dorling, D. *A New Social Atlas of Britain*. London: Wiley, 1995.

Floud, R., J. Humphries, and P. Johnson, eds. *The Cambridge Economic History of Modern Britain. II. 1870 to the Present*. Cambridge: Cambridge University Press, 2014.

Fraser, W. H. *A History of British Trade Unionism, 1700–1998*. Houndmills: Palgrave, 1999.

Goulbourne, H. *Race Relations in Britain since 1945*. Houndmills: Palgrave, 1998.

Greenwood, S. *Britain and the Cold War*. Houndmills: Palgrave, 1995.

Hall, L. *Sex, Gender and Social Change in Britain since 1880*. Houndmills: Macmillan, 2000.

Harrison, B. *Seeking a Role: The United Kingdom, 1951–1970*. Oxford: Oxford University Press, 2011.

Harrison, B. *Finding a Role? The United Kingdom, 1970–1990*. Oxford: Oxford University Press, 2010.

Hewison, R. *Culture and Consensus: England, Art and Politics since 1940*. London: Methuen, 1995.

Holt, R. *Sport and the British: A Modern History*. Oxford: Oxford University Press, 1989.

Jackson, A. *The Two Unions: Ireland, Scotland and the Survival of the United Kingdom, 1707–2007*. Oxford: Oxford University Press, 2011.

Jackson, B. and R. Saunders, eds. *Making Thatcher's Britain*. Cambridge: Cambridge University Press, 2012.

Jefferys, K. *Retreat from New Jerusalem: British Politics, 1951–64*. Houndmills: Macmillan, 1997.

McIntyre, W. D. *British Decolonisation, 1946–1997*. Houndmills: Macmillan, 1998.

Martin, J. *The Development of Modern Agriculture: British Farming since 1931*. Manchester: Manchester University Press, 1999.

Middleton, R. *The British Economy since 1945: Engaging with the Debate*. Houndmills: Macmillan, 2000.

Mingay, G. E. *Land and Society in England, 1750–1980*. London: Longman, 1994.

Needham, D. *UK Monetary Policy from Devaluation to Thatcher, 1967–82*. Houndmills: Palgrave Macmillan, 2014.

Ovendale, R. *Anglo-American Relations in the Twentieth Century*. Houndmills: Macmillan, 1998.

Pimlott, B. *Harold Wilson*. London: Harper Collins, 1992.

Pittock, M. *The Road to Independence? Scotland since the Sixties*. London: Reaktion, 2008.

Robbins, K. *England, Ireland, Scotland, Wales: The Christian Church, 1900–2000*. Oxford: Oxford University Press, 2010.

Rosen, A. *The Transformation of British Life, 1950–2000: A Social History*. Manchester: Manchester University Press, 2003.

Schofield, C. *Enoch Powell and the Making of Postcolonial Britain*. Cambridge: Cambridge University Press, 2013.

Simmons, I. G. *An Environmental History of Twentieth-Century Britain*. Houndmills: Palgrave, 2002.

INDEX

A10, 27
A14, 27
A Bigger Picture (Hockney), 115
abortion, 8, 68–69, 75, 77, 78
Abortion Act of 1967, 8, 68–69, 139
Absolute Beginners (MacInnes), 105
Absolutely Fabulous, 89
acquired immunodeficiency syndrome
    (AIDS), 9
Adams, Douglas, 25
Aden, 198, 203
*Advancing Transgender Equality: A Plan for
    Action* (2011), 73
advertising, 127
aerospace manufacturing, 36, 53
Afghanistan, military intervention in, 181
Afro-Caribbean cuisine, 100
age, 76–77
Age UK, 76
aggregate mining, 20
aging population, 2, 2
agriculture, 16–20; management, 19; mar-
    kets, 17; mechanization, 17; subsidies, 17
AIDS. *See* acquired immunodeficiency syn-
    drome (AIDS)
Airbus, 53
air quality, 87
alcohol, supermarket sales of, 26
Alfie (1966), 108
Ali, Monica, 64
Aliens Act of 1905, 59
Alliance, the, 160, 164
al-Qaeda attacks of 2001, 177
Alton Estate, Roehampton, 116
Alzheimer's disease, 9, 73, 76, 150
Amazon's drone delivery service, 6
Americanization, 26, 92, 214–15

American rock 'n' roll music, 105
Amis, Kingsley, 109, 110
ammonia, 12
Anglican Church of England, 66
anglicization, 99–100
Anglo-Irish Agreement of 1985, 198
Angry Brigade, 149–50
animal issues, 5–6
Annabel's nightclub, 43
Ann Summers shops, 69
Annual Population Survey (2015), 53
antibiotic contamination, 10
antibiotic resistance, 6
Anti-Federalist League, 222
Antiques Roadshow, 118
apartheid in South Africa, 206
Archers, The, 113
architecture, 103, 106, 109, 111, 116
Are You Being Served? (2016), 98
Armagh, 199
Arts Council, 97
Ascension Islands, 201
"A Sharp Look at the Mood of Britain"
    (1962), 92
Asian-British films, 64
Asian Infrastructure Bank, 182
assisted dying, 76
assisted living, 77
asthma, 9
A Thousand Years (Hirst), 114
Attlee, Clement, 119–25
Attlee government, 119–25
Auden, W. H., 103
austerity, 52, 124, 129
automobile manufacturing, 36, 50, 53, 54,
    106; diesel-powered, 13
automobile ownership, 24–25

Avengers, The (1961–69), 69
Away from the Flock (Hirst), 114

Baader-Meinhof Gang (West Germany), 149
baby boomers, 132
badgers, 5, 19–20
balance-of-payment crises, 209
ballot of MPs, 136
Balls, Ed, 183
banking, 42–44, 165
banking crisis of 1974, 145
Bank of England, 35, 42, 51, 54–55, 121, 179, 224
bankruptcies, 157
Banksy, 114
banned music, 110
Baptists, 66
Barbados, 206
Barclays, 44
Barclays Prosperity Map (2016), 48
Barnsley, 228
Baron, John, 225
Basingstoke, 29
Basutoland, 206
bats, 5
Battle of the River Plate, The (1956), 97
BBC (British Broadcasting Corporation), 95–96, 107, 112; BBC2, 97; vs ITV, 97–98; "Mind the Gap London vs the Rest" (2014), 32; "Matter of the North, The" (2016), 32; moving staff, 32
BBC Listener Research Department, 57
BBC Listener Research Report of 1948, 57
beach cleanliness, 23
Bean, Richard, 115
Beatles, 107–8
Bechuanaland, 206
Becket, Thomas, 68
Beckett, Samuel, 103–4
Beeching Report of 1963, 135
Behtzi Behtzi (2004), 115
Belfast, 195, 236
Benn, Tony, 96, 147, 171, 214
Berkeley, The, 54
Berio, Luciano, 103
Best Future for Britain, The, 221
Bevan, Aneurin, 123
Bevin, Ernest, 124, 202
Bhatti, Gurpeet Kaur, 115
Biffen, John, 153

"Big Bang" of 1986, 41–42
"Big Black" (Nash), 114
"big tent," 86
Bill Haley and the Comets, 105
birds, 6; British Trust for Ornithology, 12; Royal Society for the Protection of Birds (RSPB), 13
Birmingham, 44, 48–49, 109, 113, 119, 182, 195–96, 236
birth control, 8, 69, 75, 108, 140
birth rate, 2, 7–8, 76, 79, 132
Birtwistle, Harrison, 104, 116
bisexuality, 73–74
Black, Cilla, 107
Blackburn, 179
black market activities, postwar, 125
"black-on-black" killings, 84
Blackpool, 102
Black Wednesday, 171, 223
Blaenau Gwent, 228
Blair, Tony, 86, 114, 152, 154, 166, 168, 169, 173–79; conversion to Catholicism, 67
Blairism, 114
blended family, 78
blood pressure rates, 8
Bloody Sunday, 196, 198, 243
Blow-Up (1965), 108
"blue-collar plus," 58
Blunkett, David, 176
Blur (band), 114
BMW, 50
BNP. *See* British National Party (BNP)
Board of Trade, 123
Body on the Beach, The (Brett), 116–17
bomb damage, 125
book clubs, 69
Boston Consulting Group, 44
bottled water, 15
Boulez, Pierre, 103
bovine tuberculosis, 19
Bowie, David, 110, 115
Boyd, William, 76–77
Bradbury, Malcolm, 109
Bradford, 48
Bread (1986), 111
Brett, Simon, 116–17
Bretton Woods Agreement, 142–43
Brexit, 44, 91, 183–84, 192–93, 225–30
Brick Lane (2003), 64

Bridgend, 40
bridges, strains on, 26–27
Bridget Jones's Baby (2016), 69
Bridgwater, 12
Brighton, 44, 102
"bring backery," 4
Bristol, 2, 27, 44, 45, 113, 158, 179, 236
BritArt, 113, 115, 174
British Aerospace, 36
British Airways, 54
British Astronomical Association, 24
British Broadcasting Corporation (BBC).
   See BBC
British empire, 202–207
British Gas, 163
British Leyland, 36, 39
British Library, 111
British Motor Corporation, 106
British National Oil Corporation, 36
British National Party (BNP), 65, 180
Britishness in Scotland, 190
British Rail, 24
British Shipbuilders, 36
British Social Attitudes Survey (2016), 233
British Telecom, 163
British Trust for Ornithology, 12
Britpop, 114
Britten, Benjamin, 104
Brixton, 158
Broadcasting Act of 1980, 98
Broadwater Farm Estate riots, 158
Broonland (Harvie), 232
Brown, George, 137
Brown, Gordon, 41, 43, 62, 67, 154, 169,
   176–81, 231
Bruce, David, 209
Bruce-Gardyne, Jock, 215
Buddha of Suburbia, The (1991), 64
Buddhism, 68
building boom, 43
Bundesbank, 223
Burgess, Anthony, 244
Burnaston, 53
Burnley, 59, 179
Bush, George W., 178
business start-ups, 48
bus passes, 15
Butler, Rab, 126, 136, 205
"Butskellism," 75, 126, 173

butterflies, 6
Byatt, A. S., 109

Cabinet committee on modernization, 133
Callaghan, James, 139, 147–48, 154, 189,
   208, 214
Call the Midwife, 118
Cambridge, 49
Cambridgeshire, 27
Cameron, David, 57, 67, 73, 101, 178, 180–85,
   194, 226–28, 240; Brexit, 225–26
Campaign Guide 1989, The, 219
Campbell, Alistair, 175
Canary Wharf, 45
cancer, 9
cannabis use, 75
"Can't Pay, Won't Pay," 191
CAP. *See* Common Agricultural Policy
   (CAP)
capital punishment, 69, 130, 139
car culture, 25, 97
Cardiff, 39–40, 191, 199, 236
"care in the community," 87
Caretaker, The, 103
Carney, Mark, 54
car ownership, 19, 24–25
Carry On Nurse (1959), 107
Carry On Screaming (1966), 109
Carter, Jimmy, 146
"cash for honors" scandal, 176
Casino Royale (Fleming), 104
Castle, Barbara, 139
Catholic Emancipation Act of 1829, 66
Catholicism in Northern Ireland, 194–99
Catholics, 61, 199, 239
cats, 6
cattle farming, 19
CCTV (closed-circuit television), 85
cellophane works, 12
cemetery provision, 32
Central Africa, 206
centralization, 124, 162
Central Policy Review Staff, 141
Centre for Cities, 48
Centre Point, 109
Chamberlain, Neville, 126
change vs crisis, 4–5
Channel 4, 98
Charing Cross station, 116

Charles Wollaston Award, 114
Chatham, 48
cheese production, 17
Chelsea, 179
Chelsea Barracks, 111, 116
chemicals used in farming, 6
chemical works, 12
Cheshire, 20
Chesterton, A. K., 205
Chilcot Inquiry, 175
childcare, 72, 79–80, 82
child pornography, 84
"Chimeras, The" (Auden), 103
Chinese cuisine, 99–100
Chinese investment, 182
Christianity, decline of, 67; fundamental-
    ist, 68
Christians, 65–68; evangelism, 110
Christie, Agatha, 89, 104
church: and education, 66; opposition to
    homosexual marriage, 68
Churchill, Winston, 103, 119–21, 125–28, 151
Church of England, 66–67, 71, 135, 153, 239, 244
"Citizen's Charter," 170
citizenship test, 64
City, the (London), 42–43, 154, 224, 224, 232
City of Spades (MacInnes), 105
civil partnerships, 73
Claridge's, 54
Clarke, Ken, 175
Clarkson, Jeremy, 118
class, 94, 104, 119
class distinctiveness, 87–88
class structures and assumptions, 57, 86–87
cleanliness of beaches, 23
Clegg, Nick, 180
climate change, 4–6, 10–12, 17, 235
Clinton, Bill, 198
closed-circuit television (CCTV), 85
clothing, 93–94, 104, 108
coal: energy, 20–22, 132; industry, 35, 39–40,
    120, 124, 160–61; mining, 40, 157; power
    stations, 13, 21; shortage, 125; strike, 143
cockroaches, 6
Cold Feet (2016), 98
Colditz Story, The (1955), 97
Cold War, 122–23, 161, 203, 207–8, 214–15, 237
collectivism, 119, 120–21, 245
College of Europe in Bruges, 218

Committee on Higher Education, 106
Common Agricultural Policy (CAP), 212
Common Fisheries Policy, 213
Common Market Membership Treaty, 213
Commonwealth Immigrants Act of 1962, 60
communications, electronic, 93
Communism, 207; hostility to, 122
Communist Party, 146, 167
commuting, 29, 44–45, 181
competition provisions of the EU, 41
comprehensive education, 75–76
Concorde, 108
"condition of England" literature, 105
Confederation of British Industry, 42
Confessions of a Window Cleaner (1975), 110
Connaught, The, 54
conscription (national service), 77–78, 197
Conservatism, one-nation, 67, 86, 129
Conservative Central Office, 74
Conservative government: 1951–60, 125–31.
    See also Thatcherism
Conservative Party in Scotland, 190
Conservative Research Department, 133, 219
Consett, 157
Consumer Price Index, 51
container ships, 38
Continuity IRA, 199
contraceptives, 8, 69, 75, 108, 140
conviction rates, 84
Cook, Robin, 178
cookery books, 101
cookery programs, 100–1
"Cool Britannia," 174, 177
Corbyn, Jeremy, 54, 74, 77, 95, 184, 186, 233
Cornwall, 5, 11, 20
corruption, during Blair years, 175
cosmetic surgery, 56
cosmopolitanism, 99–103
council estates, 79
Council for the Protection of Rural Eng-
    land, 24
Council for Wales and Monmouthshire, 188
Countryside Alliance, 174
Countryside and Rights of Way Act of
    2000, 18
Countryside Commission's map of tranquil
    areas, 23
Coventry, 44
Coventry Cathedral, 103

Coward, Noel, 104, 105
Cowell, Simon, 118
Cox, Jo, 229
crab, 11
Crabb, Stephen, 78
Cradock, Fanny, 101
cricket, 117–18
crime, 83–85; financial, 46–47; knife, 83; and weather, 84
Criminal Justice Act of 1988, 165
crisis vs change, 4–5
cronyism, 176
Croydon, 45
crystals, 68
cuisine: Afro-Caribbean, 100; Chinese, 99–100; Indian, 99–100; Italian, 99; Japanese, 100; Korean, 100; Mexican, 100; Thai, 100
cultural changes: 1945–55, 103–4; 1956–63, 105–7; 1964–70, 107–9; 1970–79, 109–10; 1979–90, 111–12; 1990–, 112–17; generally, 92–103; sport, 117–18
Cumbria, 20, 235
current account deficit, 49, 54, 232
Currie, Edwina, 170
cyclists, 23, 25
Cyprus, 204

Dagenham, 50
Daily Express, 166
Daily Mail, 72
dairy farmers, 16–17
dance programs, 101
Dangerous Dogs Act of 1999, 5
Darling (1965), 108
Darlington, 48
Dartmoor, 24
Davidson, Ruth, 73
Davies, David, 78
Davis, David, 178
Dawlish, 11
Dayell, Tam, 194
DEA. See Department of Economic Affairs (DEA)
Death at the President's Lodging (1936), 94
debt, 49, 51–52, 54, 55, 56, 155, 179–80, 182, 232, 235
decolonization, 201, 203–4, 206, 238
deer, 6, 23

de Gaulle, Charles, 208–210
Deighton, Len, 105
deindustrialization, 38, 243
Delors, Jacques, 216–17
Department for Culture, Media, and Sport, 98
Department of Business, 53
Department of Economic Affairs (DEA), 137
Derby, 84, 158
d'Estaing, Valéry Giscard, 146, 218
Deutsche Bank, 42
devolution referenda, Scottish and Welsh, 148
Devon, 5, 11, 17, 20
diabetes, 8, 86
diesel duty, 32
diesel-powered automobiles, 13, 236
disposable income, 58
divorce, 64, 70, 77–78, 182
Divorce Reform Act of 1971, 78
DIY home improvements, 163
Dock Labour Scheme, 38
Docklands, 45–46
Docklands Light Railway, 46
docks, 38–39
dock strikes, 38
dogs, 6
domestic help, 71
domestic policy, 54
Don, Monty, 101
Douglas-Home, Alec, 126, 136–37, 152, 169, 190
Dover, 48
Downing Street Declaration, 198
Downton Abbey, 57, 113, 118
Drax, 21
Dreamland, 242
drones, 6
drug use, 9, 47, 75, 84
Druidism, 68
drunk-driving laws, 26
dubstep music, 64
Duffy, Carol Ann, 242
Duffy, Lisa, 227
Dunfermline Building Society, 41
Durham, 141, 228
Durham Miners' Gala, 144
Durham University, 153
duty on diesel, 32
Dylan, Bob, 105

Earthly Powers (Burgess), 244
East Cleveland, 20
Eastenders (1985–), 113
Easyjet, 102
Ecclestone, Bernie, 175
EC Commission, 216
economic dynamism in Wales, 39–40
economic output per head of population,
    41, 48
economics, 33–55; Keynesian, 145, 147, 154;
    Thatcherite, 155–56
Eden, Anthony, 126, 128, 203
Edinburgh, 44, 112, 236
Edinburgh Festival, 112
education, 165; and church, 66; compre-
    hensive, 75–76; of foreign students, 53;
    reforms, 140, 165
Education Reform Act of 1988, 165
EEC. *See* European Economic Community
    (EEC)
82 Portraits and 1 Still Life (Hockney), 115
electoral history, 233–34
Electricians Union, 47
electronic communications, 93
Elgin, 99
Emin, Tracey, 114
emissions, high-stack, 12
Empire magazine, 46
employment rates, 51, 71–72, 83
EMU. *See* European Monetary Union
    (EMU)
endogamy, 72
energy, 20–22
England People Very Nice (2009), 115
English Heritage, 116
English-language proficiency, 63
English Longitudinal Study of Ageing, 76
English People, The (Orwell), 241
"entryism," 146, 148
environment, 4–6
Environment Act of 1995, 236
Environment Agency, 10
environmental changes, 10–12
Equality and Human Rights Commission,
    64, 176–77
Equal Pay Act of 1970, 69
ERM. *See* Exchange Rate Mechanism (ERM)
Establishment Club, The, 106
estrogens in river water, 10

ethnic transition, 58
EU competition provisions, 41
EU referendum. *See* Brexit
euro, 214, 223
Europe, relations in, 208–25
European Anti-Maastricht Alliance, 222
European Atomic Energy Community, 213
European Coal and Steel Community,
    208, 213
European Communities Act of 1972, 213
European Communities (Amendment) Act
    of 1986, 216, 221
European Community (EC). *See* European
    Economic Community (EEC)
European Economic Community (EEC), 42,
    133, 138, 142, 204, 208–25, 210
European Foundation, 222
European Monetary Union (EMU), 222
European Single Market, 216
European Union (EU). *See* European Eco-
    nomic Community (EEC)
Euroskeptic Right, 169, 222
Eurostar rail terminal at Waterloo, 116
Eurotunnel, 102
Eurozone, 44, 55
evangelicalism, 121
Evans, Gwynfor, 189
Ewing, Winifred, 189–90
Exchange Rate Mechanism (ERM), 42, 167,
    171, 211, 214, 220, 223
Exeter, 5, 24, 34, 100, 109
exhaust emissions, 9

FA League Championships, 117
Falkender, Lady Marcia, 139
Falkland Islands, 201
Falklands War, 158–59, 162, 171, 196, 198, 215
family farming, 16
family structure, 78
Farage, Nigel, 183, 228
farmers: dairy, 16–17; pig, 19
farming, 15–20
Felixstowe, 38
female: judges, 70; Members of Parliament
    (MPs), 74; ministers, 71; priests, 71; ser-
    vants, 71
feminism, 58, 68–74
feminist theater, Making Mischief, 69
feminization, 72, 244

ferrets, hunting with, 18
ferries, 102
Festival of Britain (1951), 103, 112
Fife, 39
Fifty Shades of Grey, 69
finance, 41–44
financial crime, 46–47
Financial Services Agency, 176
Financial Services Ombudsman, 177
Fisher, Geoffrey, 67
fishing, 20, 53
fishing industry, 212
fixed terms, 120
Fleet Street, 47
Fleming, Ian, 104
Flintshire, 53
flooding, 10–11, 235
Flybe, 102
Folk Songs for the Four Seasons, 103
food banks, 182
Food Foundation, 182
food production, homegrown, 212
Food Standards Agency, 176
Foot, Michael, 147, 158, 160
foot-and-mouth disease, 19
football, 117
Football League, 117
forced marriage, 65
Ford, 50
foreign books, 102
foreign films, 102
foreign investments, 48, 54–55
formality, decline of, 93
Foster, Norman, 116
4G access, 46
foxes, 5–6, 20, 23
fox hunting with hounds, banning of, 18, 174
fracking, 4, 22, 185, 193
fraud, 46
Free Welsh Army, 189
freight, 27
French plays, 102–3
French politics, 217–18
Friedman, Milton, 154
From Home (2014), 98
Full Monty, The (1997), 73
fundamentalist Christianity, 68
Furness General Hospital, 153
"Future Policy" paper of 1959, 204

future trajectory, 199, 231–36
Fyfe, Sir David Maxwell, 128

Gaitskell, Hugh, 123, 126, 136, 173, 209
Gambia, 206
Game, The (Byatt), 109
Gaming Act of 1968, 140
"Gang of Four," 158
gangs, 47, 84
garbage, 5, 22–23
Gardeners' Question Time, 101
gardening programs, 101
gasoline rationing, 125
Gateshead, 113, 141
Gatwick Airport environmental impact, 12
GDP. *See* gross domestic product (GDP)
gender: and politics, 74; relations, 68–74;
    stereotypes, 94
generational change, 89
genetically modified (GM) crops, 185, 193
genital mutilation, 64
Genscher, Hans-Dietrich, 219
gentrification, inner-city, 75
German unification, 217, 219
Ghana, 204
GI brides, 59
Gilmour, Sir Ian, 152
Girl (1974), 73
Glasgow, 2, 39, 44, 48, 63, 109, 112, 119, 236
GLC. *See* Greater London Council (GLC)
globalization, 34, 40, 47, 91–93, 117, 162
global warming, 10–11, 235
Going to the Match (Lowry), 118
Goldfinger, Erno, 109
Goldsmith, James, 47, 223
Good Country Index, 242
Good Friday Agreement of 1998, 198
Good Housekeeping Cookery Book (1948), 101
Gowan, James, 106
Graham, Billy, 110
grammar schools expansion, 174
Gransnet, 83
Great British Bake-Off, The (2010), 100
Greater London Authority Act of 1999, 174
Greater London Authority building, 116
Greater London Council (GLC), 162, 174
Greater Manchester, 2, 81–82, 84, 236
Great Expectations (1946), 103
"green agenda," 12–13

Green Belts, 29
Greening, Justine, 73
green policies, 21–22
"Green Wedges," 29
grime music, 64
Grimethorpe Aria (Birtwistle), 116
Grimshaw, Nicholas, 116
gross domestic product (GDP): per capita,
    129; per hour worked, 53; spent on defence,
    77; UK annual growth in, 36
Grunwick, 148
Gulf War: first, 171, 221; second, 171, 178
gun ownership, 83–84

habitat loss, 6
Hackney South, 179
Hadid, Zaha, 116
Hague, William, 175
Hailsham, Quintin, 136
Halifax, 44
Hamilton, Guy, 107
Hannan, Daniel, 228
Hare, David, 111
Harrods, 54
Hartlepool, 228
Harvey, Marcus, 114
Harvie, Christopher, 232
Hayek, Friedrich, 154
Healey, Denis, 147, 212
health, 6–10
hearing problems, 24
heart disease, 8, 86, 235
Heath, Edward, 36, 60, 67, 110, 134, 136, 138,
    141–45, 147, 152, 204, 210–12
Heathrow Airport, 54; environmental
    impact, 12; expansion, 3
hedgehogs, 20
Heimats, 31
Hemerdon, 20
Henderson, Nicholas, 145
herbicides, 6
Heseltine, Michael, 152, 167
high-speed train lines, 28
high-stack emissions, 12
High Wycombe, 158
Hindley, Myra, 114
Hindus, 59, 63
Hinkley Point B power station, 22
Hirst, Damien, 113–14

History Man, The (Bradbury), 109
Hitchhiker's Guide to the Galaxy, The (Doug-
    las), 25
Hoare, David, 88
Hockney, David, 115
Hodgkin, Howard, 115
Holly, Buddy, 105
Holsworthy, 17
home improvements, DIY, 163
Home Office, 53, 61–62
home ownership, 81–82, 163
homosexual acts, law against, 128, 130
homosexuality, 73
homosexual marriage, opposition to by
    church, 68
Honda, 53
honor-based violence, 65
Hoskins, Bob, 46
hotel industry, 54
hot water costs, 14
House of Cards, 167
House of Commons Select Committee, 23
House of Fraser, 54
House of Ghostly Memory (Whiteread), 114
housing, 28–31, 79–82; costs, 28, 81; council,
    30, 80–81; crisis, 81; demands, 28; in for-
    mer pubs, 26; inadequacy, 81; prices, 232
Housing Act of 1988, 30, 80–81
Housing Act of 1958, 134
Housing Act of 1980, 163
Housing Association Provision, 81
Howard, Michael, 178
Howe, Geoffrey, 166, 220
HSBC, 44
HST-2, 28
Huddersfield, 48
Hull, 59, 179
Human Rights Act, 181
Hunter, Alan, 105
hunting, 18
Hurd, Douglas, 167, 219
Hussein, Nadiya, 100
hybrid society, 112

identity cards, 85
Ilfracombe, 102
illegitimacy, attitudes toward, 69–70
I Love Lucy, 97
IMF, 147

immigration, 56, 58–65, 68, 71, 229, 232–33;
   Commonwealth Immigrants Act of 1962,
   60; English-language proficiency, 63; EU
   nationals, 61; housing, 30–31; Polish, 62;
   population, 1–2; "primary purpose rule,"
   61; restrictions on, 60–61
import/export, 41
imprisonment, 83
income, disposable, 58
income tax, 142, 157, 165
Independent Broadcasting Authority, 98
Independent Television (ITV), 96–97, 127; vs
   BBC, 97–98
India, decolonization of, 202
Indian cuisine, 99–100
Industrial Charter, The (1947), 126
industrialization, 33–55
industrial problems, 36–41
industrial productivity, 138
Industrial Relations Act, 146
Industrial Training Act, 134
infestations, 5–6
inflation, 130, 138, 141–42
Ingram, Bernard, 219
inheritance tax, 181
inner-city gentrification, 75
"In Place of Strife," 139
Institute for Fiscal Studies, 90
Institute of Contemporary Art, 114
Institute of Education, 111
Integrated Household Survey (2013), 73–74
interest rates, 31, 48, 51–52, 76, 90–91, 155, 157,
   171–72, 223
intergenerational living, 82
international capitalism, 93
investigative journalism, 46
investment, inward, 40, 42–43
Ipswich, 29, 49
IRA. See Provisional Irish Republican Army
   (IRA)
Iraq, attack on (2003), 178
iron industry nationalization, 123
irrigation, 14
Islamic law, 63
Isle of Wight Festival, 108
Issigonis, Alec, 106
Italian Cooking (1979), 101
Italian cuisine, 99
ITN News, 96

Itsu restaurants, 100
ITV. See Independent Television (ITV)
I Want It Now (Amis), 109

Jaguar, 50
Jake's Thing (Amis), 110
Jamaica, 204
James Bond: films, 98; novels, 104
Jamie's Italy (2005), 101
Japanese cuisine, 100
jellyfish, 11
Jenkins, Roy, 139, 158, 213
journalism, investigative, 46
J. P. Morgan, 43
judges, female, 70
Junior Imperial League, 205

Kaufman, Gerald, 160
"Keep Sunday Special," 66
Kent, 106
Kenya, 202, 204
Keynesian economics, 154
KGB, 150
Khan, Sadiq, 58, 87, 236
Kinnock, Neil, 165–66, 170, 189
Kirchner, Nestor, 215
Kissinger, Henry, 147
Kitchen, The (1957), 105
"kitchen-sink drama," 104–5
knife crime, 83
Knights Companion of the Order, 70
Kohl, Helmut, 218
Korean cuisine, 100
Korean War, 207
Krays, 47
Kureishi, Hanif, 64
Labour government: 1945–51, 119–25; oppo-
   sition to, 122; policies under Attlee, 122;
   popularity, 124; religious background
   to, 121
Labour ideology changes, 173
"lame ducks," 142
Lamont, Norman, 171, 224
Lancashire, 4
Lancashire League Cricket Match
   (Lowry), 118
Landed Gently (Hunter), 106
land use, 3, 17
land values, 80

Lasdun, Denys, 111
Lawson, Nigel, 166–67, 220
Lazard, 164
League of Empire Loyalists, The, 205
Lean, David, 103
Le Corbusier, 106
Leeds, 48, 81, 228, 235
legislature: 1735 Witchcraft Act, 66; 1957
    Rent Act, 80; 1970 Equal Pay Act, 69; 1988
    Housing Act, 30, 80–81; 2002 Nationality,
    Immigration, and Asylum Act, 63; Abor-
    tion Act of 1967, 68–69; Aliens Act of 1905,
    59; Broadcasting Act of 1980, 98; Catholic
    Emancipation Act of 1829, 65; Common-
    wealth Immigrants Act of 1962, 60; Coun-
    tryside and Rights of Way Act of 2000, 18;
    Criminal Justice Act of 1988, 165; Danger-
    ous Dogs Act of 1999, 6; Divorce Reform
    Act of 1971, 78; Education Reform Act of
    1988, 165; Environment Act of 1995, 233;
    European Communities Act of 1972, 210;
    European Communities (Amendment)
    Act of 1986, 213, 219; Gaming Act of 1968,
    140; Greater London Authority Act of
    1999, 174; Housing Act of 1958, 134; Hous-
    ing Act of 1980, 163; Human Rights Act,
    180; Industrial Relations Act, 146; Indus-
    trial Training Act, 134; Local Government
    Act of 1972, 141; Marriage (Same Sex) Bill
    of 2013, 73; National Insurance Act of 1946,
    123; New Towns Act, 29; Offices and Shops
    Act of 1963, 134; Old Age Pensions Act
    of 1908, 123; Parliament Act of 1949, 122;
    Race Relations Act of 1965, 140; Rate Act
    of 1984, 162; Redundancy Payments Act,
    134; Rent Act of 1957, 140; Succession of the
    Crown Act, 241; Town and Country Plan-
    ning Act of 1947, 29; Town and Country
    Planning Act of 1959, 134; Witchcraft Act
    of 1735, 66
Leicester, 59
Leicester City football team, 117
Leicester University, Engineering Build-
    ing, 106
life expectancy, 2, 8, 76–77
light pollution, 23–24
"Lion and the Unicorn, The" (Orwell), 241
Litter and Flytipping in England (2015), 23
littering, 23
Liver Birds, The (1969), 108

Liverpool, 2, 38–39, 44, 49, 61, 79, 107, 117, 158,
    179, 236
Livingstone, Ken, 162
living wills, 76
Llandudno, 102
Lloyd, Selwyn, 18
Lloyds, 44
Local Government Act of 1972, 141
Local Government Association, 48
local government weakening, 124
London, 49, 79, 82, 109, 158, 236; cycle paths,
    25; housing crisis, 81; office development
    in, 45; population, 2, 3, 62; port of, 38;
    transport strains, 27
Londonstani (2006), 64
London Tube, 46, 177
Long Good Friday, The (1980), 46
Look Back in Anger (1956), 105
Lord of the Rings (Tolkien), 115
Love Actually (2003), 102
Lowry, L. S., 118
Lyme disease, 6

M1, 27
M11, 27
M25, 27
M40, 27
Maastricht Treaty, 221, 223
MacInnes, Colin, 105
Macleod, Iain, 136, 203–5
Macmillan, Harold, 106, 126, 128–30, 133–34,
    136, 152–53, 169, 188, 203–204, 208
Major, John, 118, 167, 169–72, 211–13, 220–25
Making Mischief feminist theater, 69
Malaya, 204
Malayan Emergency, 202
Malaysian Confrontation of 1963–66, 206
Maldives, 206
Malkani, Gautam, 64
Manchester, 2, 48–49, 113, 119, 179, 181
Mandelson, Peter, 175
Manent, Pierre, 228
manufacturing, 33–55; decline in, 34, 231–32
"march of the makers," 52
Margate, 48, 102
marital rape, 65, 70
markets, agriculture, 17
Marks and Spencer, 101
Marley, Bob, 110
Marples, Ernest, 135

marriage, 64, 65, 73, 77–78
Marriage (Same Sex) Bill of 2013, 73
Marxists, 106, 146
Massow, Ivan, 114
"Matter of the North, The" (2016), 32
Maudling, Reginald, 47, 136, 204–5
Mau Mau Uprising, 202
Mauritius, 206
Maxwell, Robert, 47
May, Theresa, 61–62, 67, 70, 72, 74, 86, 88, 185–86
means of address, 93
mechanization, agricultural, 17
Medium Term Financial Strategy, 157
melanoma, 9
Meldrum, 20
Members of Parliament (MPs), female, 74
mental hospitals, 87
"Mersey beat," 107
Mersey Docks and Harbour Board, 142
Merseyside, 38, 40, 81, 182
Merthyr Tydfil, 40, 181, 228
metal smelting industry, 40
Meters (Duffy), 242
methicillin-resistant S. aureus (MRSA), 6
Methodists, 66
Mexican cuisine, 100
Meyer, Sir Anthony, 166
MI6 building, 116
mice, 6
middle class expansion, 58
Midsomer Murders, 57
Mid-Staffordshire Hospital scandal, 7
Miliband, Ed, 182–84
Militant Tendency, 146
Milk Marketing Board for England and Wales, 16
milk production, 16–17
Milton Keynes, 44–45, 179, 242
Minder, 85
Minehead, 102
miners' strikes, 132
mines: aggregate, 20; coal, 40, 157; potash, 20; salt, 20; tin, 20; tungsten, 20
minimum wage, 217
Ministry for Welsh Affairs, 188
Ministry of Technology, 137
Mirror, 148
Misperton, Kirby, 185
Mitterrand, Francois, 159, 217–18

Mo, Timothy, 98
mobile phone networks, 46
modernism, 103, 106, 109, 111
modernist functionalism, 109
modernization, 133–34, 174
modernization, Cabinet committee on, 133
moles, 6
Mona Lisa (1986), 111
monarchy, respect for, 57, 94
Morecambe and Wise Show, 98
Morgan Grenfell, 42
Morrison, Herbert, 121, 123
Mortimer, John, 130
mosques, 63
mosquitoes, 10
Motherwell, 40
Mousetrap (1952), 104
MRSA, 6
multiculturalism, 63–64, 94, 177
multicultural London English, 63–64
multidrug-resistant tuberculosis, 6
murder rate, 83
Murdoch, Iris, 109
Murdoch, Rupert, 47, 223
music: American rock 'n' roll, 105; banned, 110; dubstep, 64; grime, 64; "Oi!", 110; pop, 107–8
Musicians Union, 105
Muslims, 63; influence in schools, 240; non-integration, 64, 227; women, 93
Muzak, 24

NADFAS. See National Association of Decorative and Fine Art Societies (NADFAS)
Nash, David, 114
National Association of Decorative and Fine Art Societies (NADFAS), 115
National Board for Prices and Incomes, 137
National Catering Inquiry, 99–100
national days of prayer, 66
National Economic Development Council, 133
National Gallery, 111
National Grid, 98
National Health Service (NHS), 7, 36, 66, 77, 79, 87, 96, 124, 134, 141, 153, 156, 165, 167, 176–77, 181, 184; establishment of, 7, 120, 122 –23
National Incomes Commission, 133
National Insurance Act of 1946, 123

nationalism, 31, 99–103, 197, 236
Nationality, Immigration, and Asylum Act
    of 2002, 63
nationalization, 35–36, 121; of the iron indus-
    try, 123; of the steel industry, 122, 123
National Joint Committee of Working
    Women's Organisation, 69–70
National Liberation Front, 205
National Lottery, 118
National Plan, 137
national road network, strains on, 26
national service (conscription), 77–78, 197
National Theatre, 111, 115
National Trust, 19
National Union of Miners (NUM), 21,
    143, 160
NATO. See North Atlantic Treaty Organiza-
    tion (NATO)
natural gas production. See North Sea oil
    and natural gas production
Nauru, 206
Neave, Airey, 196
neoliberalism, 42, 89, 156
Netflix, 99
New Age religions, 68
"New Brutalism," 106, 111
Newcastle, 45, 48, 49, 80, 109, 113, 141, 179,
    181, 228
New Elizabethan Age, 104
New Labour, 112, 123, 140, 166, 173, 179, 191
Newport, 40
News of the World, 104
New Towns, 29
New Towns Act, 29
Nigeria, 204
nightclubs, 75
nimbyism, 3–4
Nineteen Eighty-Four (Orwell), 127
Nissan, 50, 53
nitrogen oxides, 12, 235
Nixon, Richard, 110, 143, 208, 211
noise pollution, 23–24
Norfolk, 8, 17
Northampton, 29, 44
North Atlantic Treaty Organization
    (NATO), 127, 207, 234
Northern Ireland, 81, 140, 143, 145, 149, 190,
    194–99, 243
Northern Powerhouse, 28, 52

North Norfolk, 2
North Sea oil and natural gas production, 21,
    36–37, 42, 161, 164, 174, 188, 191
North Yorkshire Council, 185
"not in my backyard," 3–4
Nottingham, 2, 181, 236
nuclear energy, 20–22
nuclear family, 78–80
nuclear plant, 22
NUM. See National Union of Miners (NUM)

Obama, Barack, 218
obesity, 8–9, 26, 86
Ofcom, 176
office development in London, 45
Office for National Statistics (ONS), 74,
    90, 232
Offices and Shops Act of 1963, 134
Ofsted, 88, 170
oil production, 21, 36–37
oil spills, 12
"Oi!" music, 110
Old Age Pensions Act of 1908, 123
Oliver, Jamie, 101
Olympics, 118, 238
One Canada Square, 45
one-nation Conservatism, 67, 86, 129
One Nation Group, 126
Only Fools and Horses, 85
ONS. See Office for National Statistics (ONS)
openness, 53–54
Open University, establishment of, 140
Operation Motorman, 195
Order of the Garter, 70
Orgreave, 161
Ornithology, British Trust for, 12
Orwell, George, 105, 127, 241–42
Osborne, George, 28, 32, 43, 52, 54, 154–55
Osborne, John, 104
Owen, David, 158, 164
Oxford, 48, 84, 186, 239
Oxford English Dictionary, 74
Oxfordshire, 11
Oxford University, 153

pain relief, 9
Paisley, Ian, 143
Pakistani immigration, 60
Parker Morris standards, 29

parking issues, 25, 30
Parliament Act of 1949, 122
partisanship, 176
Passport to Pimlico (1949), 125
patriotism, 31
pay bargaining, 146
payday lending, 87
peace settlement, Northern Ireland, 197
pedophilia, 84
pension: equalization, 70; graduated, 134;
    personal plans, 163
Pensions Regulator, 176
Pentland Firth, 21
pesticides, 6
Peterlee, 29
petrol taxation, 18
Phillips, Trevor, 64
photochemical smog, 12
*Physical Impossibility of Death in the Mind of
    Someone Living, The* (Hirst), 113–14
pig farming, 19
Pinter, Harold, 103, 104
Plaid Cymru, 183, 189–90, 192
plankton, 11
plastic bag charges, 23
Plenty, 111
Plymouth, 24, 186
police corruption, 109
Polish immigration, 62
politicization in culture, 112
politics: 1945–51, 119–25; 1951–60, 125–31;
    1961–79, 132–50; 1990–2016, 169–99; Cam-
    eron years, 180–85; Thatcherism, 1979–90,
    151–68
politics: and gender, 74; and religion, 66–67;
    and TV programming, 113
poll tax, 165–67, 191
pollution, 12–13, 236; light, 23–24; noise,
    23–24
Pompidou, Georges, 110, 210
pop music, 107–8
population: aging, 2, 8; Annual Population
    Survey (2015), 54; birth rate, 8; density, 32;
    growth, 56; immigration, 1–2; life expec-
    tancy, 8; regional differences, 2; statistics,
    1–3; trends and projections, 1–2
"pork barrel" politics, 41
pornography, 84
Porridge (2016), 98

Portsmouth, 41, 236
Port Talbot steelworks, 40
"positive discrimination," 72
Post Office Tower, 108
potash mining, 20
pound sterling, 43, 54, 102, 138, 145, 157, 164,
    171, 202–3, 214, 223
poverty, 48, 85, 87
Powell, Enoch, 60, 129, 136, 210, 214
power cuts, 132, 143
powers of attorney, 76
power workers strikes, 132
prayer, national days of, 66
Prescott, John, 176
prescription charges, 134, 193
Preston, 49, 179
price inflation, 142
"primary purpose rule," 61
Prime Minister's Questions, 95
printing industry, 34, 47, 48
print unions, 47
Private Eye, 106
productivity, 36–38, 45, 49–51; industrial, 138
Profumo Affair, 137
"Project Fear," 52, 227
property lending boom, 145
prostate cancer, 9
Protestantism in Northern Ireland, 195–99
Protestant nonconformity, 120–21
Provisional Irish Republican Army (IRA),
    46, 112, 149, 194–99, 229
public restroom closures, 181
public-sector net borrowing, 232
public-sector net debt, 232
public spending cuts under Thatcher, 27
pubs: closing of, 26, 242; effect of drunk
    driving laws on, 26; sold for housing, 26
Pym, Francis, 152, 213

Qatar, 54
"quality of life" debate, 170
quantitative easing, 51–52
Queen's Golden Jubilee, 64

Race and Faith: The Deafening Silence
    (2016), 64
race issues, 158
Race Relations Act of 1965, 140
Rachmanism, 80

rail transport, 27
rail workers, 39
rape, 84; marital, 65, 70
Rate Act of 1984, 162
rationing, 127; gasoline, 125
rats, 6
Rattigan, Terence, 104, 105
RBS, 44
Reading, 49, 236
Reagan, Ronald, 154, 218
recession, 35, 51–52, 109, 146, 154, 157, 159, 165, 170, 179, 224; postwar, 145
recycled water, 15
recycling, 23
Red Brigade (Italy), 149
Redundancy Payments Act, 134
Redwood, John, 169
Referendum Party, 47, 173, 223–25
Regional Development Fund, 137
regional dimensions in economics, 44–46
regions, creation of, 192
regulatory bodies, 176
religion, 65–68; and the Labour party, 121; in politics, 66
religious change, 63
religious evangelicalism, 121
religious practice, shifts in, 65–68
renewable energy, 21
Rent Act of 1957, 80, 140
rent controls, 80
resale price maintenance (RPM), end of, 134–35
restrooms, public, closure of, 181
Revolutionary Socialist League, 146
Reynolds, Albert, 198
Rhode, John, 29
Rhodes, Cecil, 239
Richard, Cliff, 107
Richardson, Charlie, 47
Richmond Park, 23
rickets, 85
Ridley, Nicholas, 219
right-to-buy revolution for council housing, 30; council housing sales, 163
"Right to Roam," 18
rioting, 61, 105, 115, 158, 182
river water contamination, 10
road rage, 25

roadways, 25–26
Robbins, Lord, 106
Robson, James, 73
Rogers, Richard, 116
rolling plate mill at Motherwell, 40
Rosyth, 41
Rotherham, 84
Rotterdam, 38
Royal Academy, 114–15
Royal College of Surgeons, 87
Royal Society for the Protection of Birds (RSPB), 13
Royal Ulster Constabulary, Special Branch of, 196
Royle Family, The, 111
RSPB. *See* Royal Society for the Protection of Birds (RSPB)
Rudd, Amber, 78
rugby, 117
Runcie, Robert, 159
rural effects of car ownership, 24–25
rural values, 19
Rusk, Dean, 209
Russian Civil War of 1919–20, 207
Ryanair, 102

Sacred and Profane Love Machine, The (Murdoch), 109
Saint Helena, 201
salmon exports from Scotland, 193
Saltley Gate, 161
salt mining, 20
Santander, 44
satire boom, 106
Scarborough, 102
Scargill, Arthur, 160
Scarman Inquiry, 158
Scotland, 1–2, 8, 21, 188–93, 199, 228–29, 238
Scotland, rejected independence, 192–93
Scotland and Wales Bill, 190
Scottish and Welsh devolution referenda, 148
Scottish Episcopal Church, 66
Scottish Nationalists, 141
Scottish National Party (SNP), 178, 189–90
Scottish Office, 188
Scottish Parliament, 174
Scunthorpe, 40
SDP. *See* Social Democratic Party (SDP)

Sea and Ships Pavilion, 103
seagulls, 5, 20, 23
sea temperature increase, 11
second homes, 18–19
Secretary of State for Wales, 188
secularism, 241
Seifert, Richard, 109
self-employed workforce, 51, 89, 144
self-expression, 69
Selsdon Park, 142
"Sensation" show at the Royal Academy, 114
Serpentine Gallery, 116
service industries, 39–41, 53
Seven Days to Noon (1951), 103
Severn Bridge, 40, 189
Sex in the City (2010s), 69
Sex Pistols, 110
sexual behaviour, gender stereotypes in, 73
sexual revolution, 108
Shadow Cabinet, 69–70, 184
Shard, the, 116
Sharman, Helen, 70
Sheffield, 48, 81
Shelter charity, 232
shipbuilding, 34, 37–38
Shoreditch, 179
shortages, coal, 125
short-termism in manufacturing, 20, 34
Shostakovich, Dmitri, 103
Sierra Leone, 204
Sikhs, 59, 63
Sillitoe, Alan, 104
Sinn Fein, 198
Skegness, 102
skin cancer, 9
Skylon, 103
Sky Television, 163; subscriptions, 87
sleep disturbances, 24
Slough, 91
slum clearance, 79
Smith, John, 224
Smith, Owen, 77
Smith, Zadie, 64
smog, photochemical, 12
smoking, 9, 23, 77; gender differences in, 72
snails, 6
SNP. See Scottish National Party (SNP)
soap operas, 96–97

social: change, 56–91; context, 79–82; conventions, 89; differentiation, 25; media, 99; placing, 57–58; policy, 77–78; structures, 85–91
Social Democratic Party (SDP), 158
socialism, 120–22
"social revolution," 109
social welfare, 119, 122, 134, 181; payments, 177
Society for Constructive Birth Control, 8
solar panels, 13, 21
Somerset, 22
"sound money," 154–56
Sour Sweet (1983), 98
Southern Rhodesia, 204, 206
South Africa, apartheid in, 206–7
Southampton, 236
Southend, 44
Southern Railway, 39
Spanish tapas, 101
Special Branch of the Royal Ulster Constabulary, 194
Spectator, 219
speculative building boom, 43
Spence, Basil, 103
Spencer, Colin, 73
Spitting Image, 166
sport culture, 117–18
squirrels, 6, 23
staycations, 102
Steel, David, 164
steel industry, 40, 157; nationalization of, 36, 122–23
Stein, Rick, 101
Stevenage, 29
Stewart, J. I. M., 94
Stirling, James, 106
Stoke on Trent, 236
Stonehouse, John, 47
Stopes, Marie, 8
Stormont, 195
Strictly Come Dancing (2010), 101, 118
strikes, 142, 146, 148; dock, 38; miners, 132, 160–61; power workers, 132; Tube, 46; union, 38
Sturgeon, Nicola, 47, 70
subsidies, agricultural, 17
Succession of the Crown Act, 244–45
Suez Crisis, 126, 128, 202–3

sugary drinks, 88

suicide, 76

suicide bombing attacks in London, 177

Sun, 48, 148, 171, 223

Sunday Post, 232

Sunday Times, 92

Sunderland, 53, 54, 141, 158, 179, 228

sun-powered units, 13

supermarket sales of alcohol, 26

support ratio, 8

survival rates for cancer, 9

Sussex, 106

Swansea, 40

Swaziland, 206

Sweeney, The (1975–78), 109

Sweet Caress (2015), 76–77

Swindon, 53

swine, 19

Swiss Re Tower, 116

Taggart (1983–2010), 109

Tanganyika, 204

tapas, Spanish, 101

Tate Modern, 116

taxation, 121–23, 146–47, 157, 165

taxation policies of Brown, 178

tax cuts: under Major, 170; under Thatcher, 163

technology, 47–48

Teesside, 12

television: color, 98; culture, 95–99; and film influences, 57

Temple, William, 66

tennis, 118

"Ten Years of Tax: How Cities Contribute to the National Exchequer" (2016), 48

terms, fixed, 120

terrorism, 85, 150, 177; in Northern Ireland, 195–96

Terry, Quinlan, 111

textile industry, 37

Thai cuisine, 100

Thames Barrier, 45

Thames Water, 54

Thatcher, Margaret, 36, 61, 67, 70, 110–12, 143, 147, 149, 207–8, 214–21. *See also* Thatcher government; Thatcherism; election of, 147; fall of, 166–67

Thatcher government: fall of, 166–67; public spending cuts under, 26

Thatcherism, 42, 86, 110–12, 120, 129, 151–68, 173

Thatcherite economics, 155–56

Thatcherite liberalization, 53

Thatcherite monetarism, 52

That Was the Week That Was, 106

theater of the absurd, 103

Thorneycroft, Peter, 129

Thorpe, Jeremy, 143, 145

three-day work week, 143

ticks, 6

tidal energy farm, 21

Tilbury, 38

Till Death Us Do Part (1965–75), 113

Times, the, 48, 74, 215

tin mines, 20

Tippett, Michael, 104

Titchmarsh, Alan, 101

Tiverton, 135

Tolkien, J. R. R., 115

Top Gear, 118

Torbay, 102

"Tory Maoism," 153

tourism, 54, 116; British to foreign countries, 101–2

Tower Hamlets, 2, 48

Town and Country Planning Act of 1947, 29

Town and Country Planning Act of 1959, 134

Toxteth, 158

Toyota, 53

trade, 50

Trades Union Congress (TUC), 144, 146, 168; Conference, Bournemouth, 218

trade union, 38, 126, 146, 148–50, 155; collectivism, 119–20, 123; reforms, 162

traffic noise, 23

trains, 27

tranquil areas, Countryside Commission's map of, 23

transfer payments, 40–41

transgender issues, 73

transportation, 24–28

Transport for London budget, 27

travel industry, 102

travel speeds, decline in average, 181

Treaty of Rome of 1957, 208

Treaty on European Union, The. *See* Maastricht Treaty
Trellick Tower, 109
Trotskyites, 139
Truss, Liz, 22, 67, 70, 187
Trussell Trust, 82
Tube, 46
tuberculosis, 9; bovine, 19; multidrug-resistant, 6
TUC. *See* Trades Union Congress (TUC)
tungsten mines, 20
turbines, wind, 13, 21
Turner Prize, 114
TV-AM, 98
TV programming and politics, 113
TV rights, 117
Tyne, River, 141
Tyneside, 228, 236
typesetting, 47

Uganda, 60, 204
UK Independence Party (UKIP), 70–71, 130, 173, 180, 183, 222, 225–26, 233
UKIP. *See* UK Independence Party (UKIP)
UK Sport, 118
Ulster Unionists, 143
"Ulster Workers' Strike," 195
underclass, 87
unemployment rates, 51, 59, 80, 87, 142–43, 145, 154, 157–59, 179, 227
unions, 47–48, 124, 142. *See also* trade unions
union strikes, 38
university admissions, gender gap, 72
unmarried motherhood, 69–70, 155
US support, 203
utility privitization, 14

venereal disease, 9
Viagra, 78
Victorian Poor Law, 134
Vietnam War, 138, 142, 207–8
vitamin D deficiency, 85
voter turnout, 185
voting age, lowering of, 75

wage inflation, 146
Waiting for Godot, 103
Wakefield, 179

Wales, 186–91, 200, 229; economic dynamism in, 39–40
Wandsworth, 162
Wantage, 29
Wapping, 47
Warwick, 106
waste. *See* garbage
water, 13–15; contamination, 10; features, resurgence of, 10; metering, 14; quality, 15; supplies, pressures on, 14
watercolor paintings, 115
Waterloo, 116
Watford, 34
Wear, River, 141
weather and crime, 84
welfare benefits, 90
Wells, 6
Welsh Assembly, 74
Welsh language, 189
Welsh local politics, 189
Welsh Office, 188
Wesker, Arnold, 104
West Lothian question, 180, 194
West Midlands, 2, 8, 41, 48, 81
West Somerset, 2
West Yorkshire, 81–82
Which magazine, 71
Whitelaw, William, 147
Whiteread, Rachel, 114
White Teeth (2000), 64
Whitley Bay, 102
wildlife, 5–6
Willetts, David, 4
Williams, Rowan, 64
Williams, Vaughan, 103
wills, living, 76
Wilson, Harold, 108, 123, 136–39, 141–47, 150, 152, 174, 205–9
Wilson, Jen, 73
Wilson, Lord, of Culworth, 78
Wimbledon, 179
"Wind of Change" speech (Macmillan), 204
wind turbines, 13, 21
"winter of discontent" (1978–79), 148
Witchcraft Act of 1735, 66
Wodehouse, P. G., 104
Wolfenden, Lord, 130
Wolverhampton, 59, 109

women priests and bishops, 67
Women's Institute, 70
Women's Rugby Football Union, 70
woodlice, 6
wood pellets burning, 21
Woolwich, 235
working elderly, 76
work week, shortened, 143
World Cup, 117
World Economic Forum, 52
Wrexham, 40

xenophobia, 99
X Factor, The, 118

Yom Kippur War, 143
YouGov polls, 113, 229
Young Conservatives, 205
Young Ones, The (1962), 107
youth drinking, 75
youth issues, 74–76, 158
YouTube, 99

JEREMY BLACK
is a British historian and
professor of history at the
University of Exeter. His many
books include *The Holocaust:
History and Memory, Geopolitics
and the Quest for Dominance,*
and *Plotting Power: Strategy
in the Eighteenth Century.*

FOR INDIANA UNIVERSITY PRESS

Tony Brewer *Artist and Book Designer*

Dan Crissman *Trade and Regional Acquisitions Editor*

Samantha Heffner *Trade Acquisitions Assistant*

Brenna Hosman *Production Coordinator*

Katie Huggins *Production Manager*

Darja Malcolm-Clarke *Project Manager/Editor*

Dan Pyle *Online Publishing Manager*

Leyla Salamova *Artist and Book Designer*

Stephen Williams *Marketing and Publicity Manager*